£21-00N

American Psychopathological Association Series

STRESS AND MENTAL DISORDER

American Psychopathological Association Series

Critical Issues in Psychiatric Diagnosis
Robert L. Spitzer and Donald F. Klein, editors, 355 pp., 1978

Psychopathology and Brain Dysfunction
Charles Shagass, Samuel Gershon, and Arnold J. Friedhoff, editors, 399 pp., 1977

Hormones, Behavior, and Psychopathology
Edward J. Sachar, editor, 325 pp., 1976

American Psychopathological Association Series

Stress and Mental Disorder

Editor:

James E. Barrett, M.D.
Associate Professor of Psychiatry
Boston University School of Medicine
Boston, Massachusetts

Associate Editors:

Robert M. Rose, M.D.
Professor and Chairman
Department of Psychiatry and
  Behavioral Sciences
University of Texas Medical Branch
Galveston, Texas

Gerald L. Klerman, M.D.
Professor of Psychiatry
Harvard Medical School
Boston, Massachusetts

Raven Press ■ New York

Raven Press, 1140 Avenue of the Americas, New York, New York 10036

Made in the United States of America

Library of Congress Cataloging in Publication Data

American Psychopathological Association.
    Stress and mental disorder.

    Formal presentations at the sixty-eighth annual meeting of the American Psychopathological Association.
    Includes bibliographies and index.
    1. Psychology, Pathological—Congresses. 2. Stress (Psychology)—Congresses. I. Barrett, James E.
II. Rose, Robert M. III. Klerman, Gerald L.,
1928–   IV. Title.[DNLM: 1. Life change events—Congresses. 2. Mental Disorders—Etiology—Congresses.
3. Stress, Psychological—Complications—Congresses.
WM172 A512s 1978.]
RC454.4.A46 1979   616.8'9'071   79–13767
ISBN 0-89004-384-1

Preface

The relationship of stress to illness is an area which has long fascinated clinician and researcher alike. In the past decade, with improvements in the methods for assessing stress, research in this area has multiplied. The relationship of stress factors to particular physic disorders, such as hypertension or cardiac heart disease, is now well established. Knowledge about the relationship of stress to mental disorders has also advanced, although at a slower pace and with less certainty about the interpretation of the findings. The Sixty-Eighth Annual Meeting of the American Psychopathological Association was devoted to examining the state of this knowledge. The chapters that follow are the formal presentations at that conference, together with the critical discussion, both formal and informal, that those presentations provoked.

This volume reports and examines advances of the past decade in seeking relationships between stress and mental disorder. In Part I the focus is on the methodology for assessing stress. Dohrenwend critically reviews major issues in the assessment of stress and in establishing causal links between stress and psychopathology. Hurst, in a detailed and careful presentation, focuses on issues related to the scales themselves. Drawing both on earlier data and on new data from his recent work, he examines the effects of variations in scale content, scoring, and item clustering. Holmes reviews the origin of the Social Readjustment Rating Scale, establishing its roots in psychophysiology, and updates its recent usage.

In Part II attention shifts to a specific group of disorders, depressive disorders, in which stress factors appear to play an established role. Paykel examines the mounting evidence that stress, and in particular certain classes of events, relates to onset of depressive episodes. Barrett extends that concept further, relating some classes of events to onset of particular subtypes of depressive disorders and other classes of events to onset of anxiety disorders, leading him to speculate about the interaction between particular stressors and individual vulnerability factors. The vulnerability concept is further advanced in the chapter by Brown; he argues eloquently for a multifactored model in the etiology of depression, presenting data that specific early experiences predispose to depression in adult life, as well as drawing attention to the role of societal factors in preventing or ameliorating depressive episodes. Clayton and Darvish report natural history data on a universal stress experience, that of bereavement. In the Samuel Hamilton Address, Gerald Klerman continues the examination of stress and the affective disorders; he considers the adaptational function of the depressed state and sees its onset as a failure of the organism to cope with certain stress experiences.

v

The chapters in Part III turn to a macroscopic perspective, that of the role of societal factors in mental disorders. Brenner presents data on the effects of economic cycles on disease incidence. Kasl examines the effects of job loss and retirement on mental health; in his careful analysis of a plant closing he comes up with some surprising findings. Srole, using longitudinal data from the Midtown Manhattan Study, examines the impact of macro- and micro-social crises in the lives of individuals. The Paul Hoch Address, given by Lee N. Robins, is included with these chapters. In this thoughtful and provocative presentation she draws together findings from her work over two decades on antisocial personality, in particular the search for those experiences and behaviors in childhood that predict adult outcome. Vulnerability, or the fact that under the same stress conditions some develop disorders and some do not, is a theme that returns again when the findings of the contributors to this section are considered together.

Part IV has as its focus those variables that interact with stress to produce a disease state. Rose and his associates, in a study of air traffic controllers, are able in this remarkable data set to move back and forth between the physiologic and the psychologic domains, and by so doing they are able to examine the relationship of physiologic response, seen as a mediator of stress, to the development of psychiatric symptoms. His findings reassure us that the complexity of stress effects are researchable and that such multidisciplinary designs are necessary for knowledge of the mechanisms of stress effects to advance. Wender gives a reminder not to overlook genetic contributions in examining the interaction between stress and the development of a disorder. In the final chapter, Jenkins develops a systems model, considering the interplay between variables from biological, psychological, interpersonal, and societal conceptual levels in understanding a given individual's response to stress, leaving us with a theoretical framework by which we can approach the role of psychosocial factors in the development of a disease state.

The volume closes with an overview by Joseph Zubin. Drawing on his extensive background in assessment and in psychopathology, he further elaborates on vulnerability concepts and how they must be included in further research. His summary underscores the fact that, although it is reasonably well established that stress factors play an important role in the onset of certain mental disorders, the mechanisms by which this role is mediated remain to be clarified. In this volume the contributors have tried to clarify some of these mechanisms, and the direction for future research—the identification of vulnerability factors and how they are formed and transmitted—has been charted.

The Editors

Contents

Part III: Social System Stress and Psychopathology

Part IV: Future Directions for Integration of Stress Research

Contributors

James E. Barrett, M.D.
Department of Psychiatry
Boston University School of
*   Medicine*
Boston, Massachusetts 02118

M. Harvey Brenner, Ph.D.
Department of Behavioral Science
Johns Hopkins University
Baltimore, Maryland 21218

George W. Brown, Ph.D.
Social Research Unit
Bedford College
The University of London
London, W1N 1DD England

Paula J. Clayton, M.D.
Department of Psychiatry
Washington University School of
*   Medicine*
St. Louis, Missouri 63110

Harriet S. Darvish, M.A.
Department of Psychiatry
Washington University School of
*   Medicine*
St. Louis, Missouri 63110

Barbara S. Dohrenwend, Ph.D.
Division of Sociomedical Sciences
School of Public Health
Columbia University
New York, New York 10032

Bruce P. Dohrenwend, Ph.D.
Social Psychiatry Research Unit
College of Physicians and Surgeons
Columbia University
New York, New York 10032

J. Alan Herd, M.D.
New England Primate Research Center,
*   and Harvard Medical School*
Boston, Massachusetts 02115

Thomas H. Holmes, M.D.
Department of Psychiatry and Behavioral
*   Sciences*
University of Washington School of
*   Medicine*
Seattle, Washington 98195

Michael W. Hurst, Ed.D.
Department of Behavioral Epidemiology
Boston University School of Medicine
Boston, Massachusetts 02118

C. David Jenkins, Ph.D.
Department of Behavioral Epidemiology
Boston University School of Medicine
Boston, Massachusetts 02118

Stanislav V. Kasl, Ph.D.
Department of Epidemiology and Public
*   Health*
Yale University
New Haven, Connecticut 06510

Gerald L. Klerman, M.D.
Alcohol, Drug Abuse, and Mental Health
*   Administration*
Rockville, Maryland 20852

Eugene S. Paykel, M.D., FRCP,
**   FRCPsych.**
St. George's Hospital Medical School
The University of London
London, S.W. 17 England

Lee N. Robins, Ph.D.
Department of Psychiatry
Washington University School of Medicine
St. Louis, Missouri 63110

Robert M. Rose, M.D.
Department of Psychiatry and Behavioral
  Sciences
University of Texas Medical Branch
Galveston, Texas 77550

Arthur P. Schless, M.D.
Depression Research Unit
Veteran's Administration Hospital
Philadelphia, Pennsylvania 19104

Leo Srole, Ph.D.
Social Sciences Research Unit
College of Physicians and Surgeons
Columbia University
New York, New York 10032

E. H. Uhlenhuth, M.D.
Department of Psychiatry
The University of Chicago
Chicago, Illinois 60637

Paul H. Wender, M.D.
Department of Psychiatry
The University of Utah College of
  Medicine
Salt Lake City, Utah 84132

Joseph Zubin, Ph.D.
Neuropsychology Research
Veterans Administration Hospital
Pittsburgh, Pennsylvania 15206

Stress and Mental Disorder,
edited by James E. Barrett et al.
Raven Press, New York © 1979.

Stressful Life Events and Psychopathology: Some Issues of Theory and Method

Bruce P. Dohrenwend

College of Physicians and Surgeons, Columbia University, New York, New York 10032

Reponses to the question, "How important are stressful life events in the causation of psychopathology?" would probably be equally distributed among four or five graded categories ranging from "very important" to "not important at all." Undoubtedly, there would also be angry comments about the vagueness and imprecision of the question. We would be asked, for example, what types of stressful life events we were talking about: Did we mean natural or man-made disasters that affect special groups of people at any particular time? Did we mean single events, such as bereavement or physical illness, that affect most people at some time during their lives? Or were we thinking of combinations of such more usual life events occurring simultaneously or in close temporal proximity to one another in the lives of some people at some particular time? And what did we mean by "psychopathology?" Were we aware that psychopathology is not a unitary phenomenon but rather that there are various types of psychopathology, some more and some less likely to be caused by environmentally induced stress?

PSYCHOPATHOLOGY IN THE GENERAL POPULATION

The last point concerns the nature of the phenomena we are trying to explain in this inquiry about the role of stressful life events in etiology. We come to the problem with an epidemiological orientation. Accordingly, we are concerned with explaining why certain types of psychiatric disorders and distress syndromes occur with certain frequencies and are distributed in certain ways in general populations. Since our focus is on the role of environmentally induced stress, we are concerned first with the so-called functional psychiatric disorders, those with no known organic cause.

At least 60 community studies of the true prevalence of psychiatric disorders have been published since 1950 (14). The rates reported are much higher than those of earlier investigations. They reflect the expanded psychiatric nomenclatures that were developed following World War II but prior to DSM-III, which is a recent development as far as epidemiological research is concerned. Although most of the studies arrived at case counts and classifications on the basis of

1

judgments by physicians, 17 used psychiatric screening scales similar to the Psychosomatic Scale of the Neuropsychiatric Screening Adjunct developed during World War II. Analyses of the results of the latter types of studies indicate that the scales are imperfectly and often only indirectly related to clinical psychiatric disorders (16). Rather, they measure a kind of psychological and physiological distress that is well described by Frank's (22) concept of "demoralization."

Despite the methodological problems stemming from lack of consensus about how to conceptualize and measure psychopathology that have plagued epidemiological investigators (see ref. 14), we can get a very rough estimate of the extent of various types of psychopathology by looking at the aggregated results of these more recent studies. Table 1 presents the medians and ranges of rates for each major classification of functional psychiatric disorder from studies conducted in communities all over the world and published in 1950 or later. The rates should be considered descriptions of prevalence during short periods of time ranging between a few months and 1 year. As is evident, the overall median of about 14% for the functional disorders suggests that these disorders are not rare in general populations. Consider an additional set of findings from a recent study in New Haven by Weissman et al. (60) using SADS interviews and RDC criteria relevant to DSM-III. These investigators report an overall point prevalence rate of 17.8% for functional disorders.

The median of more than 25% "demoralized" in Table 1 suggests that even larger proportions of general populations show a level of distress that is characteristic of mixed samples of psychiatric outpatients and inpatients (16). We have estimated that about half of the demoralized subjects do not have clinical psychiatric disorders (40).

Taken together, these results suggest that it would not be unusual to find 14% of a sample of subjects from the general population suffering from some type of functional psychiatric disorder plus about that many who were showing evidence of severe psychological distress. Our best evidence, then, is that psychopathology of the types in which environmentally induced stress may be important is far from rare in general populations.

TABLE 1. *Medians and ranges of percentages of functional psychiatric disorders reported in epidemiological studies of "true" prevalence published in 1950 or later*[a]

Type of disorder	Median	Range	No. of studies
Schizophrenia	0.76	0.0023–1.96	17
Affective psychosis	0.43	0.0000–1.59	12
Neurosis	5.95	0.305–75.0[b]	25
Personality disorders	4.19	0.23–14.5[b]	19
Overall functional disorders	14.05	1.25–63.5	27
"Demoralization"	27.5	3.4–69.0	17

[a] Note that all percentages are adjusted for sex differences except for rates of "demoralization." Medians and ranges calculated from detailed tables and bibliography prepared to supplement refs. 14 and 15.

[b] Includes Stirling County Study "symptom patterns" that are not necessarily considered "cases" in that study (39).

STRESSFUL LIFE EVENTS

With respect to our question of whether stressful life events are important in the causation of such psychopathology in the general population, the best evidence is indirect. The reason is that this evidence comes not from epidemiological studies of community populations under ordinary conditions but rather from studies of individuals and groups under extraordinary conditions imposed by natural and man-made disasters, especially the disaster of war.

Extreme Situations

Studies of such extreme situations have provided compelling evidence that the stressful events involved can produce psychopathology in previously normal persons (see refs. 1,8,30, and 35). For example, on the basis of a series of studies using scales from the Neuropsychiatric Screening Adjunct during World War II, Star (54) concluded that (p. 455):

> . . . the fear and anxiety implicit in combat brought forth the psychosomatic manifestations in so many men that these [symptom scales] served less and less to discriminate between men who were labeled psychiatric casualties and those who were not.

Although elevation in symptom levels was not necessarily accompanied by breakdown in performance, under some conditions breakdown became endemic. In a study of 2,630 soldiers who had broken down during combat in the Normandy campaign during World War II, Swank (56) estimated that the onset of combat exhaustion occurred even in previously normal soldiers when about 65% of their companions had been killed or wounded, or had otherwise become casualties. Swank emphasized that the men in this study had been highly selected for health and ability to cope. He describes them as follows (p. 476):

> They were of better than average stability and willingness by virtue of the fact that they had passed the various training tests (induction, overseas assignment, battle simulation exercises), had been selected for combat units, and had proved their mettle by remaining in combat varying lengths of time.

While men who were stable prior to combat remained in combat longer without breaking down, such prior stability did not prevent the eventual onset of combat exhaustion.

Nor are the symptoms caused by such situations of extreme stress limited to those included under the heading of traumatic war neurosis, combat fatigue, and combat exhaustion. Psychotic symptoms can appear in the form of what have been called "three-day" psychoses (36). It is even possible that extreme situations can play a major role in inducing outright psychotic disorder since, as Paster (46) found, there was far less evidence of individual predisposing factors among combat soldiers who became psychotic than among soldiers in whom psychotic disorders developed in less stressful circumstances. In fact, it would seem that most of the varied signs and symptoms observed in psychiatric patients in civilian settings have also been observed as reactions to combat (see, e.g., ref. 36, pp. 436–438). In this sense, war has been indeed "a laboratory which manufactures psychological dysfunction" (26, p. vii).

The extent to which symptomatology and disturbance of functioning produced by extreme situations in previously normal persons are transient and self-limiting is a matter of controversy (see ref. 35). Most observers have emphasized the transience of the symptoms (see ref. 13, pp. 110–130). At the same time, studies in which persons exposed to these extraordinary events have been examined years later have repeatedly found some individuals with more or less severe pathology that apparently began at the time the stressful experience occurred (see ref. 35, pp. 445–448). Certainly at the extreme of exposure to the brutalities of Nazi concentration camps, there is strong evidence that not only does severe stress-induced psychopathology persist in the survivors (20) but also that the survivors are more prone to physical illness and early death (21).

More Usual Stressful Life Events

Fortunately, relatively few individuals in most societies are ever exposed to natural disasters or to extremely severe combat conditions. It is the lot of most people, however, to have to cope at one time or another with stressful life events of more usual kinds; events such as birth of a first child, physical illness or injury, and death of a loved one.

Quite separate bodies of research have dealt with such events as they may be related to psychopathology in general populations. One has focused more on the impact that certain remote events occurring in their childhoods may have on adults; another stressed events recently experienced by adults. The separation has had to do more with research traditions and with practicality than with logic. For example, researchers focusing on recent life events have limited their concern to recent occurrences in order to minimize problems of recall (58). Some researchers have studied particular events, such as bereavement, while others have attempted to sample a range and variety of stressful life events. Some examples of these different types of investigations follow.

Remote Events

A substantial number of studies of relationships between remote events and adult psychopathology has focused on loss of one or both parents by death or other causes during childhood (see refs. 5,25,28, and 49). Until recently, however, the results seemed inconsistent from study to study (25). This may have been due to insufficient attention to whether bereavement took place earlier or later in childhood. There are now at least three studies suggesting that death of one or both parents before age 11 is associated with depression (4) and/or severe psychological distress (12,38) among adults in samples from the general population.

Single Recent Events

Perhaps bereavement is also the clearest example of single recent events, beside the types of natural and man-made disasters discussed earlier that can produce severe symptomatology in previously normal adults. Temporarily, at least, such symptomatology is indistinguishable from the symptomatology of depressive disorders (6).

An increasing number of researchers have been investigating relationships between episodes of physical illness and episodes of emotional disturbance (19, 29,53). For the most part, these investigations are not studies of samples or groups from the general population; rather, they are studies of patient populations in which the investigators often use case-control designs. They include data from a wide variety of patients, ranging from those chosen on the basis of the presence of a particular type of physical illness or psychiatric disorder to the families comprising the patients of various general practitioners in Great Britain and the United States. The findings from these diverse studies are remarkably consistent; there is a strong positive association between physical illness and emotional disturbance (see ref. 41).

Beside bereavement and severe physical illness or injury, however, it is difficult to find consistent evidence that other types of single life events can produce psychopathology in previously normal adults in societies free from war and other natural disasters. Consider, for example, the event of unemployment. Brenner (2) has presented striking empirical evidence that unemployment is related to mental hospital admissions for a variety of serious psychiatric disorders. He discovered relationships between fluctuations in the economy and mental hospital admissions in New York State over a period of more than 100 years. Unfortunately, the data were mental hospital admissions rather than true rates of disorder. As Brenner himself realized, the results may be due to increased intolerance of deviance at times of high unemployment or to use of hospitals as almshouses by unemployed persons rather than to the precipitation of psychiatric symptoms.

As in extreme situations, the most compelling evidence that a particular type of more usual stressful life event is important would be provided by verification of the hypothesis that the event produces psychopathology in previously normal persons. Such tests require a focus not on patients but on nonpatient groups in the general population. One of the most careful case studies of the health effects of unemployment on such groups was done by Cobb and Kasl (7). The subjects of their study were 100 male blue collar workers at two plants that were scheduled to be permanently shut down, together with 74 men from two unthreatened plants who were selected as controls. The median length of unemployment in the closed plant was 5 weeks. Data were collected at various intervals on both physical and mental health, the latter by means of structured questionnaires that included questions on depressed mood, low self-esteem, anxiety, psychophysiological symptoms, and suspicion. A subset of these items were from the Langner (37) scale and similar screening instruments dating from the Psychosomatic Scale of Neuropsychiatric Screening Adjunct developed during World War II (55). Taken together, these items probably provide a satisfactory measure of demoralization.

With respect to the outcomes on these psychological measures, Cobb and Kasl (7) concluded (p. 180):

> In the psychological sphere the personal anguish experienced by the men and their families does not seem adequately documented by the statistics of deprivation and change in affective state . . . . Two things probably account for this. First, the measurement techniques for subjective states are imperfect; and second, the adaptive capacities of man . . . to reduce the effects are striking. Indeed, in some . . . [the effects] may have been so transitory as to have been missed.

Imperfect as they undoubtedly are, we would nevertheless not expect the measures used in this study to miss altogether any major outbreak of psychopathology that occurred in response to unemployment. The hypothesis about the strong adaptive capacities of these men seems all the more persuasive for this reason. In sum, the findings suggest that relatively brief unemployment alone is not an important etiological factor in severe or persistent psychological distress, much less severe psychiatric disorder, in the general population.

Consider an example of still another type of stressful event consisting of divorce or marital separation. Here the findings are consistent that there is more psychopathology among divorced or separated persons than among the married (see ref. 45). The problem is one of interpretation: Is divorce or separation a cause or a consequence of psychopathology? Even where there are data over time so that the measure of marital disruption precedes the measure of psychopathology, there is a problem of interpretation, since many types of psychiatric disorders are chronic and/or of insidious onset. In divorce or separation, we have an event for whose occurrence the individual is likely to be responsible. It is thus unlike the other more fateful events we have been considering, such as forced unemployment, bereavement, exposure to combat, a natural disaster, being struck by serious physical illness, or some types of injury. Events such as divorce and separation are less likely to be independent of the individual's psychiatric condition. For this reason alone, correlations between such events as divorce or marital separation and psychopathology are always difficult to interpret without more information about the circumstances under which they occur.

Recent Experience with Multiple Life Events

Although not as rare in the experience of most people as natural disasters and combat, events such as death of spouse, forced unemployment, and even serious physical illness or injury are rare occurrences if we look at the recent experiences of members of a community population studied at a particular point in time, as most epidemiological studies have done. For example, few wives will have lost their husbands in, say, the year preceding the study, and few men or women will have lost their jobs because of plant shutdowns. Yet we know from the results of the epidemiological studies summarized in Table 1 that psychopathology is not rare in general populations. If stressful events play an important part, it must be that different events are involved for different people and/or that various combinations of events play a part.

More researchers have been investigating this proposition in relation to both psychopathology and physical illness (see refs. 17 and 27). They have used a variety of comprehensive lists of stressful life events with which to collect a record of the recent stressful experiences of their subjects. The most widely used of these lists was developed by Holmes and Rahe (31) on the basis of study of the types of events reported by more than 5,000 medical patients as clustering close to the time of disease onset. It consists of 43 events, large and small, including "death of spouse," "divorce," "personal illness or injury," "sex difficulties," "trouble with in-laws," and "vacation."

To date, a wide variety of correlations between psychopathology and such events has been reported. For example, Brown (3), Paykel (47), and Cooper and Sylph (9) have provided evidence that acute schizophrenia, depression, and neurosis may follow life events. The range of correlates has been expanded to include associations with symptom scales that measure various types of psychological distress, including demoralization, rather than outright disorder. Markush and Favero (42) found that relatively mild symptoms of depression as well as a symptom scale of less specific psychological distress were related to measures of life events. Uhlenhuth et al. (59) have reported similar findings. Myers et al. (44) have shown with still another measure of symptomatic distress that symptom scores will fluctuate over time with fluctuations in the nature and number of life events experienced.

Unfortunately, however, the correlations are often only modest at best (see ref. 48); there are inconsistent findings (e.g., refs. 3 and 33). Moreover, especially in the research on psychopathology, some of the findings are extremely difficult to interpret due to a probable confounding of the measurement of life events with the measurement of psychopathology when, as Schless and his colleagues (51) suggest of their own findings (pp. 21–22): "the events we are measuring may be symptoms of the illness rather than antecedents."

This last problem is an example of what Kasl (34) has described as "a self-serving methodological trap" that has tended to "trivialize" a great deal of the research on relationships between environmental stress and subjective distress. It is a central danger in the use of lists of recent life events to investigate the causal role of environmentally induced stress in psychopathology. Let me further illustrate the problem with reference to some of the events on the Holmes and Rahe list, which has strongly influenced most others. Subjective events on this list, such as "sexual difficulties," "major change in number of arguments with spouse," and "major changes in sleeping habits," taken at face value, are more likely to be manifestations of or responses to, rather than causes of, underlying psychopathology. Moreover, the problem is not limited to subjective events of this type since negative objective events, such as "divorce" and "being fired from work," are as likely to be consequences as causes of psychopathology, depending on the investigator's ability to date their onset in relation to the onset of the pathology and to learn something about whether the occurrences of the events are within or outside the control of the subject. For example, it is just such events whose occurrence is brought about by the behavior of individuals that Fontana and his colleagues (23) have found to differentiate recently hospitalized psychiatric patients at a Veterans Administration hospital from controls. He refers to them appropriately as "contingent events" since the patient played a part in bringing them about. Often they were also "involved events" when the event was part of the problem for which the patient was hospitalized.

The above examples of events from the Holmes and Rahe (31) list illustrate rather than exhaust the problem of possible confounding of events with psychopathology. There are quite a few other events that could be included. According to Hudgens (32), 29 of the 43 events on the list constructed by Holmes and Rahe (31) "are often the symptoms or consequences of illness." As Brown (3) and Dohrenwend (11) have pointed out, this kind of bias in a sample of life events seriously limits the kind of inferences that can be drawn from a correlation between the number or magnitude of events experienced and illness. The limitation on causal inference is especially severe in investigations of psychiatric disorders that are often of insidious onset and long duration.

In view of these considerations, it is incredible that some researchers have advocated scoring the magnitude of life events (the amount of readjustment, change, or upset involved) in terms of subjective ratings by the individuals whose stress experiences in relation to their psychopathology are being studied (e.g., ref. 24). This procedure is virtually guaranteed to confound the relationship between stress and psychopathology. Typically, for example, psychiatric patients rate such events as more stressful than nonpatients (24,50,57), just as persons who have experienced heart attacks after a particular life event or series of life events are likely to rate such events as more stressful than a person who has survived the events without a heart attack (57). It is a certainty that if they could talk, those members of a group of rats in a stress experiment who were disrupted by an electric shock would probably also argue that the voltage involved was greater than would rats exposed to the same objective stress who were not disrupted.

This is not to say that the subjective appraisals of the magnitude of the events that the individual experiences are useless. If the particular study is prospective, we may be able to learn something about vulnerability from subjective ratings of this type, provided that we have objective measures as well. If the study is retrospective, we can learn something about rationalization. We should not confuse these matters with adequate measurement of the stress to which the individual has been exposed.

Careful attention to matters of the possible confounding of the measurement of stress and the measurement of psychopathology is all the more important given the inevitable complexity involved in relationships between stressful life events and psychopathology in the general population by contrast with the relationship between stress and psychopathology in special groups in extreme situations. Fortunately, what we know about extreme situations, such as combat, holds important clues to our problem.

Consider the circumstances under which combinations of ordinary stressful life events might induce an approximation of the conditions involved in extreme situations, such as prolonged exposure to heavy combat. Such extreme situations involve being faced with unanticipated events whose occurrences are outside the control of the individual experiencing them (e.g., death of comrades). They involve the individual's own physical exhaustion, and they strip him of the social support of his comrades as the casualty rate rises. Events in civilian life, such as loss of loved ones, serious physical illness or injury, and events that disrupt social supports (e.g., a move to a new community or a change to a new place of employment) may, if they occur in close proximity to one another, create conditions of environmentally induced stress resembling those of extreme situations. Here, we hypothesize, we may have a triad of events whose occurrence may induce psychopathology in previously normal persons in much the same way that extreme situations involved in natural or man-made disasters are known to do.

A PARADIGM OF THE STRESS RESPONSE

Perhaps reference at this point to a general paradigm of the stress response based on Selye's (52) formulations and translated into social and psychological terms (10) will clarify the matter. The paradigm consists of four main elements: (a) an antecedent stressor, often a toxic agent or electric shock in Selye's experiments with animals, (b) conditioning or mediating factors, such as climate or diet, that increase or decrease the impact of the stressor, (c) the General Adaptation Syndrome of nonspecific physical and chemical changes, indicating the intervening state of stress in an organism over time, and (d) consequent adaptive or, in cases where there is a "derailment" of the mechanism of adaptation, maladaptive responses in the form of what Selye calls "diseases of adaptation."

By stripping these four kinds of elements of particular examples, it is possible to arrive at the general paradigm of the individual organism's stress response shown in Fig. 1. This general paradigm, in turn, can be translated into social and psychological terms for its various elements. For example, stressors can range from extreme situations, such as natural and man-made disasters, to the more ordinary stressful life events that we have been considering. Mediating factors can be expanded to include both inner resources and deficits (e.g., intellectual abilities, physical health, inherited vulnerabilities, and vulnerabilities ac-

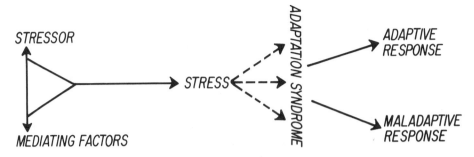

FIG. 1. General paradigm of the stress response. (From ref. 10.)

quired from, say, death of a parent before age 11) and external resources or deficits (e.g., material wealth, social support in the form of family and friends, or the absence of such assets).

Whether there is a General Adaptation Syndrome of nonspecific physical and chemical changes has been questioned (43). Whether there is anything directly analogous to it in social and psychological terms is an open issue; therefore, we have omitted the adjective "general" in Fig. 1. Certainly, however, sociopsychological adaptation syndromes must have affective elements of adaptation rooted in the arousal responses of fear and anger, and conative elements of adaptation involving change or reemphasis in activities, abandoning some activities, taking up others, and increasing or decreasing still other activities. Finally, adaptation is also likely to involve changes in orientation involving assimilation of new information, alteration of beliefs, and so on. When adaptation fails or the mechanisms underlying it become derailed, we can look for maladaptive responses in the form of transient or persistent psychopathology, with demoralization perhaps being a constant but by no means exclusive component.

In regard to the antecedent conditions producing stress as portrayed in Fig. 1, we can envision two extremes on the basis of the preceding analysis. At one extreme would be the pathogenic triad of stressors composed of fateful loss events, physical illness and injury, and other events that disrupt social supports. We hypothesize that the impact of such a triad of events would override internal and external mediating factors, as in extreme situations, and lead directly to derailment of the mechanisms of adaptation and consequent psychopathology in previously normal persons.

At the other extreme, we can envision chronic psychiatric patients, such as those whose admissions to a Veterans Administration hospital were studied by Fontana and colleagues (23). The types of stressors that differentiate such persons from controls are events that are contingent upon their own actions and/or directly involved in the process of bringing them to the hospital. Such events (e.g., quitting a job, provoking an argument with a spouse, or an arrest) are best interpreted not as antecedents to the patient's disorder or to its exacerbation but rather, in Fontana's plausible view, as attempts to cope with onsets or exacerbations of disorder by behaving in such a way as to insure hospitalization. Clearly, recent environmentally induced stress is unimportant as an etiological factor in such cases, and stressors in the paradigm in Fig. 1 can be discounted. Rather, it is the mediating factors, especially those internal mediating factors that have made the individual vulnerable, that are the causal factors in the psychopathology leading to hospitalization.

Only small minorities of individuals in a general population sample are likely to be chronic psychiatric patients with multiple hospital admissions, as in the case of most patients in Veterans Administration hospitals. Similarly, our best estimate is that only a small portion of such a sample will have recently experienced the particular triad of events that, we hypothesize, are pathogenic. For example, in a study of a sample of 166 adults from the general population of New York City, we used a comprehensive list of 101 life events to investigate experiences with stress in the year preceding the interview (18). Preliminary analyses indicate that no more than 5% experienced serious events from all three elements of the triad in the preceding year. Yet, as seen in Table 1, functional psychiatric disorders and cases of severe demoralization are far more frequent in general populations. If stressful events play a large part, then combinations of them that are less potent than the pathogenic triad but not as negligible as those Fontana shows are confounded with psychiatric condition must be involved. If so, and if the above analysis is correct, such combinations of events of intermediate potency must play their part in conjunction with internal and external mediating factors. In examining the role of such intermediate combinations of events, it is necessary to look at their interaction with mediating factors. Given our focus on the role of socioenvironmental factors, not only would such external mediating factors as those involving social supports and material resources be of special interest, but so too would internal mediating factors that may involve vulnerability stemming from early experiences with stressful events. Of particular interest here would be further investigation of the role played by loss of one or both parents before age 11 in making individuals vulnerable to loss events later in life.

CONCLUSIONS

Life events are eminently researchable. They are important to the people we study, things that they are interested in and can tell us about. If environmentally induced stress is an important factor in psychopathology in the general population, then life events are strategic phenomena on which to focus as major sources of such stress.

The problem, however, is to ask the right questions about whether and to what extent life events are causally related to psychopathology. We have introduced the paradigm of the stress response shown in Fig. 1 as an aid to asking these questions.

We hypothesize that under one set of circumstances, a pathogenic triad of events involving physical illness or injury, other fateful loss events, and events that disrupt the individual's usual social supports will override the mediating factors shown in Fig. 1 and lead directly to maladaptive responses in the form of various types of psychopathology. Under another set of circumstances, any events experienced will be brought about by the individual's behavior and occur as a function of his or her prior psychopathology or predisposition to psychopathology. Under such circumstances, internal mediating factors in the form of predispositions to the maladaptive outcomes rather than the stressful events will be the important causal agents.

It is the middle range, circumstances between these extremes, that provides the greatest challenge for investigating the role of stressful life events in psychopathology in the general population. Here a pathogenic triad does not override mediating factors, nor do internal mediating factors or predispositions by themselves account for the occurrence of psychopathology. Rather, it is more likely that the nature of the interactions between stressful events and the internal and external factors that mediate their impact is decisive. Our question becomes: "What kinds of life events, in what combinations, over what period of time, and under what circumstances are causally implicated in various types of psychopathology?"

The problem of examining the great variety of combinations of life events in this intermediate range together with their relationship to internal and external mediating factors that may often be of remote origin increases the complexity of our question. The central methodological problem in our search for answers is to avoid confounding the antecedent and consequent variables shown in Fig. 1 in our decisions about how to measure stressful life events.

Fortunately, there are at least three major reasons to expend the considerable effort required to come to terms with the problems involved. First the large majority of the general population will be experiencing life events in this intermediate range within any given period of time. Second, in examining mediating factors for such events, clues to the conditions that bring about one rather than another type of psychopathology are likely to be found. Finally, by investigating interactions with some types of mediating factors, such as those providing social supports, we may be able to gain our best leads for environmentally oriented attempts at primary prevention. Thus, while the increased complexity undoubtedly has its costs, it may have substantial benefits as well.

ACKNOWLEDGMENTS

This work was supported in part by research grant MH 10328 and by Research Scientist Award K05-MH 14663 from the National Institute of Mental Health. It was also supported by the Foundations' Fund for Research in Psychiatry.

I would like to thank Bruce G. Link for his able help analyzing the results summarized in Table 1 and Barbara Snell Dohrenwend for valuable criticism.

REFERENCES

1. Arthur, R. J. (1974): Extreme stress in adult life and psychic and psychophysiological consequences. In: *Life Stress and Illness,* edited by E. K. E. Gunderson and R. H. Rahe, pp. 195–207. Charles C Thomas, Springfield, Illinois.
2. Brenner, M. H. (1973): *Mental Illness and the Economy.* Harvard University Press, Cambridge, Massachusetts.
3. Brown, G. W. (1974): Meaning, measurement, and stress of life events. In: *Stressful Life Events: Their Nature and Effects,* edited by B. S. Dohrenwend and B. P. Dohrenwend, pp. 217–243. Wiley, New York.
4. Brown, G. W., Harris, T., and Copeland, J. R. (1977): Depression and loss. *Br. J. Psychiatry,* 130:1–18.
5. Chen, E., and Cobb, S. (1960): Family Structure in relation to health and disease. *J. Chronic Dis.,* 12:544–567.
6. Clayton, P. J., Herjanic, M., Murphy, G. E., and Woodruff, R., Jr. (1974): Mourning and depression: Their similarities and differences. *Can. Psychiatr. Assoc. J.,* 19:309–312.
7. Cobb, S., and Kasl, S. V. (1977): *Termination: The Consequence of Job Loss.* DHEW publication no. (NIOSH) 77–224. Washington, D.C.
8. Cooper, B., and Shepherd, M. (1970): Life change, stress and mental disorder: The ecological approach. In: *Modern Trends in Psychological Medicine, Vol. 2,* edited by J. H. Price, pp. 102–130. Butterworths, London.
9. Cooper, B., and Sylph, J. (1973): Life events and the onset of neurotic illness: An investigation in general practice. *Psychol. Med.,* 3:421–435.
10. Dohrenwend, B. P. (1961): The social psychological nature of stress: A framework for causal injury. *J. Abnorm. Soc. Psychol.,* 62:294–302.
11. Dohrenwend, B. P. (1974): Problems in defining and sampling the relevant population of stressful life events. In: *Stressful Life Events: Their Nature and Effects,* edited by B. S. Dohrenwend and B. P. Dohrenwend, pp. 275–310. Wiley, New York.
12. Dohrenwend, B. P., and de Figueiredo, J. M. (1978): Stressful events of the life course. Paper presented at *Symposium on Aging from Birth to Death,* Annual Meeting of the American Association for the Advancement of Science, February 12–17, Washington, D.C.
13. Dohrenwend, B. P., and Dohrenwend, B. S. (1969): *Social Status and Psychological Disorder.* Wiley, New York.
14. Dohrenwend, B. P., and Dohrenwend, B. S. (1974): Social and cultural influences on psychopathology. *Ann. Rev. Psychol.,* 25:417–452.
15. Dohrenwend, B. P., and Dohrenwend, B. S. (1976): Sex differences and psychiatric disorder. *Am. J. Sociol.,* 81:1447–1454.
16. Dohrenwend, B. P., Oksenberg, L. E., Shrout, P. E., Dohrenwend, B. S., and Cook, D. (1979): What psychiatric screening scales measure in the general population. *(In preparation.)*
17. Dohrenwend, B. S., and Dohrenwend, B. P. (editors) (1974): *Stressful Life Events: Their Nature and Effects.* Wiley, New York.
18. Dohrenwend, B. S., Krasnoff, L., Askenasy, A. R., and Dohrenwend, B. P. (1978): Exemplification of a method for scaling life events: The PERI life events scale. *J. Health Soc. Behav.,* 19:205–229.
19. Eastwood, M. R. (1975): *The Relation Between Physical and Mental Illness.* University of Toronto Press, Toronto.
20. Eitinger, L. (1964): *Concentration Camp Survivors in Norway and Israel.* Allen and Unwin, London.
21. Eitinger, L. (1973): A follow-up of the Norwegian concentration camp survivors' mortality and morbidity. *Isr. Ann. Psychiatry,* 11:199–209.
22. Frank, J. D. (1973): *Persuasion and Healing.* The Johns Hopkins University Press, Baltimore.
23. Fontana, A. F., Marcus, J. L., Noel, B., and Rakusin, J. M. (1972): Prehospitalization coping styles of psychiatric patients: The goal-directedness of life events. *J. Nerv. Ment. Dis.,* 155:311–321.

24. Grant, I., Gerst, M., and Yager, J. (1976): Scaling of life events by psychiatric patients and normals. *J. Psychosom. Res.*, 20:141–149.
25. Granville-Grossman, K. L. (1968): The early environment in affective disorder. *Br. J. Psychiatry*, 2:65–79.
26. Grinker, R. R., and Spiegel, J. P. (1963): *Men Under Stress*. McGraw-Hill, New York.
27. Gunderson, E. K. E., and Rahe, R. H. (editors) (1974): *Life Stress and Illness*. Charles C Thomas, Springfield, Illinois.
28. Heinicke, C. M. (1973): Parental deprivation in early childhood. In: *Separation and Depression*, edited by J. P. Scott and E. C. Senay, pp. 141–160. American Association for the Advancement of Science, publication no. 94, Washington, D.C.
29. Hinkle, L. E., and Wolff, H. G. (1957): Health and the social environment: In: *Explorations in Social Psychiatry*, edited by A. H. Leighton, J. A. Clausen, and R. N. Wilson, pp. 105–137. Basic Books, New York.
30. Hocking, F. (1970): Extreme environmental stress and its significance for psychopathology. *Am. J. Psychother.*, 24:4–26.
31. Holmes, T. H., and Rahe, R. H. (1967): The social readjustment rating scale. *J. Psychosom. Med.*, 11:213–218.
32. Hudgens, R. W. (1974): Personal catastrophe and depression: A consideration of the subject with respect to medically ill adolescents, and a requiem for retrospective life-event studies. In: *Stressful Life Events: Their Nature and Effects*, edited by B. S. Dohrenwend and B. P. Dohrenwend, pp. 119–134. Wiley, New York.
33. Jacobs, S., and Myers, J. (1976): Recent life events and acute schizophrenic psychosis: A controlled study. *J. Nerv. Ment. Dis.*, 162:75–87.
34. Kasl, S. V. (1978): Stress at work: Epidemiological contributions to the study of work stress. In: *Stress at Work*, edited by C. L. Cooper and R. Payne, pp. 3–50. Wiley, New York.
35. Kinston, W., and Rosser, R. (1974): Disaster: Effects on mental and physical state. *J. Psychosom. Res.*, 18:437–456.
36. Kolb, L. C. (1973): *Modern Clinical Psychiatry*. Saunders, Philadelphia.
37. Langner, T. S. (1962): A twenty-two item screening score of psychiatric symptoms indicating impairment. *J. Health Soc. Behav.*, 3:269–276.
38. Langner, T. S., and Michael, S. T. (1963): *Life Stress and Mental Health*. The Free Press of Glencoe, London.
39. Leighton, D. C., Harding, J. S., Macklin, D. B., Macmillan, A. M., and Leighton, A. H. (1963): *The Character of Danger*. Basic Books, New York.
40. Link, B. G., and Dohrenwend, B. P. (1979): Formulation of hypotheses about the true prevalence of demoralization in the United States. In: *Mental Illness in the United States—An Epidemiological Analysis of the Scope of the Problem*, edited by B. P. Dohrenwend, B. S. Dohrenwend, M. S. Gould, B. G. Link, R. Neugebauer, and R. Wunsch. *(In preparation.)*
41. Lipowski, Z. J. (1975): Psychiatry of somatic diseases: Epidemiology, pathogenesis, classification. *Compr. Psychiatry*, 16:105–124.
42. Markush, R. E., and Favero, R. V. (1974): Epidemiologic assessment of stressful life events, depressed mood, and psychophysiological symptoms—a preliminary report. In: *Stressful Life Events: Their Nature and Effects*, edited by B. S. Dohrenwend and B. P. Dohrenwend, pp. 171–190. Wiley, New York.
43. Mason, J. W. (1975): A historical view of the stress field. *J. Human Stress*, 1:6–12.
44. Myers, J. K., Lindenthal, J. J., and Pepper, M. P. (1974): Social class, life events, and psychiatric symptoms. A longitudinal study. In: *Stressful Life Events: Their Nature and Effects*, edited by B. S. Dohrenwend and B. P. Dohrenwend, pp. 191–205. Wiley, New York.
45. National Institute of Mental Health (1975): *Marital Status and Mental Disorder: An Analytical Review*. DHEW publication no. (ADM) 75–217, Washington, D.C.
46. Paster, S. (1948): Psychotic reactions among soldiers of World War II. *J. Nerv. Ment. Dis.*, 108:54–66.
47. Paykel, E. S. (1974): Life stress and psychiatric disorder: Application of the clinical approach. In: *Stressful Life Events: Their Nature and Effects*, edited by B. S. Dohrenwend and B. P. Dohrenwend, pp. 135–149. Wiley, New York.
48. Rabkin, J. G., and Struening, E. L. (1976): Life events, stress, and illness. *Science*, 194:1013–1020.
49. Rutter, M. (1974): *The Qualities of Mothering: Maternal Deprivation Reassessed*. Jason Aronson, New York.

50. Schless, A. P., Schwartz, L., Goetz, C., and Mendels, J. (1974): How depressives view the significance of life events. *Br. J. Psychiatry*, 125:406–410.
51. Schless, A. R., Teichman, A., Mendels, J., and DiGiacomo, J. N. (1977): The role of stress as a precipitating factor of psychiatric illness. *Br. J. Psychiatry*, 130:19–22.
52. Selye, H. (1956): *The Stress of Life.* McGraw-Hill, New York.
53. Shepherd, M., Cooper, B., Brown, A. C., and Kalton, G. W. (1966): *Psychiatric Illness in General Practice.* Oxford University Press, London.
54. Star, S. A. (1949): Psychoneurotic symptoms in the army. In: *Studies in Social Psychology in World War II. The American Soldier: Combat and its Aftermath,* edited by S. A. Stoufer, L. Guttman, E. A. Suchman, P. F. Lazarsfeld, S. A. Star, and J. A. Clausen, pp. 411–455. Princeton University Press, New Jersey.
55. Star, S. A. (1950): The screening of psychoneurotics in the army: Technical development of tests. In: *Measurement and Prediction,* edited by S. A. Stouffer, L. Guttman, E. A. Suchman, P. F. Lazarsfeld, S. A. Star, and J. A. Clausen, pp. 486–547. Princeton University Press, New Jersey.
56. Swank, R. L. (1949): Combat exhaustion. *J. Nerv. Ment. Dis.,* 109:475–508.
57. Theorell, T. (1974): Life events before and after the onset of a premature myocardial infarction. In: *Stressful Life Events: Their Nature and Effects,* edited by B. S. Dohrenwend and B. P. Dohrenwend, pp. 101–115. Wiley, New York.
58. Uhlenhuth, E. H., Balter, M. D., Lipman, R. S., and Haberman, S. J. (1977): Remembering life events. In: *The Origins and Course of Psychopathology,* edited by J. S. Strauss, H. M. Babigian, and M. Roff, pp. 117–132. Plenum Press, New York.
59. Uhlenhuth, E., Lipman, R. S., Balter, M. B., and Stern, M. (1974): Symptom intensity and life stress in the city. *Arch. Gen. Psychiatry,* 31:759–764.
60. Weissman, M. M., Myers, J. K., and Harding, P. S. (1978): Psychiatric disorders in a U.S. urban community: 1975–76. *Am. J. Psychiatry,* 135:459–462.

Stress and Mental Disorder,
edited by James E. Barrett et al.
Raven Press, New York © 1979.

Life Changes and Psychiatric Symptom Development: Issues of Content, Scoring, and Clustering

Michael W. Hurst

Boston University School of Medicine, Boston, Massachusetts 02118

The pioneering work of Holmes, Rahe, and others (12,14,27) in the development of methodology for the assessment of life event stress provided a beginning from which the role of life events in the etiology of mental disorders might be unraveled by persistent research, particularly scientific studies of a prospective nature. The new methodology was an exciting breakthrough for scientists in this field. The numerous studies that have been published as a consequence have yielded considerable evidence supporting the clinical impression that life events play an important role in the etiology of both mental and somatic disorders (4,8,9,12,17,23,27,32,33,37–39). Despite the breadth of findings from these numerous studies, much work remains to be done to produce an understanding based firmly on scientifically acceptable methodology, particularly regarding the assessment of life event stress (1,4–7,10,14,31).

The burden of scientific work is to provide theories and hypotheses that help us to understand, explain, and predict natural phenomena. Essential to the discharge of this function are the methods and instruments by which the theories, hypotheses, and predictions can be tested. In this chapter, issues of methodology and instrumentation for the assessment of life event stress are described and evaluated with the hope that such an evaluation will help to advance the testing of theories, hypotheses, and predictions linking life events and mental disorders.

This chapter focuses on three major issues in the assessment of life event stress: (a) the content of the life event inventories, (b) the scoring of the life events, and (c) clustering of life events. Since methodology and assessment can be a rather dry and technical focus, the attempt is to provide meaning and substance to these issues by concentrating on the question: "Do they make a difference?"

Although the issues involving methodology and instrumentation could be discussed from a totally theoretical standpoint, it would be more useful to present data that speak to the theoretical positions and demonstrate that methodology is an important concern. This chapter is organized to present both theoretical and applied issues in life change assessment. The first three sections present and discuss content, scoring, and clustering issues from a theoretical standpoint, with selected data augmenting the arguments. The last section presents a series of findings based on an attempt to take into account the theoretical issues.

CONTENT OF LIFE EVENT INVENTORIES

The content of a life event inventory is critical to its usefulness as a possible predictor instrument (1,5,23,31). A general principle for the construction or selection of life event questionnaires could be proposed: *The life events listed in a life events inventory must be ones for which the individuals in a study population would be at risk in the time span over which the study respondents would be required to report; i.e., the items must be relevant to the lives of the respondents.*

For example, one could propose a study of the relationship between life events and mental disorders among Americans in which the life event inventory included only the following items: (a) moving to the Antarctic, (b) taking a spaceship trip to the moon, (c) experiencing a 24-hr total isolation from all stimuli, and (d) experiencing your own death. Clearly, research using this life events inventory is going to be doomed in trying to establish any relationship between life events and mental disorder. The probability of these events occurring to Americans would be so low that neither a mentally disordered nor a "normal" person would be likely to experience them.

Recent life event questionnaires have been developed to expand their content in areas relevant to the population being studied. For example, when student studies were initiated, investigators found that the events listed for patients or working class persons were not experienced very frequently by their subject populations (20,23); this infrequency made it more difficult to study the effects of life change stress on student health. Expanded inventories were developed which included more relevant events, such as examinations, dropping courses, and changing advisors.

In addition, studies presently underway have recognized the fact that most currently recognized life event inventories also are relatively inappropriate for salespeople (16) or prisoners (13), because either most of the events listed in recognized inventories do not occur in their lives or they occur at such low frequency that no relationship between their occurrence and mental disorder could be shown. Sometimes, too, the typical life event inventories do not reflect the events of greatest concern and prevalence to particular groups. Thus one must bear in mind that the events in an inventory are only a sample of the universe of life events, and any given sample of events cannot be expected to fully or adequately represent all events.

An immediate question is whether the events themselves are important or whether it is their characteristics or the characteristics they have in common that are important. One could say that a trip to Antarctica, for example, was a loss of one's current psychosocial support system; or that a trip to the moon or a 24-hr isolation experiment was a similar loss. Would it be, therefore, the loss rather than the event itself that represents the stress? Unfortunately, any type of life event can be labeled with almost any type of etiologically significant meaning on a *post hoc* basis and maybe even on an *a priori* basis. This issue of content interpretation is discussed below. The important point is that events in a life events questionnaire must have some reasonable possibility of occurring in the population being studied. Otherwise, an investigator cannot evaluate the etiological roles for those events or the importance of their characteristics with respect to mental or other illnesses.

A second major point with respect to the content of life event inventories is that the event must have some meaning for the population studied. To establish a list of events that has meaning for a given study population, there are basically two choices. First, one can evaluate the list after the respondents have indicated which events have occurred to them and how they felt about those events. This *post hoc* analysis, however, has the disadvantage that significant events

TABLE 1. *Special list of relevant life events for salespeople and brokers*

1. Loss of a major account
2. An order cannot be traced
3. Principals make demands that cannot be met
4. Marital separation due to arguments
5. Interview with prospective principal
6. Cancellation of an appointment with important principals present
7. Merger with another broker
8. An employee leaves and takes at least one important account
9. An account discontinues a significant item or line of products
10. A bulletin was sent but the account claims they did not receive it
11. Unauthorized deductions by employees
12. Broker unable to pay anticipated bonus to employees
13. Three or more days in a row away from one's family on business
14. Request for kickbacks from principals or accounts
15. Work on commissions
16. A major account has a serious business loss
17. Seasonal merchandise is returned
18. Buyer makes a request which is contrary to policy or principals
19. Deliveries are adversely affected
20. Loss of account sales but account continues
21. Principal notifies broker of error or deficiency in performance
22. A change in buyers for an account
23. New product introduction which management feels will fail
24. Sales meeting with principal
25. Take a vacation
26. You take a large loan ($10,000 or more)
27. Move your household to another city
28. One of your children dies
29. Major personal physical illness
30. New person moves into household
31. Severe arguments with co-workers
32. Divorce
33. Law suit is filed against you
34. A change in principal's representative
35. You personally develop major financial difficulties

may not have been listed and therefore the investigator would not know if these events were missed. A second choice is to interview a number of subjects within the study population prior to devising or choosing a life events questionnaire. In this manner, one can learn from the subjects the types of events that are reasonably prevalent, as well as those that may cause particular concern.

The second strategy was used in devising a questionnaire for salespeople and sales representatives (16). As illustrated in Table 1, most of the events that they considered particularly "stressful" and relevant had little in common with the events that are typically listed in most life events questionnaires. One should note, too, that 10 of the events in this list were chosen from the Schedule of Recent Experience (SRE) of Holmes and Rahe (14).

These 10 were placed in the life event list to act as control items. If one devises new inventories with content that is considerably different from published inventories, it is important to use a few published items to check the comparability of item prevalence and life event ratings.

For example, the 10 SRE life events were selected from the original 43. The frequency of these events and the mean ratings assigned to them by a special group can be used to describe general differences in reporting tendencies by the special group compared to normative groups.

ISSUES IN SCORING

There are at least six major issues with respect to scoring life events for "stress:" (a) what is scored, (b) by whom the scoring is done, (c) what reference population is used, (d) how the events are scored and rated, (e) what summary scores should be used, and (f) what scores (total scores, subscores, cluster scores) are used for predictive purposes. Some of these issues have been raised by others (1,4,8,10,18,19,21,22,26,31–34,36,41,42), but they bear further analysis.

Depending on the particular life event inventory and the theoretical orientation of the investigator, subjects have been asked to rate adjustment (14,22,24), distress or upset (28,29), "stress" (15), or sometimes a combination of these three concepts (6,18,36). Research in our laboratory (18) has indicated that the correlations between scores based on distress and those based on adjustment ratings range between 0.85 and 0.95. These high correlations can be caused by a number of factors, but they certainly suggest that what is rated does not make much difference with respect to the general rank order of the life events.

On the other hand, a previously published study showed that a sample of air traffic controllers gave adjustment ratings that were significantly higher than the normative group on the SRE, but the controllers gave distress ratings that were significantly lower than the original groups tested on the Paykel, Uhlenhuth, and Prusoff (PUP) inventory (18). Thus, using adjustment scores, one would conclude that air traffic controllers experience significantly more adjustment, but significantly less distress, due to life events than a normative group. Therefore, what is rated may make a difference in the comparisons that an investigator makes and what conclusions would be drawn from the comparisons.

The second major issue is who makes the ratings that are used for scoring. A number of studies have indicated that there can be substantial differences in mean ratings between males and females, among certain sociocultural groups, and, perhaps most importantly, between subjects who have experienced events and those who have not (4,7,11,15,21,25,28,29,31,42).

Paykel et al. (28,29) have shown that, for their questionnaire, 15 of their 61 events were rated significantly differently by subjects who had and those who had not experienced the events. Horowitz et al. (15) found that two clusters of events were rated significantly more stressful by subjects who experienced the events. Other research has indicated that air traffic controllers who experienced an event gave ratings that were significantly different from the normative group for 26 of 36 life events on the SRE that could be compared and on 31 of 46 possible comparisons of life events on the PUP inventory (18). Thus it is clear that it does make a difference as to who is making the ratings that are used to score life change stress. Ratings obtained with one type of group may not be generalized to other groups.

The third major issue of scoring is one of selecting the reference population (1,18). Subjects could rate or score the life events (a) in terms of how much adjustment they feel people in general would have (14), (b) with respect to people they know (such as people in their occupational group), or (c) in terms of how much adjustment they themselves would experience (18–20). Again we ask: Does it make a difference?

Table 2 presents correlations among life event scores based on simple unit sums, ratings for people in general, average ratings of the study group, and the personal ratings of the individuals responding to the questionnaire. These data originated from a prospective study of 114 Harvard undergraduates by Locke et al. (20). The subjects completed a life event questionnaire covering the past year; 2 weeks later, they filled out the Johns Hopkins Symptom Check List (SCL-58). Note that the correlation between the life event scores and the SCL scores rises as one progresses from scores based on people in general to scores based on the individual's own ratings. Consequently, the reference population on which scores for life events are based does make a difference in terms

TABLE 2. *Correlations between different summary scores for life events and Johns Hopkins SCL scores 2 weeks later[a]*

Symptom score	Correlations with life event scores for events in past year			
	Simple unit sum	SRE weights summed for SRE items	Group mean weights summed for events that occurred	Individuals' own ratings summed for events that occurred
SCL total	0.33	0.32	0.35	0.38
SCL depression	0.28	0.29	0.31	0.38
SCL anxiety	0.19	0.17	0.21	0.21

[a] $N = 112$. All correlations were significant at $p = 0.05$, 2-tailed.

of the predictive relationship of life events to psychiatric and somatic symptoms.

The fourth major issue is whether the structure of how events are recorded and rated makes any difference. There are at least two structural tasks. Respondents to life event questionnaires are asked to indicate whether or not events have occurred, but also they are asked whether these events have occurred within a particular time span, e.g., in the last 6 months, the last year, or the last 2 years. In addition, they can be asked to rate the events according to an open-ended scale, ranging from zero to infinity, for example, or they can be asked to make ratings on a closed scale, such as from 0 to 20. Thus the major structural issues revolve around the time span within which the events are supposed to occur and the type of scale which a respondent is supposed to use. Do either of these two issues make a difference?

In summary, our research and that of others (4,26,32,33) indicate that the longer the period being recalled, the greater the reliability. On the other hand, however, the results also show that the more distant the period of recall, the more likely it is that life change stress is underestimated (3,15,19,32). For example, if a subject is asked to recall a 1-year period of time and 6 months later is asked to recall that same 1-year period, his reliability of recall will be higher than if he is asked to recall a 1-month period and 6 months later is examined regarding that same month. Conversely, if we keep the period of recall constant (e.g., a 1-month time span) but we vary the time elapsed since that period from 6 to 12 months, the respondent with an elapsed time of 6 months will tend to recall more than a respondent with an elapsed time of 12 months (3,15). With our present methodology, test-retest stability is increased by using a longer period of recall for life events, but the accuracy and validity of recall is inversely proportional to the remoteness of the time period being recalled (2,3,40).

The original scaling methodology of Masuda and Holmes (24) was an open-ended proportional system. The subjects made ratings from zero to infinity, relative to marriage, which was defined as 500 points. Thus a rating of 5,000 would be assigned to a life event that caused 10 times as much adjustment as marriage. In contrast, Paykel et al. and Hurst et al. have used closed scales with upper limits of 20 and 99, respectively. No attempt is made to imply that an event rated for example, 20, causes twice as much distress as one rated 10. Does this difference in possible implications make a difference?

To my knowledge, no study has been done to determine if the difference in inferences available from open-ended scaling in contrast to closed scaling changes anything. However, there are possible advantages and disadvantages. Open-ended proportional scaling may result in a true ratio scale. The work of Masuda and Holmes (24) suggested that this may be so and that open-ended proportional scaling follows Steven's Law of Psychophysics. This would be a theoretical advantage, but future research may disclose a practical advantage.

On the other hand, there may be statistical disadvantages to open-ended proportional scaling since the standard error of a mean would be particularly inflated by extraneous high ratings. In addition, the extraneous high ratings may really reflect response sets or personality styles rather than true adjustment or distress. Therefore, given only a theoretical advantage and two practical disadvantages, open-ended proportional ratings may be less useful than closed scaling techniques.

A fifth major issue in scoring is which summary measures of life change stress should be used. One could use total scores based on summing weights for life events that have occurred, where the weights are (a) unity, (b) the mean values assigned by an external population, (c) the mean values assigned by the sample group, or (d) the weights assigned by an individual subject. Each of these has its own advantages and disadvantages.

Using summary scores that are based on means derived from an external population has the advantage that one can compare the results in a study group with the results of another population. Furthermore, in a retrospective study, the use of external population mean scores as the weights for life events has the unique advantage of avoiding circular research (24,28,29,32,33). Retrospective studies could become circular in their findings if individuals' own ratings were used; they would also be giving their retrospective report of their psychiatric status and history and possibly would be rating life events according to their preconceived notions that some events were related to some of their difficulties. This particular problem is avoided completely by using external population scores.

A major disadvantage of using external population scores is that the external population may not be representative of one's study sample (1,18). In addition, research has indicated that total scores based on using external population ratings are highly related to the simple number of events that have occurred. Rahe (33) pointed this out in 1974, and we have confirmed it for both the SRE and the PUP inventory (18). This particular disadvantage is a major one since findings based on total scores which have resulted from summing external population mean ratings can be interpreted most parsimoniously as a consequence of the number of life changes rather than the stress caused by those life changes.

Basing the total scores on sums of the mean ratings derived from one's sample group for those events that occurred has the advantage that the experience of the study population is reflected rather than that of some external population. In retrospective studies, one would have the difficulty of somewhat circular reasoning for overall group results, although not for subgroups or individual results. Using sample group mean ratings is an advantage for prospective research in that the total scores reflect the impact of the various events on the particular group. This advantage requires considerable homogeneity of the group membership such that the impact of the events was experienced quite similarly.

Finally, one could use total scores that are based on summing an individual's own ratings for those events that have occurred to that individual. These ratings are completely inappropriate in retrospective designs because of the circularity of reasoning involved. On the other hand, they may be the best total scores to use in prospective research since they clearly reflect the impact of the life events on the life of the individual from the individual's own perspective (1,18). In addition, total scores based on summing individuals' own ratings require the fewest number of assumptions regarding the meaning of the total scores and their generalizability.

Research has indicated that there is a tremendous individual variability in the ratings of life events (18,24,31). Hence a score for a given event based on a mean of either the study sample or an external population assumes that this is the correct weight for all individuals in the study; but it has been clearly demonstrated that this is not the case. For example, in our study of air traffic controllers, the death of a pet received ratings of distress ranging from 1 to 99 (18). The average rating was low, but the average certainly did not adequately represent the distress experienced by each person whose pet died.

The final issue to be considered with respect to the scoring of life events is whether the events should be summed up into one grand total as just discussed, or whether some form of clustering may be more appropriate (1,4,10,15,26, 30,34,38,39,41). Resolution of this issue requires a clear understanding of the hypothesis being tested and the theories being used to interpret the results. For example, if the hypothesis is simply that life events have some predictive relationship to the later development of psychiatric symptoms, then a total score would be appropriate if that total score was based on a reasonably valid and reliable sampling of all of the events that might occur to the individuals in one's study population. Clearly, that is an enormous assumption.

Clusters of events could be used instead, for example, to test more specific hypotheses. One might hypothesize that the events affecting one's family are related to the development of psychiatric symptoms. For this example, we no longer have to assume that the life event inventory adequately samples all of the possible life events that happen to the individuals, but rather we make the smaller assumption that the events that could occur to one's family have been adequately sampled. It is preferable to make as few assumptions as possible in any research, including research on the role of life events and psychiatric disorders. Before turning to the focal question of whether it makes a difference, let us consider the issue of how one might cluster life events.

ISSUES IN LIFE EVENT CLUSTERING

Life events basically can be clustered by their theoretical or actual similarities to one another.

To cluster life events in terms of theoretical similarities means that one interprets the meaning of the event and then classifies the events into groups with common meanings. For example, Paykel, Uhlenhuth, and others (27–29,38,39) have classified events into exits and entrances. In this scheme for clustering, a loss, such as the death of a friend, would be interpreted as an exit, whereas a birth would be classified as an entrance. In addition, Dohrenwend and others (6,10,41) have added the dimension of desirable and undesirable life events.

In this type of clustering, the investigator interprets the meaning of the event *a priori;* if a difference in prevalence or predictive relationships is found between clusters, then the difference might be attributed to the difference in meaning assigned to the life event clusters.

A major problem with this method of clustering arises since the meaning of events may be quite different between respondents and investigators. Although a difference in cluster relationships to outcomes may be found, it may be due not to differences in meanings as interpreted by the investigators but rather to differences in the meaning of those events to the respondents.

It would be interesting if respondents to a questionnaire would rate the degree of loss or undesirability or the degree of pleasant or unpleasant affects associated with the life events. Furthermore, it would be of considerable interest for investigators to use bipolar rather than unipolar rating scales. In other words, subjects could rate on a scale ranging from undesirable to desirable. The events then would be clustered on the actual perceptions of the respondents.

Another method of clustering according to theoretical similarities is to use the similarities of events in terms of their locus in life. Again, an investigator must make the judgment; but, for example, events can be grouped if they occur surrounding particular but not necessarily distinct areas in life. Our laboratory has been using life event inventories, and we have clustered events according to their content as we interpret that content in particular areas of life (see Table 3).

The method of content clustering according to the locus of events in the

TABLE 3. *Number of life events in content clusters within three life event inventories*

Content cluster	Life event inventory		
	SRE	PUP	ROLE
Marital	6[a]	12	18
Family	9	4	16
Work	6	6	14
Financial	6	4	10
Losses	3	6	8
Children	1	7	7
Health	4	2	7
Legal	2	4	5
Dating	0	4	5
Relocation	1	2	3
Education	1	1	3
Anticipated events	0	0	2
Summary events	0	0	4
Events not applicable to ATCs	4	9	0
Total events/inventory	43	61	102

[a]Numbers refer to number of events.

real world has the advantage that there is a face understanding of what the events might be, and less interpretation is involved. However, it is still possible for investigators and subjects to interpret the loci of events quite differently with the result that the investigators may draw an improper interpretation of results.

One can also cluster life events according to actual similarities as found in the results of the respondents. For example, Rahe, Pugh, Ericson, Gunderson, Rubin, and others (26,30,34) applied statistical cluster analysis, which helps to improve the internal consistency of the clustering and the overall reliability of the cluster. However, these procedures require that there be correlations in the occurrence of differing life events. Although causality is never deducible from correlations *per se,* it is at least implied, even though the direction of causality may not be known. Consequently, statistical techniques for clustering events based on varying types of correlation analysis automatically imply that some of the life events are consequences of other life events. However, as has been noted before (8), one of our tasks should be to unravel the primary events and etiology of mental disorders and/or the chain of events that lead to onset of psychiatric disorder. Statistical clustering techniques which depend on the covariance of event occurrences almost make this impossible.

On the other hand, statistical clustering techniques might yield more reliable estimates of the life change distress in a particular area (26,34). Consequently, they have an advantage over all other clustering techniques in that there is a more clear identification of the types of life events that have actual similarities or relationships to one another for a particular group of subjects. In essence, the statistical clustering techniques identify the groups of events within which future studies might focus their search for provocative life events in the etiology of mental disorders.

Statistical clustering might be used in another way that does not depend on the covariance of event occurrences. One could cluster on the basis of the subject ratings. Clusters formed in this way would have the unique characteristic that they would be composed of events with common effects on individuals. One then could interpret the etiologic meaning of the events within these clusters that seemingly result in similar effects or responses.

ILLUSTRATIVE RESULTS IN A PROSPECTIVE ONSET STUDY

Five years ago, our group began a prospective study of health change in air traffic controllers. The design of this study and our methodology have been extensively discussed and have been published elsewhere (35). For the purpose of this chapter, only a brief outline is needed.

In this study, 416 men were initially enrolled. They represented 80% of a stratified random sampling of air traffic controllers in eight facilities in New York and New England. They had an average age of 36 (ranging from 25 to 49 years of age) and an average of 11 years of experience (ranging from 3 to

20 years). These men were evaluated comprehensively at Boston University five times over the course of 3 years. Among other assessments at each evaluation, every man was administered the Psychiatric Status Schedule (PSS) by a trained clinical psychologist and the Review of Life Events (ROLE).

The PSS is a structured interview of psychiatric status covering 321 possible symptoms rated by the interviewer. The items are scored into 50 scales, among which are four factor scales and five role scales. In our study, we concentrated on two of the four factor scales: (a) subjective distress, which assesses primarily anxiety and depression, and (b) impulse control disturbances, which assesses overt anger, acting out, and psychotropic and illicit drug abuse. We focused primarily on one of the five PSS role scales: wage earner role disturbances, which assesses disturbances in occupational functioning because of psychiatric problems. Finally, we attended to the independent symptom scale of alcohol abuse, which assesses symptoms of abuse as opposed to simply quantity or frequency of alcohol consumption.

Many other PSS symptom scales were available, but the subjective distress, impulse control, work role, and alcohol abuse scales assessed the most prevalent problems of our subjects. Subjects were categorized as either symptomatic or asymptomatic in each of these areas according to criterion cut-off scores which we established in comparison to psychiatric inpatients and outpatients, rehabilitation patients, and other urban normal controls. These criterion scores corresponded to the average score for psychiatric outpatients which in turn were 1 SD higher than the average scores for an urban community sample of nonpatients and 2 SD higher than the average scores for a group of community leaders.

The ROLE is a composite questionnaire including 39 of the 43 items in the SRE and 52 of 61 items listed in the PUP life event inventory. In addition, 19 items were devised that seemed important but had not been assessed in the SRE or PUP inventories.

Table 4 shows that the ROLE was constructed in such a way that some items were broken down into subcomponents. There were 25 items that were

TABLE 4. *Comparison of item overlap among ROLE, SRE, and PUP life event inventories*

No. of ROLE items used to define corresponding items	Single, unique items from SRE[b]	Single, unique items from PUP inventory[a]	Single items shared by SRE and PUP[a,b]	Single items unique to ROLE	Total ROLE items
1	10	22	13	19	64
2	4	3	8	NA	25[c]
3	0	2	3	NA	9[d]
4	0	0	1	NA	4
10	14	27	25	19	102

[a] Total PUP items defined = 27 (unique) + 25 (shared) = 52.
[b] Total SRE items defined = 14 (unique) + 25 (shared) = 39.
[c] 25 unique ROLE items overlap in doublets to define the 15 SRE and PUP items.
[d] 9 unique ROLE items overlap in triplets to define the 5 SRE and PUP items.

TABLE 5. *Sample overlap of ROLE items used to define one SRE item and one PUP item*

A positive response on any or all of these four ROLE items was considered equivalent -	to these single SRE and PUP items
1. Have you increased the average number of hours that you work per day? 2. Have you decreased the average number of hours that you work per day? 3. Have you taken on a second job? 4. Have you given up a second job?	SRE: Have you recently changed the number of hours that you work a day (either to more hours or to less hours per day)? PUP: Substantial change in work hours (includes taking on a second job).

identical in the SRE and PUP inventory, and 19 unique items in the ROLE. There were 14 unique SRE items and 27 unique PUP items. Basically, the ROLE included all SRE and PUP items that could occur to air traffic controllers but excluded the others that could not occur for our all-male, working sample (e.g., pregnancy).

Table 5 displays a sample item, which for the Holmes and Rahe (14) instrument was "changing the number of hours worked in a day," and for the PUP inventory was listed as "a substantial change in work hours." Four ROLE items were devised to cover the possible changes involved in these single SRE or PUP items, as can be seen.

In Table 3, note that the items were clustered into subscales according to their locus in life. Each of the ROLE subscales included all of the corresponding items in the subscales of the SRE and the PUP life event inventories. In addition, the ROLE subscales had the new items and item components.

Total scores were calculated by summing the Holmes and Rahe weights (24) for the events originating in the SRE and which occurred for the controller in the previous 9 months. A total PUP score was calculated by summing the weights published by Paykel and Uhlenhuth for their original group (29) for the corresponding items experienced by our controllers. Finally, we had our controllers give their own distress ratings from 1 to 99 for each event that they experienced. The total distress score was calculated by summing a man's own distress ratings for all the events that occurred to him among the 102 listed.

Finally, to study the predictive value of the life events with respect to the development of significant psychiatric symptomatology, a method was devised which we called a "sliding interval" analysis (see Table 6).

The basic principle is that a case was defined as a man in whom psychiatric symptomatology developed for the first time within our 3 years of assessment. A man would be excluded from these analyses if he had preexisting problems at intake, if he had unremitting problems, or if he was not asymptomatic at

TABLE 6. *Sliding interval onset analysis*[a]

Example	1 (Intake)	2	3	4	5 (Exit)
A	O	X	O	O	O
B	X	—	—	—	—
C	O	O	X	O	X
D	O	O	O	X	—
E	X	X	X	X	X
F	O	X	X	X	X
G	O	O	O	O	O

Exclusion criteria

Experimental group	Control group
1. Men with preexisting problems at intake (e.g., men B and E)	1. Men with any criterion problem at any examinaticn (e.g., men A-F)
2. Men with unremitting problems (e.g., man E)	2. Men who were not asymptomatic at all five examinations
3. Men who were not asymptomatic for every examination prior to the first occurrence of a symptomatic examination	

Predictors

Predictor variables were taken from the asymptomatic evaluation preceding the symptomatic evaluation.

[a] Psychiatric status at examination: O, asymptomatic; X, symptomatic; —, not assessed.

every examination prior to the first occurrence of a symptomatic examination. Examples of men who would be considered cases are those with the patterns underlined in Table 6.

Controls were defined as men who had no psychiatric symptomatology above our criterion level at any examination. Thus the control group was composed of those who were asymptomatic at every examination. In Table 6, example G would have been used as a control.

The sliding interval analysis refers to the method of selecting predictor variables such that the time between predictor assessment and the onset of symptomatology is relatively constant. Predictor variables, in this case the life events scores, were taken from the examination 9 months prior to the first onset of psychiatric symptomatology. By definition, the predictor variables were assessed at a time that a case was asymptomatic. Thus no matter where within the series of examinations the first onset occurred, predictor variables were always sampled from the preceding asymptomatic examination, hence the "sliding interval." Since the time between examinations averaged 9 months, the time before symptom onset for these analyses was 9 months.

The predictor variable selections for the control group cases were more problematic since by definition they never had an examination with significant symptomatology. We could not just take the intake examination data since the predictor variables may have changed over the course of the study for reasons beyond our control. Therefore, a random proportional sampling of predictor variables was made according to the proportion of men who were cases at any given examination. Thus, for example, if 20% of the men were cases at the second examination, then 20% of the possible controls were sampled for their first examination predictor variables. Similarly, if 20% of the cases occurred at the fifth examination, 20% of the controls were sampled from the fourth examination for their predictor variables.

This methodology does not confound the prediction of problems by the presence of problems at the preceding examination. It is extremely important to remember, in the results presented next, that the predictor variable data for all subjects, both cases and controls, refer to a time when they were asymptomatic. Cases are distinguished from controls for these analyses only in that significant psychiatric symptomatology developed in cases 9 months later.

One might argue that the asymptomatic examination from which predictor variables, e.g., the life event scores, were extracted could have taken place at a time during which later cases were in remission or were in a preclinical state. If this had been so, then the self-rated life event scores from that time might have been affected by the cases' remitted or preclinical status, and the resulting analysis would be concurrent rather than prospective. However, inspection of the PSS scale score distributions in the case and control groups at the asymptomatic examination revealed that about 10% of the subjects in both groups had scores bordering on the cut-off criterion for significant symptomatology. These preclinical cases were few and equally distributed between the two groups; hence any confounding effect of preclinical status on life event ratings would have been equally distributed as well. Therefore, insofar as the PSS scores reflected a preclinical condition, a preclinical or remitted status was not a distinguishing characteristic between the groups; the main and overwhelming difference was that significant symptomatology developed in cases but not in controls 9 months later.

Table 7 presents the comparison between cases and controls using subjective distress on the PSS as the psychiatric outcome, and the life event clusters and total life change scores from the SRE, the PUP inventory, and the ROLE as the predictor variables. For this analysis, there were 25 cases and 133 controls.

The life event cluster of work items was a significant predictor of cases but only for those items listed in the PUP and ROLE inventories. The work item cluster in the SRE did not significantly discriminate between cases and controls. These results clearly demonstrated that the events listed in an inventory may make a difference in terms of the conclusions one might draw. If one were using just the SRE, one would have concluded that work-related life events did not significantly predict subjective distress symptomatology 9 months later, which would have been an incorrect inference given the PUP and ROLE results.

The marital life change scores for each of the instruments were significantly different between cases and controls for subjective distress symptomatology.

TABLE 7. *Life event content cluster: Differences in the development of subjective distress disorders[a]*

Life event cluster		Instrument					
		SRE		PUP inventory		ROLE	
		Cases	Controls	Cases	Controls	Cases	Controls
Work	Mean	31.0	22.2	8.8	5.0	47.2	25.6
	SD	31.3	18.4	10.8	6.1	77.6	32.2
	t		1.92		2.47		2.27
	p		NS		< 0.02		< 0.03
Marriage	Mean	27.7	9.6	11.4	1.9	86.1	14.2
	SD	38.6	22.1	19.1	5.7	118.2	49.4
	t		3.28		4.79		4.94
	p		< 0.002		< 0.0001		< 0.0001
Total	Mean	152.6	101.2	49.0	28.7	380.6	179.4
life change	SD	100.1	67.9	33.9	24.0	303.6	155.4
scores	*t*		3.21		3.61		4.98
	p		< 0.002		< 0.0007		< 0.0001

[a] 25 cases, 133 controls.
Education, relocation, legal, financial, health, losses, children, family, and dating events were not significantly different ($p > 0.05$) between cases and controls for any instrument's items.

Cases had between 50 and 100% more life change stress in their marital situations than did controls prior to the onset of significant psychiatric symptomatology.

Finally, a number of types of life event clusters were not significantly different between cases and controls. However, one cannot conclude that these types of events have no role in the etiology of subjective distress. Among other reasons, the instruments may not have adequately sampled those domains.

Table 8 displays the life change stress differences among 67 cases of impulse control disorders and 132 controls. Again, work-related life events were not significantly different between cases and controls for the items listed in the SRE, but those of the PUP inventory and the ROLE did significantly discriminate between cases and controls. Cases scored 30 to 40% higher than controls on the work-related cluster of life events prior to the onset of impulse control disorders.

The marital life event cluster discriminated between cases of impulse control disorders and controls when using the SRE and the ROLE but not when using the PUP inventory. This result clearly indicates the importance of content when testing life events as an etiologic factor. In general, cases of impulse control disorders scored 100 to almost 300% higher than controls on the marital life event cluster.

The items regarding dating in the PUP and ROLE inventories were significantly different between cases of impulse control problems and controls. There were no dating events in the SRE, and therefore this finding would have been missed. Finally, the ROLE and PUP total scores were significantly different

TABLE 8. *Life event content cluster: Differences in the development of impulse control disorders*[a]

Life event cluster		SRE		PUP inventory		ROLE	
		Cases	Controls	Cases	Controls	Cases	Controls
Work	Mean	31.1	25.5	8.3	6.2	59.3	40.9
	SD	26.4	22.2	7.7	6.9	60.2	55.5
	t		1.59		1.98		2.09
	p		NS		<0.05		<0.05
Marriage	Mean	19.7	9.4	5.1	2.6	49.9	17.4
	SD	36.1	20.9	9.9	7.7	99.2	43.1
	t		2.56		1.93		3.15
	p		<0.02		NS		<0.003
Dating	Mean		NA	2.2	1.0	9.5	2.2
	SD			5.5	2.0	29.2	10.0
	t				3.06		2.51
	p				<0.003		<0.02
Total	Mean	126.5	108.7	39.4	31.2	295.5	207.2
	SD	85.4	70.3	25.2	23.5	256.3	197.0
	t		1.58		2.27		2.71
	p		NS		<0.03		<0.008

[a]67 cases, 132 controls.
Education, relocation, legal, financial, health, losses, children, and family events were not significantly different ($p > 0.05$) between cases and controls for any instrument's items.

between onset cases of impulse control disorders and the asymptomatic controls, whereas there was no significant difference in the SRE total score.

The null result for the SRE total life change score with respect to impulse control symptomatology points up the advantage of using some kind of cluster when investigating the etiology of psychiatric disorders. The total life change score from the SRE was not significantly different between cases and controls; one might have concluded falsely that life change stress measured by the SRE has no relationship to the onset of impulse control problems. On the other hand, the SRE marital life event cluster was significantly different between cases and controls. This result was disguised by the many more clusters which were not different between cases and controls when using the SRE.

Table 9 compares the life event scores between 75 cases of work role disorder and 134 controls. Interestingly, the PUP inventory clusters of work, marital, and dating events were not significantly different between cases and controls, whereas these clusters were significantly different between groups when using the events listed in the ROLE. The marital life event cluster was significantly different when using the SRE. Again, the improved predictive relationship is apparent when using relevant content, particular clusters, and individual ratings.

Table 10 shows the comparison of life event clusters between 44 cases of alcohol abuse and 135 controls. There were mixed results, depending on the inventory used. The work-related life event cluster was significantly different

TABLE 9. *Life event content cluster: Differences in the development of work role disorders*[a]

Life event cluster		SRE		PUP inventory		ROLE	
		Cases	Controls	Cases	Controls	Cases	Controls
Work	Mean	27.5	22.9	7.9	6.2	58.2	35.7
	SD	24.1	21.2	8.6	7.5	66.2	46.6
	t	1.44		1.50		2.83	
	p	NS		NS		< 0.006	
Marriage	Mean	20.1	10.4	4.0	2.4	34.7	15.8
	SD	34.8	24.7	9.2	6.6	78.9	39.4
	t	2.34		1.46		2.28	
	p	< 0.02		NS		< 0.03	
Dating	Mean	NA		1.3	1.0	6.5	1.3
	SD			4.4	2.4	26.0	8.9
	t			1.66		2.07	
	p			NS		< 0.04	
Total life change score	Mean	129.6	106.6	38.2	31.5	290.6	198.7
	SD	80.2	78.2	27.3	25.4	229.9	177.7
	t	2.05		1.79		3.24	
	p	< 0.04		NS		< 0.002	

[a] 75 cases, 134 controls.

Education, relocation, legal, financial, health, losses, children, and family events were not significantly different ($p > 0.05$) between cases and controls for any instrument's items.

TABLE 10. *Life event content cluster: Differences in the development of alcohol abuse disorders*[a]

Life event cluster		SRE		PUP inventory		ROLE	
		Cases	Controls	Cases	Controls	Cases	Controls
Work	Mean	28.0	23.0	8.1	5.8	56.4	32.7
	SD	24.8	20.1	8.8	6.8	64.7	44.2
	t	1.33		1.82		2.71	
	p	NS		NS		< 0.008	
Health	Mean	18.7	10.5	3.0	1.9	31.0	21.3
	SD	24.1	19.6	6.1	4.8	43.4	31.9
	t	2.27		1.26		1.59	
	p	< 0.03		NS		NS	
Marriage	Mean	27.3	11.0	9.9	2.2	46.2	19.1
	SD	43.8	23.7	14.1	5.6	89.5	55.4
	t	3.17		5.25		2.37	
	p	< 0.003		< 0.0001		< 0.02	
Total life change scores	Mean	139.8	107.9	45.0	30.5	304.3	200.1
	SD	94.6	76.7	33.3	26.2	225.0	194.3
	t	2.26		2.97		2.99	
	p	< 0.03		< 0.004		< 0.004	

[a] 44 cases, 135 controls.

Education, relocation, legal, financial, losses, children, family, and dating events were not significantly different ($p > 0.05$) between cases and controls for any instrument's items.

between cases and controls only for the ROLE item clusters. The health-related life events were significantly different between cases and controls only for the items of the SRE. The marital life events were significantly different between cases and controls for the items in all three inventories. Finally, the total life change scores were significantly higher for the cases than for the controls for all three inventories. In this instance, any one of the total scores would have supported an etiologic role for life event stress.

SUMMARY

In summary, results have been presented in support of the importance of issues of content, scoring, and clustering of life events. The results shown in Tables 7 through 10 are perhaps the most important because they demonstrate the gains one might make by taking into account most of the issues discussed thus far.

The main focus of this chapter was to discuss methodologic issues in life change assessment with respect to the question: "Does it make a difference?" The results from our onset study would seem to provide an answer; namely, these issues in the methodology of assessment do make a difference.

One can ask how much of a difference these changes make in content scoring and clustering. To begin answering this question, step-forward and step-backward discriminant and classification analyses have been performed on these data for the psychiatric onset outcome of subjective distress. Among all the variables that were assessed in our study, the most powerful predictor of the onset of subjective distress symptomatology was the ROLE total life change distress score. Once this life change score was taken into account in the discriminant solution, the other indices of life change stress had no additional contribution to the prediction. Hence, despite similarities in the three assessment technologies, the modifications that were made resulted in the most powerful method for detecting events of etiologic significance. In other words, the methodology makes a lot of difference.

ACKNOWLEDGMENTS

This chapter was prepared under the support of contract no. DOT-FA73-WA-3211 from the Department of Transportation, Federal Aviation Administration, awarded to Boston University. The contents of this report are the sole responsibility of the author and do not necessarily reflect the views of the Department of Transportation, Federal Aviation Administration, or Boston University.

The assistance of James A. Lomastro, Ph.D., in conducting the psychiatric Status Schedule interviews and many of the statistical analyses is gratefully acknowledged and appreciated. The concept of sliding interval analyses was proposed originally by C. David Jenkins, Ph.D., and refined in discussions with Robert M. Rose, M.D., C. David Jenkins, Ph.D., and the author.

REFERENCES

1. Caplan, R. D. (1975): A less heretical view of life change and hospitalization. *J. Psychosom. Res.*, 19:247–250.
2. Cash, W. S., and Moss, A. J. (1972): Optimum recall period for reporting persons injured in motor vehicle accidents. In: *Data Evaluation and Methods Research*, series 2, no. 50, DHEW, publication no. (HSM) 72–1050. Rockville, Maryland.
3. Casey, R. L., Masuda, M., and Holmes, T. H. (1967): Quantitative study of recall of life events. *J. Psychosom. Res.*, 11:239–247.
4. Cleary, P. J. (1974): Life events and disease: A review of methodology and findings. In: *Reports from the Laboratory for Clinical Stress Research.* Karolinska Institute, Stockholm.
5. Dohrenwend, B. P. (1974): Problems in defining and sampling the relevant population of stressful life events. In: *Stressful Life Events: Their Nature and Effects*, pp. 275–310. Wiley, New York.
6. Dohrenwend, B. S. (1973): Life events as stressors: A methodological inquiry. *J. Health Soc. Behav.*, 14:167–175.
7. Dohrenwend, B. S. (1973): Social status and stressful life events. *J. Pers. Soc. Psychol.*, 28:225–235.
8. Dohrenwend, B. S., and Dohrenwend, B. P. (editors) (1974): *Stressful Life Events: Their Nature and Effects.* Wiley, New York.
9. Garrity, T. F., Somes, G. W., and Marx, M. (1977): Personality factors in resistance to illness after recent life changes. *J. Psychosom. Res.*, 21:23–32.
10. Goldberg, E. L., and Comstock, G. W. (1976): Life events and subsequent illness. *Am. J. Epidemiol.*, 104:146–158.
11. Harmon, D. K., Masuda, M., and Holmes, T. H. (1970): The social readjustment rating scale: A cross-cultural study of Western Europeans and Americans. *J. Psychosom. Res.*, 14:391–400.
12. Hawkins, N. G., Davies, R., and Holmes, T. H. (1957): Evidence of psychosocial factors in the development of pulmonary tuberculosis. *Am. Rev. Tuberc. Pulmon. Dis.*, 75:768–780.
13. Heisel, S. (1978): Life event questionnaire for prisoners. *Unpublished manuscript*, Harvard University.
14. Holmes, T. H., and Rahe, R. H. (1967): The social readjustment rating scale. *J. Psychosom. Res.*, 11:213–218.
15. Horowitz, M. J., Schaefer, C., and Looney, P. (1974): Life event scaling for recency of experience. In: *Life Stress and Illness*, edited by E. Gunderson and R. H. Rahe, pp. 125–133. Charles C. Thomas, Springfield, Ill.
16. Hurst, M. (1978): Life event questionnaire for salesmen and food brokers. *Unpublished manuscript*, Boston University.
17. Hurst, M., Jenkins, C., and Rose, R. (1976): The relation of psychological stress to onset of medical illness. *Ann. Rev. Med.*, 27:301–312.
18. Hurst, M., Jenkins, C., and Rose, R. (1978): The assessment of life change stress: A comparative and methodological inquiry. *Psychosom. Med.*, 40:127–142.
19. Jenkins, C., Hurst, M., and Rose, R. (1978): Life change: Do people really remember? *Arch. Gen. Psychiatry (in press).*
20. Locke, S., Heisel, S., Williams, R., and Hurst, M. (1978): The effect of life change stress on the human immune response. Paper presented at the AAAS Annual Meeting, Feb. 12–17, Washington, D.C.
21. Lundberg, U., and Theorell, T. (1976): Scaling of life changes: Differences between three diagnostic groups and between recently experienced and nonexperienced events. *J. Human Stress*, 2:7–17.
22. Lundberg, U., Theorell, T., and Lind, E. (1975): Life changes and myocardial infarction: Individual differences in life change scaling. *J. Psychosom. Res.*, 19:27–32.
23. Marx, M. B., Garrity, T. F., and Bowers, F. R. (1975): The influence of recent life experiences on the health of college freshmen. *J. Psychosom. Res.*, 19:87–98.
24. Masuda, M., and Holmes, T. H. (1967): Magnitude estimations of social readjustments. *J. Psychosom. Res.*, 11:219–225.
25. Masuda, M., and Holmes, T. H. (1967): The social readjustment rating scale: A cross-cultural study of Japanese and Americans. *J. Psychosom. Res.*, 11:227–237.
26. McDonald, B. W., Pugh, W. M., Gunderson, E. K. E., and Rahe, R. H. (1972): Reliability of life change cluster scores. *Br. J. Soc. Clin. Psychol.*, 11:407–409.

27. Paykel, E. S. (1976): Life stress, depression, and suicide. *J. Human Stress,* 2:3–14.
28. Paykel, E. S., and Uhlenhuth, E. H. (1972): Rating the magnitude of life stress. *Can. Psychiatr. Assoc. J.,* 17:93–100.
29. Paykel, E. S., Prusoff, B. A., and Uhlenhuth, E. H. (1971): Scaling of life events. *Arch. Gen. Psychiatry,* 25:340–347.
30. Pugh, W. M., Erickson, J., Rubin, R. T., Gunderson, E. K. E., and Rahe, R. H. (1971): Cluster analyses of life changes. II. Method and replication. *Arch. Gen. Psychiatry,* 25:333–339.
31. Rabkin, J. G., and Struening, E. L. (1976): Life events, stress, and illness. *Science,* 194:1013–1020.
32. Rahe, R. H. (1976): Epidemiological studies of life change and illness. *Int. J. Psychiatr. Med.,* 8:133–146.
33. Rahe, R. H. (1974): The pathway between subjects' recent life changes and their near future illness reports: Representative results and methodological issues. In: *Stressful Life Events: Their Nature and Effects,* edited by B. S. Dohrenwend and B. P. Dohrenwend, pp. 73–86. Wiley, New York.
34. Rahe, R. H., Pugh, W. M., Erickson, J., Gunderson, E. K. E., and Rubin, R. T. (1971): Cluster analysis of life changes. I. Consistency of clusters across large Navy samples. *Arch. Gen. Psychiatry,* 25:330–332.
35. Rose, R. M., Jenkins, C., and Hurst, M. (1978): Health change in air traffic controllers: A prospective study. I. Background and description. *Psychosom. Med.,* 40:143–165.
36. Ruch, L. O, and Holmes, T. H. (1971): Scaling of life change: Comparison of direct and indirect methods. *J. Psychosom. Res.,* 15:221–227.
37. Spilken, A. Z., and Jacobs, M. A. (1971): Prediction of illness behavior from measures of life crisis, manifest distress and maladaptive coping. *Psychosom. Med.,* 33:251–264.
38. Uhlenhuth, E. H., and Paykel, E. S. (1973): Symptom configuration and life events. *Arch. Gen. Psychiatry,* 28:744–748.
39. Uhlenhuth, E. H., and Paykel, E. S. (1973): Symptom intensity and life events. *Arch. Gen. Psychiatry,* 28:473–477.
40. U.S. Dept. of HEW (1965): Health interview responses compared with medical records. *National Center for Health Statistics,* series 2, no. 7, U.S. Government Printing Office, Washington, D.C.
41. Winokur, A., and Selzer, M. L. (1975): Desirable versus undesirable life events: Their relationship to stress and mental distress. *J. Pers. Soc. Psychol.,* 32:329–337.
42. Wyatt, G. E. (1977): A comparison of the scaling of Afro-Americans' life change events. *J. Human Stress,* 3:13–18.

Stress and Mental Disorder,
edited by James E. Barrett et al.
Raven Press, New York © 1979.

Development and Application of a Quantitative Measure of Life Change Magnitude

Thomas H. Holmes

University of Washington School of Medicine, Seattle, Washington 98195

In 1967, the Social Readjustment Rating Scale (SRRS), composed of 43 life events, was published in the Journal of Psychosomatic Research (14). In the next few pages, we attempt to explain what sources of information were used to decide on the 43 life events which we felt were of potential importance in the lives of all of us. That is to say, we abstracted these life events as playing a crucial role in the predisposition for future illness. This list was drawn from more than 5,000 individual case histories. In addition, we conducted numerous laboratory experiments in which a particular life event was introduced as a potentially noxious stimulus and the individual's psychologic and physiologic responses were monitored as a reflection of the importance of a particular life event. Thus each event had been frequently observed to be a salient part of the life situation in which disease had its onset historically; in the laboratory, it was observed to initiate significant physiologic or psychologic responses which could be hypothesized as leading to tissue damage and disease.

In the development of the rating scale, each event was assigned a magnitude of change in the adjustment required, as rated by the individual. This method, used to derive a quantitative definition of life change, was used initially in psychophysics, that branch of psychology which investigates a person's ability to make subjective magnitude estimations about certain experiences (31). By utilizing this methodology, a ratio scale is obtained which supports the interpretation that social judgments about life events may operate by similar mechanisms as those utilized in the quantification of various perceptions, e.g., judgments of the intensity of sound and light and number of objects.

Since 1967 when it was published, the SRRS has been the most frequently cited reference in this area of endeavor. It has been the basis of approximately 1,000 publications ranging from scientific investigations to books, popular magazines, and newspaper articles. The purpose of this chapter is to document in historic perspective the clinical and experimental studies that led to the development of the SRRS.

For almost 35 years, we in this laboratory have been addressing ourselves to the assertion of Alexander Pope about 300 years ago that: "The proper study of mankind is man." We are interested in the natural history of disease; these are some of the questions we ask: What are the distant and proximate antecedents or precipitants of disease onset? What is the nature of the reaction when disease does occur? What are some of the factors that influence or modify the course of disease? Why do people get one disease rather than another? Can one discern any generalizations that enable us to predict disease and to use prediction of disease as a basis for possible preventive intervention?

We have done many kinds of experiments in our study of the natural history of disease. In each, the technique or method used to generate data has depended on the question asked and the context of the problem encountered. The research presented here begins, as Pope suggested, with people and takes advantage of the doctor-patient relationship to study sick people at the bedside or in the clinic. We then move from the patient in the diagnostic or treatment situation into the laboratory, where we make observations while conducting experiments, for example, in which certain kinds of stimuli are held constant while the subject's mood and behavior are varied. We then proceed to studies of the individual not as a patient or laboratory subject but as a member of the community, in order to see what can be learned about the relationship of life style to the natural history of disease. After studying the patient as an individual in the clinic, the laboratory, and the community, we consider the patient as a member of a population, applying some epidemiologic principles and techniques to the study of people and humankind. Finally, we look at possibilities for prevention of disease.

The starting point is the clinic and a device invented by Dr. Adolf Meyer, psychobiologist and psychiatrist at Johns Hopkins (21). Meyer was interested in the relationship of three open-ended disciplines—biology, psychology, and sociology—to the processes of human health and disease. To schematize those relationships, he created the life chart, a device that organizes medical data as a dynamic biography. Information is provided by the patient and is arranged by year and the patient's corresponding age. The entries on the life chart describe life situations—experiences dealing with growth, development, maturation, and senescence—as well as the patient's emotional responses to those situations. Certain life experiences we arbitrarily call disease are listed in a separate column. In this approach to patients and their problems, "disease" applies to change in health status and includes a broad spectrum of medical, surgical, and psychiatric disorders. The life chart thus allows us to take into account not only the occurrence of disease but also the setting in which it occurs.

The first patient discussed is a female born in Holland, married, and without children (11). She has a long history of headaches, head colds, sinus disease, and other diseases. She is tense and frustrated, and a review of her life documents the recurrence of episodes of bitter weeping, with feelings of helplessness associated with conflicts, doubts, and misgivings. It is in this setting that illness occurs. We now take patients like this into the laboratory to see what we can learn about the relationship between the onset of the patient's illness and the setting in which it occurs.

Observations are made of blood flow, secretions, swelling, and obstruction to breathing in the nasal mucous membranes before, during, and after an interview; biopsies are also taken before and during the interview. At the same time these observations are being made, we begin the interview, asking questions about the subject's life situation: "How do you feel? What do you see as happening to you? What position does that put you in? What does it feel like inside?" When we ask these questions, we get responses such as: "I feel helpless. Unable to face the situation. I wish it would go away, leave me alone. I feel left out in the cold."

As the individual discusses feeling "left out in the cold," we observe hyperemia, hypersecretion, and swelling in the mucous membranes, and obstruction to breathing is reported. An increase in the secretion of eosinophils and polymorphonuclear leukocytes is documented. When we compare a biopsy taken when the mucous membranes are in a reasonably normal state to one taken at the height of the reaction during the interview, we see that discussion of things having to do with coping in real life situations produces edema of the nasal tissue and other pathologic tissue change. Thus in the laboratory we have produced nasal disease by introducing a sensitive topic about boss, mother-in-law, financial difficulties, or any number of other disturbing life situations.

We explore further this relationship between nasal hyperfunction and coping in life situations by again going into the laboratory, this time to ask a question about adaptation to being left out in the cold. In these experiments, human subjects are exposed to low ambient temperatures (32). The results of measuring the temperature of the inspired air as it progresses toward the nasopharynx shows that the nose is an effective air conditioning unit. Increased blood flow rapidly warms the inspired air so that by the time it reaches the pharynx, the air is warmed from $-25°$ C to room tempreature. The nasal hyperfunction observed is, speaking teleologically, nature's way of protecting the organism from frostbite of the lungs. We can say, then, that this pattern of hyperemia, hypersecretion, swelling, and obstruction to breathing is a biologically appropriate protective reaction when the organism is exposed to cold air or noxious chemical fumes but that it is a biologically inappropriate reaction as an attempt to shut out, neutralize, and wash away an unsympathetic spouse or anyone else who makes one feel "left out in the cold."

During the course of daily observations on one subject (11), his mother-in-law comes to visit shortly after the birth of his first baby. During the following 7 days, the subject's nasal tissues exhibit progressive hyperemia, hypersecretion, and swelling. Chronic nasal disease is the consequence. The swelling is intense and the mucous membranes appear boggy and pit in response to probing. Discharge of nasal secretions is continuous. In addition, at the height of the mother-in-law situation, pain develops in the head and face of the individual.

Experiments of pain mechanisms of the nasal and paranasal tissues indicate that the sinus mucous membranes are relatively pain insensitive. The nasal tissues, on the other hand, are exquisitely pain sensitive and, when stimulated, evoke high-intensity pain. The sinus headache is really a nasal headache. Pain is generated by the pathologic tissue change in the nasal tissues and is referred to that part of the head which is also supplied by two divisions of the fifth cranial nerve, the opthalmic and the maxillary. The pain over the face can be eliminated by anesthetizing the nasal mucous membranes.

Up to this point we have been looking into the genesis of head pain associated with nasal disease. We began in the clinic where the individual identified and described his pain, and then moved into the laboratory where we stimulated the nasal tissues under carefully controlled conditions. We found that the individual's psychologic state, his attitude toward the situation in which he finds himself, is demonstrably linked to the nature of the physiologic reaction generating illness. To look at another pain mechanism, we turn now from nasal function to skeletal muscle function.

One of the most common pain syndromes seen in clinical medicine is the backache syndrome, and probably the most common source of pain in chronic intractable pain syndromes is skeletal muscle (17). In the laboratory, we again attempt to define the patients' psychologic state as the discussion of life situations takes place. The backache patient's attitude toward the situation in which he finds himself is quite different from that of the weeping patient's: The backache patient says that when mother-in-law comes to visit, he wants to run away. He cannot tolerate her and he cannot fight back; all he can do is avoid the situation by running away. He feels this very strongly but cannot take action: he is held motionless with his skeletal muscles mobilized to move.

Many laboratory experiments were performed in which backache was produced during discussions of salient life situations with the individual. As the interview begins, we see the genesis of muscle tension as recorded by electromyogram and, after a short latency, the report of backache. When we change to neutral topics, the muscle tension subsides and the pain goes away. We then reintroduce the sensitive topic; muscle tension and pain return. We are, in effect, demonstrating the nonbacterial equivalent of Koch's postulates, by manipulating the experimental situation by directing the interview toward and away from sensitive topics.

In addition to muscle tension, blood flow is another parameter in the genesis of backache pain. During the course of skeletal muscle tension or contraction, blood circulation is decreased in proportion to the strength of the contractions (4). In strong contractions, pain develops rapidly and assumes high intensity, and the endurance of the sustained contraction is reduced. When the tense contracting muscles are relaxed, the blood flow is reestablished with a rapid surge in volume, and pain promptly disappears. The pain threshold is rapidly restored to normal, endurance returns, and blood flow returns to normal.

In these skeletal muscle tension and blood flow experiments, we see another biologically inappropriate pattern of responses evoked as an attempt to cope with a disturbing life situation. In this case, the individual who wants to run away from the situation prepares for action: muscles get tense, blood flow is reduced, and pain occurs. It is not unlike Sir Thomas Lewis's (20) formulation of the genesis of pain of intermittent claudication and angina. He suggested that a metabolic factor P (for pain factor) was produced during sustained anaerobic muscle contraction which accounted for the initiation of pain. The available evidence suggests that potassium is the pain factor (4).

We turn to one final example of our investigations into a clearer understanding of clinical pain syndromes (15). Our subject is a 55-year-old male who has two illnesses with widely varying pathophysiologic processes coexisting. He has the backache syndrome, with pain, tenderness, and muscle spasm as the cardinal features. He has had backache on and off for many years and now is in the hospital with intractable abdominal pain. To find out what is going on, we give the subject a small amount of intravenous sodium amytal to make him relax. Soon all the muscle tension, pain, and tenderness are essentially gone. We now discover a mass in the left upper quadrant. The patient is completely comfortable; he feels no pain, but when one lightly manipulates the mass, high-intensity pain returns. The pain goes away when manipulation ceases. Clearly, there are two different pain mechanisms at work here.

The abdominal mass, a hypernephroma, initiates noxious afferent impulses, which travel into the spinal cord and elicit reflex muscle contractions. The mass also sends afferent impulses to the brain, where the sensation of pain is registered. The subject reacts with anxiety and tension: he would like to run away from the situation but he cannot, and this reaction sends down more motor impulses to the anterior horn cell, which stimulates the skeletal muscle to contract further. This sustained contraction gives rise to pain by the mechanisms we defined in the previous experiments. The noxious afferent impulses from the sustained muscle contraction feed back into the central nervous system (CNS); the result is chronic pain.

The sodium amytal allows us to distinguish the two pain mechanisms. It has no direct effect on pain, muscle, or cancer tissue, but it does relieve the subject's tension. When the subject relaxes, most of the efferent outflow from the CNS to the skeletal muscles is reduced. As the skeletal muscles relax, blood flow is reestablished and the pain from the muscle tension goes away. The subject still has the cancer, but to activate the pain-sensitive mechanisms associated with it one must displace or exert traction on the cancer tissue. This manipulation then provides a demonstration of the other pain mechanisms.

Thus multiple diseases may coexist, some of which are functional. We are not yet sure how cancer starts, but we can see that the skeletal muscle tension just examined is an example of functional pathophysiology.

We now turn to studies done in collaboration with Dudley et al. (5) of people with diffuse obstructive pulmonary disease. These subjects frequently experienced shortness of breath, or dyspnea. One of the first things observed about these subjects was that there was no predictable relationship between the respiratory physiologic variables and the occurrence of dyspnea. Since this did not make sense, we took our subjects back into the laboratory to look at their psychologic state as well as their physiologic state. We found a pattern. Subjects were apt to feel short of breath only on days when they felt "bad." We began to analyze more carefully the particular psychophysiologic state of each subject on dyspneic days. We found that on some "bad" days they were feeling angry or anxious, or both, and action oriented. On other dyspneic days, they felt depressed, apathetic, withdrawn, and nonaction oriented. When we distinguish these mood states and analyze them separately, we get a beautiful correlation between respiratory variables and the mood state and dyspnea.

The physiologic state associated with anger and anxiety, or action-oriented behavior, is hyperventilation (increased ventilation and decreased alveolar carbon dioxide). Under these circumstances, our subjects complained of dyspnea. The observations of dyspnea with depression or other nonaction-oriented behaviors show just the opposite state. When subjects felt depressed, action was the farthest thing from their intent. The physiologic change associated with that attitude is hypoventilation (reduced ventilation and alveolar oxygen and increased alveolar carbon dioxide).

Our next experiments (16) take us into another area of the natural history of disease. Here we study the relationship of two noxious agents acting simultaneously on the host and observe the effects of the two. Our subject in this experiment has somewhat mild hay fever. An assumption is that the constitutional dimension of hay fever is a constant. The two noxious agents we observe at work here are pollen and the home situation. After making controlled observations of the nasal mucous membranes in both left and right nasal chambers when the subject is calm, secure, and relaxed, we introduce the subject into the pollen room. The response is mild hay fever. About 20 min later, we introduce the second noxious agent by interviewing the subject about a situation at home which has engendered much conflict. The subject feels tense and helpless. The reaction of the nasal mucous membranes to this added insult is one of enhanced hyperfunction and hay fever symptoms. After 30 min of discussing the sensitive domestic situation with the subject, we redirect the interview and give him reassurance, support, and understanding. The effects of "psychotherapy," of talking things out and of reassurance and emotional support, become evident. Although the pollen is still present in the laboratory, the subject's acute reaction subsides.

Let us look at the neural mechanisms involved in the nasal hyperfunction just observed. In another experiment with a hay fever subject (16), after making controlled observations of nasal mucous membranes in both nasal chambers, we inject into the left stellate ganglion a solution of 2% procaine. The left stellate ganglion is part of the sympathetic nerve chain that gives rise to the sympathetic nerve supply to one side of the head, and the procaine blocks the flow of sympathetic impulses from the spinal cord up to the left side of the head, including the tissues of the left nasal chamber. This interference in the nerve supply to the head produces a Horner syndrome: along with the changes in the eye and the face, the mucous membranes in the left nasal chamber get red, wet, and swollen. We have now a control side, the right nasal chamber, which still receives sympathetic nerve impulses, and an experimental side, the left nasal chamber, which receives only parasympathetic nerve supply. The hyperfunction in the left nasal mucous membrane is now the result of parasympathetic impulses from the brain to the nose. This is the mechanism by which environmental stimuli, such as mother-in-law, evoke nasal mucous membrane reactions.

When we add pollen to both left and right nasal cavities, we observe two distinct reactions. In the left nasal chamber, we see the effect of adding the antigen, pollen, to the neuromechanism of mother-in-law: adding the noxious agent pollen to the already hyperfunctioning mucous membranes produces a typical hay fever reaction in the left side of the nose. The insult of pollen also produces a reaction in the right nasal cavity, but it is transient and of low magnitude, not enough to produce symptoms. The dramatically intensified hyperfunction associated with two noxious agents, such as pollen and the life situation, shows that they exert a summative or additive effect. We are dealing with solid, readily demonstrable neuromechanisms. What the brain can control, the environmental situation with its afferent input to the brain can also control. Pollen alone was not sufficient to produce symptoms in our hay fever subject, but the combined assault of pollen and life situation was.

These different reactions in the same hay fever subject led us to ask questions about resistance to attack by noxious agents. We begin asking questions in the laboratory and then move back to the clinic where we pursue this line of inquiry by studying patients' resistance to attack by a specific noxious stimulus, the pulmonary tuberculosis germ.

In experimental studies of skin inflammation, we introduced a constant amount of noxious agent and varied mood and behavior (6). The noxious agent in this instance was trypsin, a proteolytic enzyme, which we injected intradermally. The results were mild tissue damage and a sterile inflammatory reaction. We measured the magnitude of the inflammatory reaction and correlated the intensity of this reaction with the mood and behavior of the individual on a given day. In a composite plotting of our observations, we distinguished the intensity of reactions associated with three distinct mood states. The inflammatory reaction was greatest on days when subjects felt calm and secure. When subjects were tense and preoccupied, they had a much more intense inflammatory reaction than when they were low in energy and spirits. We see here dramatic changes in "resistance" to attack by the same amount of noxious agent, depending on mood and behavior.

Formulated in teleological perspective, the more acute inflammatory reaction observed in the calm-secure and the tense-anxious is protective of the host. It walls off, localizes, and destroys the invading noxious agent. Systemic dissemination of the invading agent and its ominous consequences for the patient is much more apt to occur in the state of low energy and spirits, or depression. Nature preserves the whole by sacrificing the part.

In the clinic, we apply what we have observed in the laboratory to studies of the natural history of tuberculosis. We once again hold the noxious stimulus constant—here it is the pulmonary tuberculosis germ—while varying mood and behavior. We chose 17-ketosteroid excretion rate as our index of resistance to inflammation because it reflects adrenocortical function.

At the bedside, we studied a man with far advanced bilateral, acute, exudative pulmonary tuberculosis and carefully followed his progress under treatment (3). When he entered the hospital he was depressed, withdrawn, inactive, and felt overwhelmed. He had steroid excretion rates of 2 mg/24 hr, which were about the level one would expect in someone with Addison disease (although he did not have this). The patient was given antibiotics immediately, but for the first 3 months of treatment he did not get better. Improvement did not occur until his mood and behavior changed from feelings of depression to a more optimistic and outgoing behavior, and the ketosteroid level increased toward normal. At 9 months, improvement stopped as he became depressed again, but within several months he was improved and was finally discharged. What we see here is a particular disease state (far advanced tuberculosis) associated with a particular biologic state of reduced resistance (reduced ketosteroid excretion levels) and a particular psychologic state (depression and being overwhelmed). Improvement in this patient's disease state was associated with a changed biologic state (ketosteroid level increased to normal) and a changed psychologic state (from depression to optimism).

Studies of the hospital course of 206 tuberculosis patients (3) revealed associations between the biologic, psychologic, and disease states. The 17-ketosteroid levels are associated with the state of the disease. In general, with minimal tuberculosis, the average steroid excretion is relatively high; with moderate tuberculosis, it is a little lower; and with far advanced tuberculosis, it is lower still. We also noticed that the daily steroid excretion levels within all three groups ranged from very low to very high.

When we correlated the progress of the disease, the level of the index of resistance to infection or inflammation, and the psychologic state expressed in mood and behavior, some interesting relationships emerged (3). Those patients with the far advanced, acute, exudative tuberculosis are depressed, overwhelmed, older males with considerably reduced steroid excretion. At the other end of the spectrum are those with minimal tuberculosis who have steroids above normal (corrected for age and sex). They are tense, anxious, conflict-ridden, predominantly younger females.

Taking into account the relationship of the acid-fast bacillus and the mood and behavior associated with the disease state, we now consider the social situation (9,10). We introduced our subject into the community at large to study the relationship of life style to the natural history of tuberculosis. The community we studied was the city of Seattle, and we used area of residence as determined by census tract as our index of life style. We divided the city into four areas: I, a "skid road" residential area (or city center or "ghetto"); II, a "blue collar" residential area; III, a "white collar" residential area; and IV, a "better socioeconomic" residential area. We then correlated tuberculosis morbidity rates with residential areas, our index of life style (12).

Whites who live in area I, the city center, have a high morbidity rate, but it progressively decreases in areas II, III, and IV. For nonwhites, the morbidity rate is even higher than for whites in the city center, is cut in half in the blue collar (II) and white collar (III) residential areas, but is one-third higher in area IV than in area I. There are also clear differences between nonwhite females and nonwhite males. The morbidity rate for the nonwhite females is exactly the same in area IV as in area I, while nonwhite males have almost twice the risk of getting tuberculosis when they live in area IV, the better socioeconomic residential area, than in area I, the city center.

What we are seeing for the whites in area I is the role of their marginal social status, and for the nonwhites in area IV, the culture conflict engendered by the close residential juxtaposition of a minority and a majority population. Such conflicts in life style evoke depression, withdrawal, and feelings of being overwhelmed, thereby reducing resistance to infection or inflammation and making it possible for the germ, if present, to produce the tissue reaction of tuberculosis.

At this point in our study of people, we are ready to ask another kind of question. Given all these things we know now about the natural history of disease, is it possible to make predictions about the onset of illness? Can we discover why people get sick when they do—not with *what* they get sick but *when* they get sick? We have worked on this question for many years. When we began to ask our questions about predicting the onset of illness, our clinical model, the life chart, suggested the direction our inquiries should take. In pursuing the problem of prediction, we made a systematic study of the social or life events that require change in adjustment or of coping style in the individual. We studied thousands of these situations to see what we could learn about the types of social events that require change in adjustment, their frequency of occurrence, the magnitude of change they require, and their relationship to the onset of disease.

First we return to the study of a patient with tuberculosis, noting the occurrence of job changes, residential changes, financial changes, health change, and jail terms for 12 years prior to admission to the hospital with tuberculosis. As time of admission to the hospital is approached, there is a mounting frequency of these social events. In the 2-year period prior to admission to the hospital, there is a "life crisis" or a veritable crescendo of life change events, which is the setting for the onset of tuberculosis.

From individual patient studies, we moved to studies of many samples of tuberculosis patients, and the accumulation of life events in the setting of hospitalization was a striking and consistent finding. We conducted control experiments in which we matched patients who got tuberculosis while working in the hospital with fellow hospital employees who had equal probability of exposure to the tuberculosis germ but who did not get the disease (8). Each member of the tuberculosis group was individually matched to a member of the control group so that they were the same socially in age, sex, race, marital status, income, education, length of employment, number of people in the household, and relevant health records. Time of onset was determined from routine quarterly chest X-rays done on all employees in the hospital. We then gathered data about the life changes for each group in the previous 10 years. We found that in the 2 years prior to onset of tuberculosis, a highly significant increase in the number of life changes was experienced by those who got the disease as compared to those who did not. We used a similar research design to study pregnancy and other diseases, such as heart disease, hernia, skin disease, and found similar relationships (28). In summary, it appeared from these retrospective studies that one of the important factors determining the time of onset of disease or health change is the accumulation of many life changes.

Here we began our systematic study in earnest. We analyzed approximately 5,000 case histories over many years, noting the life change events present in patients' lives at time of illness onset. We compiled a list of 43 life events empirically observed to occur just prior to the time of onset of disease, including, for example, marriage, trouble with the boss, jail term, death of spouse, change in sleeping habits, retirement, death in the family, and vacation (14). At this point, to be in a better position to predict disease onset, we needed a quantitative way of defining the salience of these life events. To accomplish this, we used a technique for the quantification of someone's experience derived from that branch of psychology called psychophysics (31).

A sample of convenience composed of 394 subjects completed the Social Readjustment Rating Questionnaire (SRRQ), a paper-and-pencil test listing the 43 items (14). The following written instructions were given to each subject:

A. Social readjustment includes the amount and duration of change in one's accustomed pattern of life resulting from various life events. As defined, social readjustment measures the intensity and length of time necessary to accommodate to a life event, *regardless of the desirability of this event.*

B. You are asked to rate a series of life events as to their relative degrees of necessary readjustment. In scoring, *use all of your experience* in arriving at your answer. This means personal experience where it applies as well as what you have learned to be the case for others. Some persons accommodate to change more readily than others; some persons adjust with particular ease or difficulty to only certain events. Therefore, strive to give your opinion of the average degree of readjustment necessary for each event rather than the extreme.

C. The mechanics of ratings are these: Event 1, Marriage, has been given an arbitrary value of 500. As you complete each of the remaining events think to yourself, "Is this event indicative of more or less readjustment than marriage?" "Would the readjustment take longer or shorter to accomplish?" If you decide the readjustment is more intense and protracted, then choose a *proportionately larger* number and place it in the blank directly opposite the event in the column marked "VAL-

UES." If you decide the event represents less and shorter readjustment than marriage then indicate how much less by placing a *proportionately smaller* number in the opposite blank. (If an event requires intense readjustment over a short time span, it may approximate in value an event requiring less intense readjustment over a long period of time.) If the event is equal in social readjustment to marriage, record the number 500 opposite the event.

Table 1 reproduces our SRRS, based on the 43 life events observed to occur prior to illness onset. For convenience, we divided the mean score for each item by 10, and thus our module item of marriage has a value of 50. We call these numerical values "life change units" or LCUs. All 43 items in the scale are now arranged in rank order. Death of spouse leads all the rest with a value of 100, while minor violations of the law is at the bottom of the selected items. Death of a family member ranks fifth, and jail term is about the same. The numerical scores allow us to compare magnitude of change required by the events. Thus change in sleeping habits does not require as much adjustment as trouble with the boss, but it does require more change and adjustment than a vacation. Mother-in-law, for example, ranks 24th in the SRRS, and she requires about one-third as much adjustment and change as death of spouse.

As one looks at the items themselves, one sees that some of the items are socially undesirable, like death or jail term, but other items are, in general, socially desirable, like getting married or a vacation. Thus desirable as well as undesirable events correlate with the onset of illness. What we are studying here is the amount of change required by these 43 life events. The relative importance of each item is determined not by the item's desirability, by the emotions associated with the item, nor by the meaning of the item for the individual; it is the amount of change that we are studying and the relationship of the amount of change to the onset of illness.

Once we had the scale, we needed to attempt to validate our method for quantification. Unlike the psychophysicist, we could not compare some physical attribute of the experience with the subjective magnitude estimation, but we could correlate the magnitudes assigned by discrete subsamples in our population. We compared males to females, single people to married people, and people of one age group to those of another. The correlations were all 0.90 and more (14).

We attempted further validation of our quantification method by doing cross-cultural studies. We studied how the Japanese in Japan assigned magnitudes to the 43 items as compared to white, middle class Americans (22). We studied the relationship of Seattle samples to samples in Hawaii (29), to blacks and to Chicanos in city centers (19), to Spanish-speaking people in Central America (30), Peru (18), and Spain (2), to French-speaking people in France, Belgium, and Switzerland (7), and to Scandinavians (25). Essentially, worldwide, death of a spouse requires about twice as much change in adjustment as marriage and 10 times as much change and adjustment as a traffic ticket. All the coefficients of correlation ranged between 0.65 to 0.98.

TABLE 1. *The Social Readjustment Rating Scale*[a]

Life event	Mean value
1. Death of spouse	100
2. Divorce	73
3. Marital separation from mate	65
4. Detention in jail or other institution	63
5. Death of a close family member	63
6. Major personal injury or illness	53
7. Marriage	50
8. Being fired at work	47
9. Marital reconciliation with mate	45
10. Retirement from work	45
11. Major change in the health or behavior of a family member	44
12. Pregnancy	40
13. Sexual difficulties	39
14. Gaining a new family member (e.g., through birth, adoption, oldster moving in, etc.)	39
15. Major business readjustment (e.g., merger, reorganization, bankruptcy, etc.)	39
16. Major change in financial state (e.g., a lot worse off or a lot better off than usual)	38
17. Death of a close friend	37
18. Changing to a different line of work	36
19. Major change in the number of arguments with spouse (e.g., either a lot more or a lot less than usual regarding childrearing, personal habits, etc.)	35
20. Taking on a mortgage greater than $10,000 (e.g., purchasing a home, business, etc.)	31
21. Foreclosure on a mortgage or loan	30
22. Major change in responsibilities at work (e.g., promotion, demotion, lateral transfer)	29
23. Son or daughter leaving home (e.g., marriage, attending college, etc.)	29
24. In-law troubles	29
25. Outstanding personal achievement	28
26. Wife beginning or ceasing work outside the home	26
27. Beginning or ceasing formal schooling	26
28. Major change in living conditions (e.g., building a new home, remodeling, deterioration of home or neighborhood)	25
29. Revision of personal habits (dress, manners, associations, etc.)	24
30. Troubles with the boss	23
31. Major change in working hours or conditions	20
32. Change in residence	20
33. Changing to a new school	20
34. Major change in usual type and/or amount of recreation	19
35. Major change in church activities (e.g., a lot more or a lot less than usual)	19
36. Major change in social activities (e.g., clubs, dancing, movies, visiting, etc.)	18
37. Taking on a mortgage or loan less than $10,000 (e.g., purchasing a car, TV, freezer, etc.)	17
38. Major change in sleeping habits (a lot more or a lot less sleep, or change in part of day when asleep)	16
39. Major change in number of family get-togethers (e.g., a lot more or a lot less than usual)	15
40. Major change in eating habits (a lot more or a lot less food intake, or very different meal hours or surroundings)	15
41. Vacation	13
42. Christmas	12
43. Minor violations of the law (e.g., traffic tickets, jaywalking, disturbing the peace, etc.)	11

[a] From ref. 14.

The life event items contained in the SRRS had previously been used in our laboratory to construct a Schedule of Recent Experience (SRE) (8,28). This instrument, a self-administered questionnaire, allows the respondent to document, for specified time periods, the frequency of occurrence of the various life events. With the development of the scale of magnitudes for the life event items (SRRS), we could now use these values to score the SRE to provide a unique method for a quantitative definition of a life crisis.

Using the SRE, we gathered retrospective life change data on subjects for a 10-year period (26). We plotted the life change score for each time period and superimposed on this profile the occurrence of illnesses. A variety of illnesses was noted to coincide with high life change magnitude. In our earlier empirical studies, we found that accumulation of many life changes in a preceding 2-year period appeared to be related to the onset of tuberculosis. When we quantify life change, we see that high life change scores are associated in time with the occurrence of a variety of different illnesses.

This retrospective study was one of many. In later studies of populations using the same methods for quantifying life change, we did both retrospective and prospective studies of the relationship between life change magnitude and the occurrence of illness (13,26). Consider first the retrospective studies. We found that in the 2 years at risk—the 2-year period derived from earlier empirical studies—30 to 35% of the people with low life change became ill. About 50% of the people who were in the intermediate range of life change became ill in the 2 years at risk. About 80% of those in the high range of life change became ill in the 2-year period of risk (26). In our prospective studies, we began with the amount of life change, predicted what was going to happen, and then studied what actually did happen in the following 2 years. We got a similar picture in these prospective studies (13,26).

In one prospective study in which we held risk of injury, age, and sex as constants, we used as an experimental group 100 college athletes who filled out a special SRE, called Athletic Schedule of Recent Experience, before the start of the football season. At the end of the season, we gathered data about injuries. We found that of those players who were in the high risk group (in the 300 range of LCU) at the start of the football season, 70% got an injury during the course of the 3-month season (1). Of those in the medium risk group (200 LCU range), about 50% got an injury. Only about one-third of those in the low risk group (100 LCU range) got an injury during the season. Interestingly enough, there were players with multiple injuries, and of the 11 players with more than one injury during the season, nine were in the high risk group. That is to say, if the athlete played football all season, had more than 300 LCUs in the year prior to the season, and got an injury and continued to play, the probability was that he would get at least one other injury.

In another prospective study of Navy personnel, Rahe et al. (27), who worked with me in the early stages of development of this life change research, found a linear relationship between mean illness rate and the magnitude of life change.

Petrich and Holmes (24) summarized the findings of a variety of studies, which again indicate a positive relationship of life change to onset of a number of psychiatric, medical, and surgical diseases.

Having reached this stage in our studies of life change magnitude and the onset of health changes, we began to investigate the relationship of magnitude of life change and seriousness of illness. To conduct such studies, we had to devise a scale for the seriousness of illness using the same psychophysics technique employed to generate the SRRS. We asked a group of doctors and a group of laypeople to rate the seriousness of a list of 126 specified illnesses (33). We said:

> The seriousness of the disease Peptic Ulcer has been given an arbitrary value of 500. You are asked to compare the seriousness of each of the other diseases to peptic ulcer. As you rate each of the remaining diseases think to yourself, "Is this disease more or less serious than an ulcer?" If, for example, you decide the disease is more serious than a peptic ulcer, then choose a *proportionately larger* number than 500. . . . If you decide the disease is less serious, indicate how much less serious by placing a *proportionately* smaller number than 500 in the column. . . ."

The Seriousness of Illness Rating Scale (SIRS) presents the medical rank order of the diseases and the magnitude of seriousness assigned by laypeople and doctors (33). Cancer and leukemia turn out to have a seriousness of about 1,000, or twice as much as peptic ulcer, and about 100 times as much as warts and dandruff. There is a coefficient of correlation of 0.935 between doctors and laypeople. When we compared one group of doctors with another, we got a coefficient of correlation of 0.98 (34). Cross-cultural studies of populations in Ireland (23), Spain (2), Central America (30), and the United States (33) yielded correlations of 0.90.

When we had our SIRS, we studied the relationship of magnitude of life change and seriousness of illness (35). We arranged in rank order of seriousness the SIRS values for each of a selection of illnesses and the average life change magnitude experienced by patients during the 6-month, 1-year, and 2-year periods prior to onset of disease. There was a positive correlation for chronic disease of 0.65. What this study tells us is that if a person has had more than 300 LCUs in the last year and gets sick in the near future, the probability is that he or she will get diabetes, schizophrenia, heart attack, or cancer rather than headache, mononucleosis, anxiety reaction, or asthma. On the other hand, if in the past year a person has had less than 100 LCUs and gets sick in the near future, he or she will be more apt to get one of the less serious diseases.

We have found that not only are people more likely to get sick when they experience increased life change but also that the greater the magnitude of the life change, the more serious the illness is likely to be if they do get sick. Knowing what we now know about prediction of illness, the next question to ask is: What can we do about prevention?

Some time ago I appeared on a national television talk show and explained much of what I have discussed in this chapter. I made an effort to adapt it to the people who listen to 10:00 A.M. talk shows: homemakers, retired people, and people who work night shifts. During the 1-hr program, I spelled out the background of our research and the relationship between magnitude of life change and illness onset and seriousness of illness. Many viewers wrote in and asked for the scale; I wrote back and asked them if they would participate in a prospective study of prevention. Of the several thousand people who wrote in, 225 randomly selected subjects were chosen to participate in the study, and these were the people we followed up.

This was a study of the effects of primary intervention—using an educational approach, telling people what the experimental data are and what the probabilities are in the relationship of life change and illness onset. The results indicated that 15% more people stayed well in the year following the intervention than in the year preceding intervention. The number of people who got one illness stayed about the same, and those who got two or more illnesses showed a dramatic reduction of 20% in morbidity. In essence, using an intervention technique of 1 hr, we get a saving in morbidity of between 15 and 20%.

When people write to me today and ask for information about life change and illness onset, I often include the following list of preventive measures, which we sent to the participants of the preventive study:

1. Become familiar with the life events and the amount of change they require.
2. Put the Scale where you and the family can see it easily several times a day.
3. With practice you can recognize when a life event happens.
4. Think about the meaning of the event for you and try to identify some of the feelings you experience.
5. Think about the different ways you might best adjust to the event.
6. Take your time in arriving at decisions.
7. Anticipate life changes and plan for them well in advance, if possible.
8. Pace yourself. It can be done even if you are in a hurry.
9. Look at the accomplishment of a task as a part of daily living and avoid looking at such an achievement as a "stopping point" or a time for letting down.
10. *Remember,* the more change you have, the more likely you are to get sick. Of those people with over 300 Life Change Units for the past year, almost 80% get sick in the near future; with 150 to 299 Life Change Units, about 50% get sick in the near future; and with less than 150 Life Change Units, only about 30% get sick in the near future. So, the higher your Life Change Score, the harder you should work to stay well.

My message is direct. There are a lot of things that are worse than illness. One of them may be not taking a promotion, or not letting your mother-in-law come to visit; but at least recognize the risk you are under and be willing to pay the price.

Let me close with a phrase that formulates what I have been saying about the natural history of disease: Disease is a by-product or epiphenomenon of our goals and the techniques we use in achieving these aspirations.

ACKNOWLEDGMENTS

I thank Marion Amundson and Ella David for their great help in the production of this manuscript.

REFERENCES

1. Bramwell, S. T., Masuda, M., Wagner, N. N., and Holmes, T. H. (1975): Psychosocial factors in athletic injuries: Development and application of the Social and Athletic Readjustment Rating Scale (SARRS). *J. Human Stress,* 1(2):6–20.
2. Celdran, H. H. (1970): *The Cross-Cultural Consistency of Two Social Consensus Scales: The Seriousness of Illness Rating Scale and The Social Readjustment Rating Scale in Spain.* Medical Thesis, University of Washington, Seattle.
3. Clarke, E. R., Zahn, D. W., and Holmes, T. H. (1954): The relationship of stress, adrenocortical function and tuberculosis. *Am. Rev. Tuberculosis,* 69:351–369.
4. Dorpat, T. L., and Holmes, T. H. (1955): Mechanisms of skeletal muscle pain and fatigue. *Arch. Neurol. Psychiatry,* 74:628–640.
5. Dudley, D. L., Martin, C. J., Masuda, M., Ripley, H. S., and Holmes, T. H. (1969): *The Psychophysiology of Respiration in Health and Disease.* Appleton-Century-Croft, New York.
6. Ely, N. E., Verhey, J. W., and Holmes, T. H. (1963): Experimental studies of skin inflammation. *Psychosom. Med.,* 25:264–284.
7. Harmon, D. K., Masuda, M., and Holmes, T. H. (1970): The Social Readjustment Rating Scale: A cross-cultural study of Western Europeans and Americans. *J. Psychosom. Res.,* 14:391–400.
8. Hawkins, N. G., Davies, R., and Holmes, T. H. (1957): Evidence of psychosocial factors in the development of pulmonary tuberculosis. *Am. Rev. Tuberculosis Pulmon. Dis.,* 75:768–780.
9. Holmes, T. H. (1956): Multidiscipline studies of tuberculosis. In: *Personality, Stress and Tuberculosis,* edited by P. J. Sparer, pp. 65–152. International Universities Press, New York.
10. Holmes, T. H. (1964): Infectious diseases and human ecology. *J. Indian Med. Prof.,* 10:4825–4829.
11. Holmes, T. H., Goodell, H., Wolf, S., and Wolff, H. G. (1950): *The Nose. An Experimental Study of Reactions Within the Nose in Human Subjects During Varying Life Experiences.* Charles C Thomas, Springfield, Illinois.
12. Holmes, T. H., Hawkins, N. G., Bowerman, C. E., Clarke, E. R., and Joffe, J. R. (1957): Psychosocial and psychophysiologic studies of tuberculosis. *Psychosom. Med.,* 19:134–143.
13. Holmes, T. S. and Holmes, T. H.: Long-range predictions of health change. *In preparation.*
14. Holmes, T. H. and Rahe, R. H. (1967): The Social Readjustment Rating Scale. *J. Psychosom. Res.,* 11:213–218.
15. Holmes, T. H., and Ripley, H. S. (1955): Experimental studies on anxiety reactions. *Am. J. Psychiatry,* 111:921–929.
16. Holmes, T. H., Treuting, T., and Wolff, H. G. (1951): Life situations, emotions and nasal disease: Evidence on summative effects exhibited in patients with "hay fever." *Psychosom. Med.,* 13:71–82.
17. Holmes, T. H., and Wolff, H. G. (1952): Life situations, emotions and backache. *Psychosom. Med.,* 14:18–33.
18. Janney, J. G., Masuda, M., and Holmes, T. H. (1977): Impact of a natural catastrophe on life events. *J. Human Stress,* 3(2):22–34.
19. Komaroff, A. L., Masuda, M., and Holmes, T. H. (1968): The Social Readjustment Rating Scale: A comparative study of Negro, Mexican, and white Americans. *J. Psychosom. Res.,* 12:121–128.
20. Lewis, T. (1942): *Pain.* Macmillan, New York.
21. Lief, A. (1948): *The Commonsense Psychiatry of Dr. Adolf Meyer.* McGraw-Hill, New York.
22. Masuda, M., and Holmes, T. H. (1967): The Social Readjustment Rating Scale: A cross-cultural study of Japanese and Americans. *J. Psychosom. Res.,* 11:227–237.
23. McMahon, B. J. (1971): *Seriousness of Illness Rating Scale: A Comparative Study of Irish and Americans.* Medical Thesis, University of Washington, Seattle.
24. Petrich, J., and Holmes, T. H. (1977): Life change and onset of illness. In: *The Medical Clinics of North America. Symposium on Psychiatry in Internal Medicine,* edited by A. Reading and T. N. Wise, pp. 825–838, Vol. 61, #4. W. B. Saunders, Philadelphia.
25. Rahe, R. H. (1969): Multi-cultural correlations of life change scaling: America, Japan, Denmark and Sweden. *J. Psychosom. Res.,* 13:191–195.
26. Rahe, R. H. (1969): Life crisis and health change. In: *Psychotropic Drug Response: Advances in Prediction,* edited by P. R. A. May and R. Whittenborn, pp. 92–125. Charles C Thomas, Springfield, Illinois.

27. Rahe, R. H., Mahan, J. L., and Arthur, R. J. (1970): Prediction of near-future health change from subjects' preceding life changes. *J. Psychosom. Res.,* 14:401–406.
28. Rahe, R. H., Meyer, M., Smith, M., Kjaer, G., and Holmes, T. H. (1964): Social stress and illness onset. *J. Psychosom. Res.* 8:35–44.
29. Ruch, L. L., and Holmes, T. H. (1971): Scaling of life change: Comparison of direct and indirect methods. *J. Psychosom. Res.,* 15:221–227.
30. Seppa, M. T. (1972): *The Social Readjustment Rating Scale and the Seriousness of Illness Rating Scale: A Comparison of Salvadorans, Spanish and Americans.* Medical Thesis, University of Washington, Seattle.
31. Stevens, S. S. (1975): *Psychophysics. Introduction to Its Perceptual, Neural, and Social Prospects,* edited by G. Stevens. Wiley, New York.
32. Webb, P. (1951): Air temperatures in respiratory tracts of resting subjects in cold. *J. Appl. Physiol.,* 4:378–382.
33. Wyler, A. R., Masuda, M., and Holmes, T. H. (1968): Seriousness of Illness Rating Scale. *J. Psychosom. Res.,* 11:363–374.
34. Wyler, A. R., Masuda, M., and Holmes, T. H. (1970): The Seriousness of Illness Rating Scale: Reproducibility. *J. Psychosom. Res.,* 14:59–64.
35. Syler, A. R., Masuda, M., and Holmes, T. H. (1971): Magnitude of life events and seriousness of illness. *Psychosom. Med.,* 33:115–122.

Stress and Mental Disorder,
edited by James E. Barrett et al.
Raven Press, New York © 1979.

Life Stress and Illness: The Search for Significance

E. H. Uhlenhuth

Department of Psychiatry, University of Chicago, Chicago, Illinois 60637

The title of this chapter may seem pretentious, applying as it does to a brief discussion of three chapters with offerings too rich to deal with adequately in a short review. These rather contrasting chapters serve to remind us that methods are critical in the context of clearly specified goals or questions.

At least two general goals may be of interest: (a) the prediction of phenomena, and (b) the understanding or explanation of these phenomena. Prediction is primarily a matter of empirical relationships between variables over time, although the term is often loosely applied even to correlations between concurrently measured variables. Explanation, on the other hand, deals in mechanisms or processes and requires a conceptual framework within which to view the data, so that the concepts themselves can be modified, if not overturned, by the empirical relationships.

From this perspective, the greatest contribution made by Holmes and Rahe (2) probably is their clear delineation of a concept of stress in everyday life— the demand for social readjustment placed on the person by events, regardless of their desirability or other properties. Although Holmes may not regard himself as a behaviorist, his list of events and rating instructions at least implies that social readjustment refers to actual changes in customary behavior required by discrete changes in circumstances. He and his colleagues, then, hypothesize that it is the burden of making these behavioral changes that increases the person's susceptibility to illness. I underscore these basic propositions only as a necessary preliminary to evaluating methods in terms of their ability to illuminate concepts.

Dohrenwend notes that measurements of both life stress and illness are critical to this area of investigation. Reliably identifying illness or "cases," particularly in studies of large samples as in survey research, is a persistent problem. Dohrenwend's shift of terminology from psychologic illness to "demoralization" seems to avoid rather than solve the problem. Clinicians ultimately will regard dimensional approaches, however sophisticated, as unsatisfactory. Answers to questions about illness and life stress will depend on the clinical evaluation and typologic diagnosis of research subjects by trained professionals, as incorporated in the study of air traffic controllers by Hurst.

Less generally appreciated is the fact that the illness criterion problem is almost equally marked in studies of life stress and somatic illness. As Minter and Kimball (4) point out after a comprehensive review of this literature, most studies depended on verbal reports or aspects of "illness behavior" that left the nature and extent of somatic pathology itself very much in question. The studies on myocardial infarction by Lind, Lindberg, Rahe, Theorell, and their colleagues (7) are prominent exceptions. Overall, however, the question remains whether the weight of the systematic evidence to date supports a relationship between stressful life events and the onset of illness in general, or only a relationship between stress and distress, especially ordinary worry and unhappiness (1).

Regarding the measurement of life stress itself, some methodologic issues that have attained great prominence turn out to be of minor practical importance. The most appropriate type of scaling, whether interval or ratio, is one of these, as noted by Hurst; but others deserve more attention within the framework posed at the outset of this discussion.

Hurst correctly points to item content as one of the signficant issues in constructing measures of life stress. His first concern is that events be chosen to produce an optimal response rate in the sample of respondents studied. An optimal (50:50) response rate is clearly desirable if the main aim is to predict symptoms on the basis of the responses to the event list. However, if the objective is to determine whether the requirement for behavioral readjustment precipitates illness, then the first concern is to choose events that fit that model. Although salespeople often may have trouble tracing orders or meeting the demands of their principals, these events soon cease to require the development of new behaviors.

To pursue the issue in Hurst's terms, hardly anyone we are likely to encounter has had the experience of moving to the Antarctic. If we are interested in predicting symptoms efficiently, we might conclude that this item is a poor predictor and that we should find a more common event. But if moving to the Antarctic is the paradigm of life stress in our theoretical scheme, then we might conclude that stress is not an important influence in the development of symptoms among our acquaintances and that we should revise our notion of what constitutes life stress. These two approaches lead to information with different kinds of significance.

Dohrenwend points to another critical aspect of item content: in the study of psychologic disorder and life events, it is especially easy to confound "causes" and "effects," since people so often initiate drastic events as a consequence of their own disorder. Indeed, events such as being fired from work are tantamount to manifestations of psychologic disorder in the area of social adjustment. It is not surprising and not especially informative (conceptually) to find even high correlations between events reflecting social maladjustment and other measures of psychologic disorder.

This problem is crucial and often neglected; I therefore submit some illustrative data from the Oakland Health Survey (8). The respondents were a random

TABLE 1. *Oakland Health Survey: Percentage of respondents with high symptom levels by sex and total number of events[a]*

	Total no. events			
Sex	0–2	3+	*p*	*N*
Men	21%	50%	<0.005	358
Women	47	67	<0.005	373
Both	34	59	<0.005	731

[a] HSCL total (12 mo) at least 0.25.

sample of noninstitutionalized residents of Oakland, California, aged 18 to 65. The 735 interviews represented a response rate of 75%. Symptom levels over the 12 months prior to interview were measured with the Hopkins Symptom Checklist (HSCL) presented as a structured interview. A total score of at least 0.25 on a scale from 0 to 3, experienced by 46% of the sample, was considered high. Life events experienced over the 18 months prior to interview were elicited by means of a questionnaire containing 41 items. These were extracted from the list of 61 events scaled by Paykel et al. (6) simply on the basis of high frequency and high stress weight.

Table 1 shows the percentage of respondents who reported high symptom levels in relation to the total number of events they experienced. In accordance with expectation, respondents who experienced at least three events reported high symptom levels more frequently than respondents who experienced less than three events. The relationship is highly significant for both men and women.

Among these 41 events, six qualify as uncontrolled or fateful events, as defined by Paykel (5), Kellam (3), and Dohrenwend: the respondent is most unlikely to influence their occurrence. Table 2 shows this list of events. With the possible exception of "laid off work," which in our list was combined with quitting the job, these clearly are catastrophic events that befall the respondent. Both

TABLE 2. *Oakland Health Survey: Fateful events*

	Event		Stress ratings		
No.	Content		Men (*N* = 142)	Women (*N* = 231)	Both (*N* = 373)
3	Injury or illness in close relative[a]		14.74	15.65	15.30
28	Quit or laid off work		15.42	15.15	15.26
32	Death of spouse		18.83	18.72	18.76
33	Death of child		19.16	19.43	19.33
34	Death of other close relative		16.76	17.49	17.21
35	Death of close friend[b]		14.31	15.71	15.18

[a] *p* < 0.05 for difference between sexes.
[b] *p* < 0.01 for difference between sexes.

TABLE 3. *Oakland Health Survey: Percentage of respondents who experienced events by type of event and sex of respondent*

| | Sex | | |
Type of event	Men ($N = 358$)	Women ($N = 373$)	p
Total no. events > 2	46%	52%	NS
Some fateful events	39	47	<0.05

men and women rate these events high on a scale from 0 to 20. The "laid off work" item is omitted from further consideration. Table 3 shows that a substantial proportion of men and women in the Oakland sample experienced at least one of the remaining five fateful events.

If events rated as severely stressful by most people are an important factor in producing psychologic distress, we certainly would expect respondents who experienced even one or two such events to report more distress than the respondents who did not experience any such events. Table 4 shows that the expected relationship does hold, at a modest level of statistical significance. This finding, however, is almost entirely due to the women in the sample. Thus the conceptual implications may be significantly different when one examines distress in relation to a heterogeneous collection of events on the one hand and in relation to a subset of clearly fateful events on the other hand.

Now I should like to go on to another aspect of methodology approached very differently by Holmes, Hurst, and Dohrenwend. This is the issue of weighting events according to their stressfulness. Hurst's data show that correlations between distress and stress are highest when the events experienced by each individual are weighted with the stress weights he personally assigns to them. This is an important observation when the main objective is to predict distress. Unfortunately, this procedure plunges us back into the very conceptual circularity from which Holmes rescued us in 1967. Dohrenwend develops this point so well that it needs only underscoring here. Defining the stressfulness of events by the individual's response obscures the nature of stress and literally precludes asking questions about factors that modify or mediate the impact of stressful

TABLE 4. *Oakland Health Survey: Percentage of respondents with high symptom levels by sex and fateful events*[a]

| | Fateful events | | | |
Sex	None	Some	p	N
Men	32%	37%	NS	358
Women	52	64	<0.05	373
Both	42	52	<0.01	731

[a]HSCL total (12 mo) at least 0.25.

events on people. Dohrenwend suggests that the individual's rating of the stress associated with events probably is a measure of his personal vulnerability to these events. This idea is worth pursuing.

Dohrenwend also suggests that significant stress may be generated by particular constellations of events, selected on a theoretical basis, such as loss of a loved one in conjunction with personal physical illness and disruption of social supports. This research strategy strikes me as potentially more illuminating than compiling stress scores from large groups of events with loose conceptual relationships. It is of passing interest that various weighting tactics do not substantially sharpen the relationships between distress and life stress. My own experience in this respect confirms the data that Hurst showed.

Our group also has given some thought to the possible importance of stressful events occurring in a setting of low social support. When one sees fateful events as the primary source of life stress, he quickly arrives at the notion that stress and fragmented social support networks are one and the same. Although a definition of life stress itself as a loss of social supports does not imply a neat behavioral mechanism of action (like the Holmes definition), it does take into account clinical experience with breakdown after losses that do not seem to impact the individual's daily behavior in any gross way.

Much effort has been expended in the study of stress and illness since Holmes and his colleagues (2) pioneered a quantitative approach firmly grounded in a theory about the nature of life stress. To many of us, it must seem that much of what followed was redundant variation on a theme. Yet reviews such as those in the preceding chapters underscore the uncertainties still remaining at the most basic level in this always fascinating and provocative area of research. As we proceed to try to fill in these gaps, we will need to be guided by a clear perception of the sort of significance we seek: the highest achievable statistical significance for accurate prediction or the significant conceptualization that brings understanding of processes and mechanisms.

ACKNOWLEDGMENTS

Preparation of this chapter was supported in part by contract number HSM 42–69–59 and by Research Scientist Award number MH-18611, both from the National Institute of Mental Health.
Robert Dingler, Linda Hicks, and Eileen Ketcherside assisted.

REFERENCES

1. Bradburn, N. M., and Caplovitz, D. (1965): *Reports on Happiness.* Aldine, Chicago.
2. Holmes, T. H., and Rahe, R. H. (1967): The social readjustment rating scale. *J. Psychosom. Res.,* 11:213–218.
3. Kellam, S. G. (1974): Stressful life events and illness: A research area in need of conceptual development. In: *Stressful Life Events: Their Nature and Effects,* edited by B. S. Dohrenwend and B. P. Dohrenwend, pp. 207–214. Wiley, New York.
4. Minter, R. E., and Kimball, C. P. (1978): Life events and illness onset: A review. *Psychosomatics,* 19:334–339.

5. Paykel, E. S. (1974): Life stress and psychiatric disorder: Applications of the clinical approach. In: *Stressful Life Events: Their Nature and Effects,* edited by B. S. Dohrenwend and B. P. Dohrenwend, pp. 135–149. Wiley, New York.
6. Paykel, E. S., Prusoff, B. A., and Uhlenhuth, E. H. (1971): Scaling of life events. *Arch. Gen. Psychiatry,* 25:340–347.
7. Theorell, T. (1974): Life events before and after the onset of a premature myocardial infarction. In: *Stressful Life Events: Their Nature and Effects,* edited by B. S. Dohrenwend and B. P. Dohrenwend, pp. 101–117. Wiley, New York.
8. Uhlenhuth, E. H., Lipman, R. S., Balter, M. B., and Stern, M. (1974): Symptom intensity and life stress in the city. *Arch. Gen. Psychiatry,* 31:759–764.

Stress and Mental Disorder,
edited by James E. Barrett et al.
Raven Press, New York © 1979.

General Discussion, Part I

Dr. Holmes: Dr. Dohrenwend referred to an economist who found that unemployment was positively associated with depressive symptoms and to admission to a mental hospital. I think those data also were positively correlated with suicide. Some further research, by an economist in California studying the Kansas City area, found that high unemployment predicted high life change, high suicide rates, high evidence of depression, and high admission to the hospital. He also looked at similar data when employment was increasing rapidly. Rapid expansion of employment predicted high life change, which predicted high suicide rates, high admission to psychiatric hospital, and high evidence of depression. I make this point to suggest that what is relevant is not whether the event is desirable or undesirable but rather how much change is involved; it is the total amount of life change that seems to be associated with health change.

Dr. Hurst: A number of people also made the point that perhaps life change stress is best viewed as a concept of vulnerability in the individual, especially in an onset study such as we have conducted. I agree with this, but I still question whether or not the individuals' own ratings are in fact circular when research is done in the way we have conducted it. We started out with people who were asymptomatic in the first place. Therefore, their own ratings and which events occurred to them could have no relationship to their subsequent symptomatology unless such a relationship existed. There is no circularity in this case. I think that self ratings, if done properly in a prospective study starting with people who are asymptomatic, give a great deal of significance to the findings that follow.

Dr. Dohrenwend: I am in such strong agreement with Dr. Uhlenhuth's discussion that my comment is almost quibbling about one point, but I think there is a misunderstanding: I was not advocating substituting demoralization for evaluation of the whole gamut of functional psychiatric disorders. I was suggesting that demoralization is interesting in its own right. I had not meant, nor do I think would Dr. Frank, to have it preempt the measurement problems in regard to all functional psychiatric disorders or the phenomena that we would like to be able to explain with our research on stress situations.

In reply to Dr. Hurst's comment, as he observes, it is far better to have data over time in this research, for many reasons. I think it should be pointed out, however, that a patient does not wear a characteristic set of symptomatology like a suit of clothes that can never be taken off. Course and type of symptomatology fluctuate in patients. Therefore, two things are necessary. One is to establish a temporal relationship, if possible. The other is to get some indication of how much the events are under the control of the individual. You would need a much longer baseline of the individual's personality and course of symptomatology to be comfortable, in my opinion, with the kind of position that you are taking.

Dr. Holmes: Another point I would like to make is best epitomized by Humpty Dumpty in *Alice in Wonderland* when he says a word means what he wants it to mean, no more and no less. The word stress has been used today in about six different ways. Stress means life events that cause something. Stress means what life events produce in the individual. Life events produce stress, which produces change in the individual, which produces change in health status. Stressors have been used as stress and as life events, but it is never quite clear which. In my chapter, I did not use the word stress at any point. I talked about life events; I talked about perception; I talked about sensory experiences; I talked about behavior and emotional states—but I did not use the word stress. The reason is because it causes confusion when used by so many different people in so many different ways. The assumption seems to be, by people who use the word stress, that "I know what I'm talking about, and therefore you know what I'm talking about," but I think this rarely occurs. Many of the points of debate and discussion in the preceding chapters could be eminently simplified if stress were either defined each time it was used or had only one definition. Better yet, use precise words that say what you want without using the word stress.

Dr. Eugene Paykel: I was struck by the similiarity among Dr. Hurst's findings using different event lists. There were significant differences, but most were quite small in magnitude. There is a more general point regarding the content of life event interview scales. I suspect that many of the differences among item lists are not as great as they appear to be. If data were collected using several different item lists on the same population, it would probably collect the same events but assign them to different items on the list.

There is a resemblance to the decision that symptom raters have to make, whether to use a highly itemized list of symptoms, in which fine atomistic distinctions are made, or rather global categories, which cover the whole spectrum of psychopathology on a small list. You record the same psychopathology; in one case you get it very precisely and in the other case less so.

I think the advantage of the atomized list is not so much in its content but its precision. However, a single atomized list will not work well with a diverse population of subjects, and that is where the global list is more useful. If you devise a finely atomized list to cover the whole spectrum of human experience, it becomes too hard to manage in an interview.

Dr. Samuel Guze: I would like to make two points in regard to Dr. Dohrenwend's and Dr. Uhlenhuth's chapters. One way to work for greater clarity in this area is to focus on vulnerable people, identified by coming from families in which other individuals have already demonstrated the illness under consideration. My second point is that the idea of life events as stress is trivialized if we see them as playing a similar role in every kind of disorder. We know from general medicine that the stress and strain of physical exertion or of climatic change are not uniform in all disorders. Climatic change, for example, will affect people with certain vulnerabilities but not with others.

My plea is that those pursuing these studies make an effort to delineate the disorders being studied. It is conceivable and probable that certain kinds of life events play an important role in precipitating certain kinds of depressions but have nothing whatsoever to do with schizophrenia. Similarly, certain events may play a role in precipitating exacerbations of alcoholism but have nothing to do with migraine headaches or asthmatic attacks.

Dr. Uhlenhuth: In response, first, I think the question of what kinds of measures of vulnerability there might be is an interesting one. I did not attempt to address that, nor did we in general. The notion of taking family history as a key to vulnerability is interesting. Another key could be a long-term medical history; that is, if a person has been vulnerable to illness before, he probably is vulnerable now. However, there are certain kinds of studies that are important to do (namely, studies in general populations, where there are well and sick people both) where some things become quite difficult to do. In survey type studies, careful clinical assessment of family history, for example, becomes difficult.

As to delineating the clinical disorders that depend on certain differential kinds of events, that is what I had in mind in commenting on the use of "demoralization" as a criterion of illness. It certainly would be important to try to pin down specific illnesses so that one can look for differential relationships and effects. That, however, also is very difficult to do in large-scale studies. I do not think Dr. Dohrenwend was advocating the use of demoralization alone as a criterion, but I grabbed that as a hobby horse to get into the notion that Dr. Guze mentioned.

I do think we can do better, and are going to do better, with this issue than we have been doing until now. Real efforts are being made to delineate discrete illnesses, particularly psychiatric illnesses, in relatively large populations in survey studies.

Dr. Hurst: We actually attempted to do that with subjective distress impulse control, work role pathology, and alcohol abuse. Many of the significant relationships were from exactly the same life event clusters for each of those different outcomes. There was not much event specificity for outcomes.

Dr. Uhlenhuth: The outcome criteria that you used are not discrete clinical illnesses, even though you used an instrument from which those could be derived. That strikes me as very curious, and I would like to see you go on and use the PSE to get at categories.

Dr. Jerome Frank: I certainly agree that demoralization differs from clinical entities. Obviously it's not the same as hysterical amnesia. How much of the effects of psychotherapy are really devoted to restoring morale as opposed to attacking symptoms? Then the question which Dr. Dohrenwend did not hit becomes relevant. He said that half the people were demoralized and half had functional disorders. What percentage with functional disorders were also demoralized?

Dr. George Winokur: Except for the rather occasional bipolar patient who can tell you that he became ill on March 22nd at 11 a.m., it is very difficult to date the onset of illness. Therefore, it becomes increasingly important to make sure that one can separate out what is cause and effect in life events. I took Holmes' Social Readjustment Rating Scale and marked off all the things that looked to me as if they could not possibly have been caused by a person—death of spouse, death of close family member, retirement from work, death of close friend, and Christmas.

Christmas poses an interesting problem; it is believed that there is such a thing as Christmas depression. As we know that depression is associated with a high suicide rate, we would assume that one way to check the validity of this comment is to see whether the suicide rate is higher during Christmas holidays. It is not; it is higher during April and May. This brings to mind the idea that maybe some of the things that have been brought out as life events are simply responses of the individual to his illness which have been poorly dated, and that maybe some of the life events are not all that important anyway.

Another viewpoint may be valid. If you look at the same kind of outcome (namely, suicide), you do see an association with farm mortgage foreclosures in Iowa. Also, you find that suicide rate changes with war. Perhaps we shouldn't be looking at specific events in the life of the individual that could be influenced; rather, we should be looking at large social events and defining the situation in that sense.

Dr. Fritz A. Freyhan: My first comment deals with the problem of recognizing the interplay between intrinsic and extrinsic factors in generating stress. I recently had to write a paper on "The Depressed Physician." Physicians are a population sample of great relevance to the foregoing section. Recent studies have shown that the incidence of affective illness among physicians is two to three times higher than that of control populations, as is their rate of suicide, alcoholism, and drug abuse. For a long time, this phenomenon has been interpreted in terms of the occupational hazard of physicians, i.e., long working hours, an excessive exposure to human tragedy, and so on. That this is too simplistic is indicated by recent screening studies of medical students, which demonstrated a high predisposition to neurotic and depressive illness. Thus we have an example that illustrates the methodological requirements for comprehensive examinations of "causes."

My second point concerns the innate resistance of people to resist not only ordinary but unusual life stress. To understand stress, we need not only know how stress contributes to subsequent disorders but we must also know more about the natural defenses that appear to be operationally successful for the large segment of the population. A woman comes to my mind who has a feeble-minded daughter, lost a son in World War II, had two sons who were assassinated, and her husband lingered on after being seriously incapacitated after a stroke. You all know whom I mean: Rose Kennedy. A man comes to my mind who according to every textbook should have been subject to serious psychopathology. As a boy, this man was rejected by a father who was cold, paranoid, homosexual, and eventually succumbed to syphilis of the brain. His mother, a charming woman, had many affairs and several ill-considered marriages. The son loved his mother in a manner that many psychiatrists would consider indicative of a neurotic symbiosis. In any event, the man did not falter. He is Winston Churchill.

In summary, neither the primarily sociological nor the psychoanalytical points of view can predict the consequences of stress. Most of our findings are after the fact. This calls for more sophisticated investigative strategies.

Dr. Holmes: I think you have identified half of two critical problems in this area of research. The first is: Why does 20% of the high risk population stay well? The other is: Why does one-third of low risk people get sick?

Dr. Julia Mayo: I would like to underscore a point mentioned already, namely, the importance of distinguishing between life events stemming from clinical psychopathology and life events precipitated by external causes. I have had occasion to use the life events scale not only with manic-depressive patients but with their spouses as well. In a study of treatment effects of lithium where the scale was given before and during treatment, we found a trend toward a domino effect in life events. After a hypomanic episode, many patients remark on the ripple effect of several related events, each of which seems to bump the other. For example, marital arguments lead to increased drinking, which leads to loss of job, which leads to loss of income, and so on. When this patient is treated with lithium and the family is treated with certain psychosocial techniques, these life events tend to disappear; what is left are life events beyond the patient's control, such as death, war, and physical illness. The point is simply this. All of us are subject to a variety of life events over time. To what degree can certain life events be eradicated by recognition of certain high risk clinical populations and applying preventive and interventive therapeutic measures?

Dr. Dohrenwend's scale is geared very definitely to middle class populations. I wonder what would be the event items, as well as the rating that would be given, if one took a lower class population, for example, class V blacks living in an urban ghetto. "Moving" to many of them is no "stress" since they move every time they cannot pay rent. Losing a job is no "stress" because many never had a job to lose. Getting in and out of marriage may not be a problem since many have had a "living together" syndrome which the middle class seems rapidly to be now adopting. Nevertheless, if one looks at content analysis, one will find that if you scale according to socioeconomic status, what is viewed as a life event or stressor for a population living in one geographic area may be entirely different when taken at a different point in time with a different population that has a different psychosocial vulnerability to start with.

Dr. Holmes: When we were studying onset of tuberculosis and did our matched sample control study where one group of employees got tuberculosis and the other group did not, both groups reported about 10 divorces over a 10-year period. The divorces in the controlled sample were randomly distributed over the 10-year period. If the person who got tuberculosis was going to get a divorce within the past 10 years, the probability was it would occur in the 2-year period prior to the onset of the disease. Thus the important thing is not that everybody experiences a particular event; it is when does it occur in combination with what other events.

With respect to blacks in the ghetto, we studied Mexican and black Americans in the ghetto of Watts in Los Angeles a year following the riot and fire. What we found was what I reported very briefly in my chapter; blacks see life events as requiring far more change in adjustment than does the white middle class. That is to say, a divorce is more salient for blacks, and a change of residences is indeed more salient for blacks than for whites.

Dr. Dohrenwend: I would like to address three of these comments. Bruce Link, my collaborator, has supplied me with the figure Dr. Frank asked about: 75% of individuals with functional disorders are also demoralized. We base this estimate on data from three studies: (a) analyses of Langner's calibration of the 22-item screening scale from the Midtown study against the psychiatrists' ratings in that study, (b) my own research in Washington Heights in which the same scale was tested against psychiatrists' rating, and (c) the Myers and Weissman comparison of results achieved with the Gurin scale by contrast with diagnoses made according to RDC criteria in New Haven.

The second thing I want to react to is Dr. Winokur's point about the very few events that would be fateful on the Holmes and Rahe list of 43 events. His assessment is close to ours as far as the Holmes and Rahe list is concerned, but I would point out that there are quite a number of longer lists. The one we constructed and have been using consists of 101 events. Moreover, the number of fateful events can be expanded by expanding the number of central figures to whom they happen. In many of the studies, this matter of central figure is left vague. Usually, the event is assumed to happen to the person himself, but a husband's loss of a job is likely to be a fateful event for the wife, whatever may have caused it for the husband.

Finally, I think Dr. Mayo's point is an excellent observation. When ratings are provided not by samples of convenience but by general population samples, I think you will find group differences in magnitude estimations. We have found some based on ratings by a full probability sample of adults. Differences proved especially sharp between Puerto Rican raters in contrast with non-Puerto Rican white raters in this study. Some differences are also evident in some of the comparisons that Dr. Holmes gave. I think that more will emerge in future investigations, especially when full probability samples of raters rather than samples of convenience are used.

Dr. Uhlenhuth: I would like to address briefly the issue of appropriateness of item scale content in relation to social class. We have found in the Oakland survey that the amounts of stress experienced over the preceding 12 months are similar among the classes, including class V. There are no significant differences. That does not dispose of the point, but it's an interesting finding.

Also, regarding the issue of confusion between stress and psychopathology, perhaps I did not underscore it clearly, but I thought Dr. Hurst's sliding interval analysis was an extremely interesting approach to that question and helps to deal with it. However, it is generally accepted that somehow prospectiveness in a study will deal with this issue adequately, but in fact it deals with it only partially. If you are depending on a criterion of illness that involves primarily verbal reports of the subjects, as many studies do, it is conceivable that you will have people who will report many life events or many stressful life events and who will also tend to report illness at a high frequency. The mere separation of the time when those two reports are made does not get you out of that bind.

Dr. Michael Hurst: I agree that it doesn't entirely. In some other studies as well as our own, there is almost always a concurrent correlation between symptom reporting and life event scores. Since our subjects were *not* reporting psychiatric symptomatology at the time of their life change assessments (by our definition of cases), this factor would seem minimal.

I would like to reemphasize a couple of other points. People seem to generalize tremendously about how other people experience certain events. This is amazing from the perspective of both a clinician and researcher. Masuda and Holmes, in their original article on scoring in 1967, showed that even for their population of 394 blue collar workers in Seattle the standard error of the mean was equal to the mean, which represents a huge variance among individuals for any given type of life event.

The same thing occurred in our air traffic controllers. The standard deviation does not equal the mean, but the standard error does. Some people rated the death of a pet as causing 1 unit of distress; other people rated it at 99. One cannot generalize about how all people experience life events. I think our group has shown that very well, and Wyatt's 1977 article in the *Journal of Human Stress* showed that Afro-Americans also rate things differently.

Dr. Robert Spitzer: I'd like to raise two methodological issues with Dr. Hurst's study which I found most compelling and interesting. One concerns the problem of the magnitude of the difference. It would seem to me, if we do accept his data, that he can confidently reject the hypothesis that there is no relationship between life events and subsequent development of signs of psychopathology. I think a rough calculation of the proportion of variance accounted for would indicate that it is somewhere in the neighborhood of 5%, which is relatively small. A skeptic might even say this lends evidence for the unimportance of life events in the development of psychopathology.

The second problem has to do with his important methodological advance of having a case defined by the subsequent development of psychopathology.

What bothers me is the possibility that one may be dealing with this kind of instance, if we take the example of alcoholism. Could we be dealing with someone who has a minor problem with alcoholism but is still below the threshold for defining him as a case? He now has alcoholism and is now also reporting many events that may be consequent to his alcoholism. At a later evaluation, his alcoholism is more fully developed. He now becomes a case, and we now retrospectively use the reports of life events not knowing that this person was mildly symptomatic prior to the life event. I would hope that there are data to indicate that that is not a likely explanation.

Dr. Hurst: Dr. Spitzer is correct about percentage of variance accounted for by life events. It was approximately 5%, and Rahe's earlier prospective studies, which were conducted with the Navy, have unfortunately shown that only 1% in the variance of illness outcomes was predictable from life events.

Our explained variance is 5 to 10%, depending on which measure of life change or psychiatric outcome used. However, once other measures are included along with life change, such as psychological, demographic, and other individual characteristics, the predictability of the outcome is greatly heightened, with the percentage of variance going up to 50, 60, or even as high as 74% in some of our analyses. Thus life change stressors are not the single most important factor.

The second point about preclinical cases confounding the results is certainly a possibility. I cannot deny that possibility because we did use an absolute cut-off for criterion definitions. On the other hand, the same criterion was used to define control cases, who seemingly had no symptomatology in any area. Therefore, control cases could have been preclinical as well, and the initial assessment of both cases and controls would have been affected. It is still true that the severity of preclinical symptoms may have been greater in the onset group when they were first assessed; not much can be done about that.

Dr. Spitzer: You could look at those data and see if they have small scores.

Dr. Hurst: We will be doing that as a check in the future.

Dr. Ernest M. Gruenberg: The law of life is change. As Holmes said, many of these events sooner or later happen to everybody; the issue is how people adapt to these changes in life. If one is not growing, not moving forward, one is trying to stand still when the world is changing, and that is impossible. If the change you are experiencing demands that you change and you are unable to change, you are going to be in trouble. That is something Dr. Frank hinted at. If your adaptation efforts are maladaptation efforts, then you are going to have a worse problem.

I want to inject a developmental attitude toward life and human personality. Perhaps the only directly relevant point concerns the concept of how much of the variance you are explaining. Why do so many people with low scores get ill, and why do so many people with high scores not get ill? Perhaps these life events are associated not only with maladaptation but with forward movement, too. Perhaps some of the difficulty of accounting for all the responses to the demands for changing would be helped if one could inject some evidence of forward movement, positive adaptation, learning, and growth into the data gathering. Then maybe one would see a bimodal distribution of responses.

Dr. Eugene I. Burdock: The amount of stress caused by a life event cannot be determined without taking into account the meaning of the event to the individual who experiences it. For example, at the top of Dr. Holmes' scale is "death of spouse." We can all think of examples, however, if only from the movies, where a spouse's death was not a traumatic event for the individual. This point is illustrated by the responses of two patients we have seen at Bellevue Hospital's trauma service, to which people are brought suffering from gunshot wounds, stab wounds, and accidents. The first case, an elderly woman who had suffered a dislocated shoulder from a fall in the street, showed very little evidence of psychological disorder when interviewed with the SCI. However, on reinterview at discharge, she showed a typical stress profile: fear-worry, agitation, and physical complaints. She was now concerned about being put back out into the community away from the sheltered environment of the hospital. The second case was a young man who had fallen off a scaffold at work and suffered multiple fractures. This man's SCI showed the stress profile on admission. At discharge, however, when his fractures had begun to heal and he felt assured that he would recover all his functions, his SCI profile was down to normal.

Thus one must take into account the meaning of the event to the individual. This point has been implicit in several of the previous comments, in particular in Dr. Hurst's and in Dr. Gruenberg's remarks, but I think it should be made explicit.

Dr. William Zung: To push further what Dr. Burdock said about the importance of definitions for stresses, vulnerability, and desirability, perhaps what is really necessary to understand is the underlying model that the investigators are presenting or have previously set up. There are two models. One is the tin cup model. All the events that have happened during a person's lifetime that are on the list "fill up" the tin cup, and after so many life events have happened, the "cup runneth over," and you "develop" a disease. An alternate model is the seesaw model. As one event occurs, it would tip the seesaw down, but when another event occurs, supposedly a stressor but identifiable as an antistressor, such as marriage, it would tip the seesaw back up.

Presently, life events are weighted negatively, and using the tin cup model, when the cup runneth over, you develop a disease. In fact, for some of these events that occur, instead of giving them a negative point, they should be given a positive point so that the end total score will be entirely different. You might come up with a minus score of 100 in the tin cup model but, if you use the seesaw model, you might have a plus 100 instead.

Dr. Hurst: That is the same as my suggestion for bipolar rather than unipolar rating scales.

Dr. Robert M. Rose: A number of these comments and discussion are not as disparate as they might first appear. When studying large numbers of individuals of diverse populations, Dr. Holmes' approach is a very valuable one. One of the conclusions that has developed from this approach is that people who have more things happening, or more things happening to them, are clearly at a greater risk for illness later on. That conclusion comes with a certain degree of epidemiological rigor.

When one wants to approach the problem from a more clinical perspective, one immediately becomes impressed with the importance of a number of other factors and the need to specify more precisely and specifically the life events that occur to which individuals, and one must weigh life change events in terms of how subjects individually perceive these events.

One has a different focus in utilizing a life event inventory to predict illness in a specific group as opposed to generalizing on the importance of life events across large populations. One confronts the fact that other variables modify the impact of life's stress, such as personality types, as individuals do differ significantly in terms of which events they experience as most stressful. I also believe that it is important to assess individuals in terms of their vulnerability both physically and psychologically, as it is not yet clear how individuals may differ in terms of their susceptibility for future illness after exposure to stressful life events.

Stress and Mental Disorder,
edited by James E. Barrett et al.
Raven Press, New York © 1979.

Causal Relationships Between Clinical Depression and Life Events

E. S. Paykel

Department of Psychiatry, St. George's Hospital Medical School, London, S.W.17, England

My data regarding life stress and the affective disorders were derived mainly from two sources. The first was a fruitful collaboration in New Haven with a number of colleagues, and the second comprises some ongoing studies in London into depression and effects of specific life events. This chapter depends mainly on the first source. I start from the premise that by now a number of studies, including our own, have demonstrated a tendency for life events to precede depression at greater than control rates. The data are viewed selectively to ask three major questions regarding the causal relationship between depression and events: (a) is depression specifically related to certain kinds of events? (b) do endogenous depressions occur, and do they show a specific symptom pattern? and (c) how important are life events in the genesis of depression?

METHODOLOGY AND OVERALL FINDINGS

The methodology of these studies has been presented fully elsewhere. The basic technique was retrospective elicitation of life events and comparison with matched controls. Retrospective studies present well-known difficulties of recall distortions due to illness, and the fact that illness itself may produce new events (4,21). To minimize these, a defined list of 61 events (condensed for some purposes to 33) was used, every event being inquired for unless clearly inapplicable and full details being obtained. The interview was postponed until acute psychiatric disturbance had subsided to diminish reporting distortions.

The first study was a controlled comparison of depressives (27). A varied and representative sample of 185 depressed patients was compared with matched controls from the general population. Overall, depressives reported about three times as many events in the 6 months before symptom onset than did the general population.

Subsequent studies have enabled comparison with other patient samples, particularly first admission schizophrenics (9) and suicide attempters (24), many of whom would not fit the criteria for the full depressive syndrome. Table 1 summarizes the mean number of events reported, using the 33-item events list,

TABLE 1. *Mean number of events reported in 6 months by different groups*

Group	Mean no.
Suicide attempters	3.3
Depressives	2.1
Schizophrenics	1.5
General population	0.8

in the 6 months prior to the onset of depression, schizophrenia, or the suicide attempt, and for general population controls. Sample characteristics and event lists differed somewhat in the original groups, but findings shown are based on comparable samples and event lists.

All patient groups reported significantly more events than did the general population. There was a rank order from suicide attempters, who reported the most events, to depressives, schizophrenics, and the general population. These differences presumably reflect, in the retrospective frame, the degree to which recent events are involved in the genesis of the illness. The findings for depressives were later supported by evidence of excess events in the 3 months prior to relapse in a different sample under maintenance treatment (29).

The month of occurrence of each event was recorded for suicide attempters, depressives, and general population subjects but not for schizophrenics. Figure 1 shows the mean number of events reported in each of the 6 months. There was a fairly even spread of events over the entire 6 months for general population

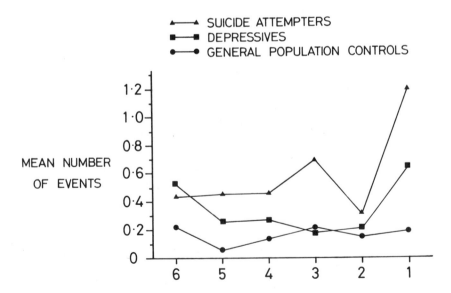

FIG. 1. Mean number of events reported during each 1-month period prior to attempted suicide, onset of illness, or interview. (From ref. 24.)

subjects. There was a marked peaking of events in the month before the attempt for suicide attempters, indicating a particularly immediate reaction. There was a mild peaking in the month before onset for depressives. The excess of events they reported, compared with general population subjects, was spread over most of the 6 months and might have extended even earlier. These findings are similar to those reported by Brown et al. (2).

SPECIFICITY

We can now examine the question of specificity. Analysis of the depressives revealed that the general excess of life events was paralleled in the pattern of most of the individual events studied. Groupings of events showed that those involving an exit from the social field of the respondent occurred much more prior to depression than in controls, but entrance events did not. Likewise, events categorized as undesirable showed a great excess prior to depression, whereas desirable events did not (27).

In addition, several items that referred to arguments or difficulties in interpersonal relationships were omitted from the final comparisons since it was felt that the patient group might report these more readily. We examined them separately, however, and they were reported much more by depressives than controls.

These findings suggested some degree of specificity in the relationship between events and depression. At best, however, the specificity was partial. A highly specific hypothesis would propose that there are certain classes of events that produce only depression. In fact, the excess among depressives included almost every event in our list, except entrances and desirable events. Many subjects reported a cluster of events, which suggested a cumulative model of stress.

Adequate investigation of the degree of specificity also requires attention to the other side of the question, the disturbance produced. When categories of events were examined for the full range of disorders, the same findings as for depression tended to hold for the other disorders, with the same ranking as before (Table 2). Exits, undesirable events, and interpersonal arguments were reported to excess before all conditions, desirable events before none. However, entrances were also reported excessively before suicide attempts, and exits were barely excessive before schizophrenia, so that the exit-entrance distinction tended to be more specific for depression. Interpersonal arguments were also reported before all conditions, but much less so for schizophrenia.

Findings for two additional categories were also available for suicide attempters and depressives (Table 2). For the first, we divided events into three groups—major, intermediate, and minor—by scores from another study in which subjects had scaled the degree to which each of the events was considered upsetting (28). Both patient groups tended to report more events than general population controls in all three categories: suicide attempters showed a further excess over depressives for major and intermediate but not minor events. The second categorization was by the degree of control or choice the respondent

TABLE 2. *Percentage of different patients groups reporting events in category at least once in 6 months*

Category	Suicide attempters	Depressives	Schizophrenics	General population controls
Exits	21[a]	25[a]	14[a]	9
Entrances	34[a]	13	16	11
Undesirable	60[a]	40[a]	42[a]	21
Desirable	15	4	8	11
Interpersonal events (full event list)	75[a]	62[a]	18[a]	3
Major upset	68[a]	45[a]	—	23
Intermediate upset	53[a]	26[a]	—	4
Minor upset	49[a]	45[a]	—	25
Uncontrolled	66[a]	40[a]	—	21
Controlled	34[a]	32[a]	—	17

[a] Patient group reports event category significantly more frequently than general population.

might exert over the initiation of the event. Some events, such as serious illness of a family member, are likely to be outside the subject's control; other events, such as marriage, may be within it. In both these categories also, depressives reported more events than the general population subjects. Suicide attempters reported significantly more uncontrolled but not controlled events than depressives. It was particularly the more threatening categories of events, scaled as major or intermediate in upset, events outside the respondent's control, and undesirable events that suicide attempters reported more than depressives.

In a further study (34) of mixed neurotic patients, there were no differences between patients with predominantly depressive and other symptom pictures regarding types of events experienced. It is clear that specificity is at best weak, and that the same event can be followed in different subjects by a variety of different disturbances. These would include somatic as well as psychiatric disorders (31). There is a limited specificity between exit events and depression. This would appear to extend more strongly into the realm of the normal reaction, most clearly seen in normal bereavement. Some disturbances do seem more strongly related to events in general than are others.

PERCEPTION OF EVENTS

What does emerge is that different types of events differ in their general propensity to produce illness. Further evidence that this is so comes from perceptions of life events. In another set of studies, we modified the technique of Holmes and Rahe (8) to scale on a 0 to 20 equal-interval scale the degree to which each of our 61 events was regarded as upsetting. Results were closely comparable in an American sample of psychiatric patients and relatives (28) and in a later English sample at St. George's Hospital (26).

Events were also found to be perceived in much the same way as they relate to psychiatric illness. Events were divided into categories and mean scores calculated for each group of events as a whole. Findings are shown in Table 3 for both American and English samples. Exits were scored much higher than entrances. In fact, when individual events were examined, there was scarcely any overlap; almost all exits were scored high and all entrances low. Undesirable events were rated as much more upsetting than desirable events. This is not altogether surprising, although the concepts of upset and undesirability are not identical: some undesirable events are trivial and score low on the upset scale. In addition, uncontrolled events were scored much higher than controlled ones. The categories of major, intermediate, and minor events are not shown in Table 3, since they were derived from the upset scale.

These findings should be interpreted cautiously, as selection among the events included in the list might influence the findings. However, they do indicate a universality in the meaning and implications of these events which extend beyond their precipitation of illness into the normal realm. This universality is further supported by the cross-cultural similarity.

ENDOGENOUS DEPRESSION

The second question concerns endogenous depressions unrelated to life stress (21). Some depressives in the original study reported no events in the 6 months preceding onset. Some of the events reported were trivial and probably unrelated to depression.

Using clinical judgment, about 15% of illnesses appeared to be unprecipitated. This judgment is not easy to make. Often there are some events but they are not sufficiently overwhelming to be a sole cause of the depression. The situation is one of partial and ambiguous precipitation, better suited to a quantitative approach.

The weights shown previously were applied to the events reported by depressed patients. As the main tool, a summed score (the total stress score) was derived

TABLE 3. *Mean scaled degree of upset for event categories*[a]

	Mean score	
Category	American study	English study
Exit	13.1	13.2
Entrance	6.2	6.5
Undesirable	13.9	14.1
Desirable	4.7	4.7
Uncontrolled	13.6	13.5
Controlled	7.4	7.2

[a] Scores are corrected for a systematic difference in levels of all events, with English scores being higher.

for each patient by adding weights for all events reported. To avoid dependence on the assumption of additivity of events, a maximum event score was also derived by taking the single weight for the highest event reported by the patient. The two scores gave closely similar results. Frequency histograms showed continuous distributions without any hint of the bimodality that would have indicated a clear separation between precipitated and unprecipitated depression (21).

As usually employed, the concept of endogenous depression involves additional issues. Endogenous depressives are considered to be distinguished not only by absence of precipitant stress but also by certain specific symptom features and by nonneurotic premorbid personalities (13). A number of studies have used factor analysis to explore this issue (17). One problem is that presence of precipitants is usually recorded as an inadequate yes-no judgment and made by the same rater who rates symptoms and personality; thus it is easy for rater bias to produce a spurious correlation.

We employed the quantified measures of precipitant stress and used separate raters. Symptoms were rated by psychiatrists at initial interview without knowledge of life event material. A principal component analysis was carried out on the symptom data alone (25). The first factor showed positive loadings on almost all items and appeared to be a factor of severity. The second factor was bipolar and closely resembled factors contrasting endogenous and neurotic depression reported by Kiloh and Garside (12) and Carney et al. (5). The third factor, also bipolar, appeared to contrast negative loadings on typical depressive symptoms and hostility with positive loadings on anxiety and hypochondriasis.

The second factor in this analysis indicated that the symptoms of endogenous and neurotic depression cluster together to form two contrasting patterns. To examine the relationship of this symptomatic distinction to stress, correlations were computed between factor scores on the three factors and the two alternative stress scores (21). These are shown in Table 4. The total stress score correlated significantly with factor II in the predicted direction that patients with endogenous symptom pattern reported less life stress, but the correlation 0.15 was so low as to account for little variance, and there was an almost significant correlation with factor III. For the maximal event score, the correlation was only with factor III but was equally low. Thus the relationship between stress and symptom pattern, although in the predicted direction, was so weak as to be trivial and was not entirely specific to the endogenous-neurotic symptom dimension.

TABLE 4. *Correlations between stress scores on upset scale and symptom factors*

Factor	Total stress score	Maximal event score
I severity	−0.08	0.04
II neurotic (+) versus endogenous (−)	0.15[a]	0.07
III anxious (+) versus depressed (−)	−0.14	−0.15[a]

[a] $p < 0.05$.

Further analyses of these data using cluster analysis techniques for grouping individuals showed evidence of four groups rather than two (20). Here again the relationship to life stress was weak.

We have recently replicated the findings regarding symptom pattern in a new English sample of 62 depressives treated with phenelzine for 4 weeks in an open predictor study (23). The life event information was limited to judgments by treating psychiatrists regarding presence of stress at onset and whether it seemed likely on clinical grounds that the illness was precipitated. In terms of this judgment, 11% of illnesses were judged definitely unprecipitated and 24%

TABLE 5. *Relationship of symptom pattern to judged precipitation in depressives treated with phenelzine*

	Not precipitated ($N= 22$)	Precipitated ($N= 40$)	F value[a]
Symptom factors			
Factor I (severity)	0.06	0.05	0.00
Factor II (neurotic +, versus endogenous −)	−0.29	0.09	2.24
Factor III (anxious +, versus depressed and hostile −)	−0.29	0.10	2.05
Symptoms (1–7 scales)			
Depressed feelings	4.59	4.70	0.32
Distinct quality	3.77	3.79	0.01
Morning worsening	2.32	2.38	0.02
Evening worsening	1.59	2.20	2.83
Reactivity	2.45	3.30	5.35[b]
Guilt	3.50	3.75	0.46
Pessimism	4.32	3.93	1.70
Suicidal trends	3.14	2.95	0.19
Depersonalization	2.09	2.13	0.01
Obsessional symptoms	1.91	1.95	0.02
Impaired work and interests	4.73	4.38	1.18
Loss of energy and fatigue	4.09	4.43	0.99
Psychic anxiety	4.41	4.45	0.03
Somatic anxiety	3.50	4.10	2.86
Anorexia	3.32	3.36	0.01
Increased appetite	1.64	1.20	3.28
Weight loss	2.76	3.31	1.11
Irritability	2.45	3.03	2.56
Initial insomnia	2.71	2.63	0.05
Middle insomnia	2.10	2.28	0.22
Delayed insomnia	2.19	2.13	0.03
Paranoid ideas	1.64	1.65	0.00
Depressive delusions	1.23	1.13	0.87
Self pity	2.73	2.58	0.22
Hypochondriasis	2.23	2.05	0.28
Hostility	1.27	1.35	0.13
Retardation	2.41	1.60	7.65[c]
Agitation	2.23	2.35	0.13
Depressed appearance	3.86	3.41	1.90

[a] 1.60 d.f.
[b] $p<0.05$.
[c] $p<0.01$.

as probably unprecipitated. The remaining 65% were considered probably or definitely precipitated. The sample here was rather different and less representative than the New Haven one in that all patients were regarded as suitable for drug treatment; the raters were English psychiatrists with a different orientation, but the findings confirm that unprecipitated depressives are in a minority.

A factor analysis in this study replicated the factors derived from the previous study. As shown in Table 5, none of the three factors showed a significant relationship to the judgment of precipitant stress. Only two of 31 individual symptoms had any relationship: unprecipitated depressions showed less reactivity in the sense of short-term fluctuations of depressed mood with environmental changes and more psychomotor retardation. The judgment of precipitant stress was relatively crude compared with the quantification of life events in the first study and was open to bias in knowledge of symptoms; this bias, however, would have been expected to inflate rather than diminish the relationship.

Overall, our findings confirm that some depressions are endogenous, although they are a minority of the total. Only very weakly are they distinguished by symptom pattern. The so-called endogenous symptom pattern certainly does occur as a group of symptoms which cluster together, but the label is unfortunate; absence of stress is not a prominent feature.

MAGNITUDE OF EFFECT

Given that life events are implicated in the genesis of most depressions, how important is the effect? It has often been pointed out that close scrutiny of the events reported by patients suggests that they can at best be only partial causes. Most of the events reported in our studies were not major crises, such as death, life-threatening illness, or financial ruin, but rather more everyday domestic disturbances, such as interpersonal arguments, marital disruptions, separation, and difficulties at work. Such events are fairly common. It seems probable that in most cases they are negotiated without illness. Some other factors must contribute to the development of depression. It is particularly easy to lose sight of base rates for the population. When the prevalence of a disease state is relatively low, single events will be of limited value in explaining it if they occur with moderate frequency in the general population (35), because most occurrences of the event will not be followed by the disease.

A previously reported calculation from the controlled study illustrated this (21). Exits were reported by 46 depressives (25%) and nine controls (5%). These differences appeared impressive. Let us try to refer this figure to the general population. Accurate figures for incidence of depression of clinical intensity in the general population are not available. We can take an estimate of 2% for new cases over the 6-month base period and apply these figures to 10,000 subjects in the general population. Among these will be 200 new depressives and 9,800 nondepressives. We can call the latter "normals," although they include some old cases of depression. In 5% of the normals (i.e., 490) and in 25% of the depressives (i.e., 50), an exit will have occurred. The total number of subjects to experience exits is 490 plus 50, or 540. Only 50 of these (9%) will become depressed; less than one-tenth of subjects who experienced exits become depressed. The greater part of the variance in determining depression must be attributed to something else.

This calculation makes a number of assumptions. In particular, the relationship would be closer if we took a higher incidence for depression. The annual incidence of 4% is high compared with most published figures although lower than some recent studies. However, the general point remains that most stressful events are not followed by psychiatrically treated depression. Some are followed by other psychiatric disorders or by somatic disorders. Incidences of other psychiatric disorders are much lower. Comparable calculations for suicide attempts, for which approximate incidence is better worked out, would indicate that perhaps 1% of exits are followed by suicide attempts (22). For schizophrenia, with low annual incidence, the proportion would be very low.

We are dealing here with an old controversy: Are the events that occur before the onset of depression mere precipitants, contributing little to causation, or are they important in the genesis of the illness? It is clear that this is an empirical question, and sufficient data are now available to answer it.

The computation given above is not a good way of looking at the question. It depends on guesswork about the incidence in the appropriate base population and the assumption that sampling has been representative. A case control study, rather than one of community incidence, could never be used to calculate the absolute amount of illness resulting from an event.

Another approach is the "brought-forward time" of Brown et al. (2). The general problem is that of nonparametric measures of association. I have been exploring use of an epidemiological concept, relative risk (22). This is the ratio of the disease rate among those exposed to a causative factor to the rate among those not exposed; i.e., it is a measure of the degree to which the factor increases the disease rate.

True calculation of the relative risk requires precise enumeration of cases of the disease in the general population or subgroups of it, so that incidences among exposed and unexposed can be determined. It can easily be shown (15) that in a case control study of an illness in which the numbers of persons affected is small compared to the number unaffected, the relative risk can be calculated approximately, as shown below, without actual knowledge of the rates.

	Cases	Controls
Cause: present	a	b
absent	c	d
Relative risk	$\dfrac{ad}{bc}$	

This approximation depends primarily on the number of persons affected by the disease being relatively small compared to the number unaffected in

TABLE 6. *Relative risks*

Group	Exits in last 6 months	All events in last 6 months
Depression	6.5	5.4
Suicide attempts	6.7	6.3
Schizophrenia	3.9	3.0

both exposed and unexposed populations (less than 20%), which is the usual situation in psychiatry. Also, neither cases nor controls should be selected with a particular bias toward individuals exposed or not exposed to the causative factor. Even where the proportion affected is more than 20%, the ratio is a useful measure of differences in disease risk between groups but better regarded as the relative odds, i.e., the ratio of affected to unaffected individuals in one group divided by the same ratio in another group. It is also possible to calculate confidence limits (7). Brown's brought-forward time can be related algebraically to the relative odds (22).

Table 6 shows relative risks from or study of depression, with those for suicide attempts and schizophrenia from the data shown previously for comparison. An exit event increases the risk of depression 6.5-fold in the next 6 months. Occurrence of any event on our list increases it on average by 5.4 times. Figures for suicide attempters are a little higher and for schizophrenia considerably lower (around 3 times). It is clear that there are differences in the extent to which different disorders are consequences of life events. Suicide attempts have the greatest association, with depression a close second, and schizophrenia considerably less.

The peaking of events in the month before the suicide attempt raises the relative risk for the month after an event to 10. Strictly speaking, each relative risk refers to a specified period after the event, since for the effects of life events (unlike, for example, the effect of carcinogens), there appears to be a rapid fall-off in the rate of illness in those exposed as time passes. There will be a fall-off of the relative risk with time. It would be possible to multiply risk by the period under consideration to derive total "risk-months," but this concept is not easily interpretable.

OTHER STUDIES

This method can also be applied to other studies in the literature. Some selected findings are shown in Table 7. Detailed derivation is described elsewhere (22). Wherever possible, the reported data have been used to calculate risks over a 6-month period for comparison with the New Haven studies (22).

The data of Brown et al. (4) are particularly well reported and suitable for depression. They give, over a 6-month standard period, a relative risk for all events of 1.9, and for markedly threatening events 5.9, close to the New Haven

TABLE 7. Relative risk estimates from other published studies

Diagnosis	Reference	Event types	Time period	Relative risk
Depression	Brown et al. (2)	All events	6 months	1.8
		Markedly threatening events	6 months	5.9
	Brown et al. (3)	Markedly threatening events	38 weeks	5.6
Schizophrenia	Brown and Birley (1)	All events	6 months	2.4
Neurosis	Cooper and Sylph (6)	All events	3 months	5.3
Psychiatric illness	Parkes (19)	Death of parent, spouse, sibling	6 months	5.9
Impairment	Myers et al. (18)	Exits	1 year	1.9
		Undesirable events	1 year	3.2

figure for exits. More recent findings from Brown et al. (3) produce a comparable but rather higher rate of 5.6 for markedly threatening events in the last 38 weeks in depressed patients. For schizophrenia, the figures of Brown and Birley (1) give a relative risk of 6.4 for the 3-week period for which the event rate was raised, but this reduces to 2.4 over 6 months.

In a study by Cooper and Sylph (6) of neurosis in general practice, the relative risk was 5.3 over a 3-month period. Risks over 6 months could not be calculated because life event rates could not be extrapolated. In a study by Parkes (19), looking at history of recent bereavement in mixed psychiatric patients, the relative risk was 6.2, remarkably close to the figures that derive for depression and exits or markedly threatening events.

One of the advantages of the relative risk is that it can be used to compare with true calculations from epidemiological studies. The last figure in Table 7 is from a community survey by Myers et al. (18). Occurrence of an exit event in the last year increased the risk of showing marked impairment on the Gurin scale of psychiatric symptoms by 1.9. Undesirable events gave a risk of 3.2. The kind of psychiatric morbidity revealed by this scale is probably milder than in most patient samples.

Another advantage is that other aspects of etiological relationships can be investigated. It is reasonable to expect, if a factor is causative, that the risk should increase as does the intensity of dose or exposure. Analyses of this kind are common in epidemiology. Brown et al. (2) report graphs from which it is possible to estimate approximate relative risk for depression over 6 months for three classes of events. The risks for markedly threatening events are 5.9, for moderately threatening events 1.7, and for events of little or no threat 1.0. These would certainly suggest a relationship to degrees of exposure.

This analogy with infectious disease serves to remind us that there are some parallels with tuberculosis, a disease that at first sight seems due to a straightforward single causative factor but which on closer scrutiny turns out to be more complex. In the preantibiotic era, it was estimated that in more than 90% of contacts, active clinical disease did not develop (30). There was a clear genetic element, with rising concordance rates with closer blood relationship and a rate in monozygotic twins more than three times that in dizygotics (11).

A MODEL FOR EFFECTS OF LIFE EVENTS

The value of measures, such as the relative risk, is to assess the importance of recent life events as factors in the genesis of depression. There does appear to be some consistency in the literature. Over 6 months, the more threatening classes of events seem to increase the risk of clinical depression approximately six times. The effects are a little less marked than for suicide attempts and considerably more than for schizophrenia. For all disorders, risks diminish with time, as reflected by declining event rates assessed retrospectively.

These findings certainly indicate effects which are of some importance. The magnitude of the effects would also be greater if individual circumstances of the event could be considered in detail. Apparently identical events can differ a good deal in their implications, and studies have usually deliberately sought to base judgments of stressfulness on external criteria rather than on the subject's own report to avoid the risk of circularity.

Nevertheless, the relationship is far from complete. It remains true that event experience is often not followed by psychiatric illness. The event is only responsible in part for the onset of clinical depression and must be regarded as interacting with a host of other factors in determining whether the outcome is an illness, and which specific illness. It is not merely the event but the soil on which it falls. The modifying factors can easily be conceived in broad outline, if not studied in detail, and Fig. 2 is an attempt to specify some of them.

At the start, the event itself may be regarded as incorporating modifying factors. What appears to be the same event may differ in circumstances and may carry a variety of implications along the dimensions already referred to in this chapter. Next, other stresses and supports in the social environment may modify the consequences. These would include such factors as outside employment, confiding relationships, presence of several young children in the home, and lower social class, as identified by Brown et al. (3). Chronic stresses, which have tended to be ignored in life event research, may perhaps sometimes have this modifying effect and sometimes act like new events.

Next we must assume a large number of personal factors reflecting vulnerabil-

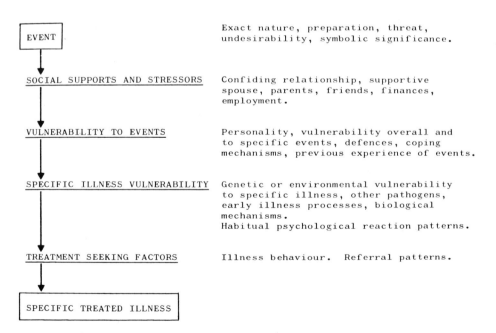

FIG. 2. Modifying factors between event and illness.

ity to events. There may be personality factors leading to greater vulnerability to events in general, such as are hypothesized in work on the neurotic constitution (33). On the other hand, specific vulnerabilities seem likely; for instance, obsessional personalities might be expected to be particularly sensitive to events involving major changes in life pattern and routine. Such vulnerabilities might be genetic or environmental in origin. There is accumulating evidence that early loss may predispose to the effects of subsequent loss in inducing depression (3) or suicide attempts (14). In this sense, all earlier life events may be seen as having persisting influences of lesser degree, both pathogenic and protective in the learning of coping behavior. Equally, the psychological effects of events, translated into their neurophysiological substrates, must interact with other neurochemical, physiological, and pharmacological aspects of central nervous system function, e.g., in the pathways regulating mood, which thus become a final common pathway for depression.

Depression is not the only possible consequence of life events. We must also envisage personal vulnerability factors leading to development of specific diseases. For affective disorder, these might include such elements as habitual psychological defense mechanisms and reaction patterns, cyclical changes in function, enzyme defects in monoamine pathways, and variations in metabolic pools of transmitter substances.

Finally, factors such as illness behavior (16) will determine whether or not an individual regards himself as ill and seeks professional treatment. Further referral patterns may also determine whether psychiatric treatment is required for those countries where there are nonpsychiatric primary givers of care. Such factors may be of great importance if, as some evidence suggests, there is a high prevalence of untreated depression in the community (3,32).

It is easy to specify some of these modifying factors in broad outline, but their interaction with events has been little investigated, and many more detailed studies are required. Prospective studies of single events have some advantages in this context.

The kind of causative chain that is indicated by this model is a multifactorial one in which many factors converge on the final state, even in a single case. Events are important, but they interact with many other factors. Rigid criteria for a reactive depression (10) and rigid separation into reactive and endogenous types become inappropriate. Most depressions may be to some extent reactive, to some extent endogenous. This kind of multifactorial etiology is complex and frustrating to purists in its blurring of clear-cut categories, but it is more in keeping with knowledge of the complexity of psychological relationships and brain mechanisms in general.

ACKNOWLEDGMENTS

Studies reported in this chapter were carried out collaboratively with a number of authors, particularly Selby Jacobs, M.D., Gerald L. Klerman, M.D., Jerome

Myers, Ph.D., Brigitte Prusoff, M.P.H., and E. H. Uhlenhuth, M.D. I am grateful to Myrna Weissman, Ph.D., for first drawing my attention to the relevance of relative risk.

REFERENCES

1. Brown, G. W., and Birley, J. L. T. (1968): Crises and life changes and the onset of schizophrenia. *J. Health Soc. Behav.,* 9:203–214.
2. Brown, G. W., Harris, T. O., and Peto, J. (1973): Life events and psychiatric disorders. Part 2: Nature of causal link. *Psychol. Med.,* 3:159–176.
3. Brown, G. W., Ni Bhrolchain, M., and Harris, T. (1975): Social class and psychiatric disturbance among women in an urban population. *Sociology,* 9:225–254.
4. Brown, G. W., Sklair, F., Harris, T. O., and Birley, J. L. T. (1973): Life events and psychiatric disorders. Part 1: Some methodological issues. *Psychol. Med.,* 3:74–87.
5. Carney, M. W. P., Roth, M., and Garside, R. F. (1965): The diagnosis of depressive syndromes and the prediction of ECT response. *Br. J. Psychiatry,* 111:659–674.
6. Cooper, B., and Sylph, J. (1973): Life events and the onset of neurotic illness: An investigation in general practice. *Psychol. Med.,* 3:421–435.
7. Everitt, B. (1977): *The Analysis of Contingency Tables.* Chapman and Hall, London.
8. Holmes, T. H., and Rahe, R. H. (1967): The social readjustment rating scale. *J. Psychosom. Res.,* 11:213–218.
9. Jacobs, S. C., Prusoff, B. A., and Paykel, E. S. (1974): Recent life events in schizophrenia and depression. *Psychol. Med.,* 4:444–453.
10. Jaspers, K. (1923): *General Psychopathology,* translated by J. Hoenig and M. W. Hamilton. Manchester University Press, Manchester.
11. Kallman, F. J., and Reisner, D. (1943): Twin studies on the significance of genetic factors in tuberculosis. *Am. Rev. Tuberculosis,* 47:549.
12. Kiloh, L. G., and Garside, R. F. (1963): The independence of neurotic depression and endogenous depression. *Br. J. Psychiatry,* 109:451–463.
13. Klerman, G. L. (1971): Clinical research in depression. *Arch. Gen. Psychiatry,* 24:305–319.
14. Levi, L. O., Fales, C. H., Stein, M., and Sharp, V. H. (1966): Separation and attempted suicide. *Arch. Gen. Psychiatry,* 15:158–165.
15. MacMahon, B., and Pugh, T. F. (1970): *Epidemiology: Principles and Methods.* Little, Brown and Company, Boston.
16. Mechanic, D. (1976): Stress, illness and illness behaviour. *J. Human Stress,* 2:2–6.
17. Mendels, J., and Cochrane, C. (1968): The nosology of depression: The endogenous-reactive concept. *Am. J. Psychiatry,* 124:1–11.
18. Myers, J. K., Lindenthal, J. J., and Pepper, M. P. (1971): Life events and psychiatric impairment. *J. Nerv. Ment. Dis.,* 152:149–157.
19. Parkes, C. M. (1964): Recent bereavement as a cause of mental illness. *Br. J. Psychiatry,* 110:198.
20. Paykel, E. S. (1971): Classification of depressed patients: A cluster analysis derived grouping. *Br. J. Psychiatry,* 118:275–288.
21. Paykel, E. S. (1974): Recent life events and clinical depression. In: *Life Stress and Illness,* edited by E. K. Gunderson and R. H. Rahe, pp. 134–163. Charles C Thomas, Springfield, Illinois.
22. Paykel, E. S. (1978): Contribution of life events to causation of psychiatric illness. *Psychol. Med.,* 8:245–253.
23. Paykel, E. S., Parker, R. R., Penrose, R., and Rassaby, E. (1979): Depressive classification and prediction of response to phenelzine. *Br. J. Psychiatry (in press).*
24. Paykel, E. S., Prusoff, B. A., and Myers, J. K. (1975): Suicide attempts and recent life events. *Arch. Gen. Psychiatry,* 32:327–333.
25. Paykel, E. S., Klerman, G. L., and Prusoff, B. A. (1970): Treatment setting and clinical depression. *Arch. Gen. Psychiatry,* 22:11–21.
26. Paykel, E. S., McGuiness, B., and Gomez, J. (1976): An Anglo-American comparison of the scaling of life events. *Br. J. Med. Psychol.,* 49:237–247.
27. Paykel, E. S., Myers, J. K., Dienelt, M. N., Klerman, G. L., Lindenthal, J. J., and Pepper,

M. P. (1969): Life events and depression: A controlled study. *Arch. Gen. Psychiatry,* 21:753–760.

28. Paykel, E. S., Prusoff, B. A., and Uhlenhuth, E. H. (1971): Scaling of life events. *Arch. Gen. Psychiatry,* 25:340–347.

29. Paykel, E. S., and Tanner, J. (1976): Life events, depressive relapse and maintenance treatment. *Psychol. Med.,* 6:481–485.

30. Pinner, M. (1945): *Pulmonary Tuberculosis in the Adult: Its Fundamental Aspects.* Charles C Thomas, Springfield, Illinois.

31. Rahe, R. H. (1968): Life-change measurement as a predictor of illness. *Proc. R. Soc. Med.,* 61:1124–1128.

32. Richman, N. (1974): The effects of housing on pre-school children and their mothers. *Dev. Med. Child Neurol.,* 16:53–58.

33. Slater, E. (1943): The neurotic constitution. *J. Neurol. Psychiatry,* 6:1–16.

34. Uhlenhuth, E. H., and Paykel, E. S. (1973): Symptom configuration and life events. *Arch. Gen. Psychiatry,* 28:743–748.

35. Wender, P. H. (1967): On necessary and sufficient conditions in psychiatric explanation. *Arch. Gen. Psychiatry,* 16:41–47.

Stress and Mental Disorder,
edited by James E. Barrett et al.
Raven Press, New York © 1979.

The Relationship of Life Events to the Onset of Neurotic Disorders

James E. Barrett

Boston University School of Medicine, Boston, Massachusetts 02118

The data to be reported in this chapter were obtained from a study designed to investigate the validity of particular psychiatric outpatient disorder categories, those with presenting symptoms of depression or anxiety, using follow-up as criterion. Life event data, the occurrence of specific life events in the 6 months prior to onset of the disorder, were included as part of the overall design. There was thus an opportunity to examine the relationship between life events, both qualitative (type of life event) and quantitative (subjective amount of life stress caused by particular events) and the onset of particular psychiatric disorders. In earlier studies investigating life events and psychiatric disorders, the criterion or dependent variable has usually been either amount of psychiatric symptomatology (9,16,36) or membership in a particular patient group classified by type—inpatients, day patients, or suicidal patients (3,15,20,23,30)—rather than by specific diagnostic group. Questions about specificity of life events as precipitants (do particular life events, or types of life events, precede the onset of particular disorders?) remained difficult to answer from the design of such studies.

The design of the present study permitted an examination of such questions for outpatient disorders presenting with symptoms of anxiety or depression. In the following material, depressive disorders are compared to anxiety disorders on life events occurring in the 6 months prior to onset of an episode of the disorder. Grouping subjects in this fashion for analysis permits comparison with published data on life events and outpatient disorders (3,18,20,23,30). Subsequently, since the present study separated subjects into specific diagnostic categories, data that examine the relationship of life events to the onset of specific psychiatric disorders are presented.

The main research questions are: (a) do depressives differ from anxiety disorders in their experience of life events, both the type of life event and the amount of subjective distress experienced, in the 6 months prior to the onset of an episode of disorder? and (b) for five specific disorders, are there differences in types of life events that occur in the 6 months prior to onset of an episode of disorder?

METHOD

Outpatient Psychiatric Disorders: Research Diagnostic Criteria

Central to the material presented in this chapter is the concept of specific diagnostic entities or disorders. In recent years, there has been considerable discussion within the psychiatric profession about psychiatric diagnosis. This discussion has included concerns about the reliability of existing categories (35), what should be the inclusion criteria for assigning a given individual to a particular diagnostic category (11,31), and, for the outpatient or "neurotic" disorders, which of the currently popular categories were valid as diagnostic entities (6, 10,27). One derivative of these discussions was the evolution of diagnostic categories for research purposes, the Research Diagnostic Criteria (RDC) (33). Stated simply, these categories represent psychiatric disorders for which there was evidence, from follow-up studies or from family studies, that each disorder was a true entity (11,33,37) and for which there were specific, defined inclusion and exclusion criteria. This system has established reliability for the individual disorders (32,33), although the validity of each disorder as an independent diagnostic entity remains to be established.

Each individual in this study received an RDC diagnosis (34); data reported are for five of those disorders. As some readers may not be familiar with RDC diagnoses, I include a brief clinical description for each of these five disorders. Three are depressive disorders. Major depressive disorder is the category for individuals who have a depressive syndrome to a relatively severe degree; such individuals might have been called severe neurotic depressive reaction or psychotic depressive reaction using older diagnostic systems. It is not identical with endogenous depression, although individuals with that syndrome would be a subset of it, for it includes less severe depression. Episodic minor depressive disorder is similar clinically to the earlier neurotic depressive reaction; it defines a milder depressive syndrome, which has a definite onset and course, with recovery to a nondepressed premorbid state. Chronic and intermittent minor depressive disorder has many similarities to the condition called depressive character. Here the individual never feels really well but reports depressive symptoms of several years' duration. These symptoms characteristically fluctuate in severity, and onset is difficult to establish. The individual may report he has been depressed for most of his adult life.

There are two anxiety disorders for which data are reported: generalized anxiety disorder and panic disorder. Clinically these disorders resemble common usage of these terms; there is persistent chronic psychic anxiety and tension in the former condition, whereas the latter requires the presence of several discrete panic attacks. There is a third RDC anxiety disorder category, phobic disorder, but there were very few individuals with this disorder who were willing to come to our offices, and thus the numbers were too small to include them in the analyses to be reported.

The interested reader is referred to the written material on the RDC categories

(34) for a detailed description, including specific inclusion and exclusion criteria, for each of the five disorders[1] considered here.

Sample Selection and Characteristics

Individual subjects studied were from a population of symptomatic volunteers. These are individuals who have definite psychiatric symptomatology and who volunteer to participate in research projects. In previous studies, such individuals were shown to be similar to psychiatric outpatients (1,2,17,28). Our subjects were selected in the following way. Advertisements were placed in local newspapers seeking individuals who were suffering from anxiety or from depression and inviting them to participate in a study investigating these symptoms. The advertisement contained a 30-item self-report inventory; included in these items were the depression and anxiety subscales of the Hopkins Symptom Checklist (HSCL) (7). Individuals interested in participating were required to fill out the symptom list and return it to our laboratory. The symptom scales were then scored, and individuals who had a score equal to or greater than 2SD above the normative mean scores published for the HSCL (8) were sent additional material explaining the nature of the follow-up study and inquiring about previous medical or psychiatric history. From those individuals who continued to respond, those who were not in psychiatric treatment and who did not have coexisting medical conditions were invited to our offices for a clinical interview. The primary purpose of this interview was to obtain sufficient psychiatric history to determine whether or not the individual met criteria for one of 10 RDC disorders.

Using the above procedure, we selected 231 subjects. Age, sex, marital status, educational status, and prior psychiatric treatment history for these subjects are shown in Table 1. This material is presented for descriptive purposes and shows that our subjects were a diverse group with sizable numbers in each of the subcategories within each demographic variable. Clinically, with respect to both their backgrounds and their presenting symptoms, the subjects in this study were similar to a private practice outpatient population.

Of these 231 subjects, 204 received a diagnosis for one of the five RDC categories described earlier, and 202 provided us with life event data. Of the remaining 27, four received the third anxiety disorder diagnosis, phobic disorder. The other 23 received diagnoses other than a depressive or anxiety disorder. Table 2 gives HSCL depression and anxiety scale scores for each of the five RDC disorder groups. Note that the groups with the highest levels of depression were indeed the three depressive disorder categories, as might be expected. Similarly, the groups with the highest anxiety scores were the two diagnosed as anxiety disorders, although two of the depressive disorder categories, major

---

[1] For ease of presentation in the text of this chapter, the following shortened names will frequently be used for these five disorders: major depression, episodic depression, chronic depression, generalized anxiety, and panic anxiety.

TABLE 1. *Symptomatic volunteers: Characteristics of subjects*[a]

Characteristic	N^b	%
Age (years)		
18–29	67	29.0
30–49	116	50.2
50–69	48	20.8
Sex		
Male	66	28.6
Female	165	71.4
Marital Status		
Single	60	26.1
Married	127	55.2
Separated, divorced, widowed	43	18.7
Education		
High school or less	59	25.5
Some college	83	35.9
College graduate	49	21.2
Graduate school	40	17.3
Psychiatric hospitalization in past		
Yes	22	9.6
No	208	90.4
Psychiatric outpatient in past		
Yes	84	36.8
No	144	63.2

[a] $N = 231$.
[b] N may not add up to 231 for some categories because question not answered by subject.

depression and chronic depression, had a mean level of anxiety similar to that of generalized anxiety. This material is presented to indicate that subjects in the study indeed were symptomatic at a level similar to that seen in actual patient groups (10,27,28). It is a basic premise in this study that whether or not an individual is or was a patient is not relevant to the questions under examination. What is relevant and crucial is that each individual must meet the specific RDC criteria for the particular disorder in order to be included in these analyses.

TABLE 2. *Scale scores (HSCL) for anxiety and depression for five RDC categories*[a]

		Anxiety		Depression	
RDC disorder	N	Mean	SD	Mean	SD
Major depressive disorder	31	1.31	0.61	1.89	0.57
Episodic minor depressive disorder	71	0.96	0.41	1.61	0.53
Chronic depressive disorder	29	1.31	0.54	1.96	0.49
Generalized anxiety disorder	53	1.31	0.44	1.14	0.60
Panic anxiety disorder	19	1.61	0.57	0.96	0.58

[a] Scale range is 0–3. Depression scale score for 2 SD above normal is 0.70. Anxiety scale score for 2 SD above normal is 0.65.

Assessment of Life Events

For each subject, a date of onset for the condition was established during the diagnostic interview. Using this date, the subject was then asked to fill out a life event scale (LES) with instructions to record those events that occurred in the 6 preceding months. Thus we attempted to limit the recording of events to only those that actually occurred 6 months prior to the agreed-upon date of onset for the condition. One of the categories, chronic depression, required symptoms for at least 2 years and thus by definition did not have a recent date of onset. Individuals in this category were asked to rate the presence of individual life events for the 6 months prior to the interview date.

The instrument used to assess life events was a 61-item inventory presented in a self-report format. The content of the 61 items was the same as that used by Paykel and his collaborators[2] in their investigations in New Haven and London (19,24). For each "yes" response to the question of whether the event occurred in the 6 previous months, the subject was asked to write in a distress rating, which could range from 1 to 99. The specific instruction was "your distress rating should reflect how much discomfort, upset, or distress the event caused you." As a guide, the subject was given three examples: low distress (1 to 10) might be "marriage of a child." Moderate distress (40 to 60) might be "additional person moves into the house." Extreme distress (90 to 99) might be "death of a child." Following this example, the subject was again reminded that this example is only a "rough guide" and that "your own ratings may take any values from 1 to 99 according to the degree of distress which the event caused you."

Analysis and Presentation of Data

In the following material, data from the LES were utilized in several ways. One set of analyses, presented in cross-tabular form, groups individual events into various life event categories, such as, for example, four of the life event categories used by Paykel et al. (exits, entrances, undesirable events, desirable events) (22). Scoring for these tables was similar to that used by Paykel. There were two possibilities: (a) one or more of the events did occur; or (b) none of the events occurred. For each life event category, these two possibilities were the predictor variables. The number of items for each life event category, and the specific content of each item, is given in Table 3 for the Paykel et al. life event categories and in Table 7 for six additional life event categories. The criterion variables used were diagnosis of any depressive disorder (major depression, episodic depression, or chronic depression grouped together) compared to any anxiety disorder (generalized anxiety and panic anxiety grouped together)

---

[2] Paykel's collaborators have included Jacobs, Klerman, Meyers, Prusoff, and Uhlenhuth. For simplicity of presentation, the categories used by these authors will be referred to as the Paykel et al. categories.

TABLE 3. *Categories of life events used by Paykel et al.: Item content*

Exit (6 items)
  Death of close family member (spouse, child, other)
  Divorce
  Marital separation
  Child leaves home
  Child marries
  Son enlisted or was drafted

Entrance (4 items)
  Became engaged
  Got married
  Birth of a child
  New person in home

Undesirable events (13 items)
  Death of close family member
  Miscarriage, still birth, or abortion
  Divorce
  Marital separation
  Serious illness of family member
  Jail sentence
  Had to appear in court
  Major financial problems
  Business failure
  Demoted
  Fired
  Unemployed 1 month or longer
  Son enlisted or is drafted

Desirable events (3 items)
  Engagement
  Marriage
  Promotion

for one set of analyses (Tables 4 and 8), or diagnosis of one of the five individual RDC disorders for another set of analyses (Tables 9 and 10). This method of presenting the data initially compares depressive disorders to anxiety disorders on the presence or absence of events in a particular life event category and then progresses to examining each individual RDC disorder with respect to these same life event categories.

A second set of analyses utilized the individual life event items and the "distress score" for each life event. Individuals were grouped, as for the cross-tabular analyses, into depressive disorders and anxiety disorders. The occurrence of each life event and the distress scores for each life event item, if it occurred (a "yes" response followed by a numerical distress rating), were then examined, again comparing depressive disorders as a group to anxiety disorders (Tables 5 and 6). A similar presentation of data for the five individual RDC disorders is not given because of the problem of low frequencies at the item level when this division is made.

TABLE 4. *Categories of life events reported by depressive disorders compared to anxiety disorders: Number of individuals reporting at least one event in each category*

Category	Depressive disorders (N = 130)		Anxiety disorders (N = 72)		Significance[a]
	N	%	N	%	
Exit	40	30.8	12	16.7	0.04
Entrance	22	16.9	15	20.8	0.62
Undesirable	75	57.7	30	41.7	0.04
Desirable	30	23.1	14	19.4	0.67

[a]Chi², with Yates correction.

RESULTS

Relationship of Four Life Event Categories to Onset of Depressive Disorders and Anxiety Disorders

Table 4 shows the results when depressive disorders were compared to anxiety disorders on the four life event categories used by Paykel et al. Two categories, exits and undesirable events, showed significant differences between depressive disorders and anxiety disorders. Of depressives, 30.8% had one or more exits in the 6 months prior to onset, compared to 16.7% of those with anxiety disorders; 57.7% of depressives experienced at least one undesirable event, compared to 41.7% of individuals with anxiety disorders.

In earlier data reported by Paykel et al. (22), 24.9% of "depressed patients" had at least one exit in the 6 months prior to onset, compared to 4.9% for a matched nondepressed control group. Of Paykel's depressives 44.3% reported at least one undesirable event in the 6 months prior to onset, compared to 16.8% for his control group. Paykel's depressive patient group thus has an intermediate position between these subject groups with respect to the occurrence of an event in these life event categories, and the subject groups in the present study appeared different from Paykel's control group. Both the depressive disorders and the anxiety disorders experienced more exits (30.8 and 16.7%, respectively) compared to Paykel's controls (4.9%), and there were similar results for undesirable events (57.7 and 41.7%, respectively, compared to 16.8%). The interesting finding in the present study, however, was that depressives differed significantly from anxiety disorders in a way that made sense clinically, e.g., more exits and undesirable events in the depressive group.

Depressive Disorders Compared to Anxiety Disorders: Item Distress Scores

From the preceding comparison with Paykel's data, we concluded that our subject groups, both the depressive disorders and the anxiety disorders, were

TABLE 5. *Average actual distress scores for individual life event items: Depressive disorders compared to anxiety disorders*

Item	Depressive disorders (N = 130)		Anxiety disorders (N = 76)		Item
	N	Average distress score	Average distress score	N	
Death of spouse	3	99.0	—	0	
Death of child	3	99.0	—	0	
	9	80.6	99.0	1	Death of family member
	6	85.5	99.0	1	Spouse unfaithful
	0	—	99.0	1	Retirement from job
	18	66.3	94.5	2	Unemployed for 1 month
	0	—	90.0	1	Child married, not approved
Spouse unfaithful	6	85.5	99.0	1	
Death of family member	9	80.6	99.0	1	
	13	71.9	89.8	6	Major financial difficulties
	8	36.9	85.2	5	Extramarital affair (self)
	7	64.3	84.8	6	Failed examination
	2	50.0	84.5	2	Dismissed from job
	5	29.2	84.5	2	Marital reconciliation
Major personal illness	14	76.7	76.5	6	
Became engaged	3	76.7	40.0	1	
Demotion	6	76.5	40.0	2	
Arguments with fiancé	23	74.7	65.4	9	
Broke engagement to marry	7	74.7	35.0	2	
Major financial difficulties	13	71.9	89.6	6	
Business failure	6	70.0	67.5	4	
Unwanted pregnancy	2	70.0	—	0	
Major personal illness	14	76.7	76.5	6	Major personal illness
	16	63.1	74.3	12	Take important examination
	43	63.6	71.5	19	Arguments with spouse
	6	58.2	70.0	1	Court appearance
	1	10.0	70.0	1	Son drafted or enlisted
Major illness, family member	40	66.3	63.5	17	

Unemployed for 1 month	18	66.3	94.5	2
Marital separation	12	64.5	55.8	5
Failed examination	7	64.3	84.8	6
Ceased steady dating	21	64.1	51.4	14
Arguments with spouse	43	63.6	71.5	19
Take important examination	16	63.1	74.3	12
Separation (significant person)	50	62.1	44.2	19
Move to another country	4	60.0	—	0
Birth of a child	3	59.7	7.5	2
Court appearance	6	58.2	70.0	1
Arguments with nonresident family members	62	56.2	65.4	39
Loss of personally valued object	34	55.6	45.0	13
Increased arguments with children	40	55.5	68.8	19
Troubles with boss or co-worker	16	53.0	68.6	8
Moderate financial difficulties	102	51.7	54.1	53
Child leaves home	15	51.3	40.0	3
Took a large loan	12	51.2	56.6	11
Change in work conditions	40	50.4	59.2	20
Dismissed from job	2	50.0	84.5	2
Wanted pregnancy	1	50.0	1.0	1

Arguments with resident family member	40	55.5	68.8	19
Troubles with boss or co-worker	16	53.0	68.6	8
Lawsuit	13	46.2	68.3	7
Business failure	6	70.0	67.5	4
Arguments with friends	62	56.2	65.4	39
Arguments with fiancé	23	74.7	65.4	9
Major illness of family member	40	66.3	63.5	17
Change in line of work	34	49.4	61.7	9
Marriage	5	26.2	60.0	1
Change in work conditions	40	50.4	59.2	20
Took a large loan	12	51.2	56.6	11
Marital separation due to problems	12	64.5	55.8	5
Moderate financial difficulties	102	51.7	54.1	53
Miscarriage or still birth	3	36.7	52.5	2
Cease steady dating	21	64.1	51.4	14
Change in schools	4	40.0	50.0	1

TABLE 6. *Life events reported by depressive disorders (N = 130) and by anxiety disorders (N = 72): Comparison of items with a frequency of occurrence of at least six*

LES item	Depressive disorders		Anxiety disorders		Significance[a]
	N	Mean distress score	N	Mean distress score	
Physical separation (from significant person)	50	62.1	19	44.2	0.01
Major financial difficulties	13	71.8	6	89.8	0.01
Arguments with resident family members	40	55.5	19	68.8	0.03
Arguments with friends	62	56.2	39	65.4	0.04
Failed exam	7	64.3	6	84.8	0.06
Lawsuit	13	46.2	7	68.3	0.08
Physical separation from spouse	19	35.8	13	49.2	0.08
Promotion	23	43.5	12	33.0	0.08
Ceased steady dating	21	64.1	14	51.4	0.08
Something valuable lost or stolen	34	55.6	13	45.0	0.09
Changed to different line of work	34	49.4	9	61.7	0.11
Change in work conditions	40	50.4	20	59.2	0.11
Arguments with boss or co-workers	16	53.0	8	68.6	0.11
Take important examination	16	63.1	12	74.3	0.12

[a] One-tailed t-test.

different from normals on the occurrence of an event in the life event categories "exits" and "undesirable events," and we noted that they were significantly different from one another on the occurrence of an event in these same life event categories. We then went on to ask: If a given event did occur, was it experienced differently, as more or less stressful, by depressive disorders compared to anxiety disorders? This material is presented in Table 5, which is arranged so that the vertical columns show average distress ratings reported for an event, if it occurred, for depressive disorders on the left, anxiety disorders on the right.[3] Frequency of occurrence of each event for each subject group is also given. The table is divided horizontally, grouping items by degree of distress experienced. Items with highest distress ratings, 90 to 99, are at the top, with subsequent divisions into distress rating groups of 80 to 89, 70 to 79, 60 to 69, and 50 to 59 (items with stress ratings below 50 are not shown). Finally, for each item in these distress rating groups, the corresponding frequency of the item and the average distress rating assigned to it can be seen for the depressive disorders compared to the anxiety disorders. Reading each side of the table vertically thus shows rank ordering of items by severity of distress for depressive disorders and for anxiety disorders, whereas reading the table horizontally permits item by item comparison on severity of distress experienced by these subject groups. In comparing the frequency of each item, the reader should remember that there are nearly twice as many subjects with a depressive disorder *(N = 130)* as with an anxiety disorder *(N = 76)*.

Certain patterns of differences between depressive disorders and anxiety disorders are suggested by the data in Table 5. Looking at the top-ranked items for depressive disorders, many of them involved changes having to do with people, with changes in relationships, e.g., deaths, engagements made or broken, and arguments with fiancé. In contrast, for the anxiety disorders, top-ranked items included many having to do with work or performance in some way, e.g., job changes (retirement, unemployment, dismissal), financial difficulties, and examination failure. Furthermore, when both subject groups experienced a particular work or performance event, the average distress score assigned it was generally higher for the anxiety group. "Unemployed for 1 month" or "major financial difficulties" received average distress ratings of 94.5 and 89.8, respectively, from the anxiety disorder group, while the same items received average distress ratings of 66.3 and 71.9, respectively, from the depressives. With the exception of deaths, which seemed universally to produce high distress, the pattern is reversed for many of the "people" items, those which reflected changes in interpersonal relationships, with depressives experiencing more distress than anxiety disorders. "Became engaged," "broke engagement," and "arguments with fiancé," for example, received average distress ratings from the depressives of 76.7, 74.7, and 74.7, respectively. For the anxiety disorders, these

---

[3] The *N* for the anxiety disorders is 76, not 72, because the four individuals with an RDC diagnosis of phobic disorder were included.

same items received distress ratings of 40.0, 35.0, and 65.4, respectively. To be sure, the frequency of occurrence for some of these items on which these average distress ratings were based was low, making truly meaningful comparisons difficult, but the pattern of anxiety disorders having high distress on performance items and of depressive disorders having high distress on certain interpersonal relationship items was suggested by these data and was of particular interest.

For those items where there were at least six "yes" responses in each subject group, distress scores of the depressive disorder group were compared to those of the anxiety disorder group. Table 6 reports the mean distress score for each of these items where the significance level (Student's t) was equal to or less than 0.1, although the levels based on items with low numbers must be interpreted with caution. At the $p \leq 0.05$ level, depressive disorders experienced a distress level significantly higher than anxiety disorders for the item "physical separation from a significant person." The reverse was true, with anxiety disorders experiencing significantly higher distress ratings than depressive disorders on "major financial difficulties," "arguments with resident family members," and "arguments with friends." When items that showed a trend toward statistical significance ($0.05 \leq p \leq 0.10$) were examined, depressive disorders experienced higher distress than anxiety disorders on the items "ceased steady dating," "something valuable lost or stolen," and "promotion," whereas the reverse was true for the items "failed examination," "became involved in a lawsuit," and "physical separation from spouse." There were four additional items for which the significance level was just above 0.10 (0.11 to 0.12); for these, "changed to different line of work," "change in work conditions," "took important examination," and "arguments at work," those with anxiety disorders experienced higher distress than those with depressive disorders.

Item content thus examined did not show a clear pattern of differences between depressives and anxiety disorders, but again items reflecting losses and changes in relationships (with the exception of "physical separation from spouse") were rated higher by depressives. Certain performance items, and arguments of many kinds—with friends, family members, boss, or co-workers—were rated higher by anxiety disorders.

Six Additional Life Event Categories: Depressive Disorders Compared to Anxiety Disorders

Responding to the suggestion, from this examination of individual item distress scores, that depressives may differ from anxiety disorders on categories that reflect types of interpersonal disruption, financial-legal disruption, or work disruption, six additional life event categories were generated and examined: (a) interpersonal disruption: death, (b) interpersonal disruption: arguments, (c) interpersonal disruption: controllable events, (d) interpersonal disruption: uncontrollable events, (e) financial-legal disruption, and (f) work disruption. The number of items in each life event category and the content of each item are given in Table 7. Those categories were then examined in the same way as the four Paykel et al. life event categories presented earlier. The focus of this analysis was thus again on the occurrence of the event in the 6 months prior to onset of the disorder, independent of whatever subjective distress it caused. Table 8 shows these data in cross-tabular form. The results were not statistically significant, with the exception of the life event category "interpersonal disruption: uncontrollable events." Of depressives, 65.4% experienced at least one event in this category in the 6 months prior to onset, compared to 50.0% of anxiety disorders.

TABLE 7. *Additional categories of life events: Item content*

Interpersonal disruption: Death (5 items)
    Death of spouse
    Death of child
    Death of family member
    Death of friend
    Divorce

Interpersonal disruption: Arguments (5 items)
    Arguments with spouse
    Arguments with fiancé
    Arguments with children
    Arguments with family member
    Arguments with boss or co-workers

Interpersonal disruption: Controllable events (4 items)
    Broke engagement
    Began an affair
    Marital separation
    Ceased steady dating

Interpersonal disruption: Uncontrollable events (5 items)
    Spouse unfaithful
    Physical separation from spouse
    Physical separation from friends
    Child marries against wishes
    Illness of family member

Financial-legal disruption (5 items)
    Serious financial difficulties
    Took a large loan
    Minor legal violation
    Had to appear in court
    Lawsuit

Work disruption (8 items)
    Changed line of work
    Demotion
    Fired
    Unemployed 1 month or longer
    Retired
    Business failure
    Failed an important examination
    Prepared for an important examination

TABLE 8. *Six additional categories of life events reported by depressive disorders compared to anxiety disorders: Number of individuals reporting at least one event in each category*

Category	Depressive disorders (N = 130)		Anxiety disorders (N = 72)		Significance[a]
	N	%	N	%	
Interpersonal disruption					
Death	37	28.5	26	36.1	0.33
Arguments	106	81.5	55	76.4	0.49
Controllable events	37	28.5	20	27.8	0.95
Uncontrollable events	85	65.4	36	50.0	0.05
Financial-legal disruption	46	35.4	22	30.6	0.59
Work disruption	51	39.2	24	33.3	0.50

[a] Chi^2, with Yates correction.

Relationship of Various Life Event Categories to Onset of Individual RDC Disorders

The analyses reported so far have been on depressive disorders as a group compared to anxiety disorders as a group, permitting comparisons with the previous work of others. As outlined initially, however, the present study permitted additional analyses not available in earlier reported work, the examination of the relationship of life events to the onset of individual RDC disorders (diagnostic categories). Using the four Paykel et al. life event categories, the relationship of the occurrence of at least one event in the various life event categories to the onset of each of the five RDC disorders was examined. The results are shown in Table 9. An interesting pattern emerged when depressive disorders and anxiety disorders were separated in this way. As before, the analyses for the two life event categories "exits" and "undesirable events" showed a significant relationship. For the life event category "exits," major depression and episodic depression appeared relatively similar with respect to the proportion of individuals experiencing at least one exit (38.7 and 33.3%, respectively). In contrast, the other depressive disorder, chronic depressive disorder, appeared similar to generalized anxiety disorder. For these disorders, 14.8 and 11.3%, respectively, of individuals experienced an exit in the 6 months prior to onset. Panic anxiety disorder, with 31.6% experiencing at least one exit, was similar to major depression and to episodic depression with respect to this "exits" variable. A similar pattern was evident in the other life event category, "undesirable events," for which there was a significant relationship. A relatively high proportion of major depression and episodic depression, 51.6 and 65.3%, respectively, experienced at least one undesirable event in the 6 months prior to onset, whereas chronic depression and generalized anxiety were again similar, with 44.4 and 37.7%, respectively. Panic anxiety, with 52.6%, was again similar to major depression.

A similar analysis was carried out for the six additional life event categories;

TABLE 9. *Categories of life events (Paykel et al.) and five RDC categories (three depressive disorders; two anxiety disorders): Number of individuals reporting at least one event in each category*

Category	Major depression (N=31)		Episodic minor depression (N=72)		Chronic minor depression (N=27)		Generalized anxiety (N=53)		Panic anxiety (N=19)		Significance[a]
	N	%	N	%	N	%	N	%	N	%	
Exit	12	38.7	24	33.3	4	14.8	6	11.3	6	31.6	0.01
Entrance	2	6.5	14	19.4	6	22.2	11	20.8	4	21.1	0.47
Undesirable	16	51.6	47	65.3	12	44.4	20	37.7	10	52.6	0.04
Desirable	7	22.6	18	25.0	5	18.5	12	22.6	2	10.5	0.73

[a] Chi^2, with Yates correction.

TABLE 10. Additional categories of life events and five RDC categories (three depressive disorders; two anxiety disorders): Number of individuals reporting at least one event in each category

Category	Major depression (N=31)		Episodic minor depression (N=72)		Chronic minor depression (N=27)		Generalized anxiety (N=53)		Panic anxiety (N=19)		Significance[a]
	N	%	N	%	N	%	N	%	N	%	
Interpersonal disruption											
Loss	10	32.3	18	25.0	9	33.3	17	32.1	9	47.4	0.449
Arguments	26	83.9	57	79.2	23	85.2	41	77.4	14	73.7	0.835
Controllable events	8	25.8	24	33.3	5	18.5	17	32.1	3	15.8	0.391
Uncontrollable events	20	64.5	54	75.0	11	40.7	24	45.3	12	63.2	0.003
Financial-legal disruption	11	35.5	27	37.5	8	29.6	18	34.0	4	21.1	0.722
Work disruption	11	35.5	28	38.9	12	44.4	19	35.8	5	26.3	0.284

[a] Chi², with Yates correction.

these results are reported in Table 10. The one life event category that previously showed a significant relationship, "interpersonal disruption: uncontrollable events," again showed a significant relationship. The pattern within Table 10 was similar to that seen for "exits" and "undesirable events." A high proportion of major depression and episodic depression, 64.5 and 75.0%, respectively, experienced at least one such event. Chronic depression and generalized anxiety had lower proportions, 40.7 and 45.3%, respectively, which were similar. The proportion for panic anxiety, 63.2%, again showed a pattern similar to major depression.

COMMENT

These results can be summarized as follows. Taken as a group, depressive disorders did differ significantly from anxiety disorders on the presence of "exits," "undesirable events," and "uncontrollable interpersonal disruptions." This difference was reflected in both the actual occurrence of events in these categories and, in some instances, the degree of distress that an event in each category caused an individual in the particular diagnostic group. These data on the amount of distress caused by particular individual events were provocative. They suggested that certain types of events, those having to do with performance, were experienced as more stressful by those with anxiety disorders compared to those with depressive disorders, whereas certain other types of events, those involving changes in important interpersonal relationships, were experienced as more stressful by those with depressive disorders compared to those with anxiety disorders.

When each RDC disorder was examined separately, there was evidence that chronic depressive disorder was different from major depressive disorder and episodic minor depressive disorder with respect to the occurrence of certain classes of events in the 6 months prior to onset of an episode. This finding is of theoretical interest, given the conceptualization of each of those diagnostic entities. Major depressive disorder and episodic depressive disorder can be considered to be on a continuum, roughly corresponding to the DSM-I categories of "psychotic depressive reaction" and "neurotic depressive reaction." As the term "reaction" implies, both of these older categories implied the presence of precipitating events; conceptually they were "exogenous" depressions. Chronic depressive disorder, on the other hand, which was derived from the unofficial but commonly used category "depressive character," implied a fluctuating but enduring symptom state; conceptually it would be one of the "endogenous" depressions, at least in the sense that the mood was unaffected by life changes. That major depressive disorder and episodic depressive disorder, compared to chronic depressive disorder, showed a relationship between onset and increased frequency of events in particular life event categories is consistent with the clinical observations that led to formulation of the categories and is a partial validation of them.

The finding that panic anxiety disorder was similar to major depressive disorder with respect to the occurrence of events in particular life event categories in the 6 months prior to onset was of theoretical interest. The symptoms of both disorders, for some patients, respond to certain antidepressant drugs (13, 14,29), leading to speculations by some researchers (13,26,29) that these disorders are variants of a common underlying disorder, despite very different presenting symptoms.

The apparent similarity between generalized anxiety disorder and chronic depressive disorder with respect to these same life event categories also deserves comment. Generalized anxiety disorder is the category derived clinically from those individuals who characteristically experienced extreme tension in many settings. This condition also tended to be long-standing, and coexisting moderate depressive symptoms were common. It is possible, perhaps probable, that the categories chronic depressive disorder and generalized anxiety disorder comprise those individuals who present with patterns of mixed anxiety and depression, and that the two are variants of the same disorder and should be grouped together.

Before making too much of these findings, one cautionary note must be sounded. When individual disorders are compared on the occurrence of events in some interval prior to onset (6 months in this case), it must be remembered that the individual disorders may be quite different on the ease and clarity with which "onset" of an episode of the disorder can be specified. For the depressive disorders considered here, onset for a particular episode is relatively easy to determine for episodic depression and for major depression. For chronic depression, as has been mentioned already, there effectively is no "episode." By definition, the symptom pattern must persist, with no periods of "normal" mood, for at least 2 years, although the symptoms can fluctuate in severity. In practice, subjects usually reported that their symptom pattern had been present for many years, although for many subjects these chronic symptoms worsened around the time they replied to our advertisement. For the anxiety disorders, onset for an episode of panic anxiety was particularly easy to specify. Subjects could often recall the day and the hour when a particular attack began. Generalized anxiety disorder, on the other hand, had a wide range in regard to specificity of onset. Some subjects could make a clear distinction when their symptoms began for an episode and were essentially well in interim periods. Others resembled chronic depression in that they experienced their symptoms "all their life," although with some waxing and waning in severity and in degree of interference with function.

Thus, for the analyses presented here as well as for those in earlier studies in which individuals with chronic or enduring symptoms were not specifically separated out, a skeptic may argue that our subject groups already differed on one of the predictor variables and that we have effectively compared apples with oranges. For one group of disorders, major depression, episodic depression, and panic anxiety, we indeed examined precipitating events, for a particular episode at least, while for chronic depression and probably for generalized anxiety we were not looking at precipitating events but rather at events occurring in a 6-month period of a chronic, continuing condition. What those events are conceptually is difficult to specify; some would consider them "maintenance" events for the condition. In the absence of a normal control group, however, the role of the events in maintaining the condition is not clear.

Taking an extreme view, the same skeptic might claim that the apparent similarities in major depression, episodic depression, and panic anxiety on the event categories "exits," "undesirable events," and "uncontrollable events" only reflected that these categories were nonspecific stressors; that is, their occurrence, for any condition in which onset of episode was easy to determine, related to that onset. This view, in which the disorders are seen as different, and therefore the life event stressors are nonspecific, contrasts with the preceding one in which the life event categories are seen as different; therefore, any relationship between a particular category and onset of particular disorders could be used as one piece of evidence that those disorders were similar and should be grouped.

Which view is "true" and should prevail? The answer must await additional data and appropriate research designs. I personally favor the view that particular classes of events do have different effects and thus do relate to onset of particular disorders. From my clinical contact with the subjects, I also believe but cannot prove that those individuals with chronic depression or generalized anxiety were experiencing an exacerbation of their symptoms when they replied to our advertisement;[4] thus, in a sense, they were experiencing an "episode" of disorder, making the comparisons reported here (relationship of life events to an episode of disorder) valid and appropriate. The question, certainly one of considerable interest, of the role of life events in initial onset (first episode) of these disorders also must await a different research design.

These data have implications for the interpretation of research findings on the role of life events in the onset of depression. For all three life event categories where there were significant relationships, the occurrence of an event in those categories was different—much less—for the RDC category chronic and inter-mittent minor depressive disorder than for the other two depressive disorders. If those with this disorder were omitted from analyses comparing "depressives" with other subject groups (normals, other diagnostic groups), the differences observed in earlier studies might have been even more striking. Certainly this would have been the case in the data presented here. Similarly, if by chance the proportion of chronic depressives had been large in the "depressive" group, the observed differences could have been reduced to the point where statistical significance was not obtained. In the prior studies reviewed by Paykel (18), overinclusion of such patients could have contributed to negative findings.

Whatever one's personal view about the issue of specificity versus nonspecificity of life events and onset of depressive disorders, for future research it would be prudent to separate chronic depressives, at least as defined by the RDC category, from other depressives. A similar argument can be made for research

---

[4] At screening interview, subjects with chronic depression or generalized anxiety were not specifically asked if their symptoms had been more severe recently, or at least this information was not recorded. Such information would have been helpful and should be included in future designs.

on the role of life events in the onset of anxiety disorders. Panic anxiety disorder should be kept separate from generalized anxiety disorder to prevent misleading results.

Returning to an examination of the role of life events in the onset of neurotic disorders, and of specific ones in particular, the evidence is that they do play some role. Considering "exits," Paykel's data show that "exits" do relate to the onset of depressive disorders when compared to normals, and the data presented here show they relate to the onset of depressive disorders compared to anxiety disorders. On the other hand, in most of the studies examined, this category of events accounted for a relatively small proportion of the variance which related to the onset of the disorder. In Paykel's data, 75% of depressives did not have an exit in the 6 months prior to onset, as was true of about 70% of depressives in these data. What is happening is that, for some people, the occurrence of an exit did relate to onset of a particular disorder, depression (particularly major depression and episodic depression), whereas for others the disorder occurred without any such event. We also know from Paykel's data on normals that some people experienced an exit without the development of a depressive disorder. What must be going on then, for some people, is a type of interaction in which exits play a role but require something else to lead to onset of a depressive disorder. This other factor has been conceptualized by some in the form of a vulnerability model. This vulnerability acts in one of two ways: either an accumulation of stressors produces an increased vulnerability to disorders in general, the nonspecific model, or particular stressors react with a predisposition to develop a particular disorder, the specificity of events model. This latter conceptualization has appeal, both from clinical experience and on common sense grounds. I would be surprised, had we included a sensitive measure of dependency (viewed as a personality trait) if we did not find that losses, or exits, in this group related more to the onset of depression than to other disorders. Brown and his collaborators (3), examining a sample of women, established a link between an early loss, loss of mother before age 11, and proneness to react to later losses by depression. Brown thus made a distinction between events as *predisposing factors* and events as *precipitating factors*. This is an important distinction, and Brown's group (4,5) has made substantial contributions to the methodology that might be employed. The important point is that however one defines the "vulnerability variables," we are probably dealing with particular people having a predisposition to respond to particular types (categories) of events with the onset of a particular disorder. We must know more about these vulnerability factors, about how to measure them reliably, and include them in subsequent research designs.

In addition to the importance of distinguishing between predisposing and precipitating events, attention should be paid to *maintenance events*. One class of events may initially precipitate the onset of a disorder in an individual predisposed to react to that type of event, while another category of events may subsequently be responsible for the maintenance of symptoms. It has already been pointed out that, for chronic depression, the symptoms were more or less continuous; events, if any, that may have related to initial onset of this disorder are in the remote past and difficult to study. Particular life events or life situations may play a role in maintaining chronic depression. The study of those events may hold promise for understanding this disorder and possibly for understanding generalized anxiety disorder as well. The important point is that maintenance events must be conceptualized separately from predisposing and precipitating events. A different set of life event items may be needed, as well as specific research designs, in approaching this issue of maintenance of symptoms.

A final set of comments about these data concerns the issue of weights or scores for life events. Many of the earlier data, those of Holmes and Rahe (12) and some of Paykel et al. (21,24,25), used hypothetical scores, e.g., "how would you react?" or "how much distress would you feel if such and such happened?" This strategy was used to establish the internal consistency of the event categories, the cross-cultural similarity of reaction to particular events, and so on. This is a valuable body of data, but the method has some potential disadvantages in examining relationships to onset of disorder in a particular individual or in groups of individuals who share a particular disorder. The actual distress experienced may be very different for an individual who actually experienced an event than what groups of people who have never actually experienced the event imagined. Selecting an example from these data, and recalling that scores reported were actual scores, with the subject acting as a sort of black box reporting the amount of distress a particular actual event actually caused, one individual experienced a divorce. He assigned it a distress rating of 10, one of the lowest scores given for any event. One can perhaps assume that he was now out of a bad marriage or was experiencing relief at finally bringing to conclusion a long, painful process. Divorce, on the Paykel et al. hypothetical ratings, consistently received one of the highest scores, 16.18 on their scale of 1 to 20 (24) and thus above 80 on my scale of 1 to 99. The hypothetical score sounds reasonable; if people in satisfactory marriages are asked how they would rate experiencing a divorce, it is not surprising that they would find it stressful. But it can be argued that the actual distress experienced should be the relevant factor relating to onset and that, in the specific vulnerability model, certain types of events may always be experienced as more stressful by one diagnostic group compared to another. In Tables 5 and 6, in which physical separation from a significant person was rated nearly 20 points higher by depressives than by those with anxiety disorders, this difference was statistically significant. Certain performance and work items (those listed at the bottom of Table 6) were rated 10 to 15 points higher by the anxiety disorder group than by the depressives. None of these latter items reached statistical significance at the 0.05 level, but I suspect they would have if the numbers of subjects had been larger.

SUMMARY

Summarizing these comments and the data presented, the presence of particular life events in the 6 months prior to onset and the degree of distress caused by those events can distinguish between particular neurotic disorders. Several suggestions for future research on the role of life events in the neurotic disorders have been presented, and I have emphasized that attention should be paid to keeping separate the individual disorders. If they are combined into broad categories, such as "depressives," meaningful differences can be obscured or lost. Conceptualization of how particular life events should relate to a particular disorder—as predisposing, precipitating, or maintaining events—should be clear in advance to guide the research strategy.

ACKNOWLEDGMENTS

This research was supported by grant MH 27865 from the National Institute of Mental Health.

The author wishes to acknowledge Seymour Fisher, Ph.D., for his encouragement in pursuing classification issues using symptomatic volunteers and for making available the facilities of the Psychopharmacology Laboratory at Boston University Medical Center.

REFERENCES

1. Barrett, J. E., and DiMascio, A. (1966): Comparative effects on anxiety of the "minor tranquilizers" in "high" and "low" anxious student volunteers. *Dis. Nerv. Syst.*, 27:483–486.
2. Brauzer, B., and Goldstein, B. J. (1973): Symptomatic volunteers, another dimension for clinical trials. *J. Clin. Pharmacol.* 13:89–98.
3. Brown, G. W., Harris, T., and Copeland, J. R. (1977): Depression and loss. *Br. J. Psychiatry,* 130:1–18.
4. Brown, G. W., Harris, T. O., and Peto, J. (1973): Life events and psychiatric disorders. Part 2: Nature of causal link. *Psychol. Med.,* 3:159–176.
5. Brown, G. W., Sklair, F., Harris, T. O., and Birley, J. L. T. (1973): Life events and psychiatric disorders. Part 1: Some methodological issues. *Psychol. Med.,* 3:74–87.
6. Derogatis, L. R., Klerman, G. L., and Lipman, R. S. (1972): Anxiety states and depressive neuroses: Issues in nosological discrimination. *J. Nerv. Ment. Dis.,* 155:392–403.
7. Derogatis, L. R., Lipman, R. S., Uhlenhuth, E. H., and Covi, L. (1974): The Hopkins Symptom Checklist (HSCL): A measure of primary symptom dimensions. In: *Modern Problems of Pharmacopsychiatry,* edited by P. Pichot, pp. 79–110. Karger, Basel.
8. Derogatis, L. R., Lipman, R. S., Rickels, K., Uhlenhuth, E. H., and Covi, L. (1973): The Hopkins Symptom Checklist (HSCL): A self-report symptom inventory. *Behav. Sci.,* 19:1–15.
9. Dohrenwend, B. P. (1974): Problems in defining and sampling the relevant population of stressful life events. In: *Stressful Life Events: Their Nature and Effects,* edited by B. S. Dohrenwend and B. P. Dohrenwend, pp. 275–310. Wiley, New York.
10. Downing, R. W., and Rickels, K. (1974): Mixed anxiety-depression: Fact or myth? *Arch. Gen. Psychiatry,* 30:312–317.
11. Feighner, J. P., Robins, E., Guze, S. B., Woodruff, R. A., Winokur, G., and Munoz, R. (1972): Diagnostic criteria for use in psychiatric research. *Arch. Gen. Psychiatry,* 26:57–63.
12. Holmes, T. H., and Rahe, R. H. (1967): The social readjustment rating scale. *J. Psychosom. Res.,* 11:213–218.
13. Klein, D. F. (1964): Delineation of two drug-responsive anxiety syndromes. *Psychopharmacologia,* 5:397–408.
14. Klein, D. F. (1969): *Diagnosis and Drug Treatment of Psychiatric Disorders.* Williams & Wilkins, Baltimore.
15. Levi, L. D. Fales, C. H., Stein, M., and Sharp, V. H. (1966): Separation and attempted suicide. *Arch. Gen. Psychiatry,* 15:158–165.

16. Myers, J. K., Lindenthal, J. J., and Pepper, M.D. (1971): Life events and psychiatric impairment. *J. Nerv. Ment. Dis.,* 152:149–157.
17. Overall, J. E., Goldstein, B. J., and Brauzer, B. (1971): Symptomatic volunteers in psychiatric research. *J. Psychiatr. Res.,* 9:31–43.
18. Paykel, E. S. (1973): Life events and acute depression. In: *Separation and Depression: Clinical and Research Aspects,* edited by J. P. Scott and E. C. Senay, pp. 215–236. American Association for the Advancement of Science, Washington, D.C.
19. Paykel, E. S. (1974): Life events and psychiatric disorder. In: *Stressful Life Events: Their Nature and Effects,* edited by B. S. Dohrenwend and B. P. Dohrenwend, pp. 135–149. Wiley, New York.
20. Paykel, E. S., Klerman, G. L., and Prusoff, B. A. (1970): Treatment setting and clinical depression. *Arch. Gen. Psychiatry,* 22:11–21.
21. Paykel, E. S., McGuiness, B., and Gomez, J. (1976): An Anglo-American comparison of the scaling of life events. *Br. J. Med. Psychol.,* 49:237–247.
22. Paykel, E.S., Myers, J. K., Lindenthal, J. J., and Pepper, M. D. (1969): Life events and depression: A controlled study. *Arch. Gen. Psychiatry,* 21:753–760.
23. Paykel, E. S., Prusoff, B. A., and Myers, J. K. (1975): Suicide attempts and recent life events: A controlled comparison. *Arch. Gen. Psychiatry,* 32:327–333.
24. Paykel, E. S., Prusoff, B. A., and Uhlenhuth, E. H. (1971): Scaling of life events. *Arch. Gen. Psychiatry,* 25:340–347.
25. Paykel, E. S., and Uhlenhuth, E. H. (1972): Rating the magnitude of life stress. *Can. Psychiatr. Assoc. J.,* SS93–SS100.
26. Pollitt, J., and Young, J. (1971): Anxiety state or masked depression? A study based on action of mono-amine oxidase inhibitors. *Br. J. Psychiatry,* 119:143–149.
27. Prusoff, B., and Klerman, G. L. (1974): Differentiating depressed from anxious neurotic outpatients. *Arch. Gen. Psychiatry,* 30:302–309.
28. Rickels, K., Csanalosi, I., Chung, H. R., Case, W. G., Pereira-Ogan, J. A., and Downing, R. W. (1974): Amitriptyline in anxious-depressed outpatients: A controlled study. *Am. J. Psychiatry,* 131:25–30.
29. Sargent, W. (1962): The treatment of anxiety states and atypical depressions by the mono-amine oxidase inhibitor drugs. *J. Neuropsychiatry [Suppl. I],* 3:96–103.
30. Sethi, B. B. (1964): Relationship of separation to depression. *Arch. Gen. Psychiatry,* 10:486–495.
31. Spitzer, R. L., Endicott, J., and Robins, E. (1975): Clinical criteria for psychiatric diagnosis and DSM-III. *Am. J. Psychiatry,* 132:1187–1192.
32. Spitzer, R. L., Endicott, J., Robins, E., Kuriansky, J., and Gurland, B. (1975): Preliminary report of the reliability of research diagnostic criteria applied to psychiatric case records. In: *Predictability in Psychopharmacology: Preclinical and Clinical Correlations,* edited by A. Sudilovsky, S. Gershon, and B. Beer, pp. 1–47. Raven Press, New York.
33. Spitzer, R. L., Endicott, J., and Robins, E. (1978): Research diagnostic criteria. *Arch. Gen. Psychiatry,* 30:312–317.
34. Spitzer, R. L., Endicott, J., and Robins, E. (1976): *Research Diagnostic Criteria for a Selected Group of Functional Disorders,* second edition. Biometrics Research, New York State Psychiatric Institute, New York.
35. Spitzer, R. L., and Fleiss, J. L. (1974): A re-analysis of the reliability of psychiatric diagnosis. *Br. J. Psychiatry,* 125:341–347.
36. Uhlenhuth, E. H., and Paykel, E. S. (1973): Symptom intensity and life events. *Arch. Gen. Psychiatry,* 28:473–477.
37. Woodruff, R. A., Goodwin, D. W., and Guze, S. B. (1974): *Psychiatric Diagnosis.* Oxford University Press, New York.

Stress and Mental Disorder,
edited by James E. Barrett et al.
Raven Press, New York © 1979.

A Three-Factor Causal Model of Depression

George W. Brown

Social Research Unit, Bedford College Annexe, London W1N 1DD England

This chapter outlines an etiological model of clinical depression developed by my colleagues and myself (for a full account, see ref. 4).

I *am* convinced that depression is largely a social phenomenon and the three main components of the model are all social—or it might be better to say psychosocial. By this I mean two things. First, the clinical depression is a cognitive phenomenon, stemming from ideas about the world—past, present and future. Second, I can conceive of societies in which clinical depression is rare. Here, I will add a rider: I have no wish to assert that genetic, constitutional and physical factors are never involved in etiology. Existing evidence for their importance remains indirect and unimpressive: if such factors can in the future be shown to play a role they can easily be incorporated into the model.

The ideas developed slowly over the last 9 to 10 years. Nonetheless, model and theory probably do not diverge much from ideas expressed elsewhere. Any claim to originality probably rests on the manner in which the three factors have been brought together in a causal model and its use to explain social class differences in the prevalence of depression. It may be of some interest to outline the main stages of the model's construction.

The research involved the study of six groups of depressed women, all aged between 18 and 65 years. Two were treated by psychiatrists, a group of inpatients and a group of outpatients, and another by general practitioners. All three lived in Camberwell in South London, a part of the Inner London borough of Southwark. There is a sizable middle-class population, but the majority are working class and the district has many of the problems of inner city populations, such as declining employment opportunities in industry. The final three groups were obtained by selecting women at random from nonpatient populations and establishing whether or not they were depressed. The first two surveys also involved women in Camberwell: in 1969 and 1974 we collected, among other things, detailed information based on a clinical-type interview about the psychiatric state of 458 women. Recently, similar information has been obtained for 354 women living in the Outer Hebrides.

The six groups of depressed women, although different in origin, have given essentially similar results. For example, like Paykel and his colleagues, we found little or no evidence of an endogenous depressive group; all the forms of depression we studied appear to be equally influenced by social factors (4, Chap. 14). What differences have occurred may prove to be explicable variations of the same basic etiological process. This chapter therefore holds for all types of depression, excluding only conditions involving definite manic features, which were not studied.

At the center of the model is a particular type of life event. Given our views on the cognitive basis of depression it was, of course, essential to deal with the meaning of life events and their immediate consequences. In current research, there is a good deal of uncertainty about what is important about life events in their role as etiological agents, although the majority of accounts appear to hold that meaning is in some way crucial. Given this, the most persistent shortcoming has been to proceed as though an event such as 'pregnancy' can be interpreted or decoded in the way that an encyclopedia will tell us the meaning of a term. For some purposes—perhaps early in a research program—it may be useful to proceed as if this kind of decoding were possible: but fundamental progress surely can only come from recognizing that events in themselves do not have meaning. A pregnancy is never a pregnancy in the way it is described in an encyclopedia. It occurs to a woman with a past, present, and future and this context has in some way to be taken into account—the fact, for example, that her husband is in prison.

Our method for doing this is not uncomplicated, but it is, I believe, misrepresented when it is described in a recent commentary as requiring an acceptance of 'a certain mystification of measurement' (7). The method demands that the interviewer-investigator takes a dominant role in the measurement process and involves a lengthy training—and neither is fashionable. The debilitating grip of the standardized questionnaire on social science research is still strong, although for the most part it is probably incapable of accurately measuring anything of complexity or emotional significance. It is in any case an approach that is only apparently 'objective.' A move from the rigidities of the questionnaire to an approach in which the investigator is trained to use rating scales, and to interview flexibly, gives back some hope of accurate and unbiased measurement (2). Once the need for lengthy developmental work and training is accepted there is no mystification. We have trained workers from all parts of the world in the use of our methods. It has so far required them to visit us; but this is a common experience with new measures, not least in the natural sciences.

Our study established the date of onset of depression in the year before we saw the women and the exact date of events before this in the year. Our procedures, though relying on the skill of trained interviewers, are highly reliable. They also appear to be valid in the basic sense of considerable agreement about the occurrence of *particular* events when the accounts of respondents, seen by different interviewers, are compared. The procedures also avoid the potential bias present in instruments relying on the use of questionnaires (2). Events to be included in the study were defined in detail *before* we began. All were capable, in our judgment, of arousing significant positive or negative emotion. For instance, the admission of a husband or child to hospital was included only if it was an emergency or the stay was seven days or more. On average such women in Camberwell had three such 'events' per year (4, Chap. 10).

On the basis of substantial background information about individual women, events are characterized in terms of two contextual scales: *short-term* threat, based on its likely threat the day it occurred, and *long-term* threat, based on the situation resulting from the event about one week after it occurred. The raters are allowed to take account of everything known about a particular woman except her psychiatric condition and how she reacted to the event. Both rate the degree of threat a woman would have been likely to feel given her particular biography and present situation. One of the most remarkable results of the entire program is that it is only the most threatening events on the *long-term* scale—what we call *severe events*—that are capable of provoking onset of depression. They formed only 16 percent of the total 'events' occurring to women in Camberwell. Events severely threatening only in the *short-term* showed not the slightest association with onset however threatening they were on the day they occurred—for example, an emergency hospital admission of a child with an extremely high temperature.

The result is methodologically significant since it argues against measurement bias. It is difficult to see why such bias should be restricted to severe events alone; that is why it should not also have led to an association between depression and events severe only on *short-term* threat. The result is theoretically significant since the majority of the severe events turned out upon inspection to involve a loss, if this term is used with a certain license to include not only loss of a person but loss of a role or loss of an idea. For example, a woman who had considered she was happily married and who found that her husband had had a love affair a year before would have experienced a severe loss event in the sense she had lost a conception of her husband and her marriage. This would be so even if the affair was over and the husband was not aware of her knowledge of the affair. Loss of an idea is probably a crucial component of most 'loss' events.

The threat ratings were only two of twenty-eight measures completed for each event and the degree of change in routine involved. But, as with the short-term threat scale, there was no suggestion that change as such or any other dimension had significance once the presence of a severe event had been taken into account.

Severe events were the major component of the first factor in our model— the *provoking agents*. The results are, of course, comparable to those of Paykel and his colleagues in New Haven (8). Using their concept of 'exit event,' the size of the effect is a good deal smaller than in the London study. But at the same time their categorization is a less sensitive indicator of *long-term threat,* that is, the type of event that appears to be critically involved in the etiology of depression. We do not include as a matter of course the 'exit' events of a child marrying or a son drafted as *severe* events, and Paykel apparently would not include as an 'exit' event a woman finding out about a husband's love affair—a severe event for us. Nonetheless the results are clearly convergent. There is, however, a second type of provoking agent. We also recorded ongoing difficulties such as poor housing which might or might not have been associated with an event. We found that certain difficulties were capable of producing depression but not with the same frequency as severe events. Such difficulties were all markedly unpleasant, had lasted at least two years, and did not involve health problems.

When severe events and such major difficulties are considered together our search for provoking agents had been as successful as we could have reasonably hoped—a large proportion of all types of depression were preceded by one or other of the provoking agents. But just as a well-established carcinogen will not always lead to cancer, so a provoking agent does not always bring about depression. Indeed only a small minority of the women in Camberwell who experienced a provoking agent became depressed. In arithmetical terms two-thirds of women who developed depression had a provoking agent of causal importance in the year before onset. This is probably a conservative estimate and takes account of the fact that some events and difficulties will be juxtaposed with onset by chance (4, p. 120; also see Chap. 9). However, in spite of the size of this association only 1 in 5 of women in Camberwell with a provoking agent developed clinical depression. Therefore while this factor determines *when* a woman develops depression, it does not tell us *who* will break down among those with a severe event or major difficulty. This is the function of the second factor of the model, which deals with the vulnerability.

Such vulnerability proved to be intimately related to social class. Fifteen percent of the women in Camberwell were suffering from a definite affective disorder in the three months before interview, almost all of depression. We have called such women *cases.* All had disorders of a severity commonly met in a psychiatric out-patient department although few had seen a psychiatrist. Twenty-three percent of the working-class women were *cases* compared with only 6 percent of the middle-class women—a fourfold difference in prevalence.

Surprisingly, although severe events and major difficulties were more common among working-class women, this explained little of this difference in risk. If we consider only women with a severe event or major difficulty in the year before we saw them, thus controlling for class differences in the incidence of the provoking agents, there was still a large difference in risk. For example, 8 percent (3/36) of middle-class women with a child who had experienced a provoking agent developed depression compared with 31 percent (21/67) of working-class women—a fourfold difference in vulnerability. For those without a provoking agent risk was only 1 percent in both groups (1/80) and (1/68), respectively.

What then is the reason for this remarkable difference in vulnerability? Anything capable of increasing risk of depression should have been revealed by our lengthy search for provoking agents. We therefore felt reasonably sure that if there were factors that increased vulnerability, they would do so *only when a woman also had* a provoking agent. We therefore began looking among these women for the second factor of our model.

Lack of an intimate, confiding relationship with a husband or boyfriend acted in exactly the way we had predicted. For the women who had had a provoking agent and who were not already depressed lack of such a tie greatly increased risk. Further, as predicted, for those *without* a provoking agent lack of intimacy was *not* associated with an increased risk of depression (Table 1).

'Intimacy' unfortunately is a 'soft' measure, at least in a cross-sectional survey, and we cannot altogether rule out the possibility of bias. We therefore looked for 'harder' indicators of vulnerability. We found three which, when considered together, gave much the same result as intimacy. They are having 3 or more children under 14 living at home, lacking employment away from home, and loss of a mother before the age of 11. The four vulnerability factors provide much of the reason why particular women get depressed following a provoking agent. They also provide most of the reason for the increased risk of working-class women. Such women are at greater risk largely because they more often have one or more of them.

Table 2 summarizes these results. Groups A and C in the table provide the extremes of protection and vulnerability for those with a provoking agent. Everyone with a confiding relationship with a husband or boyfriend is placed in group A and such a relationship is associated with a neutralizing of the effect of the three other factors. For women in group A not going out to work, for example, does not increase risk. Group B contains those without such a relationship but not a loss of mother before age 11 or 3 or more children under 14 at

TABLE 1. *Percentage of women in Camberwell who experienced onset of depression in year by whether they had a severe event or major difficulty and intimacy context*

	Intimate relationship		
Event	Yes, with husband or boyfriend	Yes, with someone seen regularly other than husband or boyfriend	No
	%	%	%
Severe event or major difficulty	10 (9/88)	26 (12/47)	41 (12/29)
No severe event or major difficulty	1 (2/193)	3 (1/39)	4 (1/23)

TABLE 2. *Proportion of women in Camberwell in whom depression developed in the year among women who experienced a severe event or major difficulty by vulnerability factors*[a]

Event	Status	With event or difficulty		Without event or difficulty	
		%	%	%	%
A. Intimate tie with husband or boyfriend regardless	Employed	9 (4/43)	10 (9/88)	1 (1/117)	1 (2/193)
	Not employed	11 (5/45)		1 (1/76)	
B. No intimate tie with husband or boyfriend, excluding early loss or 3+ children under 14 living at home	Employed	15 (6/39)		0 (0/34)	
	Not employed	30 (7/23)		11 (2/19)	
C. No intimate tie with husband or boyfriend *and* with early loss of mother or 3+ children under 14 living at home	Employed	63 (5/8)		0 (0/7)	
	Not employed	100 (6/6)		0 (0/2)	
Total		20 (33/164)		2 (4/255)	

[a] Intimacy, employment status, early loss of mother, and 3+ children under 14 at home.

home, and C the remaining women. Compared with A, risk is increased in B and still more in C. It is only in groups B and C that work outside the home serves a protective function. In both groups it almost halves the risk of depression in the presence of a severe event or major difficulty. Finally, for women without such an event or difficulty groups A, B, and C are unrelated to risk of depression.

We found nothing else that helped to explain why women developed depression. But there remained yet a further question. Provoking agent and vulnerability factor were quite unrelated to the form or the severity taken by a depressive disorder. They in no way helped to explain why some women suffered from a 'psychotic' form and others a 'neurotic' form, and why within each some were more severely disturbed than others. We therefore looked for a third, *symptom-formation* factor. We have not only.found such a factor but much the most important of its components involves social experience—the past loss of a parent or other close relative, usually in childhood and adolescence (5). Among psychiatric patients loss by death of such a relative is associated with psychotic-like depressive symptoms (and their severity). Figure 1 illustrates this by dividing

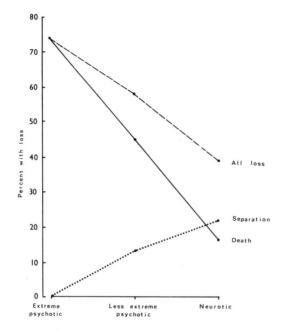

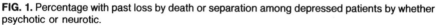

FIG. 1. Percentage with past loss by death or separation among depressed patients by whether psychotic or neurotic.

a group of depressed psychiatric patients into an extreme psychotic, a less extreme psychotic, and a neurotic group. The associations are large, have been replicated, and are not explained by background factors such as age.

It is important to note that loss of mother before 11 plays two roles—as a vulnerability factor it increases risk of depression, and as a symptom-formation factor it influences the form and the severity of depression according to whether the loss was by death or by separation.

This then is the outline of the model. Bearing various methodological innovations in mind, I believe a reasonable case has been made that the factors follow the temporal order specified and are involved in bringing about depression.

But what is going on? A causal model on its own, whatever its validity, is not enough. Consider employment. Is its protective role due to alleviation of boredom, greater variety of social contacts, or an enhanced sense of self-worth— or something else? The measures of a model do not have to be theoretically understandable in this sense—and at an early stage of development some at least will almost inevitably be theoretically ambiguous.

We have speculated that low self-esteem is the common feature behind all vulnerability factors and it is this that makes sense of our results. It is not loss itself that is important but the capacity once an important loss has occurred for a woman to hope for better things. In response to a provoking agent relatively specific feelings of hopelessness are likely to occur: the person has usually lost an important source of value—something that may have been derived from a person, a role, or an idea. If this hopelessness develops into a *general* feeling of hopelessness it may form the central feature of the depressive disorder itself.

We have come to see clinical depression as an affliction of a person's sense of values which leads, in Aaron Beck's terms, to a condition in which there is no meaning in the world, that the future is hopeless and the self worthless (1). It is after such generalization of hopelessness that the well-known affective and somatic symptoms of depression develop. Essential in any such generalization of hopelessness is a woman's ongoing self-esteem, her sense of her ability to control her world and her confidence that alternative sources of value will be at sometime available. If the woman's self-esteem is low before the onset of depression, she will be less likely to be able to see herself as emerging from her privation. And, of course, once depression has occurred feelings of confidence and self-worth can sink even lower.

It should not be overlooked that an appraisal of general hopelessness may be entirely realistic: the future for many women *is* bleak. It is probably here that our ideas depart most decisively from current opinion. We do not emphasize an inherent personality 'weakness.' While we do not rule out influence from the past—indeed we have demonstrated it has some importance—it is the link with the present that needs emphasis. Nor is it adversity or unhappiness or even loss that are central. They doubtless will always be with us, the inevitable precursors or consequences of whatever happiness we manage to achieve. Clinical depression is much less inevitable. It is a question of resources that allow a person to seek alternative sources of value and that allow her to hope that they can be found.

This interpretation is clearly relevant to factors of the model involving the current situation. It seems possible that loss in childhood and adolescence can also work through cognitive factors. For instance, the effect of loss of mother before 11 may be linked to the development of a sense of mastery. The earlier a mother is lost the more impeded is the growth of mastery and this may well permanently lower a woman's feeling of control and self-esteem. But, of course, there are other possibilities. Early loss of a mother might, for example, increase the chance of untoward experiences which are the direct antecedants of current vulnerability. Enduring feelings of insecurity may, for instance, increase the chance of marrying early an 'unsuitable' man.

For early loss acting as a symptom-formation factor we have suggested that women develop particular expectations about their environment as a result of past loss and these condition attitudes and behavior. Long-held perceptions of abandonment and helplessness may be linked to psychotic symptoms, and rejection and failure to neurotic symptoms.

For four years we have been developing new measures capable of exploring and testing these ideas, and we plan to use them in a prospective study. But we have also continued to use the existing material to explore the model. I have stated that only *severe* life-events are capable of provoking depression—

at least in the sense of producing a disorder that would not have occurred for a long period of time or not at all without the event. (Using our index of the 'brought forward time' we call this a formative causal influence in contrast to a triggering one (see 6; and 4, pp. 121–126). But events other than those rated as *severe* do play a lesser etiological role and the way they appear to do this fits our general view of depression as a cognitive disorder.

Women often endure major difficulty and disappointment for many years before developing depression. We therefore looked to see whether there was anything to suggest some kind of triggering effect about the time of onset of depression. We found, in fact, that these women do have an increased rate of quite minor events in the 5 weeks before onset. If these events served to 'bring home' to a woman the full implications of her lot, the reason for breakdown at that particular point in time would to some extent be explicable.

We see these minor events not as provoking agents in the sense outlined, but they do appear capable of triggering a depressive disorder where there has been a major loss or disappointment. For example, one woman in Camberwell, who had a very difficult marriage and was living in poor and overcrowded conditions, developed depression four weeks after she learned of her sister's engagement to be married. The likely significance of the engagement needs no underlining. Quite trivial incidents may therefore in the context of an enduring disappointment produce feelings of profound hopelessness and swiftly the psychological and physical components of clinical depression. Such a mechanism may also help to explain the existence of the minority of severe events that do not involve obvious loss. A number concerned incidents such as hospital admission for a threatening physical illness. It was notable that a number of the women also had major domestic difficulties, and it is again easy to see how such a brief separation from them might have 'brought home' the full implications of their position.

It has been common to study the effect of 'stress' on illness in general. The research in London, which has also involved studies of schizophrenia, anxiety states, and various physical conditions, suggests that this is a mistake. There is now a fair amount of evidence that when the likely meaning of events is considered there is considerable specificity in the sense used by Paykel in this volume. This may hold even within diagnostic groups. For example, a fifth of psychiatric patients with a severe event did not have one involving an obvious loss. Significantly more of these patients had a marked degree of anxiety associated with their depression (4, p. 228). The research indicates that specific types of experience should be related to particular psychiatric and physical consequences. While we argue that it is hopelessness that is critical in depression, usually provoked by some loss or disappointment, an important change in routine seems enough to bring about a florid relapse of schizophrenia symptoms (3). But it is not just a matter of different experiences leading to different conditions; it is possible that an experience protective for one condition may increase risk at the same time of another. A protective factor such as employment may help a woman to avoid depression because it raises feelings of self-worth and mastery; it may, however, because of the 'stress' of doing two 'jobs' be associated with risk of other kinds of disorder.

Probably quite disparate disorders will ultimately be shown to relate to comparable psychosocial precursors, but this needs to be demonstrated and not assumed.

A final and obvious point. It is effective theory that is desired. Working-class women away from Camberwell may not always experience so many vulnerability factors, and these may in other settings have different implications. Therefore 'refutation' or 'support' of our results must take into account the link of the elements in the model with background factors such as class and also the fact that theoretical implications of the measures may vary with the social setting. We have begun comparative research in the Outer Hebrides with the idea of forcing ourselves to face these kinds of possibilities. The population is largely rural and Gaelic-speaking. While the model has been supported to a surprising degree, there *are* some differences, and we trust these will lead to further development of measures, model, and theory. It is, I believe, from the struggle to resolve tensions between these three that new knowledge about etiology is likely to arise.

REFERENCES

1. Beck, A. T. (1967): *Depression: Clinical, Experimental and Theoretical Aspects.* Staples Press, London.
2. Brown, G. W. (1974): Meaning, measurement and stress. In: *Stressfulness of Life Events: Their Nature and Effects,* edited by B. S. Dohrenwend and B. P. Dohrenwend, pp. 217–243. Wiley, London.
3. Brown, G. W., and Birley, J. L. T. (1968): Crises and life changes and the onset of schizophrenia. *J. Health Soc. Behav.,* 9:203–214.
4. Brown, G. W., and Harris, T. (1978): *Social Origins of Depression: A Study of Psychiatric Disorder in Women.* Tavistock, London.
5. Brown, G. W., Harris, T., and Copeland, J. R. (1977): Depression and loss. *Br. J. Psychiatry,* 130:1–18.
6. Brown, G. W., Harris, T. O., and Peto, J. (1973): Life events and psychiatric disorders. Part 2: Nature of causal link. *Psychol. Med.,* 3:159–176.
7. Dohrenwend, B. P., and Dohrenwend, B. S. (1977): The conceptualization and measurement of stressful life events: An overview of the issues. In: *The Origins and Course of Psychopathology,* edited by J. S. Strauss, H. M. Babigian, and M. Roff. Plenum Press, New York.
8. Paykel, E. S. (1974): Recent life events and clinical depression. In: *Life Stress and Illness,* edited by E. K. E. Gunderson and R. D. Rahe. Charles C Thomas, Springfield, Illinois.

Stress and Mental Disorder,
edited by James E. Barrett et al.
Raven Press, New York © 1979.

Course of Depressive Symptoms Following the Stress of Bereavement

Paula J. Clayton and Harriet S. Darvish

*Department of Psychiatry, Washington University School of Medicine,
St. Louis, Missouri 63110*

Freud (8), when writing about mourning and melancholia in 1917, recognized that both psychologic and somatic depressive symptoms characterize bereavement. He listed five characteristics of mourning: (a) painful dejection, (b) cessation of interest in the outside world, (c) loss of capacity to love, (d) inhibition of all activity, and (e) absence of disturbance of self-regard (as compared to melancholia). He believed that mourning subsides after a certain lapse of time and that interference with it was useless or even harmful. Wahl (19) reports that Freud, near the end of his life, was consulted by a woman who had become depressed following the death of her husband. After listening to her, Freud quietly stated: "Madam, you do not have a neurosis, you have a misfortune."

What is the natural course of these symptoms in bereaved adults? That is an important question, as many reports of pathologic or neurotic grief following bereavement list as one of their characteristics either a prolonged or a severe course. Most papers dealing with bereavement, however, have reported only the frequency of symptoms during the previous year without considering their course.

There is one notable exception. In 1976, Blanchard et al. (2) collected data retrospectively on a volunteer sample of widowed women. They reported on the patterns of abatement of depressive symptoms in 30 highly educated women whose average age at the time of the index death was 30 and who had been widowed an average of 7 years at the time of the study. Seven women had remarried by the time of the interview. The widows were asked to state the frequency and severity of 20 symptoms thought to be associated with depression at three time periods following their husbands' deaths—a few weeks later, 1 year later, and at the time of the interview. The authors found that crying, appetite and weight loss, fatigue, sleep disturbance, loss of interest, poor memory, difficulty concentrating, decreased speed of thinking, irritability, death thoughts, visions of the husband, and hearing the husband's voice had all significantly decreased by the end of the first year. Symptoms that had not subsided within the first year were depressed mood, restlessness, dreams of the spouse, hopelessness, worthlessness, and suicidal thoughts. In fact, suicidal thoughts remained essentially unchanged throughout the 7-year period. Although symptoms were examined with respect to sudden or lingering illness in the husband, the only symptom in the widows that was significantly associated with sudden death in the husbands was suicidal thoughts.

This chapter describes a replication of the Blanchard et al. (2) analysis by examining the course of similar symptoms in a group of randomly selected widows and widowers seen within the first month of bereavement and then 1 year later. By so doing, it addresses an important methodologic question in stress research and psychiatric research in general, that is, the reliability of data gathered retrospectively.

METHODS

In 1968 and 1969, we obtained permission to use the death certificates of St. Louis City and County to gather our sample. Using a random-numbers table, we selected our sample and interviewed 76 white widows and 33 white widowers with an average age of 61. The acceptance rate was 58%. A systematic interview was used dealing with the subject's physical and mental health, marriage, social network, and actions and feelings surrounding the death. Four of the original sample (4%) died during the first year of follow-up. Of the remaining 105, 92 (88%) were reinterviewed.

Every effort was made to gather more information on those who had refused initial participation. According to the death certificates, there were no differences in the spouses' ages or causes of death between interviewed bereaved and those who had refused. At 3 months, we again tried to interview the refusers. After five refusals in five attempts, this was given up. At 1 year, a letter and a simple 1-page health questionnaire were sent to all refusers; again the response was poor.

One measure of poor health in widows and widowers frequently reported is death within the first year of widowhood. In an effort to see if the refusers were different from the subjects, death certificates were searched. No deaths were recorded in the metropolitan area for the refusers within 1 year after the deaths of their spouses. Most of the refusers were located by telephone; a few could not be located. Even if all had moved out of town and died, the death rate would not have been significantly higher in the refusers than in the accepters.

In 1973, a similar study was undertaken concentrating on people widowed under age 45. Because of fewer such cases, a consecutive series was collected from the death certificates of the city and county. Sixty-two white subjects (34 women and 28 men) with an average age of 36 were interviewed. The acceptance rate was 66%. There were no differences in the sex of the subjects who refused or, again according to the death certificates, in the mean age of the deceased or in their causes of death. At 1 year, 57 (92%) were reinterviewed. There were no deaths during the year in this group.

For both samples in the same year the prospective study was undertaken, each bereaved subject was matched with three married subjects to assure that one would be available for interview 1 year later. Controls were of the same sex, from the same voting district, and preferably from the same street. One year later, one of the three controls was interviewed concerning physical and mental health during the previous year. Thus two prospective groups of bereaved were collected with two prospective matched, married control groups. The control groups, however, are not used in this data analysis.

This analysis combines the data from the two studies *(N =* 171) since both were methodologically and substantively similar. The major causes of death in the combined groups of deceased were cancer *(N =* 58) and cardiovascular disease *(N =* 49). The younger group had a larger number of violent deaths (accidents, suicides). One-third of the combined sample *(N =* 56) had sudden deaths, with significantly more (45% versus 26%) being in the younger age group (chi-square with Yates' correction, $p \leq 0.05$). There were proportionately more male survivors in the younger compared to the older sample (45 versus 30%), and this barely missed being statistically significant.

In summary, the data of this report deal with interviews of 149 (87% of the combined original samples) widows and widowers with an average age at death of 51 who were seen within 1 month of the death of their spouses and again 1 year later. There were 96 women and 53 men. Their mean Otis Dudley Duncan socioeconomic index was 43.9 (3). This is a rating of prestige, with a scale from 2 to 96, which takes into consideration education and income. The national average in 1962 for nonblack urban residents was 43.7 (10).

For this analysis, the course of 23 depressive symptoms and nine physical symptoms was examined, as were the use of alcohol and drugs, physician visits, hospitalizations, and the presence or absence of a depressive symptom complex at the two interviews. A positive symptom complex required low mood (feeling depressed, sad, despondent, discouraged, blue, lost, or numb) plus four of the following: (a) loss of appetite or weight loss, (b) sleep difficulties, including hypersomnia, (c) fatigue, (d) feeling restless, (e) loss of interest, (f) difficulty concentrating, (g) feelings of guilt, and (h) wishing to be dead or thoughts of suicide. This cluster had to be present for 1 month.

The statistical method used was the chi-square test with the Yates' correction. For the differences in proportion in the paired sample (symptoms at time 1 and time 2), McNemar's chi-square was used (1).

RESULTS

Symptoms of Bereavement at 1 and 13 Months

Table 1 shows the frequency of positive depressive symptoms at 1 (time 1) and 13 (time 2) months. Crying, low mood, sleep disturbance, loss of appetite, fatigue, poor memory, loss of interest, difficulty concentrating, weight loss of

TABLE 1. *Frequency of depressive symptoms at 1 and 13 months*

Symptom	N= 149[a]	
	1 Month % +	13 Months % +
Crying	89	33[b]
Sleep disturbance	76	48[b]
Low mood	75	42[b]
Loss of appetite	51	16[b]
Fatigue	44	30[c]
Poor memory	41	23[b]
Loss of interest	40	23[b]
Difficulty concentrating	36	16[b]
Weight loss of 5 lbs or more	36	20[c]
Feeling guilty	31	12[b]
Restlessness *(N*= 89)	48	45
Reverse diurnal variation	26	22
Irritability	24	20
Feels someone to blame	22	22
Diurnal variation	17	10
Death wishes	16	12
Feeling hopeless	14	13
Hallucinations	12	9
Suicidal thoughts	5	3
Fear of losing mind	3	4
Suicide attempts	0	0
Feeling worthless	6	11
Feels angry about death	13	22[d]
Depressive syndrome	42	16[b]

[a] N varies from symptom to symptom, mostly 148.
[b] Significant by McNemar's chi-square, df = 1, $p \leq 0.001$.
[c] Significant by McNemar's chi-square, df = 1, $p \leq 0.01$.
[d] Significant by McNemar's chi-square, df = 1, $p \leq 0.02$.

5 lbs. or more, feeling guilty, and the depressive symptom complex all significantly decreased by the end of the first year. The frequency of many symptoms, however, was still quite high; e.g., sleep disturbance was still present in 48% of the subjects, as was low mood in 43% and restlessness in 45%. Symptoms that remained unchanged at 13 months were restlessness, reverse diurnal variation, irritability, feeling someone was to blame, diurnal variation, death wishes, feeling hopeless, hallucinations, suicidal thoughts, and a fear of losing one's mind. Two symptoms, worthlessness and feeling angry about the death, were more common at the 1-year period. The latter increase was statistically significant.

Table 2 shows the frequency of the same symptoms at 13 months according to whether or not the symptoms had been present at 1 month. It is clear that those who had had symptoms at 1 month were more likely to have the same symptoms 1 year later than were those without the symptoms originally. The

TABLE 2. *Frequency of depressive symptoms at 13 months*

Symptom	Those with symptoms at 1 month		Those without symptoms at 1 month (new symptoms)	
	% +	N	% +	N
Crying	36	132	6	16
Sleep disturbance	59	113	11	35
Low mood	49	111	22	37
Loss of appetite	28	76	4	72
Fatigue	45	65	19	83
Poor memory	34	61	15	88
Loss of interest	40	57	12	84
Difficulty concentrating	33	52	6	94
Weight loss of 5 lbs. or more	22	51	17	92
Feeling guilty	25	49	6	97
Restlessness	63	43	28	46
Reverse diurnal variation	39	38	17	109
Irritability	37	35	15	113
Feels someone to blame	63	32	11	111
Diurnal variation	24	25	7	122
Death wishes	33	24	7	124
Feeling hopeless	55	20	6	128
Hallucinations	29	17	6	131
Suicidal thoughts	0	8	3	139
Fear of losing mind	0	5	4	143
Suicide attempts	0	0	0	147
Feeling worthless	56	9	8	139
Feel angry about death	63	19	16	128
Depressive syndrome	27	63	8	86

percentage of subjects reporting new symptoms was very similar to the frequency of symptoms found in the controls, although the controls reported the presence or absence of symptoms at any time through the year and not just current symptoms (5). If the percentage of subjects who experienced a symptom for the first time at 1 year can be considered near the general population rate of that symptom (or syndrome), then the difference in percentage of the symptom in the two groups at 13 months can be considered the risk of the symptom attributable to the bereavement. Thus expressed, the symptoms that stand out most strikingly are sleep disturbance, feeling someone is to blame, and feeling angry, hopeless, and worthless.

Table 3 concerns physical symptoms and medical treatment. In general, physical symptoms were not frequent and did not change much over the year. The one exception was dysmenorrhea, which significantly decreased by the end of the first year. The use of sleeping medicines and tranquilizers also remained unchanged over the year. At time 1, subjects were coded as positive if they drank heavily, defined as three drinks per day, or were alcoholic. At time 2, amount of drinking was coded, as only a few had additional symptoms, with

TABLE 3. *Frequency of physical symptoms and treatment at 1 and 13 months*

Symptom	N = 149[a]	
	1 Month % +	13 Months % +
Headaches	26	19
Dysmenorrhea *(N = 39)*	33	10[b]
Other pains	31	30
Urinary frequency	20	18
Constipation	20	18
Dyspnea	19	16
Abdominal pain	17	16
Blurred vision	15	15
Anxiety attacks	10	7
Alcohol use	11	19[c]
Use of tranquilizers	39	31
Use of sleeping medicines	21	21
Physician visits	41	52
Hospitalizations	3	19[d]

[a] *N* varies from symptom to symptom, mostly 148.
[b] Significant by McNemar's chi-square, df $= 1$, $p \leq 0.05$.
[c] Significant by McNemar's chi-square, df $= 1$, $p \leq 0.01$.
[d] Significant by McNemar's chi-square, df $= 1$, $p \leq 0.001$.

16 ounces per week or more counted as heavy drinking. With these criteria, drinking significantly increased over the year, almost entirely in men. It should be noted that nearly one-fifth of all subjects had been hospitalized by the end of 13 months of bereavement.

Table 4 shows the same physical symptoms and treatments in reference to

TABLE 4. *Frequency of physical symptoms and treatment at 13 months*

	Those with symptoms at 1 month		Those without symptoms at 1 month (new symptoms)	
	% +	N	% +	N
Headaches	34	38	14	110
Dysmenorrhea (*N* = 39)	15	13	8	26
Other pains	52	44	20	100
Urinary frequency	41	29	13	119
Constipation	53	30	9	118
Dyspnea	43	28	10	118
Abdominal pain	42	26	11	122
Blurred vision	55	22	8	126
Anxiety attacks	20	15	5	132
Alcohol use	88	16	11	129
Use of tranquilizers	60	57	12	90
Use of sleeping medicines	52	31	13	115
Physician visits	50	48	53	68
Hospitalizations	0	5	19	144

those with or without the symptom at 1 month. Again, individuals with symptoms at 13 months were those who had had the symptoms at 1 month. Again taking the differences between the two columns as being the risk of the symptom attributable to the bereavement, use of alcohol, tranquilizers, and hypnotics is a striking practice in the first year of widowhood. The experiences of the controls from the first study of 92 widows and widowers followed for 1 year (5) may be applicable to physician visits and hospitalizations: 50% of the controls had seen a physician three or more times and 15% had been hospitalized, percentages very similar to those of the entire widowed sample here.

Bereavement Symptom Patterns in Those With or Without a Depressive Syndrome at 1 Month

Table 5 shows the pattern of symptoms in those who had experienced a depressive syndrome at 1 month compared to those who had not. Every symptom was more frequent in both time periods in those identified by having a depressive syndrome at 1 month. In those with the depressive syndrome, the change in symptoms followed the pattern shown in Tables 1 and 3. The group without the depressive syndrome showed improvement in fewer symptoms, but symptoms generally remained infrequent and unchanged.

Thus there is a group with a few symptoms who retain those few symptoms throughout the year, and the depressed group whose somatic symptoms improve but who retain the angry and self-depreciatory depressive symptoms and whose drinking increases.

Bereavement Symptom Patterns in Those With and Without Depression at 13 Months

Table 6 illustrates that there was a small group of individuals *(N = 24)* whose depressive symptoms remained essentially unchanged or increased throughout the year. Almost half of these 24 depressed at 13 months reported a severe anniversary reaction (defined as a syndrome of more than 1 day's duration with low mood described as "miserable" or its equivalent, excessive crying in places other than church or grave, and/or interruption of work function), whereas this was rare in the rest of the sample.

The nondepressed group, in general, followed the pattern noted in Table 1. They also significantly decreased their tranquilizer intake by 1 year and reported fewer hallucinations. They significantly increased their drinking at 1 year. It seems that all men, not just those who are most depressed, are at risk to increase their drinking during the first year of widowhood.

Symptoms Divided by Age, Sex, and Length of Illness

Table 7 shows the symptoms at 1 and 13 months according to the subject's age, sex, and length of deceased's illness. It is important that younger bereaved

TABLE 5. *Symptom patterns in those with and without the depressive syndrome at 1 month*

Symptom	Depressive syndrome + $N=63$		Depressive syndrome − $N=86$	
	1 Month % +	13 Months % +	1 Month % +	13 Months % +
Crying	95	42[a]	85	27[a]
Sleep disturbance	98	50[a]	61	47[c]
Low mood	95	53[a]	61	34[a]
Loss of appetite	68	24[a]	40	11[a]
Fatigue	68	37[a]	27	26
Poor memory	48	32	36	16[a]
Loss of interest	79	33[a]	14	17
Difficulty concentrating	57	27[a]	20	7[c]
Weight loss of 5 lbs. or more	48	23[b]	27	17
Feeling guilty	54	15[a]	19	11
Restlessness	74	59	21	30
Reverse diurnal variation	47	29[d]	11	18
Irritability	36	31	15	13
Feels someone to blame	27	27	19	19
Diurnal variation	29	15[d]	8	7
Death wishes	38	18[d]	4	7
Feeling hopeless	26	21	5	7
Hallucinations	16	16	9	5
Suicidal thoughts	11	5	1	1
Fear of losing mind	7	5	1	4
Feeling worthless	10	21	4	4
Feels angry about death	21	31	7	16
Alcohol use	12	22[d]	11	18
Use of tranquilizers	48	44	32	20[b]
Use of hypnotics	26	32	18	13
Physician visits	43	39	40	60[d]
Hospitalizations	5	22[c]	2	16[b]

[a]Significant by McNemar's chi-square, df $= 1$, $p \le 0.001$.
[b]Significant by McNemar's chi-square, df $= 1$, $p \le 0.01$.
[c]Significant by McNemar's chi-square, df $= 1$, $p \le 0.02$.
[d]Significant by McNemar's chi-square, df $= 1$, $p \le 0.05$.

report less low mood and more psychologic symptoms of depression at 1 month and retain the irritability and anger at 13 months. The men report striking alcohol consumption at 1 month and at 1 year and a significant increase over the year. In looking at the cause of the increase, it is clear that all heavy drinkers or alcoholics continue to drink, and almost one-third of men who previously drank less increase their drinking. There is no difference in any of the groups in the rate of the depressive syndrome at 1 or 13 months.

After 1 Year

One in six (16%) of the widowed were not doing well by 13 months. Patterns of abatement of symptoms through the year were examined, with the subjects

TABLE 6. *Symptom patterns in those with and without the depressive syndrome at 1 year*

Symptom	Depressive syndrome + N = 24		Depressive syndrome − N = 125	
	1 Month % +	13 Months % +	1 Month % +	13 Months % +
Crying	92	67[a]	89	27[c]
Sleep disturbance	96	92	73	40[c]
Low mood	83	100	73	31[c]
Loss of appetite	83	42[b]	45	11[c]
Fatigue	67	79	40	21[c]
Poor memory	46	38	40	20[c]
Loss of interest	70	57	35	17[c]
Difficulty concentrating	42	42	34	11[c]
Weight loss of 5 lbs. or more	48	43	34	15[c]
Feeling guilty	55	27	30	10[c]
Restlessness	79	86	43	37
Reverse diurnal variation	29	38	25	20
Irritability	38	42	21	16
Feels someone to blame	29	43	22	19
Diurnal variation	17	17	17	9
Death wishes	29	46	14	5
Feeling hopeless	33	38	10	8
Hallucinations	8	30	12	5[a]
Suicidal thoughts	13	8	4	2
Fear of losing mind	4	8	3	3
Feeling worthless	8	33[a]	6	7
Feels angry about death	22	44	11	19
Alcohol use	21	33	9	17[a]
Use of tranquilizers	35	39	40	29[a]
Use of hypnotics	26	35	20	19
Physician visits	35	65	43	49
Hospitalizations	4	25	3	18[c]
Severe anniversary reaction		46		14

[a]Significant by McNemar's chi-square, df = 1, $p \leq 0.05$.
[b]Significant by McNemar's chi-square, df = 1, $p \leq 0.01$.
[c]Significant by McNemar's chi-square, df = 1, $p \leq 0.001$.

divided according to the factors listed in Table 8. No striking findings emerged, although each of these factors has been implicated in poor outcome in the literature. In addition, each factor was compared to all the other "poor outcome" factors. As already shown in Table 2, depressive syndrome at time 1 was positively correlated with depressive syndrome at time 2 (27% of those depressed at time 2 were depressed at time 1, compared to 8% of those in whom the syndrome developed for the first time at time 2; $p \leq 0.004$). Having a depressive syndrome at time 1 was also positively associated with having a shorter marriage (71% of those with short marriages and only 36% of those with longer marriages were depressed in the first month, $p \leq 0.002$). This difference was lost by 1

TABLE 7. Symptoms compared by age, sex, and length of illness

	Age				Sex				Length of Illness			
	1 Month % +		13 Months % +		1 Month % +		13 Months % +		1 Month % +		13 Months % +	
Symptom	≤ 45 (N=67)	≥ 46 (N=82)	≤ 45 (N=67)	≥ 46 (N=82)	Female (N=96)	Male (N=53)	Female (N=96)	Male (N=53)	≤ 4 Days (N=50)	≥ 5 Days (N=99)	≤ 4 Days (N=50)	≥ 5 Days (N=99)
Crying	81	96[a]	28	37	91	87	42[b]	17	92	88	20	40[a]
Sleep disturbance	72	80	40	54	83[c]	64	54	38	76	77	44	50
Low mood	63	85[a]	33	53[d]	78	70	46	37	72	77	41	44
Loss of appetite	54	49	18	15	59[d]	38	17	15	64[d]	45	18	15
Fatigue	42	46	27	33	47	40	33	26	40	46	26	33
Poor memory	40	42	22	23	41	42	22	25	44	40	22	23
Loss of interest	46	36	30	17	42	38	21	28	46	38	23	24
Difficulty concentrating	43	29	22	10	34	38	12	23	40	33	16	16
Weight loss of 5 lbs. or more	39	33	21	17	46[a]	18	24	10	52[b]	27	18	19
Feeling guilty	48[d]	22	18	8	31	38	8	21[d]	46[d]	27	10	14
Restlessness	50	45	48	38	48	49	48	41	49	46	48	44
Reverse diurnal variation	33	20	18	27	27	23	31[a]	9	38	19[d]	32	18
Irritability	36[a]	14	34[b]	9	25	21	19	23	30	20	22	19
Feels someone to blame	35[a]	12	28	18	25	17	22	23	34[a]	17	26	21
Diurnal variation	21	14	10	10	17	17	7	15	20	15	4	13
Death wishes	24[d]	10	6	16	19	11	16	4	16	16	6	14
Feeling hopeless	13	14	9	16	15	11	17	6	8	16	12	13
Hallucinations	18[d]	6	13	5	14	8	8	9	12	11	10	8
Suicidal thoughts	11[d]	1	3	3	2	11[d]	3	2	8	4	4	2
Fear of losing mind	8[d]	0	6	3	4	2	5	2	8	1	2	5
Feeling worthless	8	5	8	14	8	2	11	11	6	6	10	11
Feels angry about death	21[c]	6	37[b]	10	15	10	23	21	20	9	36[a]	16

Nothing to look forward to	14	9	10	27[c]	3	26[b]	26[c]	8	4	15	20	19
Alcohol use	43	35	25	15	42	34	4	47[b]	54[c]	31	12	23
Use of tranquilizers	12	29[d]	36	26	22	19	33	26	18	23	40	26
Use of hypnotics			21	22			27	12			22	21
Physician visits	41	42	52	51	42	41	54	46	54	35	49	53
Hospitalizations	3	4	12	24	5	0	20	17	6	2	14	21
Depressive syndrome	48	38	12	20	44	40	16	17	46	40	12	18

[a] Significant by chi-square, df $= 1$, $p \le 0.01$.
[b] $p \le 0.001$.
[c] $p \le 0.02$.
[d] $p \le 0.05$.

TABLE 8. *Variables used for comparison*

Socioeconomic index of the husband prior to the death (64 with ODDs from 2–37, 85 with ODDs from 38–96)

Sex (96 women, 53 men)

Age (67 who were 45 and under; 82 who were over 45)

Years married prior to the death (28 who were married 7 years or less; 121 married more than 7 years)

Warning of impending death (50 with spouses whose illnesses were 4 days or less; 99 with long spouse illness)

Previous experience with death (19 with no previous significant deaths; 129 with some experience)

The presence or absence of a preexisting psychiatric illness, such as alcoholism, hysteria, unipolar affective disorder (46 with a previous diagnosis; 101 without)

Living alone (N = 53) or with someone (N = 93) at 1 year

Low income at 1 year (defined *a priori* as $200 per month or less—28 with such an income; 112 with higher incomes)

Ready to remarry at 1 year (18 with definite plans; 131 without)

No grave visits by 1 year (18 with none; 130 with one or more)

---

year. Thus with shorter marriages, the initial reaction was more severe, but this became muted with time.

Having a depressive syndrome at time 2 was positively correlated with having a diagnosable psychiatric illness prior to the spouse's death. At 1 month, there was no significant difference in the number with or without a psychiatric illness who reported the depressive syndrome. At 1 year, however, 64% of those who were depressed had had a preexisting psychiatric diagnosis, and only 26% of those not depressed had had such illness $(p \leq 0.001)$. The diagnoses covered the full range—alcoholism, major affective disorder, hysteria, undiagnosed psychiatric illness—with no specific illness emerging as especially predicting depressive syndrome. No other correlations were found between any variables in Table 8 and the depressive syndrome at either time period.

There was no correlation between relative youth and no warning of death with outcome as measured by depressive syndrome at time 2.

DISCUSSION

The analysis of these data is comparable to the findings of Blanchard et al. (2). The somatic symptoms of depression, as well as depressed mood and guilt (which is largely guilt of omission surrounding the illness or the death), markedly decrease by the end of the first year of widowhood. The psychologic symptoms of depression, including restlessness (agitation), irritability, blame, hopelessness, worthlessness, suicidal thoughts, and hallucinations, remain unchanged, and anger increases. Blanchard et al. (2) report only statistical findings without giving the basic data; therefore, finer comparisons are difficult. They suggested that early in bereavement the physiologic symptoms of depression predominate, but as the bereaved turns to looking toward the future and reorganizing his or her life, the psychologic symptoms become prominent. If this were true, we should expect to see different symptoms and different patterns of abatement of symptoms in those who were planning to remarry at the end of the year and those who were not. The data did not support this. The number who plan to remarry was too small to make a definitive statement about symptom change (they actually showed less change from time 1 to time 2), but the frequency of symptoms in the two groups only showed depressed mood to be significantly less common at 1 year.

Nevertheless, it is interesting that from a retrospective study with a selected population, the findings are similar to this prospective study combining a random and a consecutive sample. This may mean that the symptoms that occur around a significant life event may be vividly remembered and thus reportable years later. It emphasizes the necessity of taking the bereavement reaction into account in any study of the population prevalence of depression, as Weissman and Myers (20) have recently done. They reported a lifetime prevalence for grief reactions of 10.4%, defining a grief reaction as "symptoms that met the criteria for major depression by the SADS if they began within three months of the death of a close relative and lasted up to one year." Such reactions were more often reported in women and in those from the lower classes. The DSM-III likewise acknowledges this syndrome in its category "uncomplicated bereavement." Blanchard et al. (2) and Parkes and Brown (17) showed these symptoms to continue to improve after the first year.

Parkes (13) looked at symptoms over time in 22 widows (average age 49) referred to him for study by London practitioners. Sleep and appetite disturbance, as well as guilt, improved during the year of follow-up. Eighty-two percent reported feeling restless in the first month; this fell to 41% at the end of the year. These 1-year results are similar to those reported here. In Parkes' data, irritability and anger correlated highly with restlessness, tension, and overall affect. These findings are consistent with what was found in younger widowed here. The anger and blame that our widowed reported were not considered irrational. They were frequently directed at the deceased, hospital, physician, and so on and seldom at the survivor.

Also of note, if restlessness is a common bereavement symptom, its opposite, retardation, is not. We have never observed a "retarded" depression in bereavement, a finding similar to that of Lindemann (12) and Parkes (13).

Parkes (14) first reported that in another group of young widowed, 74% of those with short preparation for the death and 42% of those with longer preparation had a depressive symptom complex at 13 months. These figures are far in excess of the 16% of the total population reported here and are difficult to reconcile. His study population was a group of young men and women from Boston who were seen early in bereavement and followed prospectively for 2 to 4 years. The first year's interviews were open ended, with the first systematic questionnaire being applied at 13 months. His sample contained blacks and more people from lower socioeconomic classes (50% of his short preparation group was from social classes 5 and 6). Lower socioeconomic status, as seen from some of his later data and from our earlier study (4,15), does affect outcome and could partially explain his reported results.

In later papers (9,15,16) using the same study group, Parkes reported four factors which at early interviews predicted poor outcome in the young bereaved. These were (a) low socioeconomic status, (b) short terminal illness with little warning of impending death, (c) multiple life crises (particularly those involving disturbance of the marital relationship), and (d) an early reaction to the bereavement consisting of "severe distress, yearning, anger, or self-reproach." In our study, neither young age nor no warning, nor the combination, predicted outcome.

Although common sense would indicate that no warning, no anticipation, short preparation, sudden death, or any other synonymous term should be associated with poor outcome, only Parkes has been able to corroborate this. Other investigators have failed to show such an association, although only our study and Parkes' have included a significant number of young bereaved. For example, Blanchard et al. (2) found that anticipatory grief in their 30 young widowed did not affect the incidence of most depressive symptoms, except that all five women who had considered suicide did not have a chance for anticipatory grieving. They also reported that those women who experienced a sudden death and had marriages of less than 7 years experienced a more severe reaction initially, but later outcome was no different from the others. Our data partially confirm this finding, with 71% of the subjects with "shorter marriages" showing the depressive syndrome at 1 month, but only 25% by 1 year. Of those with longer marriages, 36% showed depressive syndrome at 1 month, but only 14% by 1 year. When examined by length of illness as well as by years of marriage, only years of marriage contributed to the initial impact and subsequent improvement.

In results from the Florida Health Study, Schwab et al. (18) also reported no association between age and outcome and found that extended illnesses were significantly associated with more intense grief, a repeated finding when working with older populations. They judged half the respondents interviewed more than 1 year after the death to be suffering from intense grief.

In our previous studies, symptoms of irritability and guilt in early bereavement were associated with younger age (6). This was replicated here, as seen in Table 7, which lists symptoms characteristically seen in younger widowed. The anger and irritability continue at 13 months. Perhaps people mellow with time or, alternatively and less desirable, "disengage," as Cumming and Henry (7) suggest. It could be, as Lehrman (11) has suggested, that all bereavement in young age, regardless of the length of the terminal illness, is untimely.

In the first month of bereavement, most psychologic symptoms of depression occur less frequently than do the somatic symptoms. The psychologic symptoms, however, persist while the somatic symptoms clear. There seems to be a small group of widowed (16% of the sample), not identified by age, sex, or length of the deceased's illness, with a host of depressive symptoms who would be considered clinically depressed at 13 months. There is also a group of nonde-pressed young widowed who continue to have irritability, blame, and anger at 13 months.

Of those depressed at 13 months, the syndrome developed in about 75% at 1 month, and it remained; it developed in the rest after the first month. Because depressive symptoms are common early in bereavement, symptoms alone at 1 month are not helpful in distinguishing those who will be depressed at 1 year. The presence of a preexisting psychiatric illness is associated with persistence in the depressive syndrome at 13 months. Thus those with preexisting illness are a more vulnerable group.

The association between increased physical morbidity and bereavement is still unsettled. Although physical symptoms were examined—as well as the use of tranquilizers and hypnotics, physician visits, and hospitalizations—they provided little information about the course of bereavement. Although we may have set our criteria for "significant alcohol use" by 1 year (drinking 16 ounces or more per week) too low, it still is striking that almost 50% of the men were drinking at least that much. Both previous heavy users and alcoholics, and those without such a history ("new cases"), account for this increase. Parkes (15) tried to use a physical health outcome score in his paper dealing with effects of bereavement. However, he found that physical health proved the most difficult to predict; our findings are the same. Use of medicines, physician visits, and hospitalizations seem unrelated to the presence or absence of a large number of affective symptoms, and physician visits and hospitalizations may be no more frequent in the bereaved than in the controls.

SUMMARY

Bereavement is associated with a full range of depressive symptoms. The somatic symptoms of depression tend to improve by 13 months, but the psychologic symptoms tend to persist. Sixteen percent of subjects continue to be troubled by low mood and many symptoms. This group is more likely to have a preexisting psychiatric illness. Despite this, physical symptoms, physician visits, hospitalizations, and the use of tranquilizers and hypnotics are not significantly increased in this group. The majority of bereaved improve without intervention.

ACKNOWLEDGMENTS

This work was supported in part by grants MH-13002 and MH-25430 from the National Institutes of Health.

REFERENCES

1. Bishop, Y., Fienberg, S., and Holland, P. (1976): *Discrete Multivariate Analysis: Theory and Practice.* MIT Press, Cambridge.

2. Blanchard, C. G., Blanchard, E. B., and Becker, J. V. (1976): The young widow: Depressive symptomatology throughout the grief process. *Psychiatry,* 39:394–399.
3. Blau, P. M., and Duncan, O. D. (1967): *The American Occupational Structure.* Wiley, New York.
4. Bornstein, P. E., Clayton, P. J., Halikas, J. A., Maurice, W. L., and Robins, E. (1973): The depression of widowhood after thirteen months. *Br. J. Psychiatry* 122:561–566.
5. Clayton, P. J. (1974): Mortality and morbidity in the first year of widowhood. *Arch. Gen. Psychiatry,* 30:747–750.
6. Clayton, P. J., Halikas, J. A., and Maurice, W. L. (1971): The bereavement of the widowed. *Dis. Nerv. Syst.,* 32:597–604.
7. Cumming, E., and Henry, W. E. (1961): *Growing Old.* Basic Books, New York.
8. Freud, S. (1957): Mourning and melancholia (1917). In: *The Complete Psychological Works of Sigmund Freud, Vol. XIV,* pp. 243–258. Hogarth Press, London.
9. Glick, I. O., Weiss, R. S., and Parkes, C. M. (1974): *The First Year of Bereavement.* Wiley, New York.
10. Hauser, R. M., and Featherman, D. L. (1977): *The Process of Stratification: Trends and Analyses.* Academic Press, New York.
11. Lehrman, S. R. (1956): Reactions to untimely death. *Psychiatr. Q.,* 30:564–578.
12. Lindemann, E. (1944): Symptomatology and management of acute grief. *Am. J. Psychiatry,* 101:141–148.
13. Parkes, C. M. (1970): The first year of bereavement: A longitudinal study of the reaction of London widows to the death of their husbands. *Psychiatry,* 33:444–467.
14. Parkes, C. M. (1973): Letter to the editor—Anticipatory grief and widowhood. *Br. J. Psychiatry,* 122:615.
15. Parkes, C. M. (1975): Determinants of outcome following bereavement. *Omega,* 6:303–323.
16. Parkes, C. M. (1975): Unexpected and untimely bereavement: A statistical study of young Boston widows and widowers. In: *Bereavement: Its Psychosocial Aspects,* edited by B. Schoenberg, I. Gerber, A. Wiener, A. H. Kutscher, D. Peretz, and A. C. Carr, pp. 119–138. Columbia University Press, New York.
17. Parkes, C. M., and Brown, R. J. (1972): Health after bereavement: A controlled study of young Boston widows and widowers. *Psychosom. Med.,* 34:449–461.
18. Schwab, J. J., Chalmers, J. M., Conroy, S. J., Farris, P. B., and Markush, R. E. (1975): Studies in grief: A preliminary report. In: *Bereavement: Its Psychosocial Aspects,* edited by B. Schoenberg, I. Gerber, A. Wiener, A. H. Kutscher, D. Peretz, and A. C. Carr, pp. 78–87. Columbia University Press, New York.
19. Wahl, C. W. (1970): The differential diagnosis of normal and neurotic grief following bereavement. *Psychosomatics,* 11:104–106.
20. Weissman, M., and Myers, J. (1978): Affective disorders in a US urban community: The use of research diagnostic criteria in an epidemiological survey. *Arch. Gen. Psychiatry,* 35:1304–1311.

Stress and Mental Disorder,
edited by James E. Barrett et al.
Raven Press, New York © 1979.

Discussion, Part II

Gerald L. Klerman

*Alcohol, Drug Abuse, and Mental Health Administration, Department of Health, Educa-
tion, and Welfare, Rockville, Maryland 20857*

Recently, there has been a resurgence of interest in diagnosis, and many of the contributors to this volume have been involved either in the St. Louis study or in studies in New Haven. This interest is reflected in the development of the Feighner criteria by the St. Louis group and in the use of the RDC in more current research by Weissman and Myers (1). One important issue alluded to by Brown is that of the diagnostic homogeneity of the populations called depressed. The question arises about the extent to which some of the patient samples labeled depressed in these various studies, which extend over 10 or 15 years, are diagnostically homogeneous groups.

A related concern is the extent to which these patients have symptoms of depression, which was called demoralization in the preceding chapters, or which in another context might be called human misery, or which might be based on other diagnostic criteria. In this respect, Weissman and Myers in New Haven have evidence that there is a complex relationship between individuals who have many depressive symptoms, only a fraction of which may meet, for example, the Feighner or the RDC criteria for discernible disorder.

The question may also be raised as to what extent there are differential relationships between antecedent life events and subtypes within the group of disorders. The endogenous reactive subtype discussed by Paykel has been the source of much controversy. In my opinion, it merits being relegated to the graveyard of diagnostic entities. Most evidence indicates that there is very little relationship between the presence or absence of a situational precipitant and the symptom complex called endogenous, endogenomorphic, or vital. This idea is embodied in the DSM-III and in the RDC, both of which contain discussions centering around the differences between situational depressions and the symptom complex. This lack of relationship is also suggested in the pilot research for the National Institute of Mental Health (NIMH) collaborative study on the psychobiology of depression.

Perhaps such a relationship, which has preoccupied many textbook writers and theoreticians, should be abandoned along with involutional melancholia and a number of other diagnostic entities. However, as soon as we send one group of diagnostic categories to the graveyard, our colleagues at the task force on DSM-III will generate more for other researchers to either validate or invalidate.

The more intriguing issue is, when do we consider we have evidence for causation? What is the criterion for the definition of a cause? Discussions in this volume have reflected the differences in opinion as to what is meant by relative risk and what is meant by contributing or causal factors.

In medically oriented studies there is usually an implicit, but not always explicit, model to guide the researcher and clinician in deciding which factors are necessary and sufficient to constitute causation. This has best been explicated in the scientific literature of psychiatry by Wender (2). In the area of infectious diseases, for example, for a factor or agent to be designated as causal, it must be antecedent and necessary, that is, occurring in close to 100% of the population. A popular example is tuberculosis, in which the infectious factor is necessary as an antecedent, although a number of people infected with tuberculosis bacillus may not become clinically ill.

The question is whether or not the research data about life stress, particularly data dealing with psychosocial loss and separation, conform to that disease model, or if we must give up that model, as suggested by Paykel, and substitute one that is multifactorial. While the necessary and sufficient model is a form of the multifactorial model, it specifies a certain logical and temporal sequence. The model Paykel suggests is one in which each factor involved is not in itself necessary or sufficient but may be contributory and in some degree additive. The definition of the logic of such a model and its mathematical properties are probably being worked out best in the fields of cardiovascular and gastrointestinal epidemiology, in which such contributory factors as diet, smoking, and exercise have been identified.

With that digression into epistemology, let us look at the issue of the extent to which the data presented follow the multifactorial Paykel model. Here there is clear divergence. Brown presents impressive data that some kind of loss or threat is antecedent and necessary to a depressive disorder. He also elucidates the presence of an intimate relationship, number of children, and other psychosocial resources as relevant factors. On the other hand, Paykel and others indicate that only about one-fourth of those interviewed in large surveys of depressed samples, however defined clinically, have a clear definition of loss that can be identified as an antecedent. Thus one would say that loss and separation are neither antecedent necessary nor antecedent sufficient but are contributory, which may explain why Paykel has suggested a multifactorial model.

The chapter by Clayton and Darvish, along with several others, signals the direction in which the field should go. We are arriving at a point where we have exhausted the cross-sectional method of looking at a sample of persons at one point in time to determine whether they are within a depressive category, and we have also come beyond the method of looking at all people who are ever ill to make such a determination. I would suggest that the most powerful methodological design for the future may be to take one or more factors presumed or demonstrated to be associated with higher risk, such as loss, bereavement, or the closing of a factory, and follow such a sample prospectively through time to observe the emergence of the presumed psychopathology, in this case some form of clinical depression. This means using criteria agreed upon in advance and building into the prospective study an accurate assessment of the kinds of associated variables that determine whether or not a person subjected to this pathogenic stressor will meet the criteria for the emergence of the illness.

It is a reflection of the progress of the field that in reviewing the preceding chapters, I have pulled together at least five factor categories that seem to intervene between the occurrence of the event (in this case loss and separation) and the subsequent emergence, within some subset of those exposed to the event, of the illness. There is a convergence here: of those people exposed to loss and separation, between 15 and 20% at the end of 1 year have either persistent symptoms or some clinically definable condition. That convergence is in Paykel's calculations, in Clayton's discussion of the follow-up, and in the figure mentioned by Brown.

A brief differentiation follows among the five categories of variables that intervene to make the difference between the 80% of those individuals who make some adaptation to their loss and the 20% who are still depressed in some sense, clinically or otherwise, after 1 year. One variable is a genetically determined predisposition. This is best documented for the unipolar-bipolar group with manic depressives. A second variable is early life experiences of the individual, especially early losses. These are most frequently discussed by psychoanalysts, but Brown reports the importance of a woman's loss of her mother before the age of 11. Third is the presence of certain personality traits, however they are brought about. The most prominent personality characteristic discussed in the literature on depression is interpersonal dependency; others include a propensity to guilt or increased sensitivity to psychosocial approval or disapproval. My colleague in Washington, Hirschfeld, and I have begun to identify in an NIMH study some of these attributes in detail and to explore them empirically. A fourth variable is discussed in the studies of behaviorist Peter Lewinsohn (3). He refers to an inadequate repertoire of learned social skills which renders the depressive-prone individual less able than others to elicit a social reinforcer from the interpersonal environment, such as approval and other forms of environmental support. A fifth variable, perhaps the one that has emerged most recently, is the presence or absence of social supports in the individual's environment which can provide either additional aids or a burden of the nature that Brown indicates. These may include three or more children, low financial resources, the presence or absence of an intimate companion, or other forms of personal encouragement, support, and nurturance.

In discussing the foregoing chapters, I have attempted to relate them to other issues of current importance, such as the overriding issue of diagnostic criteria for a disorder as distinct from symptoms. A second issue is what do we mean by causation and under what circumstances will we be satisfied that we have a necessary or sufficient antecedent or contributory factor? Third, how do we design a set of empirical studies to deal with a phenomenon almost universally agreed upon: that only a fraction, perhaps one-fifth, of those individuals exposed to a loss will in the subsequent year manifest some clinically discernible level of symptoms and/or disorder? Progress will surely continue at a rapid rate in understanding the interaction between personality and environmental factors and in developing appropriate methodology for investigating these factors.

REFERENCES

1. Weissman, M. M., and Myers, J. K. (1979): Affective disorders in a U.S. urban community: The use of research diagnostic criteria. *Arch. Gen. Psychiatry (in press.)*
2. Wender, P. H. (1967): On necessary and sufficient conditions in psychiatric explanation. *Arch. Gen. Psychiatry,* 16:41–47.
3. Zeiss, A. M., Lewinsohn, P. M., and Munoz, R. F. (1978): Nonspecific improvement effects in depression using interpersonal, cognitive, and pleasant events focused treatments. Paper presented at the Western Psychological Association meeting, San Francisco, California.

Stress and Mental Disorder,
edited by James E. Barrett et al.
Raven Press, New York © 1979.

Life Events and Affective Illness

Arthur P. Schless

*University of Pennsylvania and Veterans Administration Hospital,
Philadelphia, Pennsylvania 19104*

The authors of the preceding chapters, as well as many other investigators, are concerned with the etiological significance of life events to affective disorders. There has been much controversy regarding this association; many studies report no existence of such an association (1,2). More recently, however, as Paykel has indicated, there has been a preponderance of positive studies of such an association (e.g., 3,5,7).

Many of the investigators in this volume, including Brown, Paykel, Dohrenwend and Dohrenwend, have pointed out a number of methodological issues that have led to difficulties in interpreting the various studies and in comparing results. These issues, for convenience, can be divided into patient-related and data-recording problems. Patient-related issues include those concerning the subject providing the data, such as how reliable he or she is and how comprehensive the subject is in reporting previous life events. The dating of the onset of illness is crucial but difficult, due not only to recall problems but also to the problem of accurately differentiating life events preceding illness from events that have been caused by the illness. Thus when a person loses a job and "becomes" depressed he may, in fact, have been depressed and been performing poorly, resulting in his losing his position. Data-recording issues include the item content and format of the testing instrument used. In other words, how appropriate, relevant, unambiguous, and comprehensive is the instrument used for data collection?

An additional problem is whether depressives are a special group of patients, i.e., whether they perceive stress differently from a nondepressed group of patients. For example, Beck speaks of a unique cognitive set that depressives exhibit. In our study (4), 73 hospitalized depressives were administered the Holmes and Rahe Schedule of Recent Events (SRE). We found that our depressed patients (see Table 1) ranked the events similarly on admission and discharge to the way that the original Holmes and Rahe sample ranked life events. However, we found that depressed inpatients viewed life events as more stressful than a comparison group of nondepressed subjects (see Table 2). The weights assigned were independent of patient's age, sex, severity of depression, and previous experience of the event. The greater weight was still obtained when the

141

TABLE 1. *Depressives rank life events*

Event	Ranking by Holmes and Rahe	Ranking by depressed patients	
		Admission	Discharge
Death of spouse	1	1	1
Divorce	2	2	5
Marital separation	3	4	2
Jail term	4	5	8
Death—close family	5	3	3
Personal injury or illness	6	6	4

patient had symptomatically improved, suggesting that factors such as the personality of the patient are likely to influence the weighting process. This study emphasizes that the significance of the events to the individual must be understood. A depressive patient may need fewer stressful events to be equivalent in stressfulness to a given number of events than a nondepressive experiences. Barrett indicated that certain events may be more stressful for certain categories of diagnoses.

Another issue is: what is the appropriate control group for a study exploring the significance of life events to affective disorder? Should they be hospitalized or not? We approached this problem in one study (5) by having two control groups: (a) nonpsychiatrically ill medical and surgical inpatients matched for age, sex, and socioeconomic class, and (b) healthy community residents independently studied by Myers. Psychiatric patients reported significantly more events per year (6.5 ± 0.5) than did medical-surgical patients (4.6 ± 0.4), who in turn reported more than controls (2.3 ± 0.3). There was no significant difference in specific life event histories in the three groups. This study raises the possibility of using more than one control group in a given study.

To address some of the data-gathering problems and to provide an instrument that would meet some of the needs of present-day investigators, we have been

TABLE 2. *Depressives weigh life events*

Life events	Weights by Holmes and Rahe	Weights by depressed patients	
		Admission	Discharge
Death of spouse	100	113	114
Divorce	73	91	81
Marital separation	65	75	84
Jail Term	63	68	60
Death—close family	63	79	82
Personal injury or illness	53	67	82

developing a new instrument, the PERI-M. This is a modification of the Psychiatric Epidemiology Research Instrument developed by Dohrenwend and Dohrenwend. The modification is by a team headed by Dr. Robert Hirshfeld and the instrument is for use by the National Institute of Mental Health (NIMH) Collaborative Depression Study. The kinds of information gathered by this instrument include event name and number, event central figure, and date of event and relation to illness onset. A useful feature of the instrument (from the Dohrenwends) is the use of probes to elicit further information about events that have occurred, such as if the subject anticipated the event, had control over it, found the event to be desirous, or how it affected the person's self-esteem. An additional instrument we are using is a Personal Resources Inventory designed by Dr. Paula Clayton.

We have used the PERI-M as well as several other instruments to determine if we could improve the quantity of data obtained by interviewing a coinformant at the same time as the patient. A consistent finding that has emerged from 130 patients is that approximately 29% of new information is collected when a coinformant is interviewed in addition to the patient alone (6). This finding is consistent over 11 categories of events (Table 3). A validity check with knowl-

TABLE 3. *Contribution of coinformant: Percent increase in events in each category*

Event	Increase (%)	Event	Increase (%)
School	24	Money and financial	25
Work	29	Childbirth related	32
Love and marriage	33	Family and household	29
Health	25	Residence	48
Crime and legal	35	Personal	29
		Death	52

edgable third parties confirmed that approximately 80% of events reported by subjects and coinformants actually happened. We concluded that studies may benefit from separate interviews with patient and coinformant with pooling of the positive responses obtained from the two sources.

In conclusion, investigators are now exploring not only life events and specificity of these events but social supports of the individual as well as vulnerabilities and characteristics of the individual, such as personality factors, that will help explain the individual's reaction to stress.

REFERENCES

1. Hudgens, R. W., Morrison, J. R., and Barchka, R. G. (1967): Life events and onset of primary affective disorders: A study of 40 hospitalized patients and 40 controls. *Arch. Gen. Psychiatry,* 16:134–145.
2. Morrison, J. R., Hudgens, R. W., and Barchka, R. G. (1968): Life events and psychiatric illness. *Br. J. Psychiatry,* 114:423–432.

3. Paykel, E. S., Myers, J. K., Dienet, M. N., Klerman, G. L., Lindenthal, J. J., and Pepper, M. P. (1969): Life events and depression: A controlled study. *Arch. Gen. Psychiatry,* 21:753–760.
4. Schless, A. P., Schwartz, L., Goetz, C., and Mendels, J. (1974): How depressives view the significance of life events. *Br. J. Psychiatry,* 125:406–410.
5. Schless, A. P., Teichman, A., Mendels, J., and DiGiacomo, J. N. (1977): The role of stress as a precipitating factor of psychiatric illness. *Br. J. Psychiatry,* 130:19–22.
6. Schless, A. P., and Mendels, J. (1978): The value of interviewing family and friends in assessing life stressors. *Arch. Gen. Psychiatry,* 35:565–567.
7. Uhlenhuth, E. H., and Paykel, E. S. (1973): Symptom intensity and life events. *Arch. Gen. Psychiatry,* 28:473–477.

Stress and Mental Disorder,
edited by James E. Barrett et al.
Raven Press, New York © 1979.

General Discussion, Part II

Dr. George Winokur: There is a problem with precipitating factors. They are like the evanescent effect of a large thunderstorm over a cornfield in Iowa. In that sense they are trivial. It is not that they are unimportant to the individual, but they are omnipresent and seem to be found in all kinds of depressions. Therefore, I think that the important thing to ask ourselves is what the legitimate use of life events could be in further research. In my opinion, they shoud be used to separate our subcategories of psychiatric illnesses, particularly depressive illnesses. Paykel says this does not work between endogenous and reactive. We tried to evaluate the role of life events between depressive spectrum patients, i.e., depressed patients who had a family history of alcoholism versus pure depressive patients who had a family history of depression; life events did not separate these two groups either. Both had a high degree of precipitating factors, but they were not different from each other. What seemed to work in separating depression spectrum patients from pure depressives is the first cousin of the precipitating factor, namely, a stormy personal life.

When we looked at our depression spectrum patients, a large group with a family history of alcoholism (all women), they had lots of divorces, many marital problems, and frequent interpersonal difficulties. The pure depressives, a group with a family history of only depression, had none of these things. For practical purposes, the pure depressives simply had ordinary personality backgrounds.

In the long run, perhaps the response to precipitating factors would differentitate subgroups and should be evaluated. In a sense, personality problems versus precipitating factors may pertain to the difference of definition between reactive versus neurotic depression. Reactive depression implies that a person is depressed because of precipitating factors. Neurotic depression implies that a person has had a stormy life prior to the time he became depressed and may or may not have responded to precipitating factors. I think the concept of neurotic depression is closer to the one that will be usable in the long run in separating out groups. This may be the direction we should go in evaluating the effects of precipitating factors. They should be evaluated on the basis of a lifelong propensity to respond, i.e., a reactive personality.

Dr. Robert Spitzer: I think Dr. Klerman may have been incorrect in assuming that Dr. Brown's chapter supports the notion of a necessary factor. As I recall, only two-thirds of the patients with depression had these severe events, and two-thirds is not 100%.

In terms of methodology, I was pleased to note that apparently the approach taken to the measurement of a severe event is similar to the approach that we have taken in the DSM-III attempt at a multiaxial system, in that one axis measures psychosocial stress. We tried a variety of approaches and finally settled on the one that we try to estimate the severity in terms of how the hypothetically "normal" person would react given that event and the individual's total life circumstance. I gather that is similar to the approach that Dr. Brown used. Are there more details as to just how that measurement is made, and how you can keep that separate from the individual's reaction to the life events?

Dr. Brown: It is hopeless to get a general measure of stress of events. For schizophrenia, we have shown that positive events, such as falling in love, can probably contribute to a schizophrenic breakdown. Each event in the depression study was described by 28 dimensions—past experience of such an event, expectedness of the event, immediate reactions to it, and so on. For clinical depression, only one of the 28 proved to be important. That is, when severity of long-term threat was taken into account, none of the other dimensions—such as amount of change in routine brought about by the event—contributed to onset of depression. One job now, as Dr. Barrett was implying, is to go on to look at conditions, such as anxiety or depressive disorders, with particularly marked anxiety components. For such conditions, other dimensions may be important; we have already collected some evidence for this. For instance, the unresolved threat implicit in an event may be particularly important in anxiety conditions.

I have given a preliminary account of our measurement process in the Dohrenwend book and a much fuller one in our recent book *Social Origins of Depression*. Briefly, the interviewer gives to a meeting of raters the circumstances, past and present, surrounding each event, such as the fact that the woman who has just learned she is pregnant lives in one room and she has already another child. However, the interviewer holds back information about psychiatric disturbance or about how the woman reacted. We make the judgment in terms of how most women would be expected to react in terms of threat with the particular biographical circumstances surrounding the event. Thus she could sometimes tell us she was overjoyed by the pregnancy, but the raters wouldn't know that; it would be disregarded. A judgment about degree of threat would be made in terms of how most women would be expected to react. This approach gives a conservative estimate of the importance of life events. This is one reason why I said our estimate of two-thirds of depressed women having a severely threatening event of etiological importance was probably conservative. I think this kind of conclusion logically follows from the method.

Dr. Samuel Guze: Dr. Barrett, were your samples controlled for age? Different categories of life events may be significant at different ages.

With respect to assessing life stress, we have concentrated on the problems of defining a stress and of estimating the significance of a stress to the individual, but we have not dealt with defining the onset of illness. This problem is not limited to psychiatry. There are analogous problems in all of medicine. It is difficult to determine when cancer of the colon, coronary artery disease, or diabetes begin; it is difficult to date the onset of pulmonary tuberculosis. Before the advent of the chest roentgenogram, it was impossible. It may be that processes that ultimately will result in severe clinical depression or in a manic episode or in a psychotic break in schizophrenia have been set in motion many months before, so that focusing on life events in any finite period prior to the apparent onset of illness may be a mistake. Thus we must recognize that we may not be dealing with precipitating events related to the onset of illness but to those related to the intensification of symptoms or hospitalization—important observations, but obviously not the same as studying etiology.

Dr. Barrett: In relation to the particular disorders that we are examining, we are looking at age and sex as well as at other demographic variables. I can make some general remarks about the background characteristics of our subjects. Their ages ranged from 20 to 65, but more than two-thirds were in the age range 30 to 60. My impression is that there was some relationship between chronic depression and the older subjects, and that there was a relationship between panic anxiety and the relatively younger subjects. On the other hand, chronic depression (chronic and intermittent minor depressive disorder) often begins very young, or at least these subjects report their symptoms as being "lifelong." It is not clear why the younger depressives do not respond to the advertisement.

I agree that it is difficult to date the actual onset of a disorder, when the pathology begins as opposed to when the clinical syndrome became evident. In my data, let me stress again that I am dealing only with precipitating events for a particular disorder. I think in your comment you were talking about etiological events, events which were truly causative of a particular disorder. This is a very important area to study, and Dr. Brown has attempted to do so. My study, however, of necessity focused on precipitating events. Even here there were some problems. For chronic depression, for example, we were recording the occurrence of events in the previous 6 months, but they should probably not be classified as precipitants because this disorder is usually described as being lifelong, or at least persistent for many years. Having symptoms for at least 2 years is one of the defining characteristics of the category.

Panic anxiety, on the other hand, has a particularly clear date of onset. People are able to tell you the day and the hour of their first panic attack. They remember it with great vividness, often go to a hospital emergency ward because they think they are going to die, and so on. It is roughly similar for episodic minor depressive disorder; here individuals can tell you quite precisely that they were different from their usual self following a particular event, will go on to describe a full depressive syndrome which then subsides, and they then go back to their usual selves. For these latter groups, we can talk about precipitating events in the previous 6 months; but, as you say, we can say nothing about causative events or when they occurred.

Dr. Weissman: Dr. Guze made a point important to many of us trained in chronic disease epidemiology, and that is trying to date the exact time ot onset for any chronic disease. I think it is important that we begin to think of some psychiatric disorders in these categories. It's difficult, yet critical.

Dr. Paykel: I would like to respond to Dr. Guze's point. I think there are two issues; one is methodological and one substantive. The methodological issue is whether we are really recording events which are antecedents to the depression rather than those which are consequences. Certainly a large proportion of depressive onsets can be dated reasonably. With some of the other disorders, it is much harder. An alternative and very useful approach is Brown's judgment as to whether events appear to be independent of symptoms. There is a group of events that do appear to be highly external to the person so that it is hard to conceive that he would have caused them.

However, there is also a substantive issue and this is whether we should not be more subtle about our causative concepts. I found Dr. Klerman's concept of necessary and sufficient conditions very useful. It seems clear from the life event studies and indeed from the studies of almost any etiological factor in depression that there is no such thing as a necessary condition for the onset of depression. Some depressions do not appear to be preceded by life events; some do not appear to be accompanied by a family history. Whatever you look at, there are some exceptions, and you must adopt a model that sees different elements contributing to causation. One of these may be the occurrence of social stresses which occur after the onset. We are presently trying to look at this in a group of depressives. It may be that, rather like cancer, there is one point at which the cell starts to multiply, but there are other points at which the cells start to become implanted throughout the body or in which something changes immunologically. There can be a whole series of steps that lead to the fully developed condition. These should not be regarded as trivial. They may be very important in determining in whom the full condition develops and in whom it does not.

Dr. Edward Sachar: With respect to cancer, it has been demonstrated that patients with abdominal cancer often present before any medical signs with an unusual depressive syndrome consisting of vague feelings of apprehension, doom, and so on. Also, we must remember that the major depressive disorders are episodic, so that we must account for a periodic vulnerability. Here a relevant medical parallel might be an interesting disorder called periodic neutropenia in which the white cell count will suddenly drop, unbeknownst to the patients, and at that point they become extremely susceptible to infection, while at another point they do not have that vulnerability.

Dr. Clayton quite appropriately emphasized many of the similarities between a subgroup of her mourning subjects and patients with typical depressive syndromes, particularly on check-lists of presence or absence of depressive symptoms. However, I think we should be aware also that there may be qualitative differences as well. The mourning patients often experience the symptoms much more intermittently during the day than typical depressed patients. We also should not forget that the patients that we see with clinical depression, who go on to respond to imipramine, are in general quite emphatic that their depressions do not feel similar to the way they felt when they were mourning and bereaved. They can make the distinction.

Dr. Stephen Locke: I am intrigued at the direction the discussion has taken recently, particularly with reference to cancer, because we have been looking at the influence of psychosocial factors, including life change stress, on immune function, specifically, cell-mediated immunity in humans. This has some direct relevance to two areas that have come up in the discussion. One is Dr. Clayton's work on bereavement, specifically, her presentation of data suggesting that there is a subset of grieving women who manifest symptoms which, as Dr. Sachar pointed out, are often associated with the type of severe depression that should be responsive to antidepressants. What is curious about this subset of women is that they might be women who also manifest physical illnesses represented by their increased frequency of hospitalization and who, therefore, might be women who also manifest diminished immune function.

There is a study, reported in the *Lancet* last April by Bartrop and associates from Australia, which reported that recently bereaved spouses had depressed cell-mediated immunity. This group had observed that the response of white blood cells to experimental mitogens (agents that cause replication of white blood cells) was depressed significantly in spouses, both men and women, 6 weeks postbereavement in comparison to matched, nonbereaved controls.

In reference to Dr. Guze's point about the difficulty in defining outcome measures from the standpoint of defining the onset of the disease, it might be useful to think in terms of those biological measures which vary in analog fashion, taking into account periodicity and inherent biological rhythms. These biological measures may vary in association with combinations of life events and other psychosocial moderating variables and lead to alterations in responsiveness to stress.

An example of what I have in mind would be the work with the catecholamines that Dr. Shildkraut, Dr. Shatzberg, Dr. Maas, and others have been doing. It might be possible, rather than waiting for the presence of symptoms to mark the onset of disease, to begin to look at changes in biological measures (such as catecholamine metabolites) or changes in cell-mediated immune function.

Dr. Clayton: To clarify, in the subset of people who were still depressed at 1 year, there were equal percentages of men and women, and they were no more likely to be hospitalized. In fact, it was very hard to distinguish them from the rest of the group except that they were more likely to have had a history of a preexisting psychiatric illness, such as alcoholism, primary affective disorder, and hysteria. One additional thing which I have not yet done is look at the family histories of the entire group. It may be those with family histories of alcoholism or primary affective disorder would help to predict who was still depressed at 1 year.

Dr. Brown: When I first came into psychiatry 20 years ago, it was not uncommon to come across psychiatrists talking along the lines: "He couldn't have been schizophrenic because he got better." I think progress in psychiatry has been held up by the circularity of such suggestions: that outcome variables or causal variables should be taken into account in diagnostic procedures. It led to a mess from which we are only just beginning to emerge in the sense of moving from the use of categories such as "reactive" and "endogenous" depression, but there is a feeling we must create others to take their place. It is a highly illogical way of thinking about diagnosis. If we want to establish that certain kinds of depressive condition are more reactive, or the like, we should first establish categories of depression strictly on clinical grounds and, only then, see whether they relate to environmental factors, and so on. The reactive/endogenous distinction has recently done badly when this procedure has been employed. In other words, diagnosis should be a matter of symptomatology. Only when this is done should we try to establish links with other things. But in suggesting this I think I would disagree with Dr. Clayton. I cannot see any reason why the people she is talking about are not clinically depressed.

Dr. Donald F. Klein: Dr. Clayton, do you have the information concerning the recovery times of the various components of the depressive syndrome following bereavement? I distinguish between consummatory pleasures that result in a direct decrease in drive tensions, as with food and sex, and appetitive pleasures that have evolved during the course of striving for consummatory pleasures, as in pursuit or chase activities, or such derivatives as sports. The endogenomorphic depressions are characterized by inhibition of both consummatory and appetitive pleasure responses, whereas the sort of depressions often referred to as reactive, neurotic, or characterological are primarily characterized by appetitive inhibitions. Therefore, I am particularly interested in prolonged anorexia as a qualitative feature that may distinguish between normal grief and development of pathological depression. Do you have data indicating what the recovery time is for anorexia in the bereaved? This might furnish a valuable guideline as to when an intervention, such as a tricyclic antidepressant, might be called for.

Dr. Clayton: In the random sample of 109 widows and widowers, with an average age of 61, we did a 3- to 4-month follow-up on a subsample, chiefly because we were still doing intake interviews at 3 to 4 months. We did the last 65 people who entered into the study. At 1 year, we followed up the entire sample. I found that anorexia was reported at 1 month by 46% of the sample, 3 to 4 months by 25%, and at 1 year by 14%. Weight loss was reported at 1 month by 37% of the sample, at 3 to 4 months by 18%, and 1 year by 17%. Indeed, it does look as if the recovery of these functions has begun at 3 to 4 months and that it changes little over the year. The same would not be true of sleep disturbance, as it is a much more troublesome symptom.

Parkes reports:[1]

Nineteen (86%) widows claimed that they lost their appetite during the first month of bereavement, and in 15 this brought about recognized loss of weight. Six widows lost 14 lbs. or more in the course of the first month, and only one gained weight during this period. After the end of the first month, however, anorexia and weight loss were much less common, and from the third month onward it was weight gain that was more likely to be regarded as a problem.

In the book by Glick, Weiss, and Parkes, *The First Year of Bereavement,* Parkes confirms this without giving frequencies. He says:

In time some found the weight loss to be not altogether displeasing—our one year interviews suggest that they rather like the improvement in their figures, and there was not at any point fear that anorexia might be entrenched as there was in relation to insomnia.

Dr. Klein: I would like to extend what Klerman just said, that we must go from cross-sectional to longitudinal. I suggest we have to go further than that, from longitudinal to experimental.

I think some of us have doubts about whether the sort of people Dr. Brown refers to as depressed are psychiatrically ill. The major issue is autonomy of mood. What makes us think there is something pathologically wrong with the mood-regulatory mechanisms is that over and above comprehensible unhappiness is the fact that if their life

---

[1] Parkes, C. M. (1970): The first year of bereavement. *Psychiatry,* 33:461.

circumstances are changed in a positive direction, their mood still does not improve. Somebody gets fired, and clinical depression develops. The restoration of his job does not result in his mood brightening. Then we are sure there is something pathologically wrong with this person, not just realistic unhappiness. I'm not sure about Dr. Brown's subjects.

The question is, can an experimental paradigm be applied? I think Dr. Brown is quite right that the more severe type of antecedent seems to precipitate depression. However, there are irreversible severe antecedents, such as the death of a spouse, and severe antecedents, such as loss of a job, which, in principle, are reversible. I suggest that one could segregate out the potentially reversible severe antecedents and make an experimental attack on the problem. Which of these people with depressive symptomatology would not respond to an appropriate subsidy, perhaps an NIMH grant? What does Dr. Brown think would happen to the mood of his unemployed women, in their single rooms, with three children, if they received a gift of $1,000?

Dr. Brown: My colleagues and I believe (and this includes the psychiatrists who saw these women in their own homes) that they were clinically depressed. For example, the majority of the women rated as cases clearly met Feighner-like criteria. But I want to make the point that we think that the feelings of hopelessness of most of the women were justified. There were real problems; for example, those with a loss were not readily going to restore what had been lost or gain suitable alternatives. I think such an experimental approach is difficult because actually a husband has gone off, the husband is in prison, they have been rehoused from the house they have been in for 50 years, and so on. But I think the issue is an important one. Some events, of course, are reversible. As an example: one of the psychiatrists working with us went back to see one of the women 3 weeks after we had seen her. We had had no doubts that she was quite severely chronically depressed. In those 3 weeks she learned she was being rehoused and, when the psychiatrist saw her, she had far fewer symptoms. I think it is possible and useful to segregate out the reversible events. We do not know what would happen, but I suspect on occasions that a depressive disorder can be reversed very quickly given the restoration of something lost. The trouble is that for most of these women we saw, we could imagine no easy restoration without the help of God.

Stress and Mental Disorder,
edited by James E. Barrett et al.
Raven Press, New York © 1979.

Stress, Adaptation, and Affective Disorders*

Gerald L. Klerman

Alcohol, Drug Abuse, and Mental Health Administration, Rockville, Maryland 20857

It is a great pleasure for me to give the Samuel Hamilton Address. One of the unfortunate consequences of my being appointed as Administrator of the Alcohol, Drug Abuse, and Mental Health Administration was the judgment that I resign in midterm as president of the American Psychopathological Association because of a possible conflict of interest. I am indebted to the Council for extending to me the invitation to undertake the Samuel Hamilton Address which is usually the prerogative of the president.

In my chapter, I shall attempt to relate the topic of this volume, stress and mental disorder, to several recurrent problems in the study of clinical psychopathology of the affective disorders, depression and elations. Specifically, I approach the affective disorders from an adaptational approach. Adaptation is a concept common to biology, ethology, psychology, and physiology. As such it should have relevance to theoretical and clinical problems in psychopathology. Application of this concept to the data on stress and depression will integrate research findings from many areas and promote better understanding of the similarities and differences between the normal emotional state and the clinical disorder. Moreover, I believe an adaptational approach will help reconcile some of the current theoretical divisions in the field, especially the persisting controversy as to the relevance of biologic and psychosocial variables in the nature and causation of affective disorders.

THEORETICAL ASPECTS OF AFFECTIVE STATES, INCLUDING DEPRESSION

An adaptational approach views clinical states, including depressions, as a component of the adaptive responses of the human organism to its environments, including the biologic and psychosocial environments. In understanding this adaptation, we must determine whether the processes involved in both the initiation and perpetuation of the clinical disorder are similar to those processes involved in the normal emotional states, particularly depression. A definitive answer to this question would resolve a continuing controversy as to whether the clinical depressive states are quantitative extensions of the normal mood of depression encountered in everyday life, or whether they are qualitatively different.

---

* Samuel Hamilton address.

The modern concept of adaptation derives from Darwin's theory of evolution. According to the strictest criterion of evolutionary theory from the phylogenetic viewpoint, an anatomical structure, a behavior trait, or an emotion is adaptive if it promotes the survival of the species. Similarly, from the ontogenetic viewpoint, a trait or behavior is adaptive to the extent that it promotes the growth and survival of an individual member of the species. Darwin himself pioneered in the application of an evolutionary approach to behavior, including emotional responses. As Plutchik (15) has described, Darwin's theory of evolution explicitly states the thesis that there existed an evolution not only of morphologic structures but also of what Darwin called "mental and expressive capacities." To establish his general thesis, Darwin (6) collected material to document the continuity of emotional expression in lower animals, as well as primates and humans. However, these ideas and observations lay dormant for many decades.

Since World War II, there has been a remarkable upsurge of interest in the comparative biology of emotional states; in this upsurge, the field of ethology has emerged as a specialized area overlapping studies of animal behavior in psychology and zoology. Much of this research involves a significant convergence of findings from neurobiology, ethology, and comparative psychology. Studies of human infant development, particularly those following psychoanalytic theories, have paralleled this animal research. Studies of mammalian behavior, particularly of the primate infant and child development, have produced a growing body of evidence about the nature of the mother-child bond of primates. Depression and other emotional states have an important function in the regulation of these bonds.

It is now well substantiated that all mammals inherit complex behavioral systems that promote and reinforce the mother-infant attachment and, as a consequence, facilitate the formation of social groups. In this context, depression arises as the emotional response to the actual or threatened disruption of the mother-infant attachment bond. These behavioral systems and the related affective expressive behaviors have been profoundly adaptive for both the species and the individual over the millenia. They have facilitated the biologic survival of infant mammals during the long period of extrauterine development before the mammals achieve self-sufficiency. Moreover, these biobehavioral systems encourage social learning, which has also been highly adaptive in the evolutionary survival of mammals. Mammals, unlike lower species, have a large repertoire of learned responses, which has enabled them to react appropriately to changes produced by the environment, including changes in the composition of social groups. When the maternal bond of mammalian species is broken by separation and loss, a typical behavior pattern emerges in which the initial stage is characterized by anxiety, agitation, protest, and increased psychomotor activity, followed by a phase of social withdrawal and decreased motor activity. It now appears certain that the animal reactions best studied in dogs and primates in response to separation and loss are so similar to human sadness that few observers doubt the continuity between the animal and the human infant experience.

I have previously discussed the adaptive functions of affective states in general (10). The adaptive view lends importance expecially to the research on animal models, which relates stress in general and the stress of separation in particular to clinical states (19). The adaptive function of depressive affect as a signal for social communication has been demonstrated by studies in dogs (20,23), primates (8,9), and human infants. More recently, the trend in research has moved from naturalistic observations to the experimental induction of depression by various modes of separation and loss. These animal models are of great theoretical significance. Until the late 1960s, the nearest approximations of an animal model of depression were those produced pharmacologically by inducing central nervous system (CNS) depletion of amines, usually with reserpine or benzoquinoline. Although the pharmacologic model proved useful for screening antidepressant drugs in pharmaceutical firms and for the investigation of the neuropharmacologic actions of the biogenic amines, it was deficient as a behavioral model. The animal models based on separation and loss have prima facie behavioral validity. Not only do they replicate the reactions described in human infants and in animals studied naturalistically, but they provide experimental means of testing hypotheses about delayed behavioral, cognitive, and social consequences of separation in infants. Such models also provide data that would be relevant for testing the many clinical theories relating the vulnerability of adults to depression based on their early life experiences in infancy and childhood. Moreover, efforts can be made to correlate CNS biochemical and electrophysiologic changes in the animals who are experiencing separation and loss as an attempt to define the physiologic mechanisms.

Seligman (21) has proposed another animal model of depression, based on learned helplessness. At first it would appear to be difficult to reconcile these data into a universal theory of loss as a stressor specific to depression.

Discussion of the experimental animal models for depression leads to questions about the psychosocial mechanisms by which depression is initiated and mediated. Biologic evolution has produced in mammals the physiologic and biochemical capacity to generate these emotional responses. The question now arises as to the specific neuroanatomical and neurochemical mechanisms whereby these affective behaviors are initiated, perpetuated, and, perhaps even more importantly, terminated. These questions have been best investigated for anxiety and fear, emotions closely related clinically and developmentally to depression and sadness. Following the research of Cannon (3), it has been accepted that anxiety and fear serve the function of arousing the organism for preparation for "fight or flight" and that this is achieved via the complex neuroendocrine system, especially involving the central release of adrenergic substances. When we attempt a similar analysis of possible functions and mechanisms involved in depression, however, less agreement is evident. The findings in a small number of experimental studies are inconclusive. One answer to defining the physiologic function of depression has been offered by Engel (7) and Schmale (18) and their associates at the University of Rochester. Their thesis is that depression involved "conservation and withdrawal" with reduction of psychomotor activity, lowered metabolism, and increased parasympathetic activity as a mode of conserving energy in the face of threat to survival. While this hypothesis may be consistent with observations of infantile states, it is not supported by results in clinical adult disorders. Rather than being associated with conservation, depressive disorders are often accompanied by increased adrenocortical activity, signs of anxiety and tension, and increased psychomotor activity.

ADAPTIVE FUNCTION OF CLINICAL DEPRESSIONS

Separation and loss are specific forms of stress. Current interest in these stressors is part of the renewed general interest in stress research as it applies not only to mental disorders but also to medical disorders, such as cardiovascular and gastrointestinal diseases. The current research on stress has a long history. Much of it is reviewed in this volume and also at the meeting organized by Rose and his associates at Boston University in October 1977. The scientific background of this work includes the psychosomatic movement of the 1940s and early 1950s, whose clinical leaders included Franz Alexander and H. G. Wolff, and the physiologic investigations of the pituitary adrenocortical systems initiated by Selye (22).

In psychiatric thinking, the theoretical background for the concepts of stress derive from the teachings of Adolf Meyer (12), who emphasized the continuity between normal experience and clinical disorders. Meyer had been strongly influenced by Darwin, and his attempt to build a science of "psychobiology" was based on his conviction that psychiatric conditions are the reaction of human organisms to the vicissitudes of life. In Meyer's desire to enlarge the scope of relevant variables in the adaptive process, he paid great attention to factors in the social environment, and he and his students often seemed to depreciate factors of the biologic environment. Meyer's psychobiologic approach was an explicit reaction against what was then believed to be a rigid deterministic application of biology to psychiatry which relegated life experience, personality, (or, as Meyer called it, habits), and emotions to minor roles in the genesis of mental illness.

Meyer's views had particular importance in the United States and Britain in the first half of the 20th century. After the Civil War and until World War I, the dominant American concepts of nature in mental illness reflected the tenets of Social Darwinism. These claimed that the mentally ill are by heredity or social position "unfit to survive in the new industrial order." Nineteenth century psychiatrists (2) adopted these views and justified attitudes of therapeutic pessimism as "scientific" by maintaining a narrow definition of the biologic variables considered causative in mental illness. Thus Social Darwinism provided a vindication of the existing social order and justified viewing the mentally ill as failures, appropriately relegating them to the large public institutions and mental hospitals created in the second half of the 19th century.

Today, we see in the current controversies over sociobiology a similar debate over the social consequences of new biologic theory, especially genetics. My adaptational approach to depression has some similarities to the approach to social behavior developed by the Harvard sociobiologists, particularly Wilson (26) and DeVore. The newer biologic disciplines, particularly behavior genetics and neurochemistry, allow us to formulate hypotheses as to functions and mechanisms of behavior with a degree of specificity not previously available. At the same time, there has been a growth of sophistication in the social sciences, much of which is reflected in the heightened quality of research on social stress and life events as specific stressors. Nevertheless, attempts to view the scientific evidence dispassionately are often interfered with by controversies deriving from professional ideology, whether these concern sociobiology or psychobiology.

LOSS AND SEPARATION AS PRECIPITATING EVENTS FROM DEPRESSION

Although loss and separation serve as the precipitants of depression in mammals and children, the research on adults indicates that the specificity of this relationship is far from resolved. In fact, the trends reported in recent years and summarized in this volume indicate that loss and separation are not universal antecedent events in all clinical depressions; other stressors often serve as precipitants. In a significant proportion of individual depressive episodes, no apparent antecedent psychosocial external stressor can be identified. At best, loss and separation account for about 25% of precipitating events in the total sample of depressed patients. Depressed patients seem more susceptible to precipitating events at the onset of discrete episodes as compared to normal controls or schizophrenics, but loss and separation alone cannot account for the total variance.

There is evidence that depression will not develop in all individuals who are exposed to loss and separation. Obviously, other factors are involved. Loss and separation are not specific to clinical depression but may serve as precipitating events for a wide variety of clinical conditions, not only psychiatric but also general medical.

Therefore, an attempt to develop a theory based on one category of environmental stressor, psychosocial loss and separation, is insufficient. This factor is neither necessary nor sufficient to account for the clinical disorder. Loss and separation call for an adaptive response which most individuals are able to make. Only about 10 to 20% of individuals experiencing loss and separation of a family member have persistent depressive symptoms at the end of 1 year. This is the conclusion of studies of bereavement and of other loss and separations as reported by Paykel (14), Parkes and Brown (13), Clayton et al. (4), and others. Thus, as painful and disruptive as the depressive response to loss and separation in adults may be, it is usually time-limited, seldom lasting more than 6 to 9 months. Other psychosocial stressors less intense and personally significant than the death of a spouse and child are equally time-limited.

We must conclude that although environmental stressors, particularly psychosocial loss, play a role in the timing and precipitation of acute depressions, these events are neither universal nor specific. We have yet to determine why certain individuals are able to cope with stressors of loss and separation, while others fail in their adaptive efforts and subsequently develop clinical symptoms. A number of alternative factors have been proposed.

One of these factors is genetically determined hereditary predisposition, as has been documented in both unipolar and bipolar affective disorder. Another factor is individual differences in early life experiences, which may predispose the individual to conditioned sensitivity to loss and dependency. This concept has been proposed by psychodynamic theorists and documented in part by several studies of child development. We must also consider the behaviorists' contingencies which relate propensity to depression, loss of self-esteem, and feelings of helplessness or worthlessness to an inadequate repertoire of learned social skills. Still another theory deals with absence of social supports to provide substitute attachments and financial, social, and religious assistance.

My current formulation is that the adult depressive episode represents a vain attempt on the part of the individual to adapt. Clinical depressions are maladaptive outcomes of partially successful efforts at adaptation.

At this point, I wish to refer to a parallel concept in physiology, that of homeostasis. The concept of homeostasis was conceived by Cannon (3) and based on the earlier research by Bernard on the internal milieu. The concept of homeostasis has been extended to psychology to apply to the internal psychologic forces in personality akin to the physiologic balance. Richards (16,17), Nobel Laureate, argued that in studying disease it is necessary to examine the failures of homeostasis as well as those mechanisms that maintain homeostasis in normal states. He argued that there are limits to the homeostatic capabilities of the physiologic organism. Similarly, I propose that there are limits to the capability of the organism to make psychosocial adaptations.

CLINICAL ADULT DEPRESSION AS A MALADAPTIVE STATE

The question may be asked: In what way is the clinical adult depressive state maladaptive? In normals, depression serves as an important signal function to draw attention to the organism. In the clinical state, there are at least a number of considerations that lead to the conclusion that the clinical state is maladaptive.

Mortality

Survival of the species in the individual is the ultimate adaptive criterion in the Darwinian sense. Suicide is one of the forms of mortality associated with depression; as many as 15 to 30% of individuals with clinical depressions die by suicide, according to long-term follow-up studies. Recent reports from Winokur and associates (1,27) in Iowa indicate not only that death by suicide occurs but that chronically depressed individuals not treated intensively with electroconvulsive therapy and/or antidepressant drugs have a higher death rate due to cardiovascular disorders. Thus the chronically depressed individual is at greater risk for reduced survival, whether from self-inflicted attempts or from greater susceptibility to cardiovascular or other illness (11).

Fertility

Studies of marriage and fertility of patients with affective disorders indicate a general similarity of these factors to the general population. This may be due in part to the usual age of onset of depressions, which is in the 20s and 30s. In contrast to schizophrenics, who have a lower-than-normal fertility rate, affective illness does not interfere with fertility.

Child Rearing

While there may be no impairment of fertility and reproductive capacity in depressive individuals, there is strong evidence (25) that the persistence of a depressive state, particularly in the mother, interferes with the capacity for parenting, expecially the nurturance, emotional support, and affective roles within the family traditionally associated with the woman. Weissman and I (24) recently reviewed evidence that strongly indicates that women are more prone to depression, in the ratio of 2:1 or 3:1. In speculating on the possible basis of this sex difference, one line of investigation has proposed that through the centuries the psychobiologic processes reinforcing the maintenance of attachment bonds may have been selectively adaptive for females in the mammalian species who in conventional settings are responsible for child-rearing functions, at least in the child's early years. What effect modern urban living and women's liberation will have on this function remains to be determined.

Elicitation of Social Support

In the normal situation, depressed individuals elicit support, encouragement, assistance, and nurturance from the social environment, particularly from family members. Voice pattern, posture, facial expression, and verbal content serve to bring forth assistance. Recent research by social psychologists and sociologists (5), however, indicates that a biphasic sequence is involved. The assistance and support is most likely to occur in the early stages of a depressed response, and most likely with normal conditions. As time proceeds, however, the response of those in the environment is to become less supportive, increasingly hostile, irritable, and negativistic. The depressed individual is then often blamed for his or her own misfortune. Ascription of responsibility and blame and pejorative labeling may also occur.

In therapeutic settings and in sophisticated families, such labeling may include not only moralistic judgments as to the patient's worth but also statements about psychodynamic motivations and traits, such as his or her dependence, manipulation, identification with parents, and so on. While these judgments may have relevance and truth, they are of little value in helping to modify the behavior of the depressed individual; rather, they usually only reinforce the feeling of helplessness and worthlessness and serve to further distance the depressed individual. It is not clear whether this biphasic distancing phenomenon is a function merely of duration of the depressed state or of intensity, as occurs in the clinical state.

Diminished Social Participation by the Patient

Clinical depressed states distinguished from normal states involve a period of withdrawal and decreased social participation, including decreased sexual activity and socialization. It is not yet clear whether this is also reflected in decreased economic productivity, but a likely prediction would be that multiple acute episodes or chronic course would render the individual less adaptive in economic participation and would lead to slow but gradual reduction of employment stability and social status.

A related approach is to ask what possible adaptive function may be served by milder, nonclinical versions of depression. In addition to the function of depressive affect, some of our colleagues in Britain have suggested that certain personality aspects—risks associated with milder forms of disorders, such as inhibited aggression, heightened social sensitivity, ambition, and achievement— may contribute to adaptive advantage in urban modern settings and that this may account for the reports of higher incidence of manic depressive families at the higher end of the social, economic, and educational scale.

In summary, the clinical depressed state is seen as maladaptive by virtue of its increased mortality, increased social disability, impaired capacity for child rearing, distancing of the social environment, and decreased effectiveness of the individual's participation in his or her social or economic environment.

CONCLUSION

In the development of the mammalian species, particularly primates and humans, attachment bonding has been essential to protect the individual, given the fact that primates in general and humans in particular are born incompletely developed and truly dependent on parental nurturance. The depressive response is a powerful social and physiologic means of alerting the social group as well as the organism to the threat and danger from this disruption of attachment bonding.

As humans mature into adulthood, they become less dependent for their biologic survival. Nevertheless, psychosocial attachment bondings acquire new importance for human feelings of self-worth, identity, meaning, and value, providing a central focus for the cognitive sense of individual. Thus the biologic function of depression changes with the process of maturation of the human organism. Nevertheless, the psychophysiologic apparatus, which evolved through the millenia, has not been modified in its responses and capabilities; what has changed are the stimuli that initiate these powerful responses.

REFERENCES

1. Avery, D., and Winokur, G. (1976): Mortality in depressed patients treated with electroconvulsive therapy and antidepressants. *Arch. Gen. Psychiatry*, 33:1029–1037.
2. Bockoven, J. S. (1963): *Moral Treatment in American Psychiatry.* Springer, New York.
3. Cannon, W. B. (1932): *The Wisdom of the Body.* Norton, New York.
4. Clayton, P. J., Desmarais, L., and Winokur, G. (1968): A study of normal bereavement. *Am. J. Psychiatry,* 125:168–178.
5. Coyne, J. C. (1976): Toward an interactional description of depression. *Psychiatry,* 39:28–40.
6. Darwin, C. (1965): *The Expression of the Emotions in Man and Animals.* University of Chicago Press, Chicago.
7. Engel, G. L. (1962): *Psychological Development in Health and Disease.* Saunders, Philadelphia.
8. Harlow, H. F., Harlow, M. K., and Suomi, S. J. (1971): From thought to therapy: Lessons from a primate laboratory. *Am. Sci.,* 59:538–549.
9. Kaufman, I. C., and Rosenblum, L. A. (1967): The reaction to separation in infant monkeys. Anaclitic depression and conservation-withdrawal. *Psychosom. Med.,* 29:648–675.
10. Klerman, G. L. (1974): Depressions and adaptation. In: *The Psychology of Depression,* edited by R. Friedman and M. M. Katz, pp. 127–156. Winston-Wiley, Washington, D.C.
11. Klerman, G. L., and Izen, J. E. (1977): The effects of bereavement and grief on physical health and general well-being. *Adv. Psychosom. Med.,* 9:63–104.
12. Lief, A. (1948): *The Commonsense Psychiatry of Dr. Adolf Meyer.* McGraw-Hill, New York.
13. Parkes, C. M., and Brown, R. (1972): Health after bereavement. A controlled study of young Boston widows and widowers. *Psychosom. Med.,* 34:461–499.
14. Paykel, E. S. (1970): Life events and acute depression. In: *Separation and Depression, Clinical and Research Aspects,* edited by J. P. Scott and E. C. Senay, pp. 215–236, publication no. 94. American Association for the Advancement of Science, Washington, D.C.
15. Plutchik, R. (1970): Emotions, evolution, and adaptive processes. In: *Feelings and Emotions,* edited by M. B. Arnold, pp. 3–24. Academic Press, New York.
16. Richards, D. W. (1953): Homeostasis versus hyperexis: Or St. George and the dragon. *Sci. Monthly.,* 77:289.
17. Richards, D. W. (1960): Homeostasis: Its dislocations and perturbations. *Perspect. Biol. Med.,* 3:238–251.
18. Schmale, A. H. (1970): Adaptive role of depression in health and disease. In: *Separation and Depression, Clinical and Research Aspects,* edited by J. P. Scott and E. C. Senay, pp. 187–214, publication no. 94. American Association for the Advancement of Science, Washington, D.C.
19. Scott, J. P., and Senay, E. C. (1970): *Separation and Depression, Clinical and Research Aspects,* publication no. 94. American Association for the Advancement of Science, Washington, D.C.
20. Scott, J. P., Stewart, J. M., and DeGhett, V. J. (1970): Separation in infant dogs: Emotional response and motivational consequences. In: *Separation and Depression, Clinical and Research Aspects,* edited by J. P. Scott and E. C. Senay, pp. 3–32, publication no. 94. American Association for the Advancement of Science, Washington, D.C.
21. Seligman, M. E. P. (1975): Depression and learned helplessness. In: *The Psychology of Depression: Contemporary Theory and Research,* edited by R. J. Friedman and M. M. Katz. Winston-

Wiley, Washington, D.C.
22. Selye, H. (1976): *Stress in Health and Disease.* Butterworths, Boston.
23. Senay, E. C. (1966): Toward an animal model of depression. *Psychiatr. Res.,* 4:65–71.
24. Weissman, M. M., and Klerman, G. L. (1977): Sex differences and the epidemiology of depression. *Arch. Gen. Psychiatry,* 34:98–111.
25. Weissman, M. M., and Paykel, E. S. (1974): *The Depressed Woman: A Study of Social Relationships.* University of Chicago Press, Chicago.
26. Wilson, E. O. (1971): The prospects for a unified sociobiology. *Am. Sci.,* 59:400–403.
27. Winokur, G., and Tsuang, M. (1975): The Iowa 500: Suicide in mania, depression, and schizophrenia. *Am. J. Psychiatry,* 132:650–651.

Stress and Mental Disorder,
edited by James E. Barrett et al.
Raven Press, New York © 1979.

Influence of the Social Environment on Psychopathology: The Historic Perspective

M. Harvey Brenner

Division of Operations Research and Department of Behavioral Sciences, The Johns Hopkins University, Baltimore, Maryland 21218

A logical if not ideal approach to the examination of the possible impact of life stresses on illness is through the use of historic data on major aspects of societal change. Indeed, virtually all the major types of life stress can be seen to have social trends of their own, e.g., rates of financial loss, unemployment, illness, mortality, birth, migration, marriage, divorce, separation, and criminal aggression. The confluence of such trends over time, with a greater or lesser intensity, should therefore produce greater stress. Thus if stress phenomena increase the risk of morbidity or mortality either directly as agents of disease (24,37) or by increasing susceptibility (or reducing immunity) (9,23,29), then we should be able to observe such intercorrelations historically and quantitatively. There is a technology, which is now about 20 years old, that can handle the principal methodological problems encountered in multivariate time series analysis (10,17,22).

The clinical researcher who is unfamiliar with these techniques may well wonder how such "highly individualized" factors as life changes or specific stress reactions can be analyzed using macrolevel historic data. In fact, however, from the purely methodological standpoint, macrolevel historic analysis is at least an equally efficient method, as compared with microanalyses, and frequently is the only one suitable for the analysis of social stresses and their possible consequences for illness.

Perhaps the principal methodological problem in stress research encountered at the individual level of analysis is the lack of a means to discriminate the alleged causal variable from its effect. The implication is that it becomes exceedingly difficult to ascertain (a) the direction of the relationship, (b) whether the relationship is spurious (due to unobserved relationships with a third, and truly causal, variable), or (c) whether the variables are not symptomatic of the same pathological process.

The most dramatic example of these methodological problems at the individual level of analysis is found in studies of stress that use low socioeconomic status as a stress indicator. Theoretically, the lower an individual's socioeconomic position, the more exposed he or she is to deleterious life changes (especially involving economic instability and losses) and the less protected he or she is because of comparatively low financial or human support resources (1). The theory has been supported by empirical evidence that there is a statistically reliable inverse relationship between socioeconomic status and the prevalence of mental disorder. This finding has been the single most consistent empirical regularity in the field of psychiatric epidemiology for more than 40 years (13).

The difficulty has been that alternative hypotheses to the stress formulation could be raised to suggest that the relationship actually ran in the opposite direction. Thus a previous situation of mental disorder might result in diminished competence in the economic sphere. One well-known formulation of this thesis maintained that the reason the mentally ill tended to be of lower socioeconomic status is that they "drifted downward" in status as a result of earlier mental disorder (12,36). This interpretation has itself been impossible to sustain at the individual level of analysis even where there were findings that the mentally ill of lower socioeconomic status had in fact fallen in social status (14). This finding supports the stress hypothesis at least equally well because from the stress perspective it is that very loss of status that may have precipitated the currently observed mental disorder.

The only solution to this type of problem is to examine situations, as independent variables, that are not under the influence of the subjects. In stress research at the individual level, few such circumstances exist. Typically, then, when it is observed that illness tends to follow a period of several life changes or stresses, it is difficult to determine whether the factor(s) that precipitated the illness condition, (e.g., a psychopathological mental state) also precipitated the life changes (e.g., financial loss).

These problems of the direction or existence of causal relationships at the individual level of analysis are compounded further by a lack of control for factors that ordinarily influence morbidity or mortality due to specific causes. Since the person is put at risk to coronary disease, for example, by smoking, overweight, high levels of serum cholesterol, and other factors (25), proper epidemiological procedure requires that these be controlled in order to observe the impact of additional factors, including life changes, on coronary morbidity or mortality.

Such controls are rarely applied in stress research because samples are usually too small to cope with the gathering of data on life changes as well as on risk factors that would apply to the manifold outcomes of stress, ranging from the acute infectious disorders and accidents to the chronic diseases, mental disorders, and social pathologies.

There are no perfect research designs inherently free of all problems of validity and reliability. Yet for these problems, multivariate time series methods using aggregated (or macroscopic) data do provide a way out of the causal trap and allow us to control for the coincidence of multiple trends.

MACROSCOPIC HISTORIC APPROACHES IN STRESS RESEARCH

It is precisely the time series approach at the macrolevel that permitted a solution to the chicken-egg question posed by the socioeconomic status-mental illness relationship. It was necessary to find a situation in which changes in the economic situation of persons affected by income and employment losses could not, in turn, be influenced by those persons. Such a situation exists at the macrolevel, and the employment rate was selected as the independent variable. The research question was, then, to what extent are changes in the employment rate associated with changes in first admissions to mental hospitals? Theoretically, if the stress formulations used in socioeconomic status-mental illness research were correct, then a reduction in status for a population average should be associated with increased first admissions. It was found that for at least 127 years in New York State, first admissions to mental hospitals were inversely related to the rate of employment (5).

It was not possible to interpret this relationship as indicating the influence of mental disorder (or hospitalization) on the employment rate because the hospitalization, as compared with the employment rate for the state, was too small. This is obviously because severe pathological phenomena are comparatively rare in a population compared to the number earning incomes subject to inflation, or to the unemployed. Moreover, a variety of tests indicated that it was precisely those who lost the most income, whose social roles were the most seriously affected (e.g., married males), and who were living in counties hardest hit by unemployment changes who were also the most readily hospitalized during economic downturns.

These findings, published in 1973 in *Mental Illness and the Economy,* strongly supported the thesis of a causal inverse relationship based on economic stress between changes in socioeconomic status and in the level of mental disorder. Nevertheless, these findings, based on first admissions to mental hospitals, left unclear to what extent—if at all—intolerance of mental disorder, rather than psychiatric symptoms alone, was precipitated by economic stresses. It thus became useful to work with indicators of pathology which would ideally not be contaminated by factors associated with administrative dispositions or changes in family or community behavior (Figs. 1–3).

A logical choice was found in the area of cardiovascular mortality. There had been substantial theoretical speculation and a body of empirical evidence that linked cardiovascular illness to stressful events (8,11,19,26,31,39–41,44). The predicted relationship was found between adverse changes in the economy, as indicated by the unemployment rate, and various subdiagnoses of cardiovascular disease mortality, including coronary artery disease. The peak of the average mortality reaction occurred at approximately 2 years after the peak in the unemployment rate (2). These findings on approximate lag time corresponded well with those obtained by Holmes, Rahe, and colleagues (20,34,35,42) in their examination of the cumulative effect of life event changes on the onset of subsequent pathology associated with various chronic diseases.

A second study (6), using similar hypotheses and methodology, found that trends in mortality rates associated with cirrhosis of the liver also tended to peak approximately 2 years after a peak in unemployment. In that case, the multiple regression analysis also revealed that the long-term trend in cirrhosis

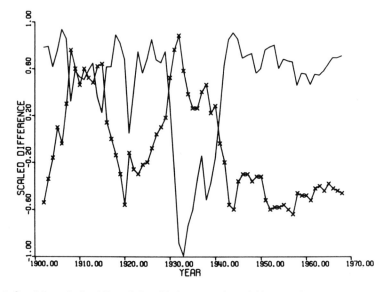

FIG. 1. Graphic analysis of the relationship between the suicide mortality rate and the employment rate, United States, 1902–1970. *Solid line,* inverted unemployment rate; *crossed line,* suicide rate. Scaled difference: Both series are scaled for viewing such that the greatest amplitude from the arithmetic mean of each series, which is set equal to zero, has been normalized to +1.00 if positive, or −1.00 if negative. Del = 0: long-term trends subtracted from the mortality series.

mortality was positively associated with the growth in real per capita disposable income. The same study also indicated that short-term increases in per capita consumption of alcohol tended to increase during economic downturns, as did arrests and trials for the crime of intoxication during automobile driving and first admissions to mental hospitals in the United States with a diagnosis related to alcohol abuse.

In a subsequent study (4), infant mortality rates in the United States were found to be related to economic recessions, as indicated by the unemployment rate, with a lag of from 1 to 2 years of the peak average mortality behind the peak of unemployment. The original hypothesis of this study specified that as a result of material deprivation and lack of medical care, in addition to psychological stress, economic decline would be associated with elevated infant mortality rates. It was suggested that the stresses of economic loss might result in maternal cardiovascular illness or in smoking or abuse of alcohol on the part of pregnant women, which are established risk factors in infant mortality.

A final group of studies, which followed from the original research on mental disorder as related to economic change, was concerned with the problem of criminal aggression. Beginning with New York State (3) and finally involving the United States, Canada, England and Wales, and Scotland (7), economic changes were studied in relation to crimes known to the police, trials, convictions, and imprisonment for each of several crimes against persons (murder, manslaughter, rape, robbery) and property (embezzlement, fraud, arson, burglary,

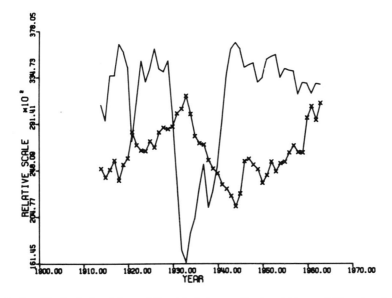

FIG. 2. Graphic Analysis of the relationship between the homicide mortality rate of white males ages 25–29 and the employment rate, United States, 1912–1965. *Solid line,* inverted unemployment rate; *crossed line,* homicide rate. Scaled difference: Both series are scaled for viewing such that the greatest amplitude from the arithmetic mean of each series, which is set equal to zero, has been normalized to +1.00 if positive, or −1.00 if negative. Del = 0: long-term trends subtracted from the mortality series.

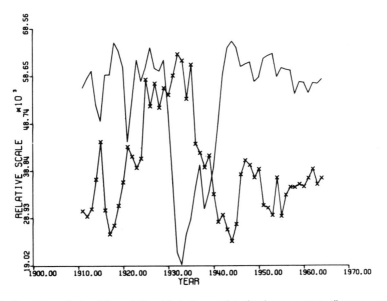

FIG. 3. Graphic analysis of the relationship between the circulatory system disease mortality rate of nonwhite males aged 35–39 at a lag of 3 years, and the employment rate, United States, 1912–1965. *Solid line,* inverted unemployment rate; *crossed line,* circulatory disease mortality rate. Scaled difference: Both series are scaled for viewing such that the greatest amplitude from the arithmetic mean of each series, which is set equal to zero, has been normalized to +1.00 if positive, or −1.00 if negative. Del = 0: long-term trends subtracted from the mortality series.

larceny). Adverse changes in employment and income were associated with increases in rates of all these crimes, controlling for the effects of urbanization, demographic changes, and changes in criminal justice system activity.

It was subsequently recognized that a single major indicator of intermediate and short-term fluctuations in the entire economy was inadequate, especially to express the full extent of economic stress even where it originated at the national level. Not only were such factors as inflation thought to have possible stressful consequences, but real income (i.e., in constant dollars), welfare, and education were thought to be important ameliorators of economic loss. In addition, questions were raised as to the more nearly precise timing of the lag in pathological reactions to changes in economic indicators. For example, increased pathology related to recession could appear to the naked eye—especially without multivariate controls—to occur as a result of the subsequent economic upturn if the lag were in the range of 2 to 4 years (15,43).

The need for more sophisticated analysis to take into account multiple economic and sociodemographic indicators became quite pragmatic when the Joint Economic Committee of the United States Congress requested that estimates be made of the amount of increased pathology that would follow from increased unemployment or the maintenance of it at a high level. To deal with this problem, it was necessary to control for the effects of those economic and sociodemographic factors that ordinarily influence the pathological phenomena in question. Also, it was crucial to know over how long a span of time the deleterious effect of unemployment might precipitate an increased incidence of pathology. It was not sufficient, therefore, to estimate the average or peak lag interval but rather the entire span over which the elevated rates of pathology would occur.

The predictive equation that was finally set up included the unemployment rate, the inflation rate, real per capita personal income, and demographic variables relating to each of the specific types of pathology. The dependent variables or indices of pathology involved the general areas of physical health, mental health, and criminal aggression. The conception was that no single type of indicator, such as depression or heart disease, would serve as a proper measure of the pathological impact of economic life stress. Rather, specific indicators relating to mental disorder and physical morbidity and mortality—involving both acute and chronic problems—would have to be involved. Also, illegal activities involving both violence and property should be included. The following indices of stress outcome were used, based on the United States as a whole: (a) first admissions to mental hospitals by sex and age, (b) total mortality by sex, race, and age, (c) suicide by sex and age, (d) homicide by sex and age, (e) cardiovascular-renal disease mortality by sex and age, (f) cirrhosis of the liver mortality by sex and age, and (g) imprisonment by age.

A sample of the resulting predictive multiple regression equations, and measures of the goodness of fit of these equations to each major type of pathology, are shown in Tables 1 and 2. It is clear that in all cases the unemployment

TABLE 1. Multiple regression of national economic indices on selected mortality rates, United States

Dependent variable	Years	Intercept	Time trend	Log time trends	Per capita income	Unemployment rate	Inflation rate	R^2	F	D.W.
General mortality rate[a] (lag 0–5)[c]										
(1) Mortality rate, total whites	1940–1974	96.2			−0.53E-2 (1.92)*	0.62 (5.05)**	0.87 (2.96)**	0.89	21.9	1.93
(2) Mortality rate, total nonwhites	1940–1974	136.4			−0.32E-1 (6.55)**	1.68 (6.95)**	2.83 (5.16)**	0.96	74.1	1.67
(3) Mortality rate, LT 1 whites	1940–1974	497.7			−0.24 (7.06)**	12.65 (8.01)**	3.59 (5.44)**	0.97	98.6	2.11
(4) Mortality rate, LT 1 nonwhites	1940–1974	936.2			−0.43 (10.48)**	17.74 (10.69)**	30.77 (6.49)**	0.99	199.6	2.40
(5) Mortality rate, 75–84 whites	1940–1974	1141.0			−0.22 (7.59)**	10.39 (7.02)**	17.56 (5.20)**	0.97	103.8	2.47
(6) Mortality rate, 75–84 nonwhites	1940–1974	767.1			−0.93E-1 (2.07)*	15.45 (6.96)**	14.80 (2.91)**	0.84	14.8	2.36
(7) Cardiovascular disease mortality rate[b] (lag 1–4)[d]	1945–1973	537.7			−0.33E-1 (2.49)**	5.46 (2.62)**	−0.04 (0.37)	0.85	11.8	2.89
(8) Cardiovascular disease mortality rate[b] (lag 1–4)[d]	1940–1973	−2836.8	−17.8 (4.70)**	1077.0 (4.76)**		2.35 (1.83)	1.04 (0.78)	0.74	6.50	2.36
(9) Cardiovascular disease mortality rate[b] (lag 1–4)[d]	1945–1973	−843.8	−7.5 (1.43)*	436.3 (1.35)*		6.15 (3.17)**	−1.10 (0.74)	0.79	6.70	2.02
(10) Cirrhosis mortality rate[b] (lag 0–5)[c]	1940–1973	−0.2			0.65E-2 (8.99)**	0.14 (4.21)**	0.16 E-3 (0.01)	0.98	114.4	1.65
(11) Cirrhosis mortality rate[b] (lag 0–5)[c]	1945–1973	−0.2			0.63E-2 (8.81)**	0.12 (3.62)**	0.29E-1 (0.37)	0.98	114.4	1.82

[a] Per 10,000 population.
[b] Per 100,000 population.
[c] Second degree polynomial distributed lag equation.
[d] Ordinary least squares equation.
† 0.10 level of significance, $t = 1.31$; $F = 1.89$.
* 0.05 level of significance; $t = 1.71$; $F = 2.28$.
** 0.10 level of significance; $t = 2.49$; $F = 3.21$.

TABLE 2. Multiple regression of national economic indices on selected pathological indices, United States

Dependent variable	Years	Intercept	Time trend	Log time trends	Dummy constant or trend	Other trends	Per capita income	Unemployment rate	Inflation rate	R²	F	D.W.
(12) Suicide rate[a] (lag 0–5)[c]	1940–1973	6.34					0.90E-3 (1.50)+	0.42 (14.23)**	0.27 (4.23)**	0.91	26.2	1.80
(13) Suicide rate[a] (lag 0–5)[c]	1945–1973	6.38					0.11E-2 (2.17)*	0.40 (17.30)**	0.25 (4.70)**	0.95	40.9	2.35
(14) Suicide rate[a] (lag 0–5)[c]	1940–1973	-0.62		2.08 (3.63)**				0.43 (12.51)**	0.31 (6.68)**	0.87	25.3	2.03
(15) Homicide rate[a] (lag 0–5)[c]	1940–1973	-7.60			DT 1967–74[e] 0.14E-1 (3.90)**	TJ[g] 0.30 (3.16)**	0.16E-2 (1.56)†	0.10 (2.38)*	0.11 (0.92)	0.99	115.6	2.29
(16) Homicide rate[a] TJ[g] (lag 0–5)[c]	1940–1973	1.02	0.65E-1 (5.30)**		DT 1967–74[e] 0.18 (3.79)**			0.54 (5.00)**	0.84 (5.30)**	0.94	47.0	1.88
(17) Imprisonment rate[a] (minus 1942–1945) (lag 0–2)[d]	1935–1965	-577.90	-3.18 (3.14)**	195.5 (3.48)**				1.59 (5.92)**	0.64 (3.35)**	0.76	10.4	1.87
(18) Imprisonment rate[a] (minus 1942–1945) (lag 0–2)[d]	1935–1973	-594.50	-2.55 (2.38)*	180.9 (2.93)**	DC 1967–71[f] -8.36 (8.33)**	TJ[g] 1.31 (4.27)**		1.52 (5.60)**	0.57 (3.07)**	0.90	23.9	1.90
(19) Mental hospital admission rate LT 65[a] (minus 1942–1945) (lag 0–5)[c]	1940–1971	-77.70					0.55E-1 (9.78)**	3.39 (9.58)**	1.78 (2.58)**	0.96	60.0	1.52
(20) Mental Hospital admission rate LT 65[a] (lag 0–5)[c]	1940–1971	-70.00					0.49E-1 (8.69)**	3.11 (8.92)**	2.19 (3.21)**	0.97	63.4	1.85

[a] Per 10,000 population.
[b] Per 100,000 population.
[c] Second degree polynomial distributed lag equation.
[d] Ordinary least squares equation.
[e] "Dummy" trend.
[f] "Dummy" constant.
[g] TJ, percentage of total male population who are ages 15–29.
† 0.10 level of significance; $t = 1.31$; $F = 1.89$.
* 0.05 level of significance; $t = 1.71$; $F = 2.28$.
** 0.01 level of significance; $t = 2.49$; $F = 3.21$. 0.05 level of significance; $t = 1.71$; $F = 2.28$.

rate is significantly positively associated with increases in each pathology over a 5-year period following the first year of impact of an increased unemployment rate. In other words, we allow the cumulative effect of increased pathology within a 6-year period to be taken into account. The assumption was that the impact of major economic stresses may occur over each of several years, with the more nearly acute reactions (e.g., mental hospitalization, imprisonment, suicide, homicide) predominating during the first 3 years and the more nearly chronic reactions (e.g., cardiovascular-renal disease, cirrhosis, and total mortality) predominating during the second 3 years.

The same procedure of estimating the 5-year distributed lag of pathology to changes in the economic indicator was used in the case of per capita income and inflation. Tables 1 and 2 show that while significant relationships were found for per capita income and inflation, the overall results were less stable,

TABLE 3. *Estimates[a] of the total effects of 1% changes in unemployment rates sustained over a 6-year period on the incidence of social trauma (based on the populations of 1970 and 1965)*

Measures of social trauma	Incidence of pathology related to 1% increase in unemployment based on 1970 population	Incidence of pathology related to 1% increase in unemployment, based on 1965 population	Total incidence of pathology, 1965	Incidence of pathology in 1965 related to 1% increase in unemployment, 1960–1965 as a proportion of total 1965 pathology
Total mortality, Whites	36,887	35,042	1,828,000	0.019
Males	12,360	11,866	911,000	0.013
Females	16,534	15,709	695,000	0.023
Nonwhites				
Males	3,829	3,599	125,000	0.028
Females	4,161	3,911	98,000	0.040
Cardiovascular mortality	20,240	19,228	1,000,787	0.019
Cirrhosis of liver mortality	495	470	24,715	0.019
Suicide	920	874	21,507	0.041
Homicide	648	616	10,712	0.057
State mental hospital first admissions[b]	4,227	4,045	117,483	0.034
Males	3,058	2,935	68,917	0.043
Females	1,169	1,110	48,566	0.023
State prison admissions	3,340	2,952	74,724	0.040

[a]Estimates are derived from equation types in Tables 1 and 2 as follows: Total mortality classified by sex and race, equation (1)–(6); cardiovascular mortality, equation (9); cirrhosis of liver mortality, equation (10); suicide, equation (14); homicide, equation (16); mental hospital admissions, equation (19); state prison admissions, equation (17).

[b]Includes only individuals under 65 years of age.

predictable, and interpretable than was the case with the unemployment rate.

From these equations, it was possible to estimate the historic impact, from 1940 to 1974, of a 1% increase in the unemployment rate on the various pathological indices (Table 3).

RAPID ECONOMIC GROWTH VERSUS UNEMPLOYMENT AS SOURCES OF ECONOMIC LIFE STRESS

In the multivariate equations described above, each of the sources of economic life stress—decreased income, inflation, and unemployment—are understood to be unidirectional in their impact on pathology; their impact is conceived as entirely deleterious. This view is traditional with respect to the literature on low socioeconomic status as a risk factor in mental disorder, morbidity and mortality, and criminal aggression. Indeed, the idea that only deleterious changes provoke pathological reaction has been traditional "common sense" as well as the professional behavioral science view.

The formulation of Selye in 1956 (37) went a considerable distance to change these traditional perspectives. It suggested that the phenomenon of change itself—beyond the capacities of the organism to adapt—is the critical precipitant of pathology. This formulation has been the guiding concept to a large number of researchers into the stress-producing potential of different types of life changes. For example, in summarizing the theoretical orientation of many researchers in this field, Levi (24) indicates that the highest stress levels are usually found at the extremes of the stimulation continuum, and thus deprivation or excess of almost any influence is provocative of stress.

However, the research evidence from studies on mental disorder (30), especially depression (32) and criminal behavior (16), show clearly that life changes viewed as undesirable showed considerably greater potency to provoke pathological responses. The weight of the evidence, when one includes traditional research pioneered by Holmes and Rahe (20,21,33) dealing in large measure with chronic physical illnesses (18), is that while all significant life changes are potential stressors, undesirable changes are predictive of higher stress levels.

If this perspective is correct, then we should observe that economic recession should show more severe and longer lasting pathological effects than periods of rapid economic growth, but that the periods of growth themselves, while desirable overall, nevertheless are stressful. A related issue, which the stress literature does not deal with systematically, is that of the interrelationship among life changes. The guiding hypothesis of the formulation in the present study is that deleterious life changes in particular are capable of producing stresses, which in turn lead to other life changes and stresses. We label this interaction among stresses the principle of acceleration of stress. An example would be the loss of a job, which may lead to financial disruption, marital and parent-child strains, and possibly the breakup of family, loss of friendships which were occupation-related, and the securing of a new job at a lower status with the requirement of moving to a home in a new area. In this formulation, the more undesirable the life change, the greater the probability of additional life changes (or stressors).

This principle of stress acceleration, which can be observed in the life of a single person, should not be confused with that of the "contagion," or multiplier, effect of one person's stresses upon those of another. Examples of the latter principle can be seen in the stress on each member of an entire family in the financial and status loss of a head of household. We therefore come to the proposition in this case that while rapid economic growth carries with it short-term stressful effects based on what may appear to be desirable life changes, the impact of economic recession—based almost entirely on undesirable effects— carries a considerably more stressful impact over a much extended span of time.

A more detailed and incisive examination of the relationship between economic change and pathology allows us to test this proposition. We can isolate the impact of long-term economic development from that of rapid economic growth periods because economic growth usually occurs in spurts of 1 to 3 years and is followed by periods of pause or recession, during which it usually slows or actually declines somewhat (27,28). We isolate the long-term, smooth, economic development trend from the rapid growth periods by fitting an exponential trend to the real per capita income data. The exponential fit then represents the long-term trend of economic development, and the residuals represent the abrupt periods of rapid economic growth and pause. We can also isolate the short-term "random" fluctuations in real per capita income by calculating the annual changes in that series.

Since there is only a moderate and unstable correlation over time between unemployment rates and per capita income in any of the forms—(a) long-term exponential trend, (b) residuals from the exponential trend, and (c) annual changes—we can add each of these components in per capita income trends to a prediction equation in which unemployment is also an independent variable. Such an equation is ideally suited to discriminate the differential impact on pathologies of rapid economic growth as compared with unemployment, short-term income losses (annual changes in per capita income), and the long-term trend of economic development.

Furthermore, since the impact of inflation on the pathological indices was observed to be highly unstable, it is useful to determine whether our predictive equation actually requires a separate variable for inflation, especially considering that we have already controlled for inflation by using real per capita income. Finally, in view of recent work showing the importance of educational level to health (38) and the probable contribution of welfare and social security and related health care benefits, it is prudent to control for trends which would measure them.

The principal hypothesis is that rapid economic growth, as well as unemployment, will be positively related to pathology. Since it is argued that economic growth will have only a short-term pathological effect, we do not require a distributed lag measure for this variable. On the other hand, we continue to suggest that the unemployment rate will show a distributed lag effect of from 0 to 5 years on pathology. All the other independent variables in the predictive equation—the exponential trend of economic growth, welfare (i.e., the percentage of government spending allocated to welfare and social security, including health, payments)—except for annual changes in per capita income, are considered without lagged effects. Since the annual changes in per capita income series has virtually no trend (i.e., zero autocorrelation), 1 year of lag has been added to the measurement procedure.

The findings (Table 4) support the principal hypothesis that rapid economic growth, unemployment, and short-term income loss are significantly related to the pathological indices. In this test, only mortality data in general and for specific causes generally associated with psychosocial stress are used, including suicide, homicide, cardiovascular disease, and cirrhosis of the liver. It can also be seen (Table 4) that the statistical significance of the lag of mortality rates by cause to changes in the unemployment rate varies by cause of death. Thus the theoretically slower reacting chronic diseases, indicated by cardiovascular, cirrhosis, and total mortality, often require that the lag estimate of average impact begin with the second year and end in the fifth. The theoretically "quick" reacting causes of death, such as suicide and homicide, require that the lag structure include the early years (0 and 1); indeed, the predominant impact is seen during those years. The implication of these findings is that, as hypothesized, while both rapid economic growth and unemployment are positively related to pathology, the impact of unemployment lasts for several additional years, particularly for the chronic illnesses. These findings further explain why it has appeared to some observers using only graphic techniques or simple correlation (i.e., not using multivariate procedures) (15,43) that the heaviest incidence of increased mortality occurs during upswings in the "economic cycle."

These findings support the position of the majority of researchers that undesirable events are likely to produce far greater stress reactions than are desirable ones. Yet the thesis is also supported that apparently desirable events (or groups of events), such as are involved in rapid economic growth, are also provocative of pathology. We must infer that the totality of changes rather than only the undesirable ones are the more appropriately used in a complete index of economic life stress.

It is also possible, however, that researchers working with life change data have made far too fine a distinction between desirable and undesirable events. In fact, it is possible that all major life changes, whether inherently agreeable or disagreeable, may possess undesirable features. In the examples of agreeable cases, e.g., marriage, birth of a child, and job promotion, each of these life transitions may involve substantially increased responsibilities for which a certain proportion of individuals may be unprepared. The unprepared persons then stand a substantial risk of role failure. We may say, in a rather straightforward

TABLE 4. Multiple regression of national economic indices on selected pathological indices, United States

Dependent variable	Years	Intercept	Time trend	% Govt. expenditures on welfare from total expenditures	No. of college graduates	% Juveniles in total population	Exponential Trend: Long-term per capita income	Residuals from long-term per capita income	One year change in per capita income[a]	Unemployment	R²	F	D.W.
Total mortality rates	1940–1973 (2–5)[c]	137.06 (5.92)**		−0.03 (−0.22)	−0.04 (−2.95)**		−0.02 (−1.65)†	0.01 (2.29)	−0.6E-2 (−0.73)	0.60 (4.72)**	0.94	38.17	2.38
	1940–1973 (0–5)	113.13 (3.85)**		0.16 (0.81)	−0.04 (−3.29)**		−0.01 (−0.51)	0.5E-2 (0.84)	−0.76 (0.89)	0.54 (3.21)**	0.94	40.34	2.55
Suicide mortality rates	1940–1973 (2–5)[a]	−24.85 (−1.59)†			−0.01 (−2.43)*	34.49 (3.08)**	0.02 (1.98)*	−0.2E-2 (−1.13)	−0.6E-2 (2.26)*	0.20 (5.13)**	0.87	15.69	1.96
	1940–1973 (0–5)	−6.27 (−0.47)			−0.9E-3 (−2.70)**	23.32 (2.52)**	0.6E-2 (0.88)	0.5E-4 (0.03)	−0.3E-2 (1.27)	0.28 (7.56)**	0.91	27.55	2.06
Homicide mortality rates	1940–1973 (2–5)	0.38 (0.04)			0.7E-3 (0.26)	38.08 (5.11)**	−0.5E-2 (−0.86)	0.4E-2 (3.03)**	−0.8E-2 (−4.33)**	0.06 (2.27)*	0.98	100.95	1.36
	1940–1973 (0–5)	−4.97 (−0.43)			−0.4E-3 (−0.13)	42.45 (5.25)**	−0.2E-2 (−0.34)	0.3E-2 (2.25)	−0.6E-2 (−3.26)**	0.07 (2.23)*	0.97	97.69	1.59
Cardiovascular mortality rates	1950–1973 (2–5)[c]	388.6 (11.92)**	24.10 (5.91)**				−0.80 (−5.56)**	0.28 (2.74)**	−0.21[e] (−1.94)	18.17 (2.62)**	0.87	13.63	2.90
	1950–1973 (0–5)[c]	367.17 (11.56)**	21.62 (5.25)**				−0.68 (−5.14)**	0.16 (2.30)*	−0.17[d] (−1.40)	8.79[e] (2.35)	0.86	10.08	2.57
Cirrhosis mortality rates	1940–1973 (2–5)[c]	1.82 (0.25)		−0.03 (−1.49)†	−0.39E-2 (−0.29)		0.48E-2 (7.93)**	0.01 (2.15)*	−0.01[f] (−5.16)	0.19[f] (4.82)	0.98	119.78	1.43
	1940–1973 (0–5)[c]	0.25 (0.26)		0.66E-1 (1.49)†	−0.1E-2 (−0.29)		0.61E-2 (7.93)**	0.5E-2 (2.15)*	−0.01 (−4.44)**	0.09 (1.30)	0.98	117.09	1.57

[a] Indicator of rapid economic growth.
[b] Indicator of very short-term income change; includes lags of 0, 1 years.
[c] Unemployment lags.
† 0.10 level of significance, $t = 1.31$; $F = 189$.
* 0.05 level of significance; $t = 1.71$; $F = 2.28$.
** 0.01 level of significance; $t = 2.49$; $F = 3.21$.

manner, that it is likely that when marriage, childbirth, and job promotion are associated with stress, it is because of anxiety over, if not the actuality of, failure. In general, then, probably all desirable life changes are potentially stressful to the extent that they carry the risk of failure, in which case, of course, they are in fact undesirable.

In terms of the present study, rapid economic growth might on the surface be thought of as inherently desirable. It involves new jobs, promotions, and increased real income, and is associated with higher marriage and birth rates (3,15,43). However, since nearly all of these changes involve potential anxieties over fulfillment of new responsibilities, for a certain proportion of persons who are anxious or who actually fail, they may be extremely undesirable.

We can practically distinguish between relatively desirable and undesirable events by (a) the probability of failure (or maladaptation) and (b) the extent to which other life changes may follow. In such a formulation, for example, death or serious illness of a husband would be considered extremely grave because of loss of job, income, and family status as well as the need of the wife to manage the family affairs, possibly take or change jobs, perhaps move to another residence, and so on. Major undesirable life changes, then, are inherently correlated with other life changes in an almost epidemic fashion.

This feature of the interrelationship of life changes, the acceleration principle of stress, is especially important in understanding the lag of several years over which mortality increases with respect to a major undesirable life change, such as unemployment. Not only must the unemployed person encounter the short-term disruption to finances, family, social network, and work life, but he or she also encounters an entirely new set of stressful life changes when reemployed. First, it is probable that the reemployed individual will be at a lower position than was previously held; thus, despite a new job, this situation really indicates downward mobility, with loss of work status, income, and social position. Second, the implications of the downward mobility for family and social relationships must be considered, as well as the possible move of residence associated with the job change.

SUMMARY AND CONCLUSIONS

We have endeavored to show that major economic life changes, as basic stressors, are associated with severe pathology in the areas of mental and physical health and criminal aggression. The hypotheses underlying the studies involved are that the number and magnitude of life changes and life changes which disrupt patterns of social organization are generative of stress. The observation was made that the pathological impact of life changes can often be more easily observed on the macro-, or societal, level of analysis than on the individual level. Several factors contribute to the special utility of stress research when conducted at the macrolevel. Most critical is that a continuous scale over time can be constructed of the occurrence of any particular life change as it affects a population in terms of rates (e.g., unemployment, migration, divorce, illness, or birth rates). The confluence of high rates of stressful events can then, through applied regression analysis over time, be tested with respect to relationships with pathological indicators. Thus quite sophisticated causal models can be investigated, including simultaneous, reciprocal, and detailed multivariate causation.

Additionally important contributions of time series analysis with macrohistoric data are that they permit the use of large population aggregates to allow controls for multiple sources of causation which may be important in disease epidemiology but minimally related to stress. Finally, these techniques permit a clearer resolution of issues of direction of causation that have proven nearly intractable in stress research using socioeconomic status or life changes as independent variables.

The use of some of these time series techniques has been reviewed with respect to the pathological impact of major economic changes, such as unemployment rates and changes in per capita income. In this chapter, data are utilized to examine the question of whether major economic changes in general, rather than only undesirable ones, were associated with mortality rates for stress-sensitive causes. It was found that in most instances, these sources of mortality responded to both rapid economic growth and increased unemployment. The response to unemployment, however, was more intense and occurred over a considerably longer period (at least 5 years for unemployment as compared with 1 year for rapid economic growth).

We conclude, therefore, that abrupt economic changes, regardless of direction, are stress provoking, but that undesirable changes, such as unemployment and income loss, are substantially more generative of pathology. Thus these macroscopic analyses confirm the importance of the overall stressful nature of extremely high stimulation, as in the formulations of Selye (37) and Levi (24), or, put another way, of a large number of stressful events, as in the Holmes and Rahe scheme (21). These analyses are also consistent with the findings of Paykel (32), Mueller et al. (30), Gersten et al. (16), and others who argue that undesirable changes are more stress-provoking than desirable ones. The findings in this chapter suggest that the undesirable events are not only inherently more stressful but have further implications for additional life stresses subsequent to the initial major event.

ACKNOWLEDGMENTS

The author gratefully acknowledges support for this research under National Institute of Mental Health grant no. MH26154, entitled "Economic Change and Social Pathologies in Urban Areas," under the Center for the Studies of Metropolitan Problems.

REFERENCES

1. Bendix, R., and Lipset, S. M. (editors) (1966): *Class, Status and Power: Social Stratification in Comparative Perspective,* second edition. Free Press, New York.
2. Brenner, M. H. (1971): Economic changes and heart disease mortality. *Am. J. Public Health,* 61:606–611.
3. Brenner, M. H. (1971): *Time Series Analysis of the Relationships Between Selected Economic and Social Indicators, Vols. I and II.* National Technical Information Service, Springfield, Virginia.
4. Brenner, M. H. (1973): Fetal, infant and maternal mortality during periods of economic instability. *Int. J. Health Serv.,* 3(2):145–159.
5. Brenner, M. H. (1973): *Mental Illness and the Economy.* Harvard University Press, Cambridge, Massachusetts.
6. Brenner, M. H. (1975): Trends in alcohol consumption and associated illnesses. *Am. J. Public Health,* 65:1279–1292.
7. Brenner, M. H. (1976): Effects of the economy on criminal behavior and the administration of criminal justice in the United States, Canada, England and Wales, and Scotland. In: *Economic Crises and Crime: Correlations Between the State of the Economy, Deviance and the Control of Deviance.* United Nations Social Defense Research Institute, Rome.
8. Cassel, J. (1967): Factors involving sociocultural incongruity and change: Appraisal and implications for theoretical development. *J. Chronic Dis.,* 45:41–45.
9. Cassel, J. (1970): Physical illness in response to stress. In: *Social Stress,* edited by S. Levine and N. A. Scotch, pp. 189–209. Aldine, Chicago.
10. Christ, C. (1966): *Econometric Models and Methods.* Wiley, New York.
11. Croog, S. H., Levine, S., and Lurie, Z. F. (1968): The heart patient and the recovery process: A review of the directions of research on social and psychological factors. *Soc. Sci. Med.,* 2:111–164.
12. Dohrenwend, B. P. (1966): Social status and psychological disorder: An issue of substance and an issue of method. *Am. Soc. Rev.,* 31:14–34.
13. Dohrenwend, B. S., and Dohrenwend, B. P. (1969): *Social Status and Psychological Disorder.* Wiley, New York.
14. Dunham, H. W., and Srinivasan, P. (1966): A research note on diagnosed mental illness and social class. *Sociol. Rev.,* 31(2):223–227.
15. Eyer, J. (1977): Prosperity as a cause of death. *Int. J. Health Serv.,* 7:125–150.
16. Gersten, J. C., Langner, T. S., Eisenberg, J. G., and Orzeck, L. (1974): Child behavior and life events: Undesirable change or change per se? In: *Stressful Life Events: Their Nature and Effects,* edited by B. S. Dohrenwend and B. P. Dohrenwend, pp. 159–170. Wiley, New York.
17. Griliches, Z. (1974): Errors in variables and other unobservables. *Econometrica,* 42:971–998.
18. Gunderson, E. K., and Rahe, R. H. (1974): *Life Stress and Illness.* Charles C Thomas, Springfield, Illinois.
19. Hinkle, L. E., Whitney, L. H., Lehman, E. W., Dunn, J., Benjamin, B., King, R., Plakun, A., and Flehinger, R. (1968): Occupation, education, and coronary heart disease. *Science,* 161:238–246.
20. Holmes, T. H., and Masuda, M. N. (1974): Life change and illness susceptibility. In: *Stressful Life Events: Their Nature and Effects,* edited by B. S. Dohrenwend and B. P. Dohrenwend, pp. 45–79. Wiley, New York.
21. Holmes, T. H., and Rahe, R. H. (1967): The social readjustment rating scale. *J. Psychosom. Res.,* 11:213–218.
22. Johnston, J. (1963): *Econometric Methods.* McGraw-Hill, New York.
23. Kaplan, B. H., Cassel J., and Gore, S. (1977): Social support and health. *Med. Care.* [*Suppl.*], 15:47–58.
24. Levi, L. (1972): Stress and distress in response to psychosocial stimuli. *Acta Med. Scand.* [*Suppl.*], 191:528.
25. Lilienfeld, A. M., and Gifford, A. J. (editors) (1966): *Chronic Diseases and Public Health.* Johns Hopkins University Press, Baltimore.
26. Marks, R. V. (1967): Factors involving social and demographic characteristics: A review of empirical findings. *J. Chronic Dis.,* 45:51–108.

27. Mitchell, W. C. (1951): *What Happens During Business Cycles: A Progress Report.* National Bureau of Economic Research, New York.
28. Moore, G. H. (editor) (1961): *Business Cycle Indicators.* Princeton University Press, Princeton, New Jersey.
29. Moss, G. E. (1973): *Illness, Stress and Social Interaction: The Dynamics of Social Resonation.* Wiley, New York.
30. Mueller, D. P., Edwards, D. W., and Yarvis, R. M. (1977): Stressful life events and psychiatric symptomatology: change or undesirability? *J. Health Soc. Behav.,* 18:307–317.
31. Ostfeld, A. M., Lebovits, B. A., Shekelle, R. B., and Paul, O. (1964): A prospective study of the relationship between personality and coronary heart disease. *J. Chronic Dis.,* 17:265–276.
32. Paykel, E. S. (1974): Recent life events and clinical depression. In: *Life Stress and Illness,* edited by E. K. Gunderson and R. H. Rahe, pp. 134–163. Charles C Thomas, Springfield, Illinois.
33. Rabkin, J. G., and Struening, E. L. (1976): Life events, stress and illness. *Science,* 194:1013–1020.
34. Rahe, R. H., Meyer, M., Smith, M., Kjaer, G., and Holmes, T. H. (1964): Social stress and illness onset. *J. Psychosom. Res.,* 8:35–44.
35. Rahe, R. H., and Romo, M. (1974): Recent life changes and the onset of myocardial infarction and coronary death in Helsinki. In: *Life Stress and Illness,* edited by E. K. Gunderson and R. H. Rahe, pp. 105–120. Charles C Thomas, Springfield, Illinois.
36. Rejd, D. D. (1961): Precipitating proximal factors in the occurrence of mental disorders: Epidemiological evidence. *Milbank Memorial Fund Q.,* 39:227–248.
37. Selye, H. (1956): *The Stress of Life.* McGraw-Hill, New York.
38. Silver, M. (1972): An economic analysis of spatial variations in mortality rates by race and sex. In: *Essays in the Economics of Health and Medical Care,* edited by V. R. Fuchs, pp. 161–227. Columbia University Press, New York.
39. Smith, T. (1967): Factors involving sociocultural incongruity and change: A review of empirical findings. *Milbank Mem. Fund.,* 45:23–38.
40. Syme, S. L., Borhani, N. O., and Buechley, R. W. (1965): Cultural mobility and coronary heart disease in an urban area. *Am. J. Epidemiol.,* 82:334–346.
41. Syme, S. L., Hyman, M. M., and Enterline, P. E. (1964): Some social and cultural factors associated with the occurrence of coronary heart disease. *J. Chronic Dis.,* 17:227–289.
42. Theorell, T., and Rahe, R. H. (1974): Psychosocial characteristics of subjects with myocardial infarction in Stockholm. In: *Life Stress and Illness,* edited by E. K. Gunderson and R. H. Rahe, pp. 90–104. Charles C Thomas, Springfield, Illinois.
43. Thomas, D. S. (1925): *Social Aspects of the Business Cycle.* Routeledge, London.
44. Wardwell, W. I., Hyman, M. M., and Bahnson, C. B. (1964): Stress and coronary heart disease in three field studies. *J. Chronic Dis.,* 17:73–84.

Stress and Mental Disorder,
edited by James E. Barrett et al.
Raven Press, New York © 1979.

Changes in Mental Health Status Associated with Job Loss and Retirement

Stanislav V. Kasl

*Department of Epidemiology and Public Health, Yale University School of Medicine,
New Haven, Connecticut 06510*

This chapter reviews and discusses some salient research literature on the mental health consequences of job loss and retirement. These two experiences, plus entering the labor force and changing one's job, are the major transitions that individuals may go through in the work role. Since unemployment and retirement are included in the commonly used lists of "stressful life events" (57,93), and since this volume is so prominently concerned with life changes, this chapter is organized to fit the general framework that has inspired the many life events studies. However, there is no theoretical framework to speak of, and much of the work on stressful life events (29,66,98) is actuated by a few simple propositions, such as: (a) life changes or events tax the adaptive capacities of an individual, and that is "stress;" (b) events differ in magnitude of change and, therefore, of stress; (c) the impact of such events is additive or cumulative; and (d) it may be useful to make some distinctions between classes of events, such as "desirable versus undesirable," and "entrances versus exits." This is, indeed, an impoverished framework which calls for enrichment in three important areas: (a) greater detail in describing the experiential aspects of the various life events (duration, unpredictability, novelty, control, and so on), (b) greater detail in characterizing the socioenvironmental aspects of the life change, and (c) a closer integration into a life cycle perspective in which the meaning of change (and of no change) can be brought into sharper focus.

The organizing framework of this chapter is the data on meaning of work and on the effects of the work environment on mental health. (a) In order to understand the effects of the loss of the work role—via either unemployment or retirement—we must first know something about the significance of the work role itself. This point could be stated even more provocatively: If the work role is unimportant for a substantial segment of the population, then may we not expect only attenuated adverse effects of job loss and retirement? (b) Many life events are firmly enmeshed in a large and deep network of prior events and decisions, of aspirations and adaptations; they are anchored to many socioenvironmental variables which describe the social and physical setting in which these events take place. Consequently, our research on stressful life events must achieve a better balance between the broadsweeping but superficial studies using a list of life events—the dominant methodology so far—and the intensive investigations of single events which can illuminate the complexity of the relationships and effects involved.

There are also limitations in my presentation. Basically, since I discuss research findings, I must go where the data are, which is predominantly on male blue collar workers. It is primarily for this group that a critical mass of evidence exists dealing with the three interconnected issues: effects of (a) work environment, (b) job loss, and (c) retirement. Moreover, because of the same limitations of evidence, I deal primarily with the noneconomic aspects of the work role and its loss.

THE MEANING OF WORK

The literature indexed under the label "meaning of work" includes two types of writings: (a) theoretical or speculative, and (b) empirical. Among the former, it would be difficult to find a writer who has not described the work role as a critical one, as a central life activity in out society. It takes up a large part of the worker's time and effort (energy) and is the major source of income. For the individual, it is probably the chief source of contact with society at large (42) and is a major influence on his self-concept or self-identity (36,88,121). From a cross-cultural perspective (128), it would appear that in almost all cultures work has significance beyond economic compensation, although individual cultures vary in the extent of valuing work. In modern American society, work is described as having certain "universal" functions: it provides money, regulates life activity, offers status or social identification, permits association with others, and makes available a meaningful life experience (123).

In contrast to these primarily theoretical or intuitive analyses of the meaning of work, a growing empirical literature points to a lesser and declining importance of the work role in contemporary American society. Although this literature is not without controversy and ambiguities in interpreting findings (45,64,65, 91,118), a suggestive picture can be painted.

In several national surveys of hopes and fears of adults in the United States (19), the category of "good job, congenial work" is mentioned among the hopes by no more than 6 to 9% of respondents, and "unemployment" among the fears by 10 to 14%. In contrast, issues of good (ill) health and better (lower) standard of living, are consistently the two most frequent hopes and fears, listed by up to 40% of respondents. Findings of highly similar import are reported in a recent study of quality of American life (17): about 38% of a national sample of respondents rate "an interesting job" as "extremely important," in contrast to 70% for "being in good health," 74% for "a happy marriage," 67% for "a good family life," and 62% for "a good country to live in." Several studies that have examined the relative contribution of job satisfaction to overall well-being and happiness conclude that family life and spare-time activities are clearly more important (17,132,134).

Some studies of the "meaning of work" have asked respondents whether they would keep on working even if they inherited enough money. Recent national data (17,39,96) suggest that two-thirds to three-quarters of respondents would continue working. Further probes for the reasons proved quite illuminating. Only about 10% said they enjoyed work, and another 10% mentioned some specific liked aspect of work or suggested that work contributed to their health or self-respect. When asked what they would miss most if they stopped working, 37% gave reasons involving co-workers, while another 29% would miss "nothing" (96). These results are closely in line with the findings from a study of retirees (83), where the question "what do you miss most about not working?" was answered by 68% of the respondents with either "nothing at all" or "my work associates."

Results with another methodology, in which the respondent is presented with a number of alternative activities and is asked which one he would miss most, suggest that only about 25% of industrial workers are "job-oriented;" that is, they choose the alternative "a day's work" (33,90,124). This is close to the results of a national time use study (101) in which 25% of respondents picked work-related activities as the most satisfying among activities of the previous day.

There is also some doubt that the work role is such a major influence on self-concept or self-identity, as asserted by many theoreticians. In a recent nationwide Quality of Employment Survey (96), respondents were asked "how much can you tell about a person just from knowing what he or she does for a living?" Approximately 48% chose the alternatives "nothing" or "a little." Similarly, when asked "how much does your job help you understand the sort of person you are?," 43% indicated "not at all" or "a little."

Overall, it would appear that lower skilled industrial workers have a rather tenuous attachment to the work role. They would continue working in the absence of financial need not because of any intrinsic satisfaction in work but because there are no meaningful alternatives. Blue collar workers still "accept the necessity of work but expect little fulfillment from their specific job" (117). Thus much of the theoretical writing on meaning of work in our society is applicable only to workers who do highly skilled and creative work (108). This is in agreement with a recent review of studies on job involvement, that is, the psychological importance of work to a person's total identity: men with high job involvement are those who have a stimulating job (high on autonomy, variety, task identity, and feedback), who participate in decisions affecting them, and who have a history of job success (97).

EFFECTS OF THE WORK ENVIRONMENT

This section deals with the data linking the work environment to mental health. The literature has been reviewed elsewhere in greater detail (67,68,70,71); I offer only selected highlights.

The first point is that one usually sees only weak associations. For example, in a nationwide study of working conditions (95), it was found that the workers' reports of presence of problems in 18 areas of labor standards concern—certainly a good general measure of the work environment—correlated in the low 0.30s with two indices of job satisfaction and even less with several mental health indices. Data from a later national survey (96) revealed that six measures of job-related stress (such as role ambiguity, underutilization, overload, and employment insecurity) had an average correlation of 0.20 with three job satisfaction measures, and an average correlation of 0.16 with three mental health indicators, reflecting depressed mood, self-esteem, and life satisfaction. Still another national sample study (78) reported the following multiple-partial correlations (controlling for education, income, and occupational status) among 12 facets of occupational conditions (involving organizational locus, occupational self-direction, job pressures, and uncertainty): job satisfaction, $r = 0.32$; anxiety, $r = 0.22$; and self-esteem, $r = 0.16$.

A similar conclusion of a weak impact of the work environment can be drawn if one simply looks at studies that correlate job satisfaction with various indicators of mental health and well-being. (a) Behavioral indicators, such as drug use, alcohol consumption, and cigarette smoking, show negligible associations with job satisfaction (20,86,96,131). (b) Indices based on somatic complaints and symptom checklists generally correlate in the 0.10 to 0.30 range (20,73, 81,84,95,102,130). (c) Affect-based measures (anxiety-tension, depression, irritation) yield still higher correlations, while indices of personal happiness and life satisfaction tend to yield the strongest associations with job satisfaction, but still averaging only in the low 0.40s (13,20,50,73,95,96). Overall, highest correlations are obtained between pairs of measures in which the shared "method variance" (18) is the greatest and where underlying response tendencies, such as defensiveness and complaining, are likely to influence both sets of measures.

Data on blue collar workers suggest that they are not appreciably different from the remainder of the United States population on somatic complaints, self-evaluated physical health, depression, self-esteem, zest, and life satisfaction (95,96). The biggest difference for these scales was on life satisfaction, where the blue collar workers were 0.29 of a standard deviation below the overall sample mean; even this overstates the difference, since this refers to the 1971 survey (95), and the 1974 data (96) yielded a smaller difference.

The major interest in blue collar workers has been in those who perform routine work, generally machine paced, requiring little skill. As a group, these workers do appear to have somewhat poorer mental health than blue collar workers in a variety of other jobs (20,44,80), but this is not always found (102). However, attempts to link this difference to specific objective aspects of work, primarily speed and intensity of machine-paced work, have not been successful (80). Since these jobs are seen as the least desirable ones in the factory, Kornhauser (80) has suggested that the poorer mental health of these workers may be better linked to the symbolic aspects of holding such jobs, that is, perceived occupational failure, rather than to specific aspects of the work environment.

A closer scrutiny of studies of these machine-paced jobs reveals (58,109) that many workers adapt so well that even the very repetitive and routine work can be satisfying. Apparently, some workers prefer mechanically paced, highly structured jobs and find some satisfaction in their very rigidity and mindless but predictable triviality. Convergent evidence on this point comes from studies of job enlargement or job enrichment (2,38,51,58). Essentially, the beneficial effects of job enlargement can be expected only for workers who are not alienated from middle-class work norms. But there is a large segment of workers, primarily the younger ones and those in the urban setting, who are indifferent to job enlargement efforts and who do not show the anticipated changes in job satisfaction, absenteeism, and turnover.

Overall, the data on blue collar workers in routine, machine-paced jobs present the following picture. Men on dull and monotonous jobs do not misperceive their work; they call their jobs dull and monotonous (12,77,111). Their levels of job satisfaction, however, do not correspond to this description, since they are not much different from other blue collar workers, and they seldom cite monotony as a reason for job dissatisfaction (20,39). When their jobs are changed (that is, enlarged), only some respond with higher job satisfaction and greater job involvement. The most plausible interpretation of these results is offered by Strauss (118), who suggests that workers:

> can adjust to non-challenging work, usually by lowering their expectations, changing their need structure, making most of social opportunitites on and off the job.

Kornhauser (80) offers a similar interpretation but with a more pessimistic emphasis:

> The unsatisfactory mental health of working people consists in no small measure of their dwarfed desires and deadened initiative, reduction of their goals and restriction of their efforts to a point where life is relatively empty and only half meaningful.

Kornhauser goes on to discuss the two dead-end options for the automobile worker: (a) maintain high expectations from work, which leads to constant frustration, or (b) limit one's expectations, which leads to a drab existence.

We must realize that the poor mental health that Kornhauser describes is from the humanistic perspective known as "positive mental health," with its emphasis on growth, development, self-actualization, and use of valued skills (62). These workers are not particularly different on more traditional indicators of psychological and somatic distress.

Also, we do not know enough about the costs of this "successful" adaptation to a dull job via disengagement. Nor do we have any good studies of the casualties of inadequate adaptation, for these are not easily detected in cross-sectional studies, or even casual longitudinal studies of an unselected group of workers. For this we need targeted prospective studies of a young cohort of workers.

Perhaps the most fundamental question underlying these issues is a metatheo-
retical one, one that cannot be tested directly. Are we postulating a human
nature with certain inherent needs (à la Maslow) or do we view the work environment (and other social settings) as a significant source of some of these needs?
If the latter, then one would view dull and boring jobs not as frustrating certain
needs but as never giving birth to them in the first place.

IMPACT OF RETIREMENT

In turning to a consideration of studies of the impact of retirement on health
and well-being, we are again addressing a large research literature from which
only selected highlights can be offered. The reader is referred to recent reviews
and the major studies for further details (4,21,22,43,69,99,100,115,120).

It must be recognized that retirement (as an event and a process) is a complex,
multidimensional transition involving many possible changes: loss of work role,
loss of income, changes in daily activities, changes in social interaction, residential
and geographical mobility, changes in self-concept and perceived public identity,
and so on. Moreover, the retirement process may be taking place in different
psychosocial contexts: within policies of voluntary versus mandatory retirement,
in conjunction with changes in health status of the retiree or of significant
others (especially spouse), in the context of a fulfilled versus unfinished work
career, and of a strong versus weak attachment to the last work setting or
company, together or apart from spouse's retirement, coinciding with increased
physical separation from offspring, and so on.

Studies of retirement decision continue the theme of tenuous attachment to
the work role (8,9,32,48,53,59,60,99,103,112,114). The majority of people look
forward to retirement and would like to retire earlier than they expect to. Financial considerations are paramount: given the availability of an early retirement
pension plan and the evaluation that postretirement income will be adequate,
the vast majority of blue collar workers choose to retire early. Evaluations of
one's health status as poor—or as declining, particularly in relation to perceived
job demands—also influence the decision to retire early. On the other hand,
work role variables, such as work commitment or job satisfaction, seldom have
any detectable influence on the decision process.

Descriptive studies of adjustment to retirement suggest that somewhere between one-quarter and one-third of respondents may be classified as poorly
adjusted to their circumstances (3,4,53). However, reduced income and decline
in health account for more than two-thirds of the reasons among the dissatisfied
minority of retirees. Only about 25 to 30% of United States retired men say
they want a job or that they should have continued working (17,110); however,
this is as much due to financial concerns as to a commitment to work. Fewer
than 20% of American retired men miss "work" in retirement, and only about
8% list loss of work as the most important aspect of retirement (110).

Studies of correlates of retirement satisfaction (8,9,17,32,100) reveal that low satisfaction will be found among those in poor financial circumstances or poor health and for those who are older, living alone, of lower education, and belonging to fewer or no organizations. Unfortunately, this list of correlates does not specifically illuminate retirement satisfaction; they are global correlates of general well-being found for working adults as well. There is some evidence that involuntary retirement is associated with lower retirement satisfaction. However, this is not because of the lack of an opportunity to continue working; rather, it is because the involuntary label includes many who were not able to retire as planned (e.g., decline in health, job loss) and the underlying association is of low satisfaction with poorer health or finances. Job satisfaction on last job, job orientation, and main source of job satisfaction ("people" versus "work itself") do not seem to influence retirement satisfaction.

An overall summary of the results of studies of the impact of retirement on health and well being leads to the following conclusions:

1. There is no evidence to suggest that the transition from work to retirement is accompanied by an adverse (on the average) impact on the physical health of the person. This comes from a variety of studies, using different designs, and measuring mortality, morbidity, and self-assessed health status (27,35,54,55,85,87,89,120,129). Even though these studies are not particularly well executed, they do not always share the same weaknesses, and thus their consistency is difficult to dismiss. Some studies (8,43,106) suggest an improvement in health status following retirement. However, they all use self-assessed health status, and there is every reason to suspect that with the removal of work role demands following retirement, the whole subjective framework for self-evaluation of health status changes. Hence I would not trust this evidence concerning presumed health benefits of retirement.

2. Similarly, there is no good evidence that retirement is associated with an adverse (on the average) impact on the mental health of the person (4,10, 11,40,46,63,115,116,119,120,125,126). Again, the quality of research in this area is not strikingly high, particularly in the area of measurement of mental health, where the studies fall short of the standards set by the well-known community studies in psychiatric epidemiology of the last two decades. Moreover, one does see an occasional result of an adverse impact but only in some very narrow domain, such as perceived usefulness, which may be lower after retirement (5). In general, however, any differences between the employed and the retired wash out when one adjusts for age, health status, income, and functional disability.

In view of this absence of demonstrated impact of retirement on health and well-being, it is useful to list the following additional conclusions which, in my opinion, are also well supported by the evidence from studies already cited.

3. Variations in postretirement outcomes are most convincingly seen as reflecting continuities of preretirement status, particularly in the areas of physical health, social and leisure activities, and general well-being and satisfaction.

4. Certain predictors of outcome, such as prior attitudes toward the process of retirement and expectations about postretirement outcomes, make their contribution primarily via their association with underlying variables, such as prior health status and financial aspects of retirement; consequently, they do not contribute independently to our understanding of outcomes.

5. Variables reflecting aspects of the work role (such as job satisfaction and work commitment) are not powerful or consistent predictors of outcomes.

6. Financial considerations dominate the entire picture and represent the most obvious target for ameliorating the condition of retired elderly. However, adaptation to reduced income is a poorly understood process, and the effects of increased income on health status and medical care utilization may be very small (34).

The above summary of major findings and conclusions is, in some sense, misleading in that it does not adequately highlight what we do not know. For example, there is no adequate study that tests the hypothesis that for individuals who are healthy and who wish to continue work, involuntary retirement has adverse effects. Looking at effects of mandatory retirement among blue collar workers who, in fact, would prefer to retire early (and do so when the retirement benefits are adequate), will not test the hypothesis. Nor is it enough to classify a cross-section of subjects as "voluntary" versus "involuntary," when the latter classification picks up mostly those in poor health, in poorer financial circumstances, with more irregular work history, and so on. We must also realize that effects of work role variables, such as work commitment, cannot be studied effectively if the only occupational groups with sufficiently great commitment to work and to their jobs—because it is fulfilling or associated with great power and prestige—are not normally forced to discontinue their activities: artists, scientists, congresspeople, judges, physicians, and so on (37,61,99,104,112,120). Other research needs include: (a) a more systematic exploration of the occupational specificity of retirement outcomes, (b) a detailed analysis of the phases of retirement adaptation (if they exist) and the nature of coping styles utilized by different individuals or subgroups, and (c) the study of retirement together with other significant events, such as bereavement and residential mobility.

EFFECTS OF JOB LOSS

Compared to retirement, job loss is an "exit" from the work role which would appear to represent a more severe experience in most aspects except its transitoriness: more unwanted and unexpected, greater financial penalty, possibility of self-blame, more negative public perceptions, and so on.

Much of the work on unemployment has been done from the economic viewpoint and is concerned with such issues as factors affecting reemployment, workers' geographic and occupational mobility, processes of finding a new job, and economic consequences (92,113,133). The literature on mental health consequences, on the other hand, is quite limited.

There appears to be a good deal of suggestive, indirect evidence linking unemployment to differences in mental health and well-being. A number of studies (15,28,31,56,94,122) have related cyclical fluctuations in the state of the economy (primarily percent unemployed) to fluctuations in rates of suicide and psychiatric hospitalizations: periods of high unemployment are claimed to coexist with, or are shortly followed by, periods of high rates of suicides and psychiatric hospitalizations. More recent reports (23,30) have analyzed data on symptoms of depression and psychophysiological distress obtained in successive monthly samples in one metropolitan community in relation to several monthly economic indices, including unemployment, inflation, and various changes in the community's economy. The results are generally consistent with the previous findings, also showing a (lagged) coincidence of fluctuations in the economic and psychological indicators.

However, it has been difficult to interpret precisely the findings from such ecological analyses and to integrate them with results from epidemiological or clinical studies of individuals. Some of the issues are of a technical nature, such as (a) how to deal with the problem of autocorrelations, (b) how to find nonarbitrary ways of selecting those secular trends which first need to be removed statistically, and (c) how to justify *a priori* the temporal period for which lagged correlations are computed, since lags of different temporal spans strikingly alter the results. Other issues concern the uncertainty regarding exactly what inferences are logically permissible from ecological analyses, given their many limitations, collectively labeled as "the ecological fallacy." Still other problems concern only some but not all of the studies; for example, rates of psychiatric hospitalization are a dubious index of incidence of mental disorder, particularly when these rates are only used as aggregates over large geographic and temporal units (e.g., yearly rates for a particular state or country). There is also the issue of nonreplication of findings based on different methodologies; for example, the link between unemployment and suicide (16) is not always replicated (82), and case analyses of attempted or actual suicides (14,52,107) have not succeeded in pinpointing the role of unemployment. In short, the ecological analyses using economic cycle data have more than their share of ambiguity and difficulty of interpretation.

Many of the relevant unemployment studies date from the late 1930s and early 1940s (6,7,24,47,79,105) and, not unexpectedly, are not quite up to the standards of social research expected today. Nevertheless, some highlights of their findings are interesting and worth noting, provided we remember that the evidence is more tentative:

    1. The employment-unemployment-reemployment cycle was not associated with strong disruptions of family structure, personality, or attitudes, except perhaps in families or individuals who were allegedly unstable from the start.

    2. The best documented effects of unemployment were in the area of self-esteem, self-respect, depression, and life satisfaction, but it is not clear how long lasting these effects were.

3. In a great many instances, the men who became unemployed blamed themselves, in both superficial and profound ways, for the loss of their jobs.

4. There is no doubt that financial difficulties profoundly altered the family life (e.g., leisure activities and daily routines) and that going into debt had additional adverse effects on self-esteem and depression. However, the effects of lack of money are difficult to disentangle from the effects of lack of a job.

The more recent correlational surveys have shown that unemployed men are more unhappy (13,17), have higher rates of psychiatric disorder (41), and believe their lives to be controlled by environmental forces instead of being in control of their own lives (127). In these cross-sectional studies of unselected groups, the direction of causality is unclear; it is impossible to estimate the contribution of prior poor mental health to the onset and duration of an episode of unemployment. A study of Packard employees after the company closed down (1), although a retrospective account of their experience, does represent a careful analysis of the data. In this study, neither life satisfaction nor alienation was found to be significantly related to length of unemployment. On the other hand, an index of economic deprivation was significantly related to both these mental health variables, suggesting that financial difficulties rather than absence of work is the more powerful variable.

The recently completed prospective study of job loss among blue collar workers (26) represents a unique attempt to document in detail the health and mental health impact of a permanent plant shutdown. In addition to the final report by Cobb and Kasl (26), a number of preliminary findings have also been reported (25,49,72,74,76). The results of this study are exceedingly complex and defy an easy summary; for example, the outcomes were frequently influenced by the urban versus rural setting of the two plants that closed down and by the degree of social support experienced by the workers who lost their jobs. Moreover, many anticipation effects were evident, that is, elevations in physiological indicators or measures of psychological distress at a time when the work loss had not yet taken place but the men were aware of the impending shutdown. In comparison to stably employed controls, men who lost their jobs had a somewhat greater incidence of dyspepsia, joint swellings, and being placed on antihypertensive and hypoglycemic medications.

The remainder of this chapter is concerned with describing the major thrust of the findings from this longitudinal study regarding the effects of job loss on mental health and well being. I cite a number of tables from the final report (26) and from some subsequent analyses of the impact by duration of the unemployment experience (75).

The measures to be considered can be grouped as follows:

1. Relative economic deprivation: a two-item index, reflecting difficulty in living on present income and the subjective comparison of own family income with that of friends and neighbors.

2. Work role "deprivation" scales: 12 dimensions in which the respondent rates his current life situation ("how things look to you now") as well as "how you would like things to be." The score reflects the difference between actual and desired situation for each of 12 dimensions, which deal with physical activity, keeping busy, doing interesting things, use of valued skills, security about future, perceived respect from others, socializing with others, being able to talk over problems with friends, and so on. These dimensions are called "work role deprivation scales" since they reflect the various possible dimensions of satisfaction which the job and the work setting may provide.

3. Indicators of mental health: the nine scales here are based on a factor analysis of a large pool of items, with about five to six items defining each scale. Because of heavy borrowing of items from existing measures, these scales may be viewed as highly typical of what is available in the research literature. The nine scales, with illustrative items in parentheses, are as follows: (a) depression ("things seem hopeless"), (b) low self-esteem ("I am inclined to feel I am a failure"), (c) anomie ("these days a person doesn't really know whom he can depend on"), (d) anxiety-tension ("I often feel tense"), (e) psychophysiological symptoms ("I am bothered by my heart beating hard"), (f) insomnia ("I have trouble falling asleep"), (g) anger-irritation ("I lose my temper easily"), (h) resentment ("I feel I get a raw deal out of life"), (i) suspicion ("I used to think most people told the truth but now I know otherwise").

The measures are scored so that a high score indicates high deprivation, high distress, poor mental health, or low sense of well-being. Moreover, all scales have been converted into standard scores (mean = 0, SD = 1.0), with the data on stably employed controls (men in comparable blue collar jobs who did not face the threat or the actuality of plant closing) used as a basis for standardization.

Table 1 summarizes some of the major findings on changes in mental health and well-being of the 100 men who went through the experience of plant closing, job loss, some unemployment (for most of them), probationary reemployment, and stable reemployment. The first column presents the mean values for the various measures based on data collected on the first home visit 4 to 7 weeks before scheduled plant closing. All men are still working on their old jobs and know of the impending shutdown. The data in the second column are based on subsequent home visits (6 weeks, 6 months, 1 year, and 2 years after plant closing) whenever the respondent was unemployed. For 51 of the men, one or more of the scheduled home visits took place when the man was unemployed; for the other 49 men, either none of the visits coincided with the time they were unemployed or they might have experienced no unemployment (12% of the sample). The data in the third column are based on all visits when the man was reemployed; five men remained unemployed during all subsequent

TABLE 1. Changes in mental health and well-being associated with anticipation of plant closing, being unemployed, and being reemployed[a]

Indicator	Mean values for anticipation (N = 100)	Mean values for all occasions when un-employed (N = 51)	Mean values for all occasions when employed (N = 95)	Amount of intra-person difference between all occasions when unemployed and when employed (N = 46)
Relative economic deprivation	−0.23	1.23	0.17	0.96
Work role "deprivation" scales				
Security about the future	0.44	0.58	−0.02	0.54
Getting ahead in the world	−0.20	0.66	−0.25	0.96
Respect from others	0.10	0.46	−0.10	0.52
Use of one's best skills	0.18	1.56	0.31	1.26
Things are interesting	0.16	0.53	0.03	0.61
Summary scale of 12 dimensions	0.25	0.94	−0.03	0.94
Mental health indicators				
Depression	0.35	0.55	0.23	0.18
Low self-esteem	0.15	0.34	0.03	0.14
Anomie	−0.04	0.05	−0.19	0.01
Anxiety-tension	0.12	0.17	−0.16	0.28
Psychophysiological symptoms	0.03	−0.09	−0.06	−0.30
Insomnia	−0.07	−0.08	−0.08	−0.14
Anger-irritation	0.03	−0.11	−0.15	0.02
Resentment	0.15	0.25	0.03	0.05
Suspicion	−0.31	−0.35	−0.38	−0.28

[a]From ref. 26. See text for description of measures and explanation of computation of mean scores.

follow-up visits. The values in columns 2 and 3 are means of 51 and 95 scores, respectively, where each score is an ipsative (intraperson) mean whenever two or more scores were available for each individual for periods of unemployment and reemployment. The last column is based on computing an intraperson difference between the ipsative mean for all occasions of unemployment and that for all occasions of employment; there were 46 individuals on whom these intraperson differences could be computed.

The first column of Table 1 shows few overall anticipation effects. The men felt more insecure about the future (almost ½ SD above controls) and somewhat more depressed (about ⅓ SD above controls) but less suspicious. More refined analyses (26) showed stronger anticipation effects among the men in the rural setting, among those low on social support, and among those whose subsequent unemployment experience was more severe.

The impact of unemployment on these indicators of mental health and well-being can be examined in several ways: (a) compare means in column 2 with controls (i.e., a mean of 0); (b) compare columns 2 and 3; (c) examine means in column 4, which may be viewed as the most sensitive approach since it compares unemployment and reemployment values intraindividually. However, all comparisons roughly tell the same story: on indices of deprivation (economic, in the work role), the impact is clear-cut and highly significant (all differences in column 4 at $p < 0.005$ or lower). Thus, for example, on "use of one's best skills," the discrepancy between "actual" and "desired" when the men are unemployed is 1.5 SD above any such discrepancy for controls and about 1.25 SD above the discrepancy values for occasions when the men are later reemployed. However, the mental health indicators reveal little impact. In column 2, only three means are suggestively different from controls: high on depression and low self-esteem, and below expected on suspicion. The last column (intraperson differences) does not yield statistically reliable differences for these three scales. In fact, in column 4 there are only two significant intraperson differences: anxiety-tension and psychophysiological symptoms. Moreover, the latter scale reveals an opposite effect: fewer symptoms were reported during periods of unemployment. Overall, the impact of unemployment on these mental health indicators seems rather weak. More refined analyses (26) suggested, among others, that unemployment had a stronger impact on the work role deprivation scales in the rural setting, and on the mental health indicators in the urban setting.

The impact of unemployment on mental health and well-being was further examined in additional analyses, which we view as perhaps the most probing way of examining the issue (75). Essentially, the procedure is as follows. Between phases 1 and 2 (anticipation to 6 weeks after plant closing) the men experience a transition from either anticipation to unemployment ($N = 53$) or anticipation to fairly prompt reemployment ($N = 46$). Any differential changes in the dependent variables may be viewed as reflecting the impact of an acute or brief "stress." For example, men experiencing the transition to unemployment may show a rise in a particular variable reflecting deprivation or distress if there was no anticipation effect, or they may stay high if there was an anticipation effect. Men experiencing the transition to prompt reemployment may be expected to stay low (or average) if there was no anticipation effect, or show a drop if there was such an effect. In any case, the two groups should show differential trends.

We followed these men through phase 3 (third round of visits 4 to 6 months after plant closing). The men unemployed at phase 2 may still be unemployed ($N = 15$) or may have found a job, a delayed reemployment group ($N = 37$). The men who were employed at phase 2 are continuing to stabilize their reemployment situation ($N = 34$). (There were also 11 men who were employed at phase 2 but by phase 3 had experienced additional job changes and/or episodes of unemployment; they do not fit the notion of stabilized reemployment and are omitted from this particular analysis.) Any differential changes in the dependent variables across these three groups would suggest the impact of more prolonged stress. In particular, the group continuing to be unemployed should continue being elevated or show some additional increases. The delayed reemployment group should show a drop in indices of deprivation and distress, while the stabilized reemployment group should continue being low or perhaps show some additional decreases. The data relevant to these expectations are presented in Tables 2 and 3.

Table 2 presents the relevant results for selected deprivation scales. Inspection shows that only one scale, relative economic deprivation, shows results fully consistent with the hypothesized impact of both brief and prolonged stress. Between first and second rounds, the men who go on to unemployment go up almost 2 SD in relative economic deprivation, while those who become promptly reemployed show essentially no change. Between rounds 2 and 3, men continuing in unemployment status show an additional slight rise, while those continuing to stabilize on their job show a slight decline. The delayed reemployment group shows, as expected, a significant decline in economic deprivation, since for them this represents a transition from unemployment to reemployment.

In striking contrast to these results are the findings for the work role deprivation scale labeled "how much time filled with things to do; how busy." Here, there is a clear-cut effect of brief stress only: men who go on to unemployment at phase 2 increase in their sense of idleness, of not having enough things to do to keep busy and fill time. This feeling of deprivation does not last with continued unemployment, and they come down almost as much as the group experiencing delayed reemployment. Two other scales ("chance to use one's best skills" and "feelings of getting ahead in the world") show the same pattern, but it is somewhat less striking.

Another variable, "chance to talk with people around you and enjoy yourself," shows still another interesting pattern. Essentially, there is no impact of the briefer stress; the prolonged stress actually benefits those continuing to be unemployed and adversely affects those in the delayed reemployment group. This would suggest that, at least, lengthier unemployment does not reduce enjoyable social interactions and may provide an opportunity for increasing them.

TABLE 2. Changes in selected deprivation scales: Differences between study groups classified by employment status at rounds 2 and 3

| Indicator | | Amount of change from | | | | |
| | | 1-Anticipation to | | 2-Unemployed to | | 2-Reemployed to |
		2-Unemployed	2-Reemployed	3-Still unemployed	3-Delayed reemployed	3-Stabilized reemployed
Relative economic deprivation	Mean change[a]	1.74	0.11	0.33	-1.02	-0.23
	Signific. of change	<0.001	NS	NS	<0.001	NS
	Signific. of group diff.	<0.001		<0.025		
Work role "deprivation" scales						
Feelings of security about the future	Mean change	-0.03	-0.37	0.00	-0.74	-0.25
	Signific. of change	NS	NS	NS	<0.025	NS
	Signific. of group diff.	NS		NS		
Feelings of getting ahead in the world	Mean change	0.98	0.02	-0.47	-1.30	0.14
	Signific. of change	<0.001	NS	NS	<0.001	NS
	Signific. of group diff.	<0.001		<0.005		
Feelings of respect from others	Mean change	0.33	-0.09	0.43	-0.97	0.31
	Signific. of change	NS	NS	NS	<0.005	NS
	Signific. of group diff.	NS		<0.01		
Chance to use one's best skills	Mean change	1.89	0.27	-0.88	-1.84	-0.25
	Signific. of change	<0.001	NS	<0.07	<0.001	NS
	Signific. of group diff.	<0.001		<0.005		
How much time filled with things to do; how busy	Mean change	1.24	-0.15	-1.07	-1.28	-0.60
	Signific. of change	<0.001	NS	<0.01	<0.001	<0.025
	Signific. of group diff.	<0.001		NS		
Chance to talk with people around you and enjoy yourself	Mean change	-0.14	0.08	-1.13	0.64	-0.53
	Signific. of change	NS	NS	<0.01	<0.05	NS
	Signific. of group diff.	NS		<0.025		

[a] Positive score indicates an increase in deprivation over time; negative score indicates a decrease. Values are in Z-scores (M = 0, SD = 1) based on normative data from controls.

TABLE 3. Changes in selected mental health and physiological indicators: Differences between study groups classified by employment status at rounds 2 and 3

Indicator		Amount of change from				
		1-Anticipation to		2-Unemployed to		2-Reemployed to
		2-Unemployed	2-Reemployed	3-Still unemployed	3-Delayed reemployed	3-Stabilized reemployed
Depression	Mean change[a]	0.30	-0.43	-0.39	-0.09	0.07
	Signific. of change	<0.10	<0.05	NS	NS	NS
	Signific. of group diff.			NS		
Anxiety-tension	Mean change	0.19	-0.45	-0.51	-0.05	-0.14
	Signific. of change	NS	<0.025	<0.10	NS	NS
	Signific. of group diff.	<0.01		NS		
Psychophysiological symptoms	Mean change	-0.18	-0.30	-0.71	0.38	0.10
	Signific. of change	NS	NS	<0.05	NS	NS
	Signific. of group diff.	<0.01		<0.05		
Suspicion	Mean change	0.17	-0.55	-0.56	0.12	-0.04
	Signific. of change	NS	<0.01	<0.05	NS	NS
	Signific. of group diff.	NS		NS		
Pulse rate (beats/min)	Mean change	2.43	-2.22	-3.36	-0.97	-1.65
	Signific. of change	<0.05	<0.05	<0.05	NS	NS
	Signific. of group diff.	<0.05		NS		
Diastolic blood pressure (mm Hg)	Mean change	1.36	-3.07	1.36	-1.65	-0.22
	Signific. of change	NS	<0.005	NS	NS	NS
	Signific. of group diff.	<0.005		NS		
Serum uric acid (mg/100 ml)	Mean change	0.09	-0.55	-0.37	-0.23	-0.01
	Signific. of change	NS	<0.001	NS	NS	NS
	Signific. of group diff.	<0.01		NS		
Serum cholesterol (mg/100 ml)	Mean change	9.24	-2.40	-6.21	-18.97	-2.63
	Signific. of change	<0.025	NS	NS	<0.001	NS
	Signific. of group diff.	<0.05		NS		

[a] Positive score indicates an increase over time; negative score indicates a decrease.

Only one of the work role deprivation scales, "feelings of respect from others," suggests the impact of the more prolonged stress: with continued unemployment, there is an increase in the sense of not being respected by others, in contrast to the perceived gain in respect among the delayed reemployment group.

Table 3 presents the relevant results for a few selected mental health indicators and for four physiological variables. The pattern of results is fairly consistent. Of the four mental health indicators, three show the predicted sensitivity to the impact of briefer stress. However, all four reveal a decline in the group that continues to be unemployed (between rounds 2 and 3); therefore, none shows the predicted sensitivity to more enduring stress.

The data on the physiological variables are included to show that this pattern of findings need not be limited to the mental health indicators. As can be seen, all four physiological variables show a sensitivity to the briefer stress, but none shows reliably different trends associated with the longer lasting stress; only diastolic blood pressure reveals a pattern of trends consistent with sensitivity to prolonged stress, but the differences are not significant.

Overall, our results suggest that these blue collar workers did not maintain a state of arousal, distress, and sense of work role deprivation as long as the unemployment experience lasted; instead, they showed evidence of adaptation. Thus, following an initial period of unemployment, those continuing to remain unemployed could not be distinguished—in terms of changes on the many indicators—from those finding a new job. It is possible that adaptation to nonwork (unemployment, retirement) among most blue collar workers does not take long, except for the economic aspects.

CONCLUSION

Modern industrial society apparently cannot provide fulfilling work for many of its citizens; that is tragic and dehumanizing. A review of the relevant literature also suggests that what may tax the adaptive capacities of blue collar workers in low skill jobs may not be job loss or retirement as much as it is coming to terms with the dull, monotonous job in the first place. If most workers adapt by giving up any expectations that work will be a meaningful human activity— and thereby compromise their "positive mental health"—then we should not be surprised that the loss of the work role (via job loss or retirement) among such disengaged workers may not be the trauma which facile generalizations from the "stressful life events" literature would seem to dictate. Of course, this personal conclusion is intended to apply only to the noneconomic aspects of the loss of the work role.

REFERENCES

1. Aiken, M., Ferman, L. A., and Sheppard, H. L. (1968): *Economic Failure, Alienation, and Extremism.* University of Michigan Press, Ann Arbor.
2. Alderfer, C. P. (1969): Job enlargement and the organizational context. *Personnel Psychol.,* 22:418–426.

3. Atchley, R. C. (1975): Adjustment to loss of job at retirement. *Int. J. Aging Hum. Dev.,* 6:17–27.
4. Atchley, R. C. (1976): *The Sociology of Retirement.* Wiley, New York.
5. Back, K. W., and Guptill, C. S. (1966): Retirement and self-ratings. In: *Social Aspects of Aging,* edited by I. H. Simpson and J. C. McKinney, pp. 120–129. Duke University Press, Durham.
6. Bakke, E. W. (1940): *Citizens Without Work.* Yale University Press, New Haven.
7. Bakke, E. W. (1940): *The Unemployed Worker.* Yale University Press, New Haven.
8. Barfield, R., and Morgan, J. N. (1969): *Early Retirement: The Decision and The Experience.* Institute for Social Research, The University of Michigan, Ann Arbor.
9. Barfield, R. E., and Morgan, J. N. (1977): Trends in planned early retirement. Institute for Social Research, The University of Michigan, Ann Arbor *(unpublished manuscript).*
10. Bell, B. D. (1974): Cognitive dissonance and the life satisfaction of older adults. *J. Gerontol.,* 29:564–571.
11. Bell, B. D. (1975): The limitations of crisis theory as an explanatory mechanism in social gerontology. *Int. J. Aging Hum. Dev.,* 6:153–168.
12. Blauner, R. (1964): *Alienation and Freedom: The Factory Worker and His Industry.* University of Chicago Press, Chicago.
13. Bradburn, N. (1969): *The Structure of Psychological Well-Being.* Aldine Press, Chicago.
14. Breed, W. (1963): Occupational mobility and suicide. *Am. Sociol. Rev.,* 28:179–188.
15. Brenner, M. H. (1973): *Mental Illness and the Economy.* Harvard University Press, Cambridge.
16. Brown, T. R., and Sheran, T. J. (1972): Suicide prediction: A review. *Life Threat. Behav.,* 2:67–98.
17. Campbell, A., Converse, P. E., and Rodgers, W. L. (1976): *The Quality of American Life.* Russell Sage Foundation, New York.
18. Campbell, D. T., and Fiske, D. W. (1959): Convergent and discriminant validation by the multitrait-multimethod matrix. *Psychol. Bull.,* 56:81–105.
19. Cantril, A. H., and Roll, C. W., Jr. (1971): *Hopes and Fears of the American People.* Universe Books, New York.
20. Caplan, R. D., Cobb, S., French, J. R. P., Jr., Harrison, R. V., and Pinneau, S. R., Jr. (1975): *Job Demands and Worker Health.* DHEW publication no. (NIOSH) 75–160, Washington, D.C.
21. Carp, F. M. (editor) (1972): *Retirement.* Behavioral Publications, New York.
22. Carp, F. M. (1977): Retirement and physical health. In: *Advances in Psychosomatic Medicine, Vol. 9: Epidemiologic Studies in Psychosomatic Medicine,* edited by S. V. Kasl and F. Reichsman, pp. 140–159. Karger, Basel.
23. Catalano, R., and Dooley, C. D. (1977): Economic predictors of depressed mood and stressful life events in a metropolitan community. *J. Health Soc. Behav.,* 18:292–307.
24. Cavan, R. S., and Ranck, K. H. (1938): *The Family and the Depression.* University of Chicago Press, Chicago.
25. Cobb, S. (1974): Physiologic changes in men whose jobs were abolished. *J. Psychosom. Res.,* 18:245–258.
26. Cobb, S., and Kasl, S. V. (1977): *Termination: The Consequences of Job Loss.* DHEW (NIOSH) publication no. 77–224, Cincinnati.
27. Crawford, M. P. (1972): Retirement as a psychosocial crisis. *J. Psychosom. Res.,* 16:375–380.
28. Dayton, N. A. (1940): *New Facts on Mental Disorder.* Charles C Thomas, Springfield, Illinois.
29. Dohrenwend, B. S., and Dohrenwend, B. P. (editors) (1974): *Stressful Life Events: Their Nature and Effects.* Wiley, New York.
30. Dooley, C. D., and Catalano, R. (1977): Economic, life, and disorder changes: Time-series analyses. Program in Social Ecology, University of California, Irvine *(unpublished manuscript).*
31. Dooley, D., and Catalano, R. (1977): Money and mental disorder: Toward behavioral cost accounting for primary prevention. *Am. J. Community Psychol.,* 5:217–227.
32. Draper, J. E., Lundgren, E. F., and Strother, G. B. (1967): *Work Attitudes and Retirement Adjustment.* University of Wisconsin, Bureau of Business Research and Service, Madison.
33. Dubin, R. (1956): Industrial workers' worlds: A study of the "central life interests" of industrial workers. *Soc. Problems,* 3:131–142.
34. Elesh, D., and Lefcowitz, M. J. (1977): The effects of the New Jersey Pennsylvania negative income tax experience on health and health care utilization. *J. Health Soc. Behav.,* 18:391–405.

35. Emerson, A. R. (1959): The first year of retirement. *Occup. Psychol.,* 33:197–208.
36. Erikson, E. H. (1956): The problem of ego identity. *J. Am. Psychoanal. Assoc.,* 4:56–121.
37. Fillenbaum, G. G. (1971): The working retired. *J. Gerontol.,* 26:82–89.
38. Ford, R. N. (1969): *Motivation Through Work Itself.* American Management Association, New York.
39. Form, W. H. (1973): Auto workers and their machines: A study of work, factory and job dissatisfaction in four countries. *Soc. Forces,* 52:1–15.
40. Fox, J. H. (1977): Effects of retirement and former work life on women's adaptation in old age. *J. Gerontol.,* 32:196–202.
41. Fried, M. (1969): Social differences in mental health. In: *Poverty and Health: A Sociological Analysis,* edited by J. Kosa, A. Antonovsky, and I. K. Zola, pp. 113–167. Harvard University Press, Cambridge.
42. Friedmann, E. A., and Havinghurst, R. J. (1954): *The Meaning of Work and Retirement.* University of Chicago Press, Chicago.
43. Friedmann, E. A., and Orbach, H. L. (1974): Adjustment to retirement. In: *American Handbook of Psychiatry, Vol. I.,* edited by S. Arieti, pp. 609–645. Basic Books, New York.
44. Gardell, B. (1971): Alienation and mental health in the modern industrial environment. In: *Society, Stress, and Disease, Vol. I.,* edited by L. Levi, pp. 148–180. Oxford University Press, London.
45. Gechman, A. S. (1974): Without work, life goes . . . *J. Occup. Med.,* 16:749–751.
46. George, L. K., and Maddox, G. L. (1977): Subjective adaptation to loss of the work role: A longitudinal study. *J. Gerontol.,* 32:456–462.
47. Ginzberg, E. (1943): *The Unemployed.* Harper, New York.
48. Glamser, F. D. (1976): Determinants of a positive attitude toward retirement. *J. Gerontol.,* 31:104–107.
49. Gore, S. (1973): *The Influence of Social Support in Ameliorating the Consequences of Job Loss.* Unpublished doctoral dissertation, University of Pennsylvania, Philadelphia.
50. Gurin, G., Veroff, J., and Feld, S. (1960): *Americans View Their Mental Health.* Basic Books, New York.
51. Hackman, J. R., and Lawler, E. E., III (1971): Employee reactions to job characteristics. *J. Appl. Psychol.,* 55:259–286.
52. Harrington, J. A., and Cross, K. W. (1959): Cases of attempted suicide admitted to a general hospital. *Br. Med. J.,* 2:463–467.
53. Harris, L. (1965): "Pleasant" retirement expected. *The Washington Post,* Nov. 28.
54. Haynes, S. G. (1975): *Mortality Around Retirement and the Socio-Medical Correlates of Early Death Among Retirees in the Rubber Industry.* Unpublished doctoral dissertation, University of North Carolina, Chapel Hill.
55. Haynes, S. G., McMichael, A. J., and Tyroler, H. A. (1977): The relationship of normal involuntary retirement to early mortality among U.S. rubber workers. *Soc. Sci Med.,* 11:105–114.
56. Henry, A. F., and Short, J. F., Jr. (1954): *Suicide and Homicide.* Free Press, Glencoe.
57. Holmes, T. H., and Rahe, R. H. (1967): The social readjustment rating scale. *J. Psychosom. Res.,* 11:213–218.
58. Hulin, C. L., and Blood, M. R. (1968): Job enlargement, individual differences and worker responses. *Psychol. Bull.,* 69:41–55.
59. Jacobson, D. (1972): Fatigue-producing factors in industrial work and pre-retirement attitudes. *Occup. Psychol.,* 46:193–200.
60. Jacobson, D. (1972): Willingness to retire in relation to job strain and type of work. *J. Industr. Gerontol.,* 13:65–74.
61. Jaffe, A. J. (1972): The retirement dilemma. *J. Industr. Gerontol.,* 14:1–89.
62. Jahoda, M. (1958): *Current Concepts of Positive Mental Health.* Basic Books, New York.
63. Jaslow, P. (1976): Employment, retirement, and morale among older women. *J. Gerontol.,* 31:212–218.
64. Kahn, R. L. (1974): On the meaning of work. *J. Occup. Med.,* 16:716–719.
65. Kahn, R. L. (1972): The meaning of work: Interpretation and proposals for measurement. In: *The Human Meaning of Social Change,* edited by A. Campbell and P. E. Converse, pp. 159–203. Russell Sage Foundation, New York.
66. Kasl, S. V. (1977): Contributions of social epidemiology to studies in psychosomatic medicine. In: *Advances in Psychosomatic Medicine, Vol. 9, Epidemiologic Studies in Psychosomatic Medicine,* edited by S. V. Kasl and F. Reichsman, pp. 160–223. Karger, Basel.

67. Kasl, S. V. (1973): Mental health and the work environment: An examination of the evidence. *J. Occup. Med.,* 15:509–518.
68. Kasl, S. V. (1978): Stress at work: Epidemiological contributions to the study of work stress. In: *Stress at Work,* edited by C. L. Cooper and R. Payne, pp. 3–48. Wiley, Sussex.
69. Kasl, S. V. (1978): *The Impact of Retirement of Health and Well-Being.* Technical report prepared for the National Institute of Aging, NIH, order no. 263-78-M-2062. Department of Epidemiology and Public Health, Yale University School of Medicine, New Haven.
70. Kasl, S. V. (1974): Work and mental health. In: *Work and the Quality of Life,* edited by J. O'Toole, pp. 171–196. MIT Press, Cambridge.
71. Kasl, S. V. (1977): Work and mental health: Contemporary research evidence. In: *A Matter of Dignity: Inquiries into the Humanization of Work,* edited by W. J. Heisler and J. W. Houck, pp. 85–110. University of Notre Dame Press, Notre Dame.
72. Kasl, S. V., and Cobb, S. (1970): Blood pressure changes in men undergoing job loss: A preliminary report. *Psychosom. Med.,* 32:19–38.
73. Kasl, S. V., and Cobb, S. (1971): Physical and mental health correlates of status incongruence. *Soc. Psychiatry,* 6:1–10.
74. Kasl, S. V., Cobb, S., and Brooks, G. W. (1968): Changes in serum uric acid and cholesterol levels in men undergoing job loss. *JAMA,* 206:1500–1507.
75. Kasl, S. V., Cobb, S., and Thompson, W. D. (1977): Duration of stressful life situation and reactivity of psychological and physiological variables: Can one extrapolate chronic changes from reactivity to acute stress? Presented at the Annual Meeting of the American Psychosomatic Society, Atlanta, March 25–27.
76. Kasl, S. V., Gore, S., and Cobb, S. (1975): The experience of losing a job: Reported changes in health, symptoms, and illness behavior. *Psychosom. Med.,* 37:1–6–122.
77. Kirsch, B. A., and Langermann, J. L. (1972): An empirical test of Robert Blauner's ideas on alienation in work as applied to different type jobs in a white collar setting. *Sociol. Soc. Res.,* 56:180–194.
78. Kohn, M. L., and Schooler, C. (1973): Occupational experience and psychological functioning: An assessment of reciprocal effects. *Am. Soc. Rev.,* 38:97–118.
79. Komarovsky, M. (1940): *The Unemployed Man and His Family.* Dryden Press, New York.
80. Kornhauser, A. (1965): *Mental Health of the Industrial Worker.* Wiley, New York.
81. Langner, T. S., and Michael, S. T. (1963): *Life Stress and Mental Health.* Free Press, Glencoe.
82. Lester, D. (1970): Suicide and unemployment. *Arch. Environ. Health,* 20:277–278.
83. Loether, H. J. (1965): The meaning of work and adjustment to retirement. In: *Blue Collar World,* edited by A. B. Shostak and W. Gomberg, pp. 525–533. Prentice-Hall, Englewood Cliffs, New Jersey.
84. McDonald, B. W., and Gunderson, E. K. E. (1974): Correlates of job satisfaction in naval environments. *J. Appl. Psychol.,* 59:371–373.
85. McMahan, C. A., and Ford, T. A. (1955): Surviving the first five years after retirement. *J. Gerontol.,* 10:212–215.
86. Mangione, T. W., and Quinn, R. P. (1975): Job satisfaction, counterproductive behavior, and drug use at work. *J. Appl. Psychol.,* 60:114–116.
87. Martin, J., and Doran, A. (1966): Evidence concerning the relationship between health and retirement. *Sociol. Rev.,* 14:329–343.
88. Miller, D. R. (1963): The study of social relationships: Situation, identity, and social interaction. In: *Psychology: A Study of a Science, Vol. 5,* edited by S. Koch, pp. 639–737. McGraw-Hill, New York.
89. Myers, R. J. (1954): Factors in interpreting mortality after retirement. *J. Am. Stat. Assoc.,* 49:499–509.
90. Orzack, L. H. (1959): Work as a "central life interest" of professionals. *Soc. Problems,* 7:125–132.
91. O'Toole, J. (1974): Work in America and the great job satisfaction controversy. *J. Occup. Med.,* 16:710–715.
92. Parnes, H. S., and King, R. (1977): Middle-aged job losers. *Industr. Gerontol.,* 4:77–95.
93. Paykel, E. S., Prusoff, B. A., and Uhlenhuth, E. H. (1971): Scaling life events. *Arch. Gen. Psychiatry,* 25:340–347.
94. Pierce, A. (1967): The economic cycle and the social suicide rate. *Am. Sociol. Rev.,* 32:457–462.
95. Quinn, R. P., Seashore, S., Kahn, R. L., Mangione, T., Campbell, D., Staines, G., and McCul-

lough, M. (1971): *Survey of Working Conditions.* document no. 2916–0001, U.S. Government Printing Office, Washington, D.C.
96. Quinn, R. P., and Shepard, L. J. (1974): *The 1972–73 Quality of Employment Survey.* The Institute for Social Research, University of Michigan, Ann Arbor.
97. Rabinowitz, S., and Hall, D. T. (1977): Organizational research on job involvement. *Psychol. Bull.,* 84:265–288.
98. Rabkin, J. G., and Struening, E. L. (1976): Life events, stress, and illness. *Science,* 194:1013–1020.
99. Riley, M. W., and Foner, A. (1968): *Aging and Society. An Inventory of Research Findings, Vol. 1.* Russell Sage Foundation, New York.
100. Riley, M. W., Johnson, M., and Foner, A. (1972): *Aging and Society. Vol. 3. A Sociology of Age Stratification.* Russell Sage Foundation, New York.
101. Robinson, J. P., and Converse, P. E. (1972): Social change reflected in the use of time. In: *The Human Meaning of Social Change,* edited by A. Campbell and P. E. Converse, pp. 17–86. Russell Sage Foundation, New York.
102. Roman, P. H., and Trice, H. M. (1972): Psychiatric impairment among "Middle Americans:" Surveys of work organizations. *Soc. Psychiatry,* 7:157–166.
103. Rose, C. L., and Mogey, J. M. (1972): Aging and preference for later retirement. *Aging Hum. Dev.,* 3:45–62.
104. Rowe, A. R. (1973): Scientists in retirement. *J. Gerontol.,* 28:345–350.
105. Rundquist, E. A., and Sletto, R. F. (1936): *Personality in the Depression.* University of Minnesota Press, Minneapolis.
106. Ryser, and Sheldon, A. (1969): Retirement and health. *J. Am. Geriat. Soc.,* 17:180–190.
107. Sainsbury, P. (1955): *Suicide in London.* Maudsley monograph no. 1, London.
108. Sayles, L., and Strauss, G. (1966): *Human Behavior in Organizations.* Prentice-Hall, Englewood Cliffs, New Jersey.
109. Sexton, W. P. (1968): Industrial work: Who calls it psychologically devastating? *Manag. Personnel Q.,* 6:2–8.
110. Shanas, E., Townsend, P., Wedderburn, O., Fribes, M., and Miethoj, P., and Stehouwer, J. (1968): *Old People in Three Industrial Societies.* Atherton Press, New York.
111. Shepard, J. M. (1971): *Automation and Alienation.* MIT Press, Cambridge.
112. Sheppard, H. L. (1976): Work and retirement. In: *Handbook of Aging and the Social Sciences,* edited by R. H. Binstock and E. Shanas, pp. 286–309. Van Nostrand, New York.
113. Sheppard, H., Belitsky, A., and Harvey, A. (1966): *The Job Hunt.* The Johns Hopkins Press, Baltimore.
114. Sheppard, H. L., and Herrick, N. Q. (1972): *Where Have All the Robots Gone? Worker Dissatisfaction in the '70's.* Free Press, New York.
115. Simpson, I. H., and McKinney, J. C. (editors) (1966): *Social Aspects of Aging.* Duke University Press, Durham.
116. Stokes, R. G., and Maddox, G. L. (1967): Some social factors on retirement adaptation. *J. Gerontol.,* 22:329–333.
117. Strauss, G. (1974): Is there a blue-collar revolt against work? In: *Work and the Quality of Life,* edited by J. O'Toole, pp. 40–69. MIT Press, Cambridge.
118. Strauss, G. (1974): Workers: Attitudes and adjustments. In: *The Worker and the Job: Coping with Change,* edited by The American Assembly, Columbia University, pp. 73–98. Prentice-Hall, Englewood Cliffs, New Jersey.
119. Streib, G. F. (1956): Morale of the retired. *Soc. Problems,* 3:270–276.
120. Streib, G. F., and Schneider, C. J. (1971): *Retirement in American Society: Impact and Process.* Cornell University Press, Ithaca.
121. Super, D. E. (1951): Vocational adjustment: Implementing a self-concept. *Occupations,* 30:88–92.
122. Swinscow, D. (1951): Some suicide statistics. *Br. Med. J.,* 1:1417–1422.
123. Tausky, C., and Piedmont, E. B. (1967/68): The meaning of work and unemployment: Implications for mental health. *Int. J. Soc. Psychiatry,* 14:44–49.
124. Taylor, L. (1968): *Occupational Sociology.* Oxford University Press, New York.
125. Thompson, G. B. (1973): Work versus leisure roles: An investigation of moral among employed and retired men. *J. Gerontol.,* 28:339–344.
126. Thompson, W. E., Streib, G. F., and Kosa, J. (1960): The effect of retirement on personal adjustment: A panel analysis. *J. Gerontol.,* 15:165–169.

127. Tiffany, D. W., Cowan, J. R., and Tiffany, P. M. (1970): *The Unemployed: A Social-Psychological Portrait.* Prentice-Hall, Englewood Cliffs, New Jersey.
128. Triandis, H. C. (1973): Work and nonwork: Intercultural perspectives. In: *Work and Non-Work in the Year 2001,* edited by M. D. Dunnette, pp. 29–52. Brooks/Cole, Monterey.
129. Tyhurst, J. S., Salk, L., and Kennedy, M. (1957): Mortality, morbidity and retirement. *Am. J. Public Health,* 47:1434–1444.
130. Veroff, J., Feld, S., and Gurin, G. (1962): Dimensions of subjective adjustment. *J. Abnorm. Soc. Psychol.,* 64:192–205.
131. Von Wiegand, R. A. (1972): Alcoholism in industry (U.S.A.) *Br. J. Addict.,* 67:181–187.
132. Wessman, A. E. (1956): *A Psychological Inquiry into Satisfaction and Happiness.* Unpublished doctoral dissertation, Princeton University. Princeton.
133. Wilcock, R. C., and Franke, W. H. (1963): *Unwanted Workers.* The Free Press, Glencoe.
134. Wilson, W. (1967): Correlates of avowed happiness. *Psychol. Bull.,* 67:294–306.

Stress and Mental Disorder,
edited by James E. Barrett et al.
Raven Press, New York © 1979.

Macrosocial and Microsocial Crises and Their Impact on the Midtown Manhattan Follow-up Panel

Leo Srole

New York State Psychiatric Institute, New York, New York 10032

The Midtown Manhattan Study, fielded in 1954 under the direction of Dr. Thomas Rennie and the writer as its senior psychiatrist and senior social scientist, respectively, was an epidemiological, cross-sectional investigation of the entire range of mental health differences and psychiatric service utilizations in a general, residential, metropolitan population between the ages of 20 and 59.

In one respect, the Midtown Study fitted the specifications of descriptive epidemiology in that it sought to delineate the differential frequencies of mental impairment and treatment facilities for it as distributed throughout the complex network of interlocking groups embedded in the enormously heterogenous Midtown population. The social policy purpose of this effort was to provide a rational, empirical basis for the long overdue expansion and redeployment of psychiatric services in the American urban community.

Beyond such demographic, descriptive mapping of unserved treatment needs, the Midtown Study was also an enterprise in etiological epidemiology. That is, it viewed a community population as a long-standing laboratory of improvised natural experiments that offered the opportunity to trace sociocultural contributions to mental health differences among the population's subgroups. The social policy purpose at this level was to provide an evidential foundation for a primary preventive psychiatry that was still in its infancy.

We were determined, however, to avoid the simplistic, sociological determinism implied in many cross-sectional investigations where a current social status or group membership is held to have previously acted in a unidirectional fashion on the current mental health of its adult members.

To take a specific illustration, numerous cross-sectional investigations, finding a correlation between adults' socioeconomic status and their mental health, have concluded that the former stands in a causal relationship to mental health. In the Midtown Study, we held that in fact adult socioeconomic status could be, and often is, a consequence as well as a "cause" of the individual's prior mental health; in other words, the two variables are locked in an interacting, reciprocal relationship, one spiraling over time.

To detour around this ambiguity, we placed primary analytic emphasis not on the respondent's own socioeconomic status in 1954 but on that of his parents when he was an adolescent. Part of our general strategy in the 1954 interviews was to comb the childhood period for etiological clues to social influences on later mental health. In this respect, what was primarily a cross-sectional, single point-of-time investigation was secondarily a longitudinal study of the retrospective kind.

When we started our planning in the early 1950s, we found ourselves with a newly established funding resource, the National Institute of Mental Health (NIMH), and new tools, probability sampling techniques and symptom inventories, with which to explore the large, recently opened research frontier provided by general populations.

In this pioneer atmosphere, we did not look beyond the newly visible horizon to consider what might lie beyond or to conceive that we would return someday for a second round with our sample of 1,660 interviewed Midtown adults. Thus we did not build into our interview instrument any of the informational links necessary to retrace the residential steps of mobile people in their post-1954 peregrinations.

Sometime in 1956, however, I encountered the first report of the Framingham, Massachusetts, prospective longitudinal investigation of the cardiovascular disorders in a general population sample of men. I monitored its subsequent publications with fascination and with envy of its large etiological pay-offs. It was Framingham's repeated examinations of the same men that ultimately disentangled sequentially much of what is now known about the major risk factors contributing to our most prevalent and lethal somatic disease. The Framingham model suggested that the Midtown Study of 1954 could be turned into the first-stage baseline for a second-stage follow-up of accessible first-stage Midtown respondents.

In the late 1960s, the NIMH Center for Epidemiological Studies supported our "Bureau of Missing Persons" operation to locate a large enough number of our first-stage people to make a follow-up satisfactory by statistical criteria. In this effort, we had the counsel of the distinguished medical epidemiologist, Dr. Richard Remington, Dean of the University of Michigan School of Public Health. Statistical criteria were met to his satisfaction and that of our NIMH Review Committee when we located 1,124 of our original respondents, 858 alive and 266 deceased, with another 100 of the unlocated actuarially predicted as also deceased.

With further funding from NIMH, we succeeded by the summer of 1974 in reinterviewing a panel of 695 of our original respondents (81% of the 858 located alive), now aged 40 to 79, and residentially scattered across the entire New York metropolitan region and state, 28 other states, and 12 countries. Dean Remington had urged, "catch everybody you possibly can, wherever they are," on the probability sampling principle that all 1,660 respondents of 1954 should have the same chance of being restudied in 1974. For example, 17 first-stage respondents were traced to homes overseas, and by extraordinary efforts we succeeded in reinterviewing 12 of them in places as distant as Morocco and Greece. We tracked one man into the People's Republic of China, but regrettably he failed to answer our letters asking to see him on his next visit to the United States. The 20-year change from local concentration to residential dispersion offers us the new variable of geographic stability-mobility to test for its bearing on mental health in 1954 as an antecedent and in 1974 as a consequence.

Our two main purposes with our panel of 695 reinterviewed respondents were (a) to establish their mental health status in 1974 on a basis comparable to that of 1954, and (b) to exploit our extended temporal perspective to the fullest depth possible.

In this chapter, I shall (a) outline the methods we applied to these ends and the conceptions prompting them, and (b) report a few preliminary findings that have thus far emerged from our analytic work.

The interviews of 1954 consisted of 380 questions and subquestions that required 135 min on the average to administer. The reinterviews of 1974 included more than 600 questions that took an average of 200 min to administer, the two sessions together aggregating almost 6 hr.

Of the entire corpus of items used in 1974, 185 were replications of those asked in 1954, chosen to permit comparison of each respondent across a 20-year time span on identically worded criteria. Of those replicated items, 83 represented the pool of validated signs and symptoms used in 1954 by our Study psychiatrists to independently assign each respondent on a six-class continuum of mental health status, based on degree of symptom formation and severity of impairment in social functioning. The six classes referred to were: (a) Asymptomatic ("Well"), (b) Mild symptom formation, (c) Moderate symptom formation, (d) Marked symptom formation at a level of some impairment in role functioning, (e) Severe symptom formation with role impairment, and (f) near or total Incapacitation in role functioning.

Although in 1974 we replicated 83 of the symptom items used originally, the most serious technical problem of the Midtown Restudy, in the absence of our original psychiatrists, was to classify the 1974 symptom information in a fashion approximating the psychiatrists' mental health ratings of 20 years earlier. By means of multiple regression techniques harnessed to the computer and applied to the 1954 symptom information, we were able to isolate a subset of symptoms, each statistically weighted according to its power to predict the psychiatrists' ratings in that year, which when summed yielded scores that reproduced the psychiatrists' judgmental ratings of that year with an accuracy suggested by a correlation coefficient of 0.83. This accomplished, we turned to the 1974 information derived from the same subset of symptom questions, to which we applied the identical weights and score cutting points to achieve a simulated mental health classification calibrated precisely to the computer-reproduced mental health classification schema of 1954. The computer-reproduced classifications of 1954 had the psychiatrists' judgmental ratings of 1954 as their reference model, and the computer-stimulated classifications of 1974 had the computer-reproduced mental health classifications of 20 years earlier as their reference model. I hereafter refer to these two standardized measures as MH 54 and MH 74, respectively.

Although the Midtown panel was 20 years older at follow-up, the Pearson correlation between MH 54 and MH 74 is 0.52. This reflects the facts that in 1974, 41% of the panelists fell into the same category on our six-class continuum of global mental health status as in 1954, and most of the rest changed only one step in either direction. More precisely, 26% of our respondents moved down to a less favorable category, and 33% moved up to a better mental health stratum.

These figures provide a documentary moving picture showing that around a plurality of apparently stabilized mental health conditions (on all six MH class levels), there has been a dynamic circulation of numerical minorities on the up and down escalators of emotional well-being across a span of two decades. However, I am not generalizing this finding to any population universe other than the reinterviewed survivors of the Midtown universe of 1954, as studied by the methods we used in 1954 and 1974. Not until we have a series of Midtown-like follow-up research projects will we be able to begin drawing such generalizations. The Midtown Longitudinal Study is a sample of one among all such possible researches; in this sense, it is an investigation of a single case.

As mentioned above, at our first stage we retrospectively probed into a substantial series of intrafamily and extrafamily facets of the childhood period of our respondents' lives.

Twenty years later, we cast a much larger net over the lifespan. Our general model was an adaptation of the individual life history, a model that evolved from two related streams of influence. The first stream had its source in the patient's "life chart" of Adolph Meyer, to which I was exposed through his former resident and associate, Thomas Rennie, the launcher of the first-stage Midtown study. The second influence was that of the University of Chicago sociologists, who had developed a less structured life history approach applied to special populations in urban community investigations, to which I was exposed as a graduate student in the 1930s.

By historic coincidence, Meyer himself had been strongly influenced by an earlier generation of Chicago sociologists when he was superintendent of a nearby state hospital before coming east to head the New York State Psychiatric Institute, which, 60 years later, was to cosponsor the second-stage Midtown Study that he had posthumously imprinted with his thought.

In 1974, we also carried out Meyer's emphasis on the individual's assets as well as his/her liabilities, locating some of these around what we called the high and low points of one's life. Parenthetically, these were largely probed through open-ended rather than multiple-choice questions, a mode of inquiry we used to a far greater extent than in 1954.

When planning the Midtown follow-up in 1972–1973, we were aware of the early applications of the Holmes and Rahe Life Events checklist that has since accelerated through the psychiatric literature with bandwagon effects. It was at first glance seductively attractive because it was quick and easy to adapt, administer, and code, and therefore highly efficient in cost terms. In my view, however, it also had a number of serious shortcomings.

First, it was constructed to catch short-term effects of life events, whereas we were primarily interested not in transitory consequences but in more or less lasting impacts on somatic, psychic, and social well-being.

Second, it explicitly incorporated the assumption that the 43 events in the list were differentially stressful and potentially pathogenic experiences for the individual. We, on the other hand, were convinced that after the initial process of settling into a change in life circumstances, the results, depending on individual differences, are often turned into a developmental advance rather than a retreat, a view consonant with Erikson's position that growth is fostered by life cycle changes and crises which are confronted and successfully mastered.

Third, the Holmes and Rahe instrument assumes that its 43 events all fall on the stimulus side of the stimulus-response equation, where the response is taken to be a change toward adverse psychological health. In my judgment, 29 of the 43 events in their checklist may not be primarily exogenous but essentially psychogenic, symptomatic manifestations arising from the same phenomenological substrate as do the health changes that ensue. Involved here is the *post hoc ergo propter hoc* fallacy entangled in the many findings which have seemed to validate the Holmes and Rahe claim that such temporally antecedent events are precipitants of illness. Obviously, an event such as divorce and the illness that follows may both have a common source in an already disturbed personality.

On these critical grounds, we decided to follow another, far more difficult and time-and budget-consuming course in constructing our 1974 interview schedule. We probed first into what we now call "microsocial crises," because they generally also involve his/her immediate small circle of kin and friends. Second, we explored reactions to a series of macrosocial crises, so designated because they involved the larger society as a quasifamily. Third, we ventured into even larger macrosocial universes in the succession of human generations, each a huge, historically discrete mix of all manner of impinging life experiences, both favorable and unfavorable.

Before elaborating on our probes of the respondent's microsocial crises, I must first indicate that earlier in the reinterviews we had routinely inquired about life cycle developments (a) in the marital status domain—dates and causes of changes, including, among the spouseless, the presence of a spouse-surrogate, (b) within the procreative domain—birth dates of children and grandchildren, their dates and causes of death, and (c) the causes, circumstances, and dates of death of parents. Intrafamily losses and gains were thus covered in a more or less systematic fashion.

We also covered the nature and dates of major medical developments, accidents, injuries, and surgeries, episodes of nervous breakdowns, near breakdowns, police arrests, and, finally, prolonged depressive or manic states, what brought them on, and whether, when, and where they had been treated. On the asset side of the ledger, we asked respondents what they regarded as the best period of their life, what was good about the current state of their health, what development, recent or past, gave them the greatest personal pleasure, and a large series of domain-specific satisfactions-dissatisfactions, including the sexual domain.

We assume that from such information, and from that gathered in 1954, we may be able to construct a taxonomy of life history patterns or types, in which the biblical figure of Job would occupy one pole. As you may recall, Job had all the blessings of life, including the transcendant one of God's view that he personally was "a perfect and upright man." Satan then sought and secured God's permission to test Job's faith by destroying all that he had, including his family, his health, and his many properties. Upon passing the test, after a period of utmost despair, Job had all that had been suddenly and inexplicably taken from him restored. Except for that happy ending, the Job type of roller-coaster life history is by no means unrepresented in our Midtown panel.

At the other extreme might be the benign, unremarkable life history, devoid of any high peaks or unbalancing falls, in which life's inevitable losses are spaced out singly, more or less in their preordained season, among modestly balancing, expected gains. As an approximation of the relatively flat life history line, we might temporarily assign this pattern the class label of "smooth" type. If the Midtown investigators' own life histories permit, one of the reporting monographs of our follow-up study may present a gallery of portraits of such types, including their health outcomes, drawn as composites from our own fascinating collection of panel characters.

As in the Book of Job, we wanted to know how life, like Satan, had tested our respondents with major misfortunes, and how each had responded to the most trying one, however generated. To this end, late in the interview we asked a series of questions, the first of which was phased as follows:

> They say that life is the school of hard knocks that we all have to take. As you think back over *your* life, what heavy blows have hit you the *hardest* and upset you the *most* for some time afterwards? What happened and how old were you at that time?

After each hard knock mentioned, a standard probe was regularly presented as to "any other heavy blows?" until the respondent had no more to report. Note that our emphasis was on "heavy blows that hit you the hardest," on criteria of the most upsetting effects for a prolonged period of time.

The number of such heavy blows reported ranged from zero to six, distributed in a more or less normal curve, with a mean of 2+. Parenthetically, about 10% of our sample reported no heavy blows. We intend to give them special analytic attention to discern from cross-validating information (derived by our routine life history coverage) the answer to our question of whether or not they approximate the "smooth" life history type.

At the Job-type pole of the continuum are 44 respondents, representing 6% of the panel, who reported a lifetime incidence of five or more heavy blows. Included is a mother with four World War II Gold Stars.

All respondents reporting one or more hard knocks were next asked:

> Of all these heavy blows that you had to take, which was the one that *hit* you the hardest, *distressed* you the most and *upset* you the longest?

As to the character of these heaviest blows, they were in descending order of frequency, intrafamily deaths and illnesses (more than half of the illnesses were clearly psychiatric), marital disruptions other than widowhood (including 43 instances of what one panelist called a "tragic love affair"), almost 100 cases related to job or career, and 22 related to entrapments of World War II.

The next question was:

> As for the emotional upset that you felt, how long (in weeks, months or years) did it take you to get over that upset and feel yourself again?

Of those asked this question, about one-third recovered from the upset within 50 weeks or less, 20% took 2 to 16 years to recover, and 26% are "not over it yet." This is one of several of our criteria of severity of an event's impact that I find lacking from the life events checklists that I have so far seen.

Among victims of the most extreme of these heavy blows were the United States Naval Intelligence Officer captured by the Japanese at Bataan and imprisoned there for the entire duration of the war, and Jewish survivors of German concentration camps, who had spouse, children, parents, and siblings all incinerated in the Nazi crematoria. I might also mention the man, near the opposite extreme of the Job type, who grew up in the Hitler Jugend, joined the Nazi party, served as a German combat naval officer, who in 1974 told us he had only one heavy blow in his lifetime, namely, "the defeat and surrender of Germany in 1945." This exception aside, he apparently has had a "smooth" life history pattern. It is therefore hardly surprising that both in 1954 and 1974 he emerged with a mental health classification of "asymptomatic," with the interviewers' observations at both points of time confirming that placement.

The chronological age when these heaviest blows fell ranged from age 5 to 79, with 185 of the blows having occurred in the preadult years. Clearly, recency of a life change is hardly a sufficient criterion of the salience or significance of that experience in the totality of the life history.

Both the single- and multiple-blow respondents were probed about such aspects of the heaviest blow as to (a) who was the person (or persons) at the center of the crisis, (b) whether the crisis happened suddenly or unfolded gradually, and (c) who "was helpful to you in the hardest part of that difficult period?"

In reply to the last question, there were 225 citations of members of the nuclear family, 174 mentions of extended kin, 120 designations of one or more friends, and 50 mentions of a professional, a number fewer than the 80 respondents who credited "nobody" or "only myself." This should roughly convey the relative supportive importance during a severely traumatic episode of different kinds of role figures in one's social network.

Unless the respondent's hardest blow was identified as a personal illness, he or she was next asked: "In the period following the (*event* named) did your health change in any way, and if so what changes took place?" Approximately 80% of the respondents asked this question did not link this hardest blow to any change in their health. Of the 89 respondents who did report a health change, 15 actually acknowledged a change for the better. Of the remaining 74 respondents, 19 developed somatic disorders, 12 reported conditions that are generally considered psychosomatic, with the other 43 members of this group developing depressions (including one Auschwitz survivor who experienced a prolonged suicidal depression), acute anxiety states, sharp losses or gains in weight, and the onset of alcohol addiction. One of the latter respondents had been severely injured in the Battle of the Bulge and was found to be functionally incapacitated by alcoholism in 1974, the identical classification assigned to him by our Study psychiatrists in 1954. The exprisoner of Bataan survives financially largely on a total disability pension. Clearly the adverse heaviest blows are nonspecific in their effects on individuals hit by them.

It may be useful to repeat that 365 respondents identified the heaviest blow of their entire life in considerable detail without having any health sequelae worthy of mention. Of the 89 respondents who did recall a change in health, one-sixth reported improved health, with the changes of the rest divided among somatic disorders, psychosomatic conditions, and psychopathological states. Some of the latter were sequelae associated with the extreme traumas of combat or brutal, prolonged imprisonments.

Three more questions were put to all respondents reporting a heaviest blow. The first one was:

> Such very heavy blows can be a turning point followed by more or less lasting change in the course of our lives, change that might not otherwise have occurred. Would you say that the (heaviest blow reported) was a turning point of change in the course of *your* life?

About 307 (53%) of the respondents asked this question did perceive the blow to be a turning point; the rest did not feel any consequential change affecting their life course. As we shall see, "turning point" is a dimension of a life crisis that clarifies its impact. These 307 people who reported a significant turn in the direction of their lives were next asked: "Looked at now, do you feel that this turning point, on the whole, changed your life for the *better* or for the *worse*? In what ways?"

Among those reporting the blow to be a turning point, 104 respondents (47%) assessed its consequences as "for the better," 110 as "for the worse," and the remainder as having mixed positive and negative elements. Of the respondents reporting a turning point "for the better," 60% specified that the improvement was in the intrapsychic realm, whereas of those reporting a turning point "for the worse," 18% reported that the adversity was centered in the intrapsychic realm.

Almost all the heaviest blows elicited in the 1974 interviews were temporally located in the years before 1954. It is therefore not surprising that the group comprehending "for the better" turning points was significantly more favorable in mental health composition, in both 1954 and 1974, than those whose heaviest blows occasioned life turning points "for the worse."

Specifically, in 1954, when none of the above life history information had been gathered, our standardized mental health classifications of the "turn for the better" and "turn for the worse" groups were distributed as shown in Table 1, which also includes their mental health distribution in 1974.

Table 1 indicates that whereas in 1954 the Impaired/Well ratios of the two criterion groups differed by a magnitude of 1:5, by 1974 they differed by a magnitude of almost 1:9. In 20 years, the original sharp contrast between the two groups has sharpened even further.

It remains for us to try to analytically parcel out from our mass of individual life history information the relative contributions of exogenous and endogenous factors in the respondents with heaviest reported blows of the two different turning-point types.

It appears that (a) the direction of the effects of the turning points is an additional dimension elucidating the quality of the impact of the heaviest blow, and (b) our strategy of open-ended probing of the individual life history has elicited several epidemiological criteria which, together, have proven power for long-range prediction and perhaps explanation of the consequences of "heaviest" adversities for mental health outcomes in a general urban population.

From the microsocial blows, I now turn to the four macrosocial crises, which, because of space limitations, must be skimmed over superficially. The most proximal one was the Constitutional crisis of Watergate, which gathered momen-

TABLE 1. *Mental health distributions of Midtown panel (*N = 695*) in "turn for better" and "turn for worse" "heaviest blow" groups*

	MH 54		MH 74	
	Better	Worse	Better	Worse
Asymptomatic (Well)	29.6%	11.8%	30.3%	8.2%
Impaired	10.5%	21.8%	9.1%	21.8%
Impaired/Well ratio	36	184	30	266
N = 100%	142	110	142	110
	Pearson's r = 0.38		r = 0.43	

tum during the 8 months of our field interviews but did not reach the apogee of Nixon's resignation until a month after our last interview was completed. The second crisis was the Kennedy assassination about 11 years before our 1974 study, the only one of the four that came with the suddenness of a lightning bolt out of a clear sky instead of as a gradually accelerating convulsion that stretched over a year or more. The third crisis was World War II, which began here in 1941. The fourth was the Great Depression, which really took large scale hold in 1931.

In bringing up each of these national episodes with our 1974 respondents, we probed into how they currently perceive its influences upon them, if any, at varying distances in time from its onset.

I had as illustration what in November 1963 E. B. White had written in *New Yorker* magazine. These, in part, were his words:

> The death of a President enters the house and becomes a death in the family. No other public death produces so personal an alteration in one's world. Tritely, one remembers the precise spot on which one stood, resisting acceptance and grief. . . . We were left in the silence of irrevocable fact, exchanging empty looks with our companions. Speech, when it returned, was not at first commensurate with national disaster, being little more than the incoherent responses of private pain common to all who have lost a father, a brother, or a son.

A decade after that cataclysmic event, some 55% of our respondents gave evidence of having been as deeply affected by it as E. B. White; 9% candidly said they had not been affected at all.

For the much more prolonged crises of World War II and the Great Depression, we explored far more details of exposure, impact, turning point, influences, and reactions, on both the personal and intrafamilial levels. We have only begun to analyze this information, which we will present in a later, separate paper.

The most macrosocial entity circumscribed in the Midtown panel is the decade-

TABLE 2. *Midtown Manhattan follow-up panel. United States born only (N = 498)*

	Decade-of-birth cohorts			
	A	C	B	D
	b ± 1900	b ± 1920	b ± 1910	b ± 1930
	Age 50–59	Age 50–59	Age 40–49	Age 40–49
	(1954)	(1974)	(1954)	(1974)
	MH 54	MH 74	MH 54	MH 74
Asymptomatic (Well)	15.8%	30.5%	21.3%	27.6%
Impaired	17.6%	9.0%	15.6%	8.5%
Impaired/Well ratio	112	34	74	30
N = 100%	(57)	(167)	(122)	(152)

[a] United States born only.
Chi-square = 24.54, 3 df, $p < 0.01$.
Cramer's $V = 0.435$.

of-birth cohort. Table 2 represents the United States-born segment of our Midtown panel, divided into four birth cohorts, the oldest one born (1895–1904) and the youngest one (1925–1934). I have juxtaposed cohorts A and C because they were each in the 50 to 59 age bracket in 1954 and 1974, respectively, just as cohorts B and D were both at age 40 to 49 in those respective years of our two-stage study.

Stated differently, groups A and C in Table 2 were born 20 years apart and on that basis can be designated as generation-separated, like-age cohorts. Note that on our standardized measure of mental health status, the later group, cohort C, is significantly better in mental health composition than cohort A, the earlier group. The mental health disparity observed between the two age 50 to 59 cohorts, A and C, is reinforced by a parallel differential between cohorts B and D, who are both aged 40 to 49. Parenthetically, we have also analyzed two other replicated indicators of well-being in the Midtown panel, namely, self-rated health and latent suicide potential, with findings to be reported in a later paper. Suffice it only to mention here that on these two indicators, as well as on mental health composition, cohorts C and D appear significantly better off than their respective like-age but generation-earlier cohorts A and B.

The consistency of the findings on all three indicators, and on both age-since-birth strata, suggest that the differences are predominantly rooted not in undefined, artifactual measurement slippages that might hypothetically have occurred between our 1954 and 1974 interviews but rather in the massive sociocultural differences experienced by the cohorts born ±1900 to ±1910 (A and B) and those born in the two succeeding decades (C and D). Our 1974 interviews amply corroborate the real improvements in life history circumstances experienced by members of the later of the two generation segments in our panel, as does a more recent national survey of "social mobility in the U.S.," its key finding summarized by a *New York Times* article (April 24, 1978) in the following words:

> For many [respondents] who described themselves as being in the middle and working classes, life is considerably better than it was a generation ago.

By its long reach back to the turn of the 20th century, the Midtown Longitudinal Study has been able to parcel out the discrete effects on well-being of temporally distinct generation groups, consequences that are independent of the discrete effects of the age-since-birth variable.

In a century of ever-more accelerating social and economic changes, interspersed with a series of macrosocial convulsions speeding up that acceleration, successive generation groups have matured in and navigated through different confluences in the stream of history, each with disparate mixes of benign and noxious currents. The developmental effects, gross and fine, of immersion in different parts of that stream at different stages of the individual life cycle are the source of the proverbial "communication gap" which sets off one generation from the next.

One of the major advances of the Midtown Longitudinal Study of 1974 over its cross-sectional baseline investigation of 1954 is that it has opened new vistas of macrosocial developments and their imprints on micropsychological outcomes across the historic procession of human generations.

I would close with the suggestion that the comparative study of generation milieus stakes out the new subspecialty domain of sociopsychiatric history.

ACKNOWLEDGMENTS

The Midtown Manhattan Follow-up Study in its first stage (1952–1959) was sponsored by the Cornell Medical College and supported by grants from NIMH (#M 515), Grant Foundation, Rockefeller Brothers Fund, Milbank Foundation, Littauer Foundation, and the Samuel Rubin Foundation. In its second stage (1972–) the Study was sponsored by the New York State Psychiatric Institute and Columbia University College of Physicians and Surgeons, Department of Psychiatry, successively chaired by Drs. Lawrence C. Kolb, Sidney Malitz, and Edward J. Sachar. Its operational grants were from the NIMH Center for Epidemiological Studies (#MH 13369) and the Foundations Fund for Research in Psychiatry. The Study is beholden to the indispensable support of all its sponsors and grantors.

This chapter owes much to my colleagues Anita K. Fischer and E. Joel Millman.

Stress and Mental Disorder,
edited by James E. Barrett et al.
Raven Press, New York © 1979.

Discussion, Part III

B. S. Dohrenwend

*Division of Sociomedical Sciences, School of Public Health, Columbia University,
New York, New York 10032*

My discussion is based mostly on some reading of earlier publications by Brenner, Kasl, and Srole and on conversations with them about their chapters.

In one respect, all three chapters provide reason for optimism about research on life stress and psychopathology. They are all products of long-term programs based on substantial commitments of resources to investigating life stress and its effects.

At a more specific level of response, my first comments regard the preceding chapter by Srole. His Table 2, which is discussed as evidence of powerful birth cohort effects distinguishing the first two decades of this century from the third and fourth, aroused but did not satisfy my curiosity. The nature of my question is described in Fig. 1. The major comparisons in Dr. Srole's table are indicated by the percentages joined by dashed lines at the top of Fig. 1. Each pair describes the percentage impaired in two birth cohorts when they were the same age. Although neither difference appears to be statistically significant, this is not a critical point since they indicate a replicated result.

The next point concerns attrition effects, which are indicated by comparing the numbers on the upper left side of Fig. 1 with those that Srole used to make his comparisons. Thus in the 1900 cohort, 32% of United States-born respondents interviewed in 1954 were reinterviewed in 1974, and the percentage impaired dropped from 27.1 in the 1954 sample to 17.6 in the 1974 sample. Although attrition affected all the groups used in Srole's comparisons, this complex phenomenon seems to deserve attention and calls for analysis to determine how it could influence conclusions based on cases in the 1974 follow-up.

Most important, however, is that the critical comparison confounds cohort effects with time of measurement effects, as indicated in Fig. 1. Thus, for the subjects who were compared when in their 40s, data on the 1910 cohort come from the 1954 study and data on the 1930 cohort from the 1974 follow-up; likewise, for those compared when in their 50s, data on the 1900 cohort come from the 1954 study and data on the 1920 cohort from the 1974 follow-up. Given this confounding, I am curious about the figures that I have labeled a, b, c, and d, with the subscripts to indicate that these percentages would be

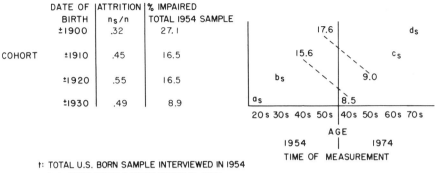

Percent of Midtown Follow-up Respondents Impaired (based on table from L. Srole, Macro-Social and Micro-Social Crises and Their Impact on the Midtown Manhattan Follow-up Panel)

FIG. 1. See text for details.

based on the subjects, in the respective cohorts, who were present in the 1974 sample. My question is whether these figures are, as indicated at the bottom of the figure, consistent with a cohort effect or with a time-of-measurement effect. First, let us assume negligible age effects, as indicated in these data. A cohort effect is indicated if a_s and b_s, the percentages impaired among the 1930 and 1920 cohort subjects in 1954, are about 8.8, that is, approximately equal to the percentages impaired in these cohorts in the 1974 follow-up. On the other hand, a pure time-of-measurement effect would make these percentages about 16.6, approximately equal to those observed in other birth cohorts measured at the same time, in 1954. The answer to this question would either strengthen the argument for a cohort effect or, if the time-of-measurement effect is found to be strong, force some rethinking of what is being measured in the midtown Manhattan follow-up study.

In the chapter by Brenner, he broke through the causal ambiguity involved in the association of low socioeconomic status and psychopathology. To this end, he chose to look at changes in the economic system that the individual who became ill or was hospitalized for psychopathology could not possibly have caused. With that tactic, however, he exposed himself to the risk of the ecological fallacy, that individuals were influenced by a social process that may not have actually affected their lives. To test the validity of his inferences concerning the relationship of changes in the economic system to individual health, we must know whether the persons who became ill actually lost their jobs at the time of economic recession or depression, or somehow suffered some major economic loss. Implicit in his work is the hypothesis that the individual who loses his job, thus suffering both a loss and a major life change, is at high risk of illness.

It is just this hypothesis that Kasl tested in his study with Cobb, which he described briefly, of the effects on individual workers of plant closings. Note that this event has the independence from individual control that Brenner called for as a means of reducing the ambiguity of causal inferences. It is, in a cold, intellectual sense, a disappointment to find that Kasl's subjects generally remained in good health. His findings did not confirm Brenner's implicit hypothesis.

Like Brenner's work, the work of Joseph Eyer involves analyses relating changes in the economic system to individual health and illness. To state the issue, an abstract of a 1977 article by Eyer (1) follows:

> The general death rate rises during business booms and falls during depressions. The causes of death involved in this variation range from infectious diseases through accidents to heart disease, cancer, and cirrhosis of the liver, and include the great majority of all causes of death. Less than 2 percent of the death rate—that for suicide and homicide—varies directly with unemployment. In the older historical data, deterioration of housing and rise of alcohol consumption on the boom may account for part of this variation. In twentieth-century cycles, the role of social stress is probably predominant. Overwork and fragmentation of community through migration are two important sources of stress which rise with the boom, and they are demonstrably related to the causes of death which show this variation.

Although Eyer's research, like Brenner's, is concerned with many outcomes besides psychopathology, and Brenner has introduced qualifications in his most recent work in terms of effects of rapid upturns in the economy, discussion of their contrasting results and similar interpretations of stress as the mediating process would contribute to our understanding of the stress processes that are the subject of this volume.

REFERENCE

1. Eyer, J. (1977): Prosperity as a cause of death. *Int. J. Health Serv.*, 7:125–150.

Stress and Mental Disorder,
edited by James E. Barrett et al.
Raven Press, New York © 1979.

General Discussion, Part III

Editors' Note: Because of changes between the publication version of some chapters and the version presented at the meeting itself, the full open discussion for Part III has been omitted. Much of that discussion was concerned with various aspects of Dr. Brenner's chapter, particularly the method of computation of the lag times. His presentation underwent substantial changes between the meeting and the version published here, but some of the open discussion questions still appeared relevant and thus are included.

Dr. Robert Rose: Dr. Brenner, is there an alternative explanation to account for these economic changes? You correctly point out that the curve was reverse sigmoid with the level of mortality dropping in the late 1930s and continuing relatively constant. The advent of antibiotics occurred after World War II, and their widespread use became disseminated. That is one alternative explanation for the drop in infant mortality that occurred; the residual constant level may be due to problems of distribution or utilization of antibiotics and/or other factors attributable to prenatal mortality.

Dr. Brenner: Various authors have examined the effects of the introduction of each of the antibiotics on all of the major infectious diseases. For the United States, at least, they attribute a decline, at most, of 2% due to their introduction and distribution. These studies were replicated for Sweden and, earlier still, in studies done in England, Wales, and New Zealand.

Dr. Stanislav Kasl: I'd like to pick up on that comment because I think there's a more bothersome problem, which is that infant mortality rates remained essentially at the same level from the 1920s to the 1940s, but there was a profound change in the unemployment rate; thus the raw data do not show any association. But, lo and behold, you detrend and suddenly, because of the detrending, the rates that were high in the 1920s are now below this linear trend. Where there was no association or one totally opposite to expectations (there was no change whatever in mortality and a profound change in the economic condition), by the process of so-called detrending there is suddenly a big association. I have seen your detrending of heart disease data where you chose to detrend differently, removing more complex nonlinear trends as well. I think the whole process of analyzing the ecological data is a wedding of an extremely sophisticated computer technology to a certain set of totally arbitrary moves that have to do with both the detrending (or the various ways of detrending) and the lagging. Earlier, your reply to a comment about this by Dr. Dohrenwend was: "Well, he chooses a different lag."

Since the economy shows minor yearly fluctuations up and down, the lag, depending on which lag one chooses, produces positive or negative association, or no association. How do we understand the apparent arbitrariness of several of these steps in your analysis?

Dr. Brenner: I did not say, in response to Dr. Dohrenwend, that Ayer uses simply a different lag or that he uses no lag and I use some different lag. What I said is that at any lag at all from zero to 9 years, the correlation will always be positive. It does not change sign; it is merely smaller.

Furthermore, the techniques of detrending are not in any way arbitrary. What they reflect is a standardized procedure, a program developed at the University of Michigan for treatment of exactly these kinds of data, in which the person investigating has no control over the type of trend involved. Instead, there is a choice made on the basis of the best-fitting linear regression, or nonlinear regression curve, which composes an equation on its own. The procedures are well developed and are replicated in this country and in others.

Dr. Kasl: That could not possibly be true; the infant mortality rates clearly were first level (straight line, zero slope) and then started to decline in a straight line. The obvious best fit is something other than a single straight line with a moderate slope. Clearly, someone chose to detrend in this nonoptimal way.

Dr. Brenner: No. In fact, the picture does not replicate the mathematics. They are two different procedures. One is useful for observation, containing a variety of discrepancies that are only brought forward. In mathematical analyses, the modern analyses, graphs are not used. For purposes of demonstration to an epidemiological audience to whom that paper was first presented, the usual observational techniques using graphic analysis were first presented. Subsequently, within that paper, the more modern analyses were attached, so that the reader had a choice of observing the effects of both types of techniques.

Stress and Mental Disorder,
edited by James E. Barrett et al.
Raven Press, New York © 1979.

Sturdy Childhood Predictors of Adult Outcomes: Replications From Longitudinal Studies*

Lee N. Robins

*Department of Psychiatry, Washington University School of Medicine,
St. Louis, Missouri 63110*

One area that has long been a problem to psychiatric nosology is where psychiatric diagnosis meets social problems—the area of conduct disorders, antisocial personality, alcoholism, and drug dependence. A question has been raised as to whether these are disorders in the same sense as schizophrenia or depression since they require neither thought disorder not internal distress. Are we just using pseudomedical jargon to refer to behavior of which we disapprove? Are we victims of a secular religion that substitutes "sickness" for "sin?" Or are we "blaming the victims" of a sick society by designating as evidence for an illness within the person behaviors that are caused by the experience of poverty and discrimination? If the latter is the case, are these behaviors "normal" for the poor but pathological when they occur in the middle class?

The answers to these puzzling questions cannot be achieved in any single study, since most are limited in the locations surveyed, the social groups studied, their age range, and the historic eras through which they have lived. Even the most complex designs, calling for multiple age cohorts followed at repeated intervals (9), are limited by the methods available at the time and by the level of theoretical sophistication of the investigator. In the long run, the best evidence for the truth of any observation lies in its replicability across studies. The more the populations studied differ, the wider the historic eras they span, the more the details of the methods vary, the more convincing becomes that replication. Thus two imperfect studies that agree are more persuasive than a single, elegant study.

This chapter discusses my own attempts to replicate the results of a study that I was involved in many years ago. The opportunities to attempt these replications in part were intentionally created and in part came along fortuitously.

The original study was a follow-up of patients who attended the Municipal Child Guidance Clinic of St. Louis in the 1920s. That study began when Dr. Patricia O'Neal came upon the records of the clinic when they were about to be destroyed. Together, we decided to see what had become of these people.

---

* Paul Hoch Award Lecture.

We focused on antisocial personality (sociopathy) as the outcome of interest because that seemed the best use for these records; the clinic started as a service for the Juvenile Court, and a large proportion of its clientele had severe antisocial behavior. We were innocent in those days of concerns about the theoretical implications of the intersection of psychiatry and social problems. Once done, however, this adventitious excursion into studying childhood predictors of adult antisocial behavior so intrigued me by challenging my own and others' preconceptions of the time that it clearly needed replication.

Our second study was a conscious effort to test the major findings of the first in a nonpatient population. It was carried out in young black men whose names had been chosen from public elementary school records. This sample was black and male because we wanted a sample from a population with a high enough rate of serious adult deviant behavior that we could study childhood predictors of adult deviance in a relatively small sample. Our research design, which required locating and interviewing the sample after many years and reviewing a host of records about them, was not well suited to large samples. A small sample unselected for sex, race, and class would have yielded too few cases of severe antisocial outcomes to enable us to study their childhood correlates.

The third study was not originally intended as a replication of the first or second but was a follow-up of a random sample of army enlisted men who left Vietnam in September 1971. This study was conducted at the request of Dr. Jerome Jaffe, then head of the Special Action Office on Drug Abuse Prevention. It was carried out in two stages, the first in 1972, less than 1 year after these men returned from Vietnam. Because we sought predictors of their continued involvement with heroin after return, we included as possible predictors the same childhood variables that had predicted heroin use in the follow-up of young black men. These childhood variables were much the same as the behavioral and family predictors of antisocial personality in the first study. Because we were interested in the effects of heroin use in Vietnam on a variety of aspects of the veterans' lives, we also included many measures of adult adjustment other than drug abuse. In short, we included sufficient childhood predictors and adult symptoms of antisocial personality to use this study as a replication of the earlier two studies, this time in a national sample, although a very young one. We realized, however, that the period immediately after return from Vietnam might not be a representative slice of their young adult lives. To serve our purposes and those of the government, it seemed wise to reinterview them after they had been back longer. We did so after they had been back in the United States for 3 years, at which time we asked them about their lives during the 2-year interval between the first and second interviews. It is this 2-year period that serves as our sample of the adult behavior of Vietnam veterans.

At the time of the second interview with the veterans, we also interviewed a group of nonveterans, matched with the veterans in terms of their place of rearing, age, and educational level at the time the veterans were inducted. The

TABLE 1. *The subjects*

Variable	Study I Ex-child guidance patients (*N* = 436)	Study II Young black men (*N* = 223)	Study III	
			Vietnam veterans (N = 571)	Matched nonveterans (*N* = 284)
Date of birth	1912[a]	1933[a]	1951[a]	1951[a]
Year of follow-up	1955–56	1966	1974	1974
Age at follow-up	43[a] years	33[a] years	23[a] years	23[a] years
Childhood	< 18 years	< 15 years	< 19[a] years	< 19[a] years
Adulthood	Age 25 +	Age 18 +	22–23[a]	22–23[a]
Place of birth	St. Louis[a]	St. Louis	National	National
Race	White	Black	All	All
Social class	Low[a]	Low[a]	Slightly low	Slightly high
IQ	> 79	> 84	Acceptable to U.S. Army	?

[a] Median or mode.

nonveterans were included to provide an estimate of what drug use and other aspects of adult adjustment of the veterans could have been expected to be if they had not served in the military. For this chapter, this nonveteran group provides an opportunity to replicate findings in that part of the male population not drafted into the military.

The four samples we compare vary by (a) race, (b) the historic periods in which they spent their childhood and adulthood, (c) geographic area, and (d) age at follow-up (Table 1). They agree on four variables: (a) all include only Americans; (b) all samples are entirely male (studies II and III) or very predominantly male (study I); (c) all samples exclude individuals with very low IQs (in the first two studies because we set limits on acceptable IQs and in the third study because the Army set such limits); and (d) all tend toward lower class status of rearing (study I children because the clinic served the Juvenile Court and various social agencies, study II children because of the low social status of blacks in the 1930s, and study III children because, despite the draft lottery, most middle-class males managed to not become army enlisted men).

RACE

Study I, the child guidance sample, is entirely white; study II, the young black men, is entirely black; and study III, the veterans and nonveterans, includes all races.

HISTORIC PERIODS

Study I children reached adolescence in the 1920s, study II children in the early 1940s, and study III children in the 1960s. Thus they grew up in eras separated by enormous technological and social changes. For instance, the first two groups attended racially segregated schools, whereas the third sample lived through various attempts at integration. Expectations for final education levels rose dramatically over the period, as did use of illicit drugs and early sexual behavior.

GEOGRAPHY

Children in studies I and II grew up in the same large midwestern city. Study III children grew up all over the United States, many in rural areas and small towns.

AGE AT INTERVIEW

At follow-up, study I subjects were middle-aged, study II subjects were in their early 30s, and study III subjects had barely entered adulthood. Thus we judged their adult behavior problems during very different age spans.

CHILDHOOD DATA

The information that we had available about the childhoods and adult lives of these samples also differed (Table 2). The child guidance clinic records provided us with a comprehensive behavioral history of all children up to the time at which they were first seen, at an average age of 13. For the few who

TABLE 2. *Data sources*

		Study III	
Study I Ex-child guidance patients	Study II Young black men	Vietnam veterans	Matched nonveterans
Source of childhood variables			
Clinic record	Interview	Interview	
Juvenile police and court	Juvenile police and court School records		
Source of adult variables			
Interview, records: police, prison, social agency, hospital, credit ratings, military, and VA, vital statistics	Interview, records: police, prison, social agency, hospital, credit ratings, military, and VA, vital statistics	Interview	
Overall evaluation: Diagnosis by consensus of 2 psychiatrists	No. symptoms applicable to diagnosis of antisocial personality	No. symptoms applicable to diagnosis of antisocial personality	

continued in treatment, there are also later behavioral records. For both study I and study II, we collected juvenile police and court records. For study II, whose cases had been picked out of elementary school records, we obtained complete transcripts of elementary and high school records. For the veterans, we depended entirely on the interview for information about their childhoods.

ADULT DATA

For all studies, we had detailed interview information about the adult history from the subjects themselves or, in studies I and II, from relatives of those who died after surviving into adulthood. For studies I and II, we also collected a great variety of objective records for the adult period, including police, prison, social agency and hospital records, credit ratings, military and VA records, vital statistics, and others. For the veterans, we had complete military records and records of VA contacts. Unfortunately, the military records do not cover the period we have designated as "adulthood." Therefore, for information about the interval between the first and second interviews, we have to rely entirely on what we were told in the second interview. The same is true for nonveterans. The records for the period in the military enabled us to test the validity of what veterans told us about their experience during that interval, and we found them to be extraordinarily honest (4). We previously reported on the candor of the subjects in studies I (3) and II (6). Good results for all three studies gave us considerable confidence in the honesty of the interview information.

OUTCOME VARIABLES

Study I data were analyzed a long time ago on a countersorter using multi-punched cards. We have not yet been able to get these cards transformed to computer-readable form for further analysis. As a result, we use as our outcome variable for study I the diagnosis based on the consensus of two psychiatrists after reading the interviews and record data. In the second study, analyzed after we had partially entered the computer age, we still had global diagnoses by psychiatrists, but in addition the diagnostic criteria items were entered into the computer. We can therefore use counts of how many diagnostic criteria for antisocial personality were met as our outcome variable. In the Vietnam study, we lack a psychiatrist's global evaluation, but we again have a count of the number of criterion symptoms met for antisocial personality.

Table 3 shows which childhood behaviors were covered in each study. Many childhood behaviors in the clinic records of study I were either very rare or were found not closely related to antisocial personality or other diagnoses and so were dropped in later studies. We added childhood drug and alcohol problems in study II, problems which had not been in the clinic's protocol, probably reflecting the rarity of these problems among children in the 1920s.

In each study, we counted the number of childhood behaviors. The average

TABLE 3. *Independent variables: A. Childhood antisocial behaviors*

Study I	Study II	Study III
No. antisocial behaviors	No. antisocial behaviors	No. antisocial behaviors
Arrests	Arrests	Arrests
Truancy	Truancy	Truancy
Drinking	Drinking	Drunk before 15
Fighting		Fighting
Sex	Sex	
Marriage	Marriage	
Dropout		Dropout
"Bad" friends	"Bad" friends	
Incarceration	Incarceration	
	Drugs	Drugs

Behaviors in only one study:
    Study I: Runaway, out late, lying, vandalism, bad language, incorrigible, reckless, no guilt, impulsive, perversions, rape, incest, exposed self, masturbation, sex play, aliases
    Study II: Alcohol problems

and range were greater in those studies that investigated more kinds of childhood antisocial behaviors.

Table 4 shows the family background variables included across studies. In study II, having family data on the computer enabled us to construct complex family variables we could not study earlier. Five family variables were available for all studies: (a) antisocial behavior in mother and father, (b) broken homes, (c) divorce, (d) separation or parents' never living together as the reason for the broken home, and (e) guardian's occupation.

Table 5 shows our measures of adult antisocial behavior. From study I we have only the three diagnoses of alchololism, drug dependence, and antisocial personality. In study II, the behaviors used to make a diagnosis of antisocial

TABLE 4. *Independent variables: B. Family*

Study I	Study II	Study III
Father antisocial or alcoholic	Father antisocial or alcoholic	Father antisocial or alcoholic
Mother antisocial or alcoholic	Mother antisocial or alcoholic	Mother antisocial or alcoholic
Home broken	Home broken	Home broken
Divorce/separation of parents	Divorce/separation of parents	Divorce/separation of parents
	Lived apart from both parents	Lived apart from both parents
Guardian's occupation	Guardian's occupation	Guardian's occupation
Slum residence	Poverty	
Supervision	Supervision	
No. siblings	No. siblings	
Discipline	Discipline	

Family variables in study II only: Age at family break up, few years with parent figures of both sexes, lived with mother only, parents' education, home ownership

TABLE 5. *Dependent variables: Adult antisocial behavior*

Study I	Study II	Study III
Diagnoses	No. of the following	No. of the following
Alcoholism	Alcoholism	Alcoholism
Drug dependence	Regular drug use	Regular drug use
Antisocial personality	Multiple divorce/separation	Divorce, separation
	Financial problems	Credit trouble
	Multiple serious arrests	Arrests
	Job trouble	Job trouble
	Violence	Violence
	Vagrancy	Vagrancy
	Impulsivity	
	Deviant life style	

personality are listed. Most of those were replicated in study III. In study I, we used a hierarchical principle in making diagnoses: diagnoses of alcoholism and drug dependence were allowed only in persons who did not qualify for the diagnosis of antisocial personality, since problem drinking and drug dependence also served as criterion symptoms of antisocial personality.

This review of the data collected in the three studies and the ways in which they were analyzed shows that the researcher as well as the study subjects were exposed to different influences in different eras. The choice of childhood variables in successive studies reflected changes in the frequencies of particular types of socially disapproved behaviors over time, changes in the technology available for creating composite variables out of the raw data provided by interviews and records, and new interests and hypotheses. Research methods as well as research subjects respond to historic change and to the need to change or redefine variables based on their performance in earlier studies.

Expecting to find stable results in this sea of change of subjects, eras, locales, data collected, choice and definition of variables, and methods of analysis may seem too stringent a test of the validity of the results from study I, done in the days of our youth and ignorance without even the blessing of the computer; but we try.

RESULTS

The most basic and essentially untested assumption of study I was that "sociopathy" was a "real" entity. The most basic finding of that study was that the antisocial behaviors of childhood also constituted an entity. Since these two entities were highly correlated, the implication was that childhood and adult antisocial behaviors were parts of the same entity, no matter how much the behaviors found at one age period differed from those found at another.

To replicate the finding that childhood antisocial behaviors form a coherent syndrome, one question to be asked is: "Do all these behaviors predict the level of adult antisocial behavior?" Table 6 lists the childhood behaviors and

TABLE 6. *Childhood behaviors tested in more than one study: Significant prediction of adult antisocial behavior*

Childhood behavior	Tested in how many samples	Significant in how many
Arrests	4	4
Truancy	4	4
Alcohol	4	3[a]
Fighting	3	3
Sex	2	2
Dropout	3	3
"Bad" friends	2	2
Incarceration	2	2
Drugs	3	3

[a] Not significant in study I.

notes in how many samples we had information for each and in how many each was significantly related to a level of adult antisocial behavior high enough to make probable a diagnosis of antisocial personality. With one exception (drinking in study I), each childhood behavior significantly predicted a high level of antisocial behavior in every study in which it was tested. The one exception was probably due to the fact that very few child guidance clinic subjects were reported to drink. Since study I childhood behaviors all came only from clinic records, we do not know whether drinking actually rarely occurred or whether it was only rarely inquired about. The fact that with this one exception every childhood antisocial behavior significantly predicted severe adult antisocial behavior in every test certainly suggests these childhood behaviors operate similarly, as elements of a syndrome should.

Table 7 considers whether the adult antisocial behaviors we studied also form a syndrome. It shows the behaviors studied, the number of samples in which

TABLE 7. *Adult behavior problems evaluated in more than one study: Which are significantly predicted by number of childhood behaviors?*

Adult behavior	Tested in how many samples	Significant in how many
Alcoholism	4	4
Drug Abuse	3	3
Violence	3	3
Job trouble	3	3
Crime	3	2[a]
Financial problems	3	2[b]
Marital	3	2[b]
Vagrancy	3	1[c]

[a] Nonveterans, $p < 0.10$.
[b] Not significant in nonveterans.
[c] Significant only in nonveterans.

they were tested, and the number of tests in which they were significantly predicted by the number of childhood antisocial behaviors. All samples agree that the first four variables (or the first five, using a one-tailed test) are significantly predicted by the level of childhood antisocial behavior. Financial and marital problems were significantly predicted by childhood antisocial behavior in young black men and veterans but not in nonveterans; and vagrancy, although showing the same trend in each sample, was significantly predicted only among nonveterans. This slightly different pattern for nonveterans shows the problems of using a small, unrepresentative sample with a low level of deviance.

It is striking that the findings for St. Louis born and reared young black men and a predominantly white national sample of veterans agree so well with the findings of study I when it is remembered that these adult symptoms were arbitrarily selected as the symptoms of antisocial personality in study I.

These findings that essentially in all four samples every type of childhood antisocial behavior predicted a high level of adult antisocial behavior and that each type of adult antisocial behavior was predicted by the number of childhood behaviors seem to argue for the unitary nature of antisocial behavior in both childhood and adulthood. These results agree with the Jessors' (1) observations on adolescents that whichever of four behaviors they began in 1 year—losing their virginity, aggression, drinking, or using marijuana—greatly increased the likelihood of their doing the other behaviors the following year. These behaviors formed a syndrome that could begin with any one of them.

We seem to have replicated the most basic premise and finding from study I—that severe adult antisocial behavior is a syndrome, as is severe childhood antisocial behavior, and that the two are closely interconnected, probably part of a single process.

There are six other findings from study I that can be examined for replicability:

1. Adults who were diagnosable as having antisocial personality had almost all been antisocial children; that is, antisocial personality rarely or never arose *de novo* in adulthood.
2. Despite the strong correlations between childhood and adult behavior, most highly antisocial children do not become highly antisocial adults; that is, while according to finding 1 antisocial childhood behavior may be a necessary condition for antisocial personality of adulthood, it is not a sufficient one.
3. The variety of childhood antisocial behaviors was a better predictor of severe adult antisocial behavior than was any particular childhood behavior.
4. The child's own behavior was a better predictor of his adult behavior than were his family characteristics or social status.
5. Family variables matter more for moderately than for severely antisocial children. In study I, severely antisocial children were found to be at high risk, no matter how good or bad their environment, but moderately antisocial children with antisocial fathers were more likely to be highly antisocial adults than were others.

The final finding we will try to replicate is:

6. Social class of rearing was a remarkably unimportant variable. It added nothing significant once the levels of the child's and his parent's antisocial behavior were taken into account in prediciting severe adult antisocial behavior. Of course, low social class might have contributed to the level of childhood antisocial behavior or could have reflected the antisocial parent's inability to earn a living, but children reared in a poor but conforming family who did not develop antisocial behavior in childhood were no more likely to show severe antisocial behavior as adults than were similar middle-class children, although they were more likely to be found in the lower class as adults.

Table 8 shows that the first of these findings, that highly antisocial adults had generally been highly antisocial children, was replicated in each study. Two-thirds or more had been highly antisocial children, and more than 90% had had some of these childhood antisocial behaviors. Thus severe adult antisocial behavior does seem to virtually require a history of antisocial behavior in childhood.

Table 9 shows that the next finding, that most highly antisocial children recover, was also confirmed in all samples. We tried various higher cutoff points than the ones appearing in Table 9, trying to raise the proportion of those who would be highly antisocial adults, but without much success. No matter where we drew the line, we could never produce a rate much higher than 50%. In study I, raising the cutoff point from six or more behaviors, which yielded 36% sociopathic as adults, to 10 or more antisocial behaviors raised the rate sociopathic only to 41%. In study II, raising the cutoff point from three or more childhood behaviors, which yielded a rate of 41% with four or more adult antisocial behaviors, to four, five, or more childhood behaviors did not push the adult rate above 51%. Thus replication confirms the finding that even highly antisocial children become highly antisocial adults in half or fewer cases.

TABLE 8. *Finding 1: "Highly antisocial adults had been highly antisocial children"*

Childhood antisocial behavior	Highly antisocial adults (%)			
			Study III	
	Study I (N = 94)	Study II (N = 53)	A (N = 118)	B (N = 17)
Low	5	12	10	6
Moderate	13	21	18	29
High	82	67	72	65

Replication: Yes.

TABLE 9. *Finding 2: "Most highly antisocial children recover"*

Children with a high level of antisocial behavior	High level of adult antisocial behaviors	
	N	%
Study I	157	36
Study II	86	41
Study III		
A. Veterans	208	41
B. Nonveterans	48	23

Replication: Yes.

Table 10 tests findings 3 and 4—that number of childhood behaviors was a better predictor of severe adult antisocial behavior than either any specific childhood behavior or than any family variable—by stepwise multiple regression. All the individual child behavior and family variables were entered, as well as the number of childhood behaviors. In studies II and III A (Vietnam veterans), the number of antisocial behaviors was the single best predictor, confirming both findings. For nonveterans, truancy was a slightly better predictor than was number of antisocial behaviors, which may again be due to our having a small and only mildly antisocial sample of nonveterans. The best predictor in every sample, including nonveterans, was childhood behaviors, not family vari-

TABLE 10. *Findings 3 and 4: "Number of childhood antisocial behaviors is a better predictor of severe adult antisocial behavior than (3) specific behaviors or (4) family variables"*

		Study III	
Variable	Study II	A	B
No. independent variables:	24	11	
Childhood behavior	9	7	
Family	15	4	
Dependent variables: 4 + adult antisocial behaviors			
	Added explained variance (%)		
Two best predictors			
No. antisocial behaviors	12	13	
Truant			11
Drugs	5		
Arrest		3	
Drunk before 15			7
Sum:	17	16	18
Total, all variables	30	19	25

Replication: Finding (3): Yes in two of three and close in the third.
                Finding (4): Yes.
Stepwise multiple regression.

ables, confirming the conclusion that childhood behavior is a better predictor of adult outcome than is family background.

Table 11 tests the finding that family variables help predict the outcomes only of less severely antisocial children. We tested this by dividing each sample into two groups according to whether they did or did not have high levels of childhood antisocial behavior. We then submitted both groups to stepwise multiple regression using all family variables as the independent variables and a high level of adult antisocial behavior as the dependent variable. This finding was not supported. Family variables were at least as useful in explaining the outcomes of highly antisocial as of less antisocial children in every sample.

We also learned from the stepwise regression the probable reason for our error. In study I, in precomputer days, we had not undertaken multivariate analyses using all family variables. Instead we chose our best family variable, father's antisocial behavior, to stand for them all. Study II confirmed that having an antisocial father was important only for the less antisocial child's future, but other family variables performed even better in predicting outcomes for highly antisocial children than antisocial fathers did for the moderately antisocial. If we get study I onto the computer, we will do a replication in reverse to see if this explanation is correct.

The final finding to be tested is that social class was unimportant in predicting outcomes as compared with childhood behavior and other family variables. We have in fact already replicated this finding by not having reported social class as a significant contributor in any of the analyses thus far reported. It has not appeared in any previous table because it never contributed even 1% to explained variance when competing with childhood behavior and other family variables in any of the samples.

How, then, are we to make sense of the universal observation that antisocial behavior is more common in the lower class? Indeed the diagnosis "antisocial personality" has been called a middle-class psychiatrist's label for patterns of behavior normal in the lower class or at least understandable in the lower

TABLE 11. *Finding 5: "Family variables contribute to the prediction of adult antisocial behavior only for less antisocial children"*

Study	Variance explained by all family variables when childhood antisocial behavior	
	High (%)	Low or moderate (%)
Study II	32	8
Study III		
A. Veterans	3	2
B. Nonveterans	8	4

Replication: No. We had looked at the wrong family variable, "antisocial father," for highly antisocial children in study II. The important ones are: placed out: 12%; poverty: 7%; years with both parents: 4%. "Antisocial father" was important (2%) only for children with low or moderate antisocial behavior.

class because of pressures of poverty and low prestige. One possibility occurred to us: Adult antisocial behavior lies along a continuum of severity, only the upper range of which is designated as evidence for psychiatric disorder. Perhaps such extreme levels of antisocial behavior are pathological in every social class. But milder levels of antisocial behavior may be "normal" in the lower class only. The results we have presented so far all concerned predicting a high level of adult antisocial behavior, a level sufficient to warrant a diagnosis of antisocial personality. If low social class predicts mild antisocial behavior, we would not have detected it.

To test this possibility, we set aside the highly antisocial adults in each of our samples and performed a stepwise multiple regression to look for significant predictors of some adult antisocial behavior rather than none. When we did this, guardian's low occupation, our index of low social class of rearing, emerged as the second best predictor for the sample of young black men, second only to having an antisocial father, but it did not appear in study III. However, the study II sample was urban, while study III was nationwide. Therefore, we repeated the test for study III subjects reared in metropolitan areas. Table 12 shows the results. Guardian's occupation now made a small significant contribution to veterans' mild adult antisocial behavior but still did not appear for those troublesome nonveterans, with their low levels of antisocial behavior. To complete this test, we hope to do a "reverse" replicability test in study I, if we can get it onto the computer. All we can claim at present is that we may have solved the riddle of why social class has never been found to be a

TABLE 12. *Does low social class predict moderate adult antisocial behavior in urban children?*[a]

Study	Predictors adding 1% + to explained variance
Study II	
Father antisocial	9
Guardian's occupation	3
	12
Study III (in urban area at induction)	
A. Veterans	
No. antisocial behaviors	4
Mother antisocial	2
Father antisocial	2
Guardian's occupation	1
	9
B. Nonveterans	
No. antisocial behaviors	13
Dropout	1
	14

[a]Omitting all cases with high levels of adult antisocial behavior. Dependent variable, some antisocial behavior. Stepwise multiple regression.

good predictor of the syndrome of adult antisocial behavior, even though we know that all the elements of that syndrome occur more often among lower- than middle-class populations. Clearly this issue needs further work.

DISCUSSION

We have now attempted to replicate some of the major findings of our first study in three samples that differ from the sample in which the original observations were made in (a) being nonpatients, (b) race, (c) era and place of rearing, (d) age at interview, (e) sources of the data, and (f) details of the way some data items were defined. Despite these awesome odds, all but one of the findings have been confirmed. Antisocial personality seems to be a real syndrome in American males, one that rarely occurs in the absence of serious antisocial behavior in childhood. It is better predicted by the variety of childhood antisocial behaviors than by any particular behavior, and childhood behaviors are better predictors than are family variables. Social class is not a family characteristic that helps in this prediction. Despite the important role that childhood antisocial behavior plays in forecasting adult antisocial behavior, most antisocial children do not grow into severely antisocial adults (although very few of them are completely free of antisocial behavior as adults).

Since spontaneous recovery is frequent, it is hoped that careful study of those circumstances surrounding recovery might suggest strategies of intervention with the 40 to 50% who do not recover spontaneously. Learning how to intervene is obviously important, not only because antisocial personality is a devastating syndrome from the viewpoint of both the actor and society, but also because of another finding that we discovered in study I (5) and replicated in study II (7,8): These patterns of childhood antisocial behavior are transmitted from one generation to the next. Figure 1 shows that elementary school truancy and high school dropout in the parents is transmitted to their children. Transmission in both studies was enhanced when the parents continued their childhood antisocial behavior into adulthood. (We have not been able to repeat this replication in study III, since the average age of the offspring of these young veterans is only 2 years.) Intervention in childhood is therefore important both for the future health of affected children and for the health of the next generation.

Despite these sturdy findings, a lot of work remains to be done. We need to know which family variables contribute most to the likelihood that childhood antisocial behavior will continue into adulthood. At least we now know that our pessimism about finding family variables that might influence the course for highly antisocial children was unwarranted.

We also need to know what conditions account for the progression into severe adult antisocial behavior of that small proportion of less severely antisocial children who do so. Although the risk for any given moderately antisocial child is low, there are so many more moderately than severely antisocial children that moderately antisocial children account for a third of all the adults with

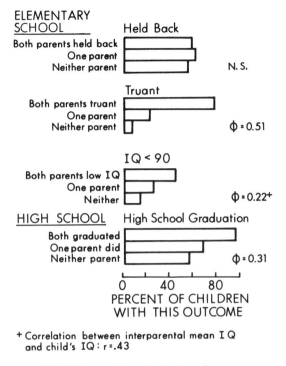

FIG. 1. Transmission of school performance.

antisocial personality. Until we can specify which segment of moderately antisocial children are at high risk, intervention remains impractical—there are too many of them to make intervention economically feasible and the risk for any given child is too low to justify interference in his life.

Finally, I'd like to come back to the question I raised originally about whether antisocial personality *is* a psychiatric disorder. I am not sure I know exactly what kinds of disconfirmatory evidence one could amass to show that it is not. However, I think it would be appropriate to close by paraphrasing a charming remark of a former winner of the Paul Hoch award (2) that if antisocial personality is a myth, it is a myth that is told over and over by different groups in different places and in different times, and the plot always seems to be the same.

POSTSCRIPT: THE RELATIONSHIP OF LONGITUDINAL STUDIES TO STRESS RESEARCH

The body of work described herein has not tried to distinguish among the possible mechanisms by which childhood behavior and family characteristics have these highly replicable effects. One mechanism could be that they lead to the child's exposure to unusually severe stresses or to an excess number of harmful life events. Other possible mechanisms are through genetic effects, the child's modeling his behavior on his parents', or the parents' selectively reinforcing (i.e., teaching) him maladaptive behaviors. He may be crippled by the low self-esteem that comes from having parents with bad reputations or himself being labeled as a "bad kid" early in life. No doubt there are many other possible mechanisms as well. Life event research has not, until now, taken into account all these possible alternative explanations. I think such neglect may have had serious consequences, best illustrated with the following example.

As we have shown, a child with severely antisocial behavior is probably being reared in a poor family in which the parents have high rates of behavior problems. When this child grows up, he or she is much more likely than the average person to marry someone with serious behavior problems and to produce children with similar behavior problems. The implications for the life events this individual will experience are that: his parents are much more likely to separate or die young than are other children's parents; his spouse and children are more likely than other people's to fall sick or die young because of their alcoholism or drug addiction, or to go to jail or to be fired because of their antisocial behavior.

From the life history researcher's point of view, each of these events—the parents' breakup, illness of the spouse, or spouse or child going to jail—appears to be a "fateful" event, one over which our proband has no direct control. The antisocial child who subsequently meets criteria for alcoholism, drug abuse, or antisocial personality will almost certainly have suffered more of these fateful life events than the average person, but his disorder may actually have occurred quite independently of these life events. In fact, we do not need to know that he has suffered these life events to predict such disorders for him. Multiplying his case by many, we would expect substantial correlations between these fateful life events and the subsequent development of alcoholism, drug dependence, and antisocial personality, not to mention premature death from heart disease, cancer, tuberculosis, pneumonia, accidents, or homicide (since early deaths from all these causes are more common in individuals with these psychiatric diagnoses than in the general population), even if such events were not in any sense causal. Indeed, it may be impossible to discover fateful events independent of the individual's susceptibility to pathology. It is their independence of that susceptibility that we must prove, not the fact that they were not directly caused by the respondent's pathological behavior, which is what we mean when we call them fateful.

To meet this complication, life events research might profit from two strategies to allow the interpretation of life events as causal factors in pathology. First, the incidence of disorder following the life event must be shown to be higher than the incidence within the same age range for individuals who did not experience the life event, even after their own behavior and family characteristics are held constant. If antisocial children with alcoholic fathers whose fathers die before they reach 12 are more likely to become alcoholic thereafter than equally antisocial children whose equally alcoholic fathers survived past their reaching age 12, then we have an argument for the significance of early parental death. Were the comparison group not matched for early behavior and father's alcoholism, there would be so many plausible alternative interpretations for the correlation between father's death and alcoholism that it would be hard to know what to make of it.

Second, the variance of the length of the interval between the occurrence of the life event and onset of disorder should be compared with the variance of age of onset itself. If the variance of the interval should be found to be markedly smaller than the variance of age of onset, this finding would be consistent with the existence of an "incubation" period between event and illness. While the absence of such a consistent interval between event and illness would not disprove the impact of the life event, the presence of such consistency would be powerful confirmatory evidence.

ACKNOWLEDGMENTS

This work was supported in part by U.S.P.H.S. grants DA 00013, MH 18864, DA 4RG 008, AA 03539, MH 14677, and DA 05043.

REFERENCES

1. Jessor, R., and Jessor, S. (1977): *Problem Behavior and Psychological Development: A Longitudinal Study of Youth.* Academic Press, New York.
2. Kety, S. S., Rosenthal, D., Wender, P. H., Schulsinger, F., and Jacobsen B. (1975): Mental illness in the biological and adoptive families of adopted individuals who have become schizophrenic: A preliminary report based on psychiatric interview. In: *Genetic Research in Psychiatry,* edited by R. R. Fieve, D. Rosenthal, and H. Brill, chapter 11, pp. 147–165. Johns Hopkins University Press, Baltimore.
3. Robins, L. N. (1966): *Deviant Children Grown Up: A Sociological and Psychiatric Study of Sociopathic Personality.* Williams & Wilkins, Baltimore.
4. Robins, L. N. (1974): *The Vietnam Drug User Returns.* Special Action Office Monograph, series A, no. 2, U.S. Government Printing Office, Washington, D.C.
5. Robins, L. N., and Lewis, R. G. (1966): The role of the antisocial family in school completion and delinquency: A three-generation study. *Sociol. Q.,* 7:500–514.
6. Robins, L. N., and Murphy, G. E. (1967): Drug use in a normal population of young Negro men. *Am. J. Public Health,* 57:1580–1596.
7. Robins, L. N., Ratcliff, K. S., and West, P. A. (1979): School achievement in two generations: A study of 88 urban black families. In: *New Directions in Children's Mental Health,* edited by S. J. Shamsie. Spectrum Publications, New York.
8. Robins, L. N., West, P. A., and Herjanic, B. (1975): Arrests and delinquency in two generations: A study of black urban families and their children. *J. Child Psychol. Psychiatry,* 16:125–140.
9. Schaie, K. W. (1975): Research strategy in development human behavior genetics. In: *Developmental Human Behavior Genetics—Nature-Nurture Redefined,* edited by K. W. Schaie, V. E. Anderson, G. E. McClearn, and J. Money, chapter 9. Lexington Books, Lexington, Massachusetts.

Stress and Mental Disorder,
edited by James E. Barrett et al.
Raven Press, New York © 1979.

Cardiovascular and Endocrine Responses to Work and the Risk for Psychiatric Symptomatology Among Air Traffic Controllers

*Robert M. Rose, **Michael W. Hurst, and †J. Alan Herd

*Department of Psychiatry and Behavioral Sciences, University of Texas Medical Branch, Galveston, Texas 77550; **Boston University School of Medicine, Boston, Massachusetts 02118; and †Harvard Medical School, Cambridge, Massachusetts 02138*

During the last 10 to 15 years, a considerable literature has appeared (16,28) documenting the sensitivity of both endocrine and cardiovascular systems to environmental stimuli. Many reports (2,30) have shown that systolic and diastolic blood pressure and heart rate are sensitive to changes in the psychosocial environment. There also is a large literature beginning with the early work of Seyle (24) in the 1950s showing the sensitivity of adrenocortical hormones to psychological stimuli (17). In more recent years, other hormones, including growth hormone (GH) (3), prolactin (20), and testosterone levels (12,21), have been shown to change as a result of exposure of the individual to stressful environments. Included among these reports have been studies that have documented that individuals show significant differences in their cardiovascular (2) or endocrine (8) responses to work. These studies have focused not only on the nature and magnitude of the work (6) but also on the context in which the work was done (4), i.e., whether the individual was paid by his productivity (piecework) or was on straight salary (29).

There have been numerous discussions in the literature (7,14) about the implications of these altered endocrine or cardiovascular states on future health. It has been postulated that one mechanism that may link exposure to stressful environments with future illness (13), either physical or psychological, may relate to long-term maladaptive physiological responses. Thus authors have hypothesized that the changes in hormone levels that are seen acutely during the viewing of a stressful movie, prior to an examination in school (10), or in response to the death of a loved one may not be just an acute response but one that recurs often and constitutes a more chronic, characteristic pattern for the individual (9). Such chronically altered endocrine levels or elevated blood pressure responses may lead to future illness in that they play a part in the pathophysiology of certain diseases (11,25).

There are two significant gaps in the proposed pathway that may link the chain of events hypothesized to relate acute physiological change to later health change. The first is whether or not individuals who show acute endocrine or cardiovascular changes under certain environmental conditions show these same changes upon reexposure to the same conditions or other provocative stimuli, i.e., whether individuals show a characteristic mode of response. The other major gap is the lack of information as to whether or not individuals who show these altered cortisol, GH, or blood pressure responses to a particular environment are at a greater risk for the development of future illness.

Few if any studies provide information on either of these two questions. Most studies have been acute in nature and describe which individuals in a given group showed changes in blood pressure or cortisol levels in response to a variety of psychosocial stimuli. Few studies have followed the same individuals over a longer period of time during reexposure to the same or other stimuli. However, no studies have followed individuals and measured their cardiovascular and endocrine responses during exposure to a potentially obnoxious environment, at the same time noting what changes, if any, occurred in their health. Therefore, the hypothesis that acute or even prolonged alterations in cardiovascular levels or endocrine changes associated with exposure to a variety of psychosocial stimuli lead to increased risk of negative health change, i.e., illness, has not yet been tested. Such a prospective study would be necessary to test whether altered endocrine or cardiovascular responses to threat or exposure to potentially stressful environments, reflecting perhaps an inability to adapt to these stimuli, function to place the individuals at greater risk for future illness. Studying individuals' responses who are already ill does not provide data about the role of these changes in cardiovascular or endocrine status in placing individuals at greater risk of becoming ill.

An opportunity to test the hypothesis that individuals who exhibit increased cardiovascular or endocrine responses to a potentially stressful environment have more physical or psychological health change was afforded by a prospective study of health changes of air traffic controllers. An outline of this study, including the general hypotheses to be tested, the nature of the study population, as well as the instruments and assessment techniques employed, was recently published (23).

Briefly, approximately 400 men were followed for 3 years, during which time they had five physical and psychological examinations—at the beginning, at the end, and at 9-month intervals. They also filled out a number of psychological test inventories, including items to assess attitudes toward work, coping mechanisms employed, and life changes. In addition, individuals were also studied while actually working on the job separating aircraft. On approximately two occasions a year, their blood pressure was measured every 20 min for 5 hrs along with observations of the amount of work performed and their behavior responses to work. On two other occasions, blood was collected continuously by use of an indwelling catheter in 20-min segments for 5 hrs along with similar observations of behavior and work load. This design afforded an opportunity to test the hypothesis that those individuals who showed increased cardiovascular or endocrine responses to air traffic control work were at a greater risk for the development of physical or psychological illness. This chapter focuses only on changes in psychological health during the course of this study. The major predictor variables reported are systolic and diastolic blood pressure and cortisol and GH levels collected while men were working. We examine the question of whether there are stable or characteristic blood pressure or endocrine responses for the individual, as well as any relationship between these responses and the development of psychiatric-psychological syndromes.

METHODS

Psychiatric Assessment

Each participant was interviewed using the Psychiatric Status Schedule (PSS) (27) on five occasions: at intake, during three interval examinations, and at the final examination. Three doctoral level psychologists and one master level psychologist were trained to use the PSS until they reached criterion levels as established by the manual and training tapes (26) made available by Dr. Jean Endicott from the biometrics group at Columbia.

Questions on the PSS are grouped to cover symptoms in areas of somatic complaints, moods, fears, interpersonal relationships, ideation, cognitive processing, suicidal tendencies, drug and alcohol use, delusions, hallucinations, behavior during the interview situation, and role functioning as a wage earner, housekeeper, student, mate, parent, and patient as applicable for a given subject. The computerized program then scored symptoms using item weights of 0, 1, 2, or 3, and converted the raw scores into T-scores (mean $= 50$, SD $= 10$) based on the results of the standardization study of 770 psychiatric patients.

A total of 50 T-scores were possible. Four scores, called macroscales because they subsumed 16 symptom scale scores, assessed subjective distress, behavioral disturbances, impulse control disturbances, and reality testing disturbances. An alcohol abuse symptom scale was scored independently. Of seven role scales assessing impairment due to psychiatric disturbances in wage earner, housekeeper, student, mate, parent, and patient (denial of illness) roles, we used only the wage earner and mate role scales.

We focused primarily on the four macroscales, the independent symptom scale alcohol abuse, and the two role scales named above. The other symptom scales were not utilized because they were subsumed by the macroscales.

A recent report by Dohrenwend et al. (5) noted that there were difficulties in using the PSS in a nonpatient population. These difficulties related to the fact that there was insufficient internal consistency in scale scores using data from a general population, and not patient groups. We also observed that the internal consistency of the 50 individual PSS scales for the air traffic controllers was lower than that of the patient sample (frequently less than 0.50). Unlike the report of Dohrenwend et al., however, we did not use individual scales but used the macroscales noted above. Internal consistency of these macroscales for the air traffic controllers was as follows: subjective distress, 0.82; behavioral disturbances, 0.47; impulse control disturbances, 0.52; wage earner, 0.28; and mate, 0.72.

It can be seen that using the macroscales, adequate internal consistency to justify the use of this instrument was present on four of the five scales, and not present only in the wage earner. These findings support the use of the PSS to determine subjective distress (depression and anxiety, primarily) and impulse control disturbances, which were quite prevalent among the air traffic controllers.

We analyzed the data from the PSS in several ways. We compared the air traffic controllers with five other groups (22): inpatients, former inpatients, pretreatment outpatients, and two nonpatient groups—an urban community sample and urban community leaders. For each of the macroscales, we established a symptomatic cutoff score, which was greater than or equal to 1 SD from the urban community sample or 2 SD above the urban community leader sample, whichever was greater. This permitted us to compare controllers who had significant symptomatology at intake (prevalence) with those who were without problems at intake. Furthermore, this dichotomization permitted us to sum across time for each individual in terms of the presence or absence of problems for all five examinations.

The PSS data were used in two ways, both as outcome variables against which cardiovascular and endocrine measures could be tested as possible predictors. The first outcome variable we labeled as susceptibility to psychiatric problems, defined as the presence of an elevated score on one or more of the five criterion scales of the PSS. Comparisons of cardiovascular and endocrine results were made among three groups: those having no psychiatric problems during the 3 years, those with problems at intake, and those in whom problems developed after intake.

The second outcome variable was the extent of psychiatric problems defined by the quantity and frequency of problems. Four groups were compared: (a) men who had no problems on any of the criterion scales during the 3 years of study, (b) mild cases with only one criterion scale abnormal at only one of the five examinations, (c) moderate cases with one or more criterion scales abnormal at two or three of the five examinations, and (d) chronic cases with one or more criterion scales abnormal at four or five examinations.

To summarize, we were asking whether individuals who had increased cardiovascular or endocrine responses at work had either more susceptibility to psychiatric problems as defined above or whether the extent of psychiatric problems was greater in those with greater physiological changes.

The other technique used to evaluate psychiatric symptomatology among the controllers was by use of the Zung depression (31) and anxiety (32) scale. These two 20-item checklists were mailed to all participants once a month to evaluate individuals' levels of depression and anxiety during the 9 months between examinations at Boston University.

Of 377 men who were eligible to participate in this aspect of the study, 354 (94%) returned all five or more questionnaires, and the vast majority returned all questionnaires.

We (1) divided the continuous scores on both the depression and anxiety scales into four categories: levels 0, 1, 2, and 3. Level 0 was established at a range indicative of insignificant symptomatology. Level 1 represented definite symptoms of depression or anxiety. Scores in this range reflected significant depression or anxiety at the symptom level. Persons scoring at this level would not be expected to obtain treatment. Level 2 was significant symptomatology equivalent to that observed in outpatient groups. Level 3 was marked symptomatology in a range equivalent to that seen in hospitalized patients.

In an attempt to compare men across time, we annualized the rates of the depression and anxiety episodes. An episode was defined as a month in which a controller had a level 1 score or above. If a man returned a minimum of five questionnaires during the 8 to 9 months between examinations at Boston University, he was classified into one of four groups based on the annual rate of response, averaged across all years. Individuals were thus divided into: (a) asymptomatic, (b) acute—an annualized rate of episodes equal to or greater than 1 month but less than 3 months per year, (c) intermittent—three but less than nine episodes per year, and (d) chronic—greater than or equal to 9 months per year. Average annualized rate of episodes were determined for both anxiety and depression. We were then able to ask whether men who had different physiological responses at work were more at risk for showing increased levels of depression or anxiety; i.e., were they asymptomatic, acute, intermittent, or chronic?

Cardiovascular Measures

A total of 1,421 days of observations were made, with each day averaging 5 hrs, yielding a total of 7,105 hr. Of the total sample of 416, 382 (92%) completed one blood pressure study in the field; 288 men (69%) had a total of three or more studies completed over the course of their participation.

We analyzed each day's blood pressure readings from a number of perspectives in an attempt to characterize which analyses might best summarize the responses that day and reflect any influences of work load. For each day's protocol, the following variables were determined: average systolic, diastolic, and heart rate, and maximum systolic, diastolic, and heart rate. In addition, we were able to compare a number of men with themselves in order to more carefully investigate any influences of increased work holding the individual across time. For these analyses, we determined the residual systolic range, which measured variability during the day controlling for initial level.

A number of findings relative to cardiovascular measures should be mentioned. Blood pressures at work were highly correlated with the blood pressure taken at the physician's office ($r = 0.65$ for both systolic and diastolic). The daily average systolic blood pressure was 129 mm Hg and daily average diastolic was 87 mm Hg. It was also noted that on the average, systolic blood varied significantly during the day, with the average range of 35 ± 12 mm Hg, and diastolic pressures ranged an average of 27 ± 8 mm Hg. This was a clear indication that the individuals were having significant changes in their blood pressure while controlling air traffic. There was also a tendency for blood pressure to be higher when men were on position compared to when they were off position. Moreover, these differences became more apparent when each man's blood pressure was calculated on the basis of his own responses.

On the average, systolic blood pressure increased 4 to 5 mm Hg and diastolic blood pressure increased 2 to 3 mm Hg under conditions of higher work load when days of varying work load were compared. It was apparent from analyzing these data that individuals were significantly different from one another with respect not only to their average blood pressure while working but to the degree to which their blood pressure increased when they were confronted with increased work, usually calculated by the number of planes under the controller's legal responsibility. These results are being published in greater detail elsewhere (22).

Endocrine Studies

We collected almost as many blood samples as cardiovascular measures. A total of 1,156 days of observation were made in which blood was drawn every 20 min for 5 hours. Of all participants, 369 men (89%) had at least 1 day in which blood was withdrawn, and 243 men (58%) had three studies or more.

Cortisol was determined by radioimmunoassay, which yielded excellent reproducibility. The average coefficient of variation for duplicates or the within-assay reproducibility was 2.96%, and the coefficient of variation between assays was 6.41%.

In general, the cortisol values for all men were equal to or somewhat greater than those reported in the literature. Similar to that observed for the blood pressure measure, men exhibited significant interindividual differences in total cortisol levels during the 5 hrs studied.

We performed a number of analyses on each day's data in order to characterize individuals' responses. We totaled the cortisol secreted during the day, averaged the number of peaks or episodes of secretion observed during the day, and averaged the total area under the peak to quantitate the magnitude of cortisol secreted in an episode. As there was a strong diurnal trend, in order to collapse across morning and afternoon studies, all values were also normalized. We calculated the average for each point in time and expressed each result in terms of its deviation from the average. The total and maximum cortisol for men who had all three studies are given in Table 1.

Similar to the results observed for systolic and diastolic blood pressure, cortisol, both total for the day and maximum cortisol, was higher when the men were working on position as compared to when they were off position. This was true for all three visits.

TABLE 1. *Average total and maximal cortisol across all visits for men who had three or more studies*

		Group		
Value	Mean	Low	Middle	High
Average for day				
Normalized	100	77–95	96–103	104–140
N	231	77	77	77
Raw cortisol value (μg/100 ml)				
Morning study	13.0	8.7–11.9	12.1–13.7	13.9–21.8
Afternoon study	9.4	4.1– 8.2	8.6– 9.8	10.2–17.0
Maximum value on position				
Normalized	120	88–112	113–125	126–180
Raw cortisol value (μg/100 ml)				
Morning study	16.5	10.3–15.8	15.8–17.8	18.3–29.0
Afternoon study	13.1	6.7–11.0	11.6–13.1	13.5–25.1

We also analyzed human GH (HGH) for all men who finished the first study and for those men who also finished the second study, with a total of 362 men in the first round and 299 for the second study.

By far the largest number of men, 92%, failed to have any HGH values above 2.0 ng/ml during the 5 hrs they were studied. Approximately 5% of the men showed one or more peak values of 2.0 to 4.9 ng/ml; 2% had a peak value of 5.0 to 10.0 ng/ml; and less than 1% showed any value greater than 10.0 ng/ml. These data indicate that there were very few men secreting increased amounts of GH during the day than are reported as occurring with exposure to acutely stressful environments.

RESULTS

The main question in this chapter is whether those men who showed increased blood pressure, cortisol, or GH responses to work showed an increased risk for developing psychiatric or psychological problems, as measured either by the PSS or by monthly Zung depression or anxiety scores. However, the design of the study also permitted us to inquire as to how stable or characteristic individuals' cardiovascular or endocrine responses were at work. As we studied a significant number of the men three times or more, we were able to look at the stability as assessed by correlations between visits of the various measures that we used to summarize both blood pressure and endocrine data.

Table 2 lists the correlations among cardiovascular measurements of controllers at work across the three studies. It can be seen from this table that the average systolic and diastolic blood pressure and heart rate are relatively stable across time, with the correlation coefficients ranging from 0.47 to 0.61 when one compares first versus second, first versus third, or second versus third studies. The maximum blood pressure readings observed at work, either systolic or

TABLE 2. *Correlations among daily cardiovascular measurements of air traffic controllers at work: Across three studies[a]*

Measurement	First versus second study	First versus third study	Second versus third study
Systolic blood pressure			
Average	0.59	0.57	0.49
Range	−0.02	0.14	0.24
Maximum	0.41	0.44	0.39
SD	0.03	0.20	0.25
Diastolic blood pressure			
Average	0.61	0.47	0.52
Range	0.00	0.12	0.04
Maximum	0.46	0.30	0.36
SD	0.04	0.15	0.09
Heart rate			
Average	0.54	0.47	0.51
Range	0.04	0.10	0.25
Maximum	0.40	0.36	0.44
SD	0.08	0.07	0.19

[a] $N = 256$–320, excluding subjects on antihypertensive medications; some correlations are based on fewer subjects than others because for some subjects there were too few observations to calculate a measure; e.g., there is no range when only one measurement was made. In addition, the correlations could only be calculated for subjects having a particular measure for all three studies.

diastolic, were also significantly correlated across time, but the average correlation was somewhat attenuated compared to the average values. It is of interest that the range of blood pressure, the range of heart rate, or the standard deviation were not significantly correlated across time. It is impressive nonetheless that individuals do tend to show considerable stability in both average and maximum blood pressures across time, accounting for approximately 25 to 35% of the variance.

Cortisol measures were less stable than those for blood pressure (Table 3). Similar to blood pressure, there was considerable consistency within a given visit between various ways of assessing cortisol response. The only measure of cortisol response that showed a significant correlation across time was that for total cortisol. The correlations of total cortisol area from visits 1 to 5 ranged from a low of 0.23 to a high of 0.40 with an average correlation across all visits of 0.29. However, when one classifies individuals into high, middle, or low groups and asks whether or not the first visit is predictive of the average of three visits, the data are somewhat more stable. The first visit does correlate 0.71 with the average of all three visits, and visits that were closer to one another in time were generally more highly correlated.

The degree of association between first visit cortisol levels and the average cortisol for all visits is presented in Table 4. In this chi-square analysis, it is

TABLE 3. *Prediction of average total cortisol (three to five visits) by first visit*

	Average cortisol all visits			Raw total
Group	High	Middle	Low	
High	50	25	4	79
	(26)	(27)	(26)	
Middle	25	32	25	82
	(27)	(28)	(27)	
Low	1	20	47	68
	23	23	23	
Total	76	77	76	229

$X^2 = 88.99$; df $= 4$; $p < 0.00001$.
Correlation visit 1 $\times$ total average $= 0.71$.

clear that individuals who were high during the initial visit were most often high or in the middle, and very rarely low, across all visits; similarly, those who were low in the first visit were most often middle or low on subsequent visits ($\chi^2 = 88.99$, df $= 4$, and $p < 0.00001$).

These data suggest that there is reasonable stability in both blood pressure and cortisol measures across time. One's ability to characterize an individual's response in either blood pressure or cortisol is considerably enhanced by studying them on more than one measure. However, if one wished to characterize an individual in terms of just one study, and if the individual could be placed in a high, middle, or low group, one is likely to be correct a significant percentage of the time as individuals rarely cross from the highest to the lowest groups

TABLE 4. *Relationship of average normalized cortisol on-the-job to overall psychiatric susceptibility status[a]*

Cortisol output		Asymptomatic	Prevalence	Incidence	F	P
Average normalized total	Mean	1,179.1	1,231.1	1,198.9	3.20	<0.05
	SD	121.8	119.2	133.2		
	N^b	95.0	60.0	64.0		
Average on-position maximum in 20 min	Mean	117.9	126.3	119.5	6.32	<0.003
	SD	14.4	15.5	15.0		
	N^c	101.0	61.0	65.0		

[a] Overall psychiatric susceptibility status groups were defined as: asymptomatic, all five PSS criterion scales were asymptomatic at all five evaluations ($N = 135$); prevalence cases, any of the five PSS criterion scales were symptomatic at intake ($N = 99$); incidence cases, any of the five PSS criterion scales were symptomatic after intake but not at intake ($N = 117$).

[b] Men who had no problems but who did not have all five PSS evaluations ($N = 65$) and men who did not have the specified cortisol assessment ($N = 132$) for three or more field studies were excluded.

[c] Men who had no problems but who did not have all five PSS evaluations ($N = 65$) and men who did not have the specified cortisol assessment ($N = 124$) for three or more field studies were excluded.

when the average of all studies over time is calculated. Many of these results do support the use of single measures to characterize individuals, although much greater stability and certainty is obtained when individuals can be studied multiple times.

Most of the analyses reported in this section utilize all the data available on individuals, i.e., the average across all studies in which the individual participated. Because of this, our analyses are limited essentially to concurrent relationships, as these blood pressure or endocrine measures were taken during the course of the study concurrent with the determination of psychiatric-psychological problems.

In general, there was little in individuals' cardiovascular or endocrine responses to work that was associated with overall psychiatric susceptibility. We employed many variables to characterize individuals' blood pressure responses, including average systolic or diastolic blood pressure, as well as more complex variables in which we compared individuals to themselves (ipsative approach), examining for any changes in blood pressure as the individual was exposed to varying work load. We also characterized cortisol and GH responses in various ways. Few of these cardiovascular or endocrine measures were found to have any association with psychiatric susceptibility.

In Table 4 we noted that there was a slight increase in average normalized total cortisol among individuals who entered the study with psychiatric problems, i.e., problem cases and those in whom new problems developed (incidence cases compared to the asymptomatic group). However, the prevalence cases were the most different from the other two in terms of either total or maximum cortisol. These data suggest that individuals who come into this study with psychiatric problems do experience increased secretion of cortisol later in the study.

Similar results were obtained, as shown in Table 5, comparing the blood pressure responses among those who were asymptomatic, prevalence, or incidence cases. The most impressive finding in these data is that the individuals who came into the study with more problems tended to have higher than average systolic blood pressure, as shown as a ratio of observed to expected in the prevalence group of 1.30. Again, there were not very significant differences between those in whom new problems developed (incidence cases) and the asymptomatic group except that the incidence group had fewer individuals with very high systolic blood pressure.

Another summary statistic employed in the analysis of the PSS data was to categorize men according to the extent of their psychiatric problems during the course of study. Men who had problems at intake and men who had incomplete examinations were excluded from these analyses. The four groups were labeled as asymptomatic, mild, moderate, or chronic new cases. We found that none of the cardiovascular or endocrine variables significantly discriminated among these four groups.

In a similar finding, none of the cardiovascular or endocrine variables were

TABLE 5. *Relationship of average systolic blood pressure at work to overall psychiatric status susceptibility groups*[a]

Blood pressure (BP)	Ratio of observed to expected numbers of subjects in each psychiatric susceptibility group[b]			Total no.
	Asymptomatic	Prevalence	Incidence	
Very low average systolic BP (less than − 1 SD) at work	1.44	0.50	0.77	41
Average systolic BP (± 1 SD) at work	0.88	1.04	1.15	193
Very high average systolic BP (greater than ± 1 SD) at work	1.18	1.30	0.50	39

[a] Men with no psychiatric problems but who were not evaluated all five times ($N = 65$) and men with less than three on-the-job blood pressure studies ($N = 145$) were excluded from this analysis. The psychiatric groups were reduced as follows: asymptomatic (135 reduced to 122), prevalences cases (99 reduced to 67), and incidence cases (117 reduced to 84).

[b] A ratio of 1.00 means that the number of men observed in a category was exactly equal to that expected by chance.

$X^2 = 13.44$; $df = 4$; $p < 0.01$.

different in men with varying rates of depression or anxiety, as categorized into asymptomatic, acute, intermittent, or chronic groups determined from scores on the Zung inventories.

DISCUSSION

These negative results were somewhat surprising to us, but there was sufficient consistency that the absence of positive relationships between cardiovascular and endocrine responses was impressive.

There were a large number of predictors of psychiatric health outcome as scored by both the PSS and the Zung anxiety and depression rating scales. Most of these predictors were ones associated with stable personality characteristics, such as type A, the amount of life change individuals experienced, attitudes toward work, especially job and self-morale, and the presence or absence of various factors that we labeled as coping efforts.

Similarly, the physiological responses that were studied were found to predict other health outcomes, especially the risk for hypertension and the frequency of occurrence of more mild illness, such as that associated with minor injuries and viral syndromes.

Our data strongly suggest that individuals show significant consistency in the blood pressure and endocrine responses to support their being classified as high, middle, or low responders. More stable classifications result from averaging responses from over several days' observations. Men who show increased cardiovascular or endocrine responses to work are not at an increased risk for developing psychiatric or psychological problems. The only relationships that we did find were that individuals who had problems at intake had higher blood pressure responses and a slightly increased level of cortisol secretion at work. This was not predictive but would be best interpreted in terms of psychological distress influencing endocrine response rather than increased endocrine or cardiovascular responses predicting risk for future psychiatric problems.

The cortisol levels we observed, along with the absence of elevated GH levels, suggest that most controllers were not under acute stress when we studied them. There are a large number of reports of increased cortisol and GH responses among individuals exposed to a variety of stimuli, but most of these are associated with more acute situations, such as parachute jumping (19) and upcoming examinations (10). Several studies in the literature indicate that after repeated exposure to stress, individuals adapt and endocrine responses return to lower levels (15,18). As a matter of fact, it was of interest that the individuals who had the lowest levels of cortisol response were at the most risk for developing more mild illness, such as flu-like syndromes, compared to those with more moderate or high endocrine responses. The significance of this finding is not yet clear but may indicate that adaptation to repeated stress by suppression may not be the most propitious homeostatic mechanism.

In a similar vein, blood pressure responses were predictive of future hypertension. We have found that individuals who showed the greatest blood pressure responses to work were at the greatest risk for developing hypertension. It was also of note that individuals with the lowest blood pressure variability, along with those who had the lowest endocrine responses, were also at increased risk for developing minor illness.

SUMMARY

A large number of more than 400 air traffic controllers were followed for 3 years, each with repeated examinations employing the PSS. In addition, the same men filled out a monthly Zung anxiety and depression checklist to assess intercurrent affective change. These individuals were also studied on an average of three or more times at work, while actually controlling traffic, with their blood pressure measured every 20 min for 5 hrs, or blood samples drawn on a similar schedule for cortisol and GH analysis.

We found that individuals who showed increased blood pressure, cortisol, or GH responses to work were not at increased risk for developing psychiatric or psychological problems. The absence of any relationship suggests that cardiovascular or endocrine responses to work are not associated with the development of psychological problems, although these responses are predictive of various physical illnesses. These findings argue for a specificity between mode of response to stress and risk for illness.

REFERENCES

1. Barrett, J., Hurst, M. W., DiScala, C., and Rose, R. M. (1978): Prevalence of depression over a 12 month period in a non-patient population. *Arch. Gen. Psychiatry,* 35:741–749.
2. Bevan, A. T., Honour, A. J., and Stott, F. H. (1969): Direct arterial pressure recording in unrestricted man. *Clin. Sci.,* 36:329–344.
3. Brown, G. M., and Reichlin, S. (1972): Psychologic and neural regulations of growth hormone secretion. *Psychosom. Med.,* 34:45–61.
4. Caplan, R. D., and Jones, K. W. (1975): Effects of work load, role ambiguity, and type A personality on anxiety, depression, and heart rate. *J. Appl. Psychol.,* 60:713–719.
5. Dohrenwend, B. P., Yager, T. J., Egri, G., and Mendelsohn, F. S. (1978): Psychiatric Status Schedule as a measure of dimensions of psychopathology in the general population. *Arch. Gen. Psychiatry,* 35:731–740.
6. Dutton, L. M., Smolensky, M. H., Leach, C. S., Lorimor, R., and Hsi, B. P. (1978): Stress levels of ambulance paramedics and fire fighters. *J. Occup. Med.,* 20:111–115.
7. Eich, R. H., Cuddy, R. P., Smulyan, H., and Lyons, R. H. (1966): Hemodynamics in labile hypertension: A follow up study. *Circulation,* 34:299–307.
8. Frankenhaeuser, M., Mellis, I., Rissler, A., Bjorkvall, C., Patkai, P. (1968): Catecholamine excretion as related to cognitive and emotional reaction patterns. *Psychosom. Med.,* 39:109–120.
9. Hofer, M., Wolff, C. T., Friedman, S. B., and Mason, J. W. (1972): A psychoendocrine study of bereavement: Part I. 17-Hydroxycorticosteroid excretion rates of parents following death of their children from leukemia. *Psychosom. Med.,* 34:481–491.
10. Jones, M. T., Bridges, P. K., and Leak, D. (1968): Relationship between the cardiovascular and sympathetic responses to the psychological stress of an examination. *Clin. Sci.,* 35:73–79.
11. Julius, F., and Schork, M. A. (1971): Borderline hypertension: A critical review. *J. Chronic Dis.,* 23:723–854.
12. Kreuz, L. E., Rose, R. M., and Jennings, J. R. (1972): Suppression of plasma testosterone levels and psychological stress: A longitudinal study of young men in officer candidate school. *Arch. Gen. Psychiatry,* 26:479–482.
13. Levi, L., and Kagan, A. (1973): A synopsis of ecology and psychiatry: Some theoretical psychosomatic considerations, review of some studies and discussion of preventive aspects. In: *Proceedings of the V World Congress of Psychiatry, Vol. 1,* edited by R. de la Fuente and M. N. Weisman, pp. 369–379. Elsevier, New York.
14. Levy, R. L., Hellman, C. C., Stroud, W. D., and White, P. D. (1944): Transient hypertension and cardiovascular renal disease *JAMA,* 126:829–833.
15. Maguire, G. P., Maclean, A. W., and Aitken, R. C. B. (1973): Adaptation on repeated exposure to film-induced stress. *Biol. Psychol.,* 1:43–51.
16. Mason, J. W. (1968): A review of psychoendocrine research on the pituitary-adrenal cortical system. *Psychosom. Med.,* 30:576–607.
17. Mason, J. W. (1975): Psychological stress and endocrine function. *Top. Psychoendocrinol.,* I: 1–15.
18. Mikulaj, L., Kvetnansky, R., Murgas, K., Parizkova, J., and Vencel, P. (1976): Catecholamines and corticosteroids in acute and repeated stress. In: *Catecholamines and Corticosteroids and Stress,* edited by E. Usdin, R. Kvetnansky, and I. Korn, pp. 445–455. Oxford, Pergamon Press.
19. Noel, G. L., Dimond, R. C., Earll, J. M., and Frantz, A. G. (1976): Prolactin, thyrotropin, and growth hormone release during stress associated with parachute jumping. *Aviat. Space Environ. Med.,* 47:543–547.
20. Noel, G. L., Suh, H. K., Stone, J. G. (1972): Human prolactin and growth hormone release during surgery and other conditions of stress. *J. Clin. Endocrinol.,* 35:840–851.
21. Rose, R. M., Gordon, T. P., and Bernstein, I. S. (1972): Plasma testosterone levels in the male rhesus: Influences of sexual and social stimuli. *Science,* 178:643–645.
22. Rose, R. M., Jenkins, C. D., and Hurst, M. W. (1978): *Air Traffic Controller Health Change Study,* edited by M. A. Levin, pp. 255–278. University of Texas Medical Branch, Galveston, Texas.
23. Rose, R. M., Jenkins, C. D., and Hurst, M. W. (1978): Health change in air traffic controllers: A prospective study. I. Background and description. *Psychosom. Med.,* 40:142–165.

24. Selye, H., and Heuser, G. (1956): *Fifth Annual Report on Stress.* MD Publications, New York.
25. Sokolow, M., Werdegar, D., Kain, H. K., and Hinman, A. T. (1966): Relationship between level of blood pressure measured casually and by portable recorders and severity of complications in essential hypertension. *Circulation,* 34:279–298.
26. Spitzer, R. L., Endicott, J., and Cohen, J. (1968): *Manual of Instructions: Psychiatric Status Schedule.* Biometrics Research, New York State Psychiatric Institute, New York.
27. Spitzer, R. L., Endicott, J., Fleiss, J. L., and Cohen, J. (1970): The Psychiatric Status Schedule. A technique for evaluating psychopathology and impairment in role functioning. *Arch. Gen. Psychiatry,* 23:41–55.
28. Taggert, P., Carother, M., and Somerville, W. (1973): Plasma catecholamines, lipids and their modification by oxprenalol when speaking before an audience. *Lancet,* 2:341–346.
29. Timio, M., and Gentili, S. (1976): Adrenosympathetic overactivity under conditions of work stress. *Br. J. Prev. Soc. Med.,* 30:262–265.
30. Ulrych, M. (1969): Change of general hemodynamics during stressful mental arithmetic and non-stressful quiet conversation and modification of the latter by beta-adrenergic blockade. *Clin. Sci.,* 36:543–561.
31. Zung, W. W. K. (1965): A self-rating depression scale. *Arch. Gen. Psychiatry,* 12:63–70.
32. Zung, W. W. K. (1971): A rating instrument for anxiety disorders. *Psychosomatics,* 12:371–379.

Stress and Mental Disorder,
edited by James E. Barrett et al.
Raven Press, New York © 1979.

Nurture and Psychopathology: Evidence from Adoption Studies

Paul H. Wender

*Department of Psychiatry, University of Utah College of Medicine,
Salt Lake City, Utah 84132*

The utilization of the natural experiment of adoption to study the role of genetics in the etiology of the schizophrenias was an idea that apparently occurred simultaneously to Dr. Leonard Heston, Dr. Seymour Kety, Dr. David Rosenthal, and myself in the early 1960s. Although initially the strategy was designed to determine whether genetic factors existed and, if they did, to measure their magnitude, it soon became apparent that this strategy could shed considerable light on the role of certain psychosocial factors in the genesis of mental illness.

Following its initial employment in the study of schizophrenia, the adoption technique has been employed to investigate affective illness, sociopathy, criminality, alcoholism, and hyperactivity in children. These studies have told us not only a good deal about the role of genetic factors in the etiology of these disorders but also something about the roles of parental psychopathology and of social class in the genesis of these forms of psychopathology.

For details about the sometimes subtle interpretative problems with which one is faced in examining data obtained from adoption studies, the interested reader is referred to the original studies (7,10,15,17). In this chapter, I first describe the ideal experimental design of an adoption study and then allude briefly to the difficulties that arise from the nonideal designs we must employ. The perfect way to perform such a study would be, over a period of a few years, to enter nurseries of newborns and switch the name tags on the cribs. This would avoid several problems: (a) The population of parents putting up their children for adoption would not be self-selected (one is concerned that such parents are deviant); (b) there would be no danger of the adoptee forming an initial tie with a parent figure and then having it broken; (this is ostensibly not pathogenic before the age of 6 months, but it would be nice to have uniformity in regard to this important variable); (c) selective placement would not exist (this refers to the attempt of some social agencies to match the attributes, including IQ and social class, of the biological and the adoptive parents, a factor which can make interpretation of adoption studies difficult); (d) it would avoid the problems that derive from adoptive parents having been specially selected by virtue of their ostensible mental health as well as their demonstrable material resources (this makes the adopting population a nonrandom one). Having switched babies in the proposed fashion, one would simply follow them for a period of 30 or 40 years. Obviously, this impeccable design entails some practical difficulties in execution. Accordingly, we decided to perform our adoption studies in Denmark where we felt the excellent record systems would avoid as many design problems as possible.

Before examining the various adoption studies, let me discuss the principal experimental designs and their weaknesses as compared with the ideal design mentioned above. The two major techniques have been labeled by Kety, Rosenthal, and myself as the "family method" and the "adoptee method." In the family method, one begins with a group of adopted individuals with a disorder to be studied, the index group, and a group of nondisordered adoptees, suitably matched, which constitutes the control group. The frequency of psychiatric illness is then investigated in the biological and adoptive families of the index and control groups. If genetic factors are operative, an increased frequency of the disorder in question will be found among the biological relatives of the index group as compared to those of the control group. If psychosocial factors or illness in the rearing parents are contributory to the disorder in question, an increased frequency of such factors or disorders will be found among the adoptive relatives of the index group as opposed to those of the control group.

What are some of the interpretive difficulties with the family method as ordinarily employed? First, the manner in which the controls are chosen and the population from which they stem tends to diminish the apparent magnitude of genetic factors. In most studies the controls are not interviewed and hence may have undetected psychiatric illness. In the Danish family study of schizophrenia, approximately one-fifth of the controls—who had been chosen on the basis of never having been formally diagnosed as having a psychiatric illness—were found to be perfectly healthy on the basis of the interviews. Thus the unscreened controls from this population are apt to have undetected illness, which if genetic will also appear in their biological relatives.

The second problem relates to the fact that individuals placing their biological children for adoption are probably a deviant population. If we make the assumption that they are and that there are genetic contributions to psychiatric illnesses, what happens? As an extreme example, suppose half the biological parents placing their children for adoption are schizophrenic. We know from nonadoption studies that approximately 50% of the offspring of schizophrenic parents will be in the "schizophrenic spectrum" and 50% will apparently be normal. In this extreme instance, half the children placed for adoption would be in the schizophrenic spectrum and half would not. On the average, all screened and clinically normal controls and all index cases would come from families in which one parent was schizophrenic. As a result, no differences would be found in the frequency of schizophrenia in the biological relatives of index cases and controls.

A third problem likewise occurs with the adoptive families. Individuals with gross psychiatric illness are screened out, but there may be individuals who are subtly psychonoxious and who have no detectable psychiatric illness on relatively cursory inspection. These parents might be driving their children schizophrenic, depressed, or alcoholic but would seem to be free of psychiatric illnesses. If such a situation exists, it would tend to diminish the apparent effect of psychological factors in the genesis of psychiatric illness. Hence an adequate evaluation of these parents might require more than a diagnostic interview.

A fourth source of possible error is based on whether case ascertainment is determined by registered pathology or on the basis of interviews. The existence in Denmark of central registries of psychopathology and criminality permitted us to conduct noninterview studies. Obviously, the use of registries introduces a systematic bias, skewing toward more severe or socially unacceptable psychopathology. It also tends to underestimate the degree of pathology in all classes of relatives since individuals with milder forms of disorder are less likely to have been hospitalized or incarcerated. In all the studies reported except the adoption studies of sociopathy and criminality, psychiatric diagnosis was based on interviews.

The next adoption strategy is the "adoptee method." An elaboration constructed by Rosenthal allows one not only to look for genetic and experiential factors but to analyze their interaction. This is done by studying four groups of adult adoptees: (a) an index group (individuals born of psychiatrically ill parents and raised by non-ill parents), (b) a control group (individuals born to nonpsychiatrically disturbed biological parents and reared by nonpsychiatrically disturbed adopting parents), (c) a cross-foster group (individuals born to nonpsychiatrically disturbed biological parents and reared by psychiatrically disturbed adopting parents), and (d) individuals born to and reared by psychiatrically disturbed parents; optimally one would employ individuals born to and adopted by such parents, but for obvious statistical reasons such a subpopulation is as difficult to locate as one of albino aardvarks. Errors introduced by the realities of this method are similar in nature to those in the family studies. Since the entire population of a country cannot be interviewed, one depends on registries of mental illness. The biological parents of the control subjects are selected on the basis of having no known psychiatric illness. The assumption that the frequency of illness in such parents is the same as that of the population at large is unjustified. A preliminary, unpublished study conducted by Rosenthal and me at the National Institute of Mental Health (NIMH) indicated that many control biological parents who were not officially registered as having psychiatric illnesses did indeed have such illnesses. If genetic factors are operative, this selection error would increase the frequency of psychiatric illness in the so-called controls, minimizing the apparent effect of genetic factors. Comparable errors might seem to be introduced when the adoptive parents of the index cases are not evaluated. However, the adopted parents of the controls likewise were not evaluated, so that with sufficient sample size this error should not prejudice the results. I now turn to the psychiatric illnesses with which these techniques have been employed and report the results that have been obtained.

SCHIZOPHRENIAS

A family study of schizophrenia was conducted in Denmark by Kety et al. (6,7). This study demonstrated the existence of genetic factors but failed to demonstrate any increased psychopathology among the adopting parents of the index cases, as compared to the adoptive parents of the controls; that is, no nurture effects were demonstrable. In the adoptee studies conducted by Rosenthal et al. (9,10) and Wender et al. (15), genetic factors could again be demonstrated but the effects of nurture could not. Individuals born of schizophrenic parents were no more severely ill when raised by those parents than when raised by nonschizophrenic adopting parents. Individuals born of normal parents manifested no more schizophrenic spectrum disorder when reared by schizophrenic parents than when reared by normal parents.

One study, conducted by Wender et al. (16) in the United States, apparently documented some environmental effects. This study employed a third method, the "adoptive parents method," in which one compares parents who have reared their own schizophrenic offspring (the biological parents), parents who have adopted a child who subsequently became schizophrenic (the adoptive parents), and a suitably chosen comparison group, controlling for the effects of either adoption or children on their parents. In this study, the biological parents of schizophrenics exhibited considerably more psychopathology than the adopting parents of schizophrenics, who manifested somewhat more psychopathology than the comparison group, the adopted parents of normals. In addition, employing the Rorschach communication evaluation techniques of Singer and Wynne, both the adopting and biological parents of schizophrenics demonstrated equal communication pathology, which was more severe than that seen in the control parents.

A possible source of difficulty in this study was the choice of a comparison group. Since the study was conducted, it has been shown that test anxiety affects communicative clarity as measured by this method, and it seemed possible that much of the communication pathology in the adoptive parents might be reactive to the serious family problems produced by a schizophrenic child. Accordingly, a replication study was conducted by Wender et al. (17) utilizing a comparison of parents expected to have familial problems on a reactive basis, the biological parents of nongenetic retardates. In this study, no nurture effects were demonstrable. The biological parents of schizophrenics demonstrated more clinical psychopathology than either the adopted parents of schizophrenics or the natural parents of retardates whose levels of psychopathology were equivalent. A similar finding held with respect to communication abnormalities as manifested on the Rorschach test. In this better designed study, no nurture effects were demonstrable.

AFFECTIVE DISORDERS

Three studies have been conducted. The first, conducted by Mendlewicz and Rainer (8), utilized the family method to investigate bipolar affective disorder. Their findings documented genetic but not nurture effects. There was an increased frequency of affective spectrum disorders only in the biological parents of the bipolar probands. A study of primary affective disorder and "neurotic" depressive disorder, employing the family method, is currently being conducted by Kety et al.; the results are not yet available. Finally, Goodwin et al. (1) utilized the adoptee method to investigate the rates of depression in the adopted and non-adopted daughters of alcoholics. In this instance, they claimed to have demonstrated a nurture effect. The nonadopted daughters of alcoholics showed a statistically increased frequency of depressive disorders (27%) as compared with the population at large (7%) but not with the adopted daughters of alcoholics (14%). Their claim is that this type of depressive disorder, termed "depressive spectrum disease" by Winokur, would seem to have an environmental component. However, since the meaningful comparison (that between the prevalence of depressive disorder in the adopted and nonadopted daughters) is statistically insignificant, their assertion is not supported. There is no evidence that adoption attenuates the risk of depression in the daughters of alcoholics.

SOCIOPATHY

Only one study has been conducted in the area of sociopathy. Schulsinger (13) utilized the family method (with case ascertainment by psychiatric registers) to investigate genetic and environmental factors in psychopathy. It is important to note that Schulsinger employed a Danish definition of psychopathy, which differs considerably from that employed in the Research Diagnostic Criteria and the preliminary edition of DSM-III. Rather than employing operational behavioral measures, the Danish definition is based on a more global assessment of personality structure depending on attributes such as behavior that is alloplastic, impulse-ridden, and with abreactions disproportionate to the precipitating stimuli. Schulsinger found an increase in psychopathy only among the biological relatives of the index cases. Psychopathy was not increased among the adopting parents of the index cases, nor was any other psychiatric illness found in excess. These results again failed to document a nurture effect.

ALCOHOLISM

Alcoholism is obviously a disorder with an environmental component. The drug must be available for any genetic diathesis to manifest itself. Chemical availability must be supplemented by cultural permissiveness. One would not expect a high frequency of the disorder in strict Mohammendan countries where alcoholic beverages are banned. Furthermore, clinical experience reveals that alcoholics are a very heterogeneous entity. Schizophrenics drink, individuals with affective disorders drink, sociopaths drink, and so do a host of other types of people. Alcoholism is certainly familial, as shown in nonadoption studies. It is a reasonable question to ask if one sort of alcoholism, not associated with any other psychiatric illness, has genetic or environmental components.

Goodwin et al. (2,3) performed a modified adoptee study of alcoholism comparing three groups: (a) adoptees born to alcoholic fathers and reared by nonalcoholic fathers, (b) adoptees whose biological fathers were not known to be alcoholic and who were reared by nonalcoholics, and (c) the siblings of the individuals in the first group who rather than being adopted away were reared by those same biological fathers. An increased prevalence of alcoholism was found in the biological sons of alcoholics. The rate was not diminished by being reared in nonalcoholic homes. For this subgroup of alcoholics, sons of alcoholic fathers, familial nurture effects could not be demonstrated. Unfortunately, a cross-fostering experiment was not performed (the effect of rearing the adopted sons of nonalcoholics by alcoholics) and the "pure" effects of nurture are unknown. It should be reemphasized that still other nurture effects are not ruled out. If prohibition existed in Denmark or if the subjects were devout Muslims, one would anticipate lower rates of alcoholism for all groups mediated through environmental but not familial variables. It is interesting that drinking patterns of rearing parents were also found to have no effect on the rate of alcoholism in a half-sib study conducted by Schuckit et al. (12).

CRIMINALITY

Another adoption study is one of criminality conducted by Hutchins and Mednick (5) in Denmark. Of all the conditions discussed, criminality is least disease-like. Criminality is a legal term applied to socially nonsanctioned behavior, which may be abnormal only in a particular cultural context. Because sociological studies clearly suggest that some forms of criminal and delinquent behavior are learned, one would be surprised not to find nurture effects in the etiology of this ill-defined group of nonacceptable behaviors. The investigators did indeed find environmental effects. Employing both the family and adoptee methods, they found that criminal behavior in the adoptee was related to such behavior in both his adoptive and biological fathers. (It is hard to stifle a small cheer for the validation of common sense.) The study, based on registry diagnosis, did not carefully distinguish among various forms of crimes and contained some other methodological difficulties which the interested reader should examine. A replication with interviews is being conducted.

SOCIAL CLASS, PARENT-CHILD RELATIONSHIPS, AND PSYCHOPATHOLOGY

The two major Danish adoption studies conducted by Kety, Rosenthal, and myself in the United States and Schulsinger and Welner in Denmark have provided us with information concerning not only the role of genetics in the etiology of the schizophrenias but the relationship of familial upbringing and social class to other forms of psychopathology as well.

Both these studies have been published (11,18) but have somehow failed to produce a large wave of excitement in the scientific community. Both were of interest to us because, despite certain inherent limitations in the method of the studies, they failed to support the assumed relationships between social class or familial relationships and the development of psychopathology.

I begin by reviewing the study in which we examined the relationship between familial upbringing and the subsequent development of psychopathology. The purpose of this study was to explore the relationship between familial atmosphere and the subsequent development of psychopathology in the offspring when genetic factors were accounted for. It has long been assumed that psychopathology in individuals is closely related to the child rearing experiences they have undergone. While the adoption studies now force all but the most obdurate to acknowledge that genetic factors play a role in several psychiatric illnesses, most psychiatrists adhere to the belief that familial experience is of critical importance in the genesis of that relatively vague group of conditions designated as "personality disorders" and "neuroses." This does not appear to be a startling assumption. There is ample naturalistic observation and social psychological data documenting that many aspects of behavior are socially transmitted. Children speak the same language as their parents and tend to share their parents' political and religious views, attitudes, and values. Empirical studies tend to show a relationship between parental attitudes, behaviors, and psychological characteristics in their children. Students of child development, psychoanalysts, and learning theorists have provided theoretical mechanisms by which such familial transmission of psychological characteristics can take place. Having shown that much of children's normal behavior can be related to the familial atmosphere to which they were exposed while growing up, it hardly seems a giant theoretical leap to assume that personality distortions and neuroses are likewise a function of the child's learning experience within the family.

The adoption studies of schizophrenia showed us that nonpsychotic personality deviations—some "borderline" schizophrenia states—had a genetic component. This led us to wonder if genetic relatedness might have contributed to the clinically observed relationship between other forms of psychopathology in parents and their offspring. Furthermore, we saw a way in which the same data utilized to examine the role of genetic factors in the etiology of schizophrenia could be employed to study the relationship between child rearing practices and psychopathology. This study was an offshoot of the adoptee studies of schizophrenia.

In these studies, we examined 258 adults who represented four selected groups: (a) index adoptees who had a biological parent with schizophrenic or manic depressive disorder and who were given up for adoption to nonbiologically related parents early in life, (b) matched control adoptees who were similarly adopted but whose biological parents had no registered psychiatric illness, (c) cross-foster subjects who did not have a biological parent with a schizophrenic or manic depressive disorder but who were adopted and reared by persons who did have such a disorder, and (d) nonadoptees who had a schizophrenic or manic depressive parent and who were reared in the parental home, at least during the first 15 years of life. These subjects received a 3- to 5-hr psychiatric interview by Welner, who was in general blind (except in the fourth group) in regard to the psychiatric status of the biological parent. During the course of the interview, he obtained information regarding the psychopathological status of the subject and historical information, which included reasonably detailed material concerning the relationship between the subject and his rearing parents.

The next step was to form independent judgments of the subject's account of his family experience and of his psychopathology. The interviews were edited by a research assistant who culled information from the interviews and compiled abstracts dealing with each subject's report of his relationship with his rearing parents. [For a more detailed presentation of specific material collected, the reader is once again referred to the original article (11).] This information was placed on index cards, and raters were given the task of sorting these cards into a forced modified normal distribution, distributing subjects on a continuum of best to worst familial relationships. There were 20 categories, "20" representing the worst and "1" representing the best parent-child relationships. Three raters were employed, and the interrater reliability showed an appreciably high degree of consensus, with correlations in the mid-80s. To illustrate the data available and the spread in types of relationships, I present an example of two sets of relationships, one very good and one very poor. First, an example of a very good relationship in childhood:

A 23-year-old man was rank 2, with one dissident judge ranking him one step higher. The conditions in the childhood home were, in general, excellent. The parents were not strict, and only a few times did the subject get a "whack on the neck." He feels that he was a bit spoiled by the mother who, however, did not fuss over him. The home was quite firm with regard to appearing on time and the like. However, the subject was allowed, all in all, to do the things that most children were allowed to do. He describes the father as a nice guy who now and then could become really furious, but the rage quickly disappeared again. The father was a very stable worker who was many years with his employers. The mother is described as very loving and good to others. The home was patriarchal, but nonetheless the parents were able to talk about things with one another. It is the subject's impression that the parents' marriage was good. As a rule, he had an excellent relationship with his parents. For most of his childhood he had a confidential relationship with his mother. When he grew up he also became close with his father. In childhood he was probably more closely attached to his mother but afterward he has become just as attached to his father. The subject did not get sexual information from his home. If he has problems, he usually tells them to his wife and to his parents. He believes that the person who knows him best is his father and the subject is used to telling about himself to a certain extent. He probably still feels most closely attached to his parents. He does not tend to get cross with his parents. Now and then he may feel that his mother mixes too much into his affairs, but this is seldom. He is very closely attached to his parents.

Next, a very poor relationship:

A 45-year-old man was ranked 18, with one dissident judge rating him one step lower. Both parents were rather mean. He stayed at home until the age 18. Both parents were unloving, restrictive, and he was often beaten. He never fitted in with his adoptive parents. He never had very good contact with the parents. He always felt that he was treated in a different way from his cousins and other children in the family, and he remembers that he felt resentment and sadness because of that. The subject never had confidence in any grown-ups. He tells that when he was about age 6, his adoptive mother tried to seduce him to intercourse. She was rather violent and broke his penis. He remembers clearly that it was extremely painful and that his mother, too, was extremely scared. [It should be mentioned that the interviewer has asked one of the chief surgeons at the hospital whether a thing like that could happen. The surgeon affirmed that it has happened, but extremely seldom.] His father died eight years ago, and the mother died two or three years ago. He didn't have close connections with them and he visited them regularly, without great pleasure and without being moody. He always felt that he wasn't treated by his parents as a child of their own flesh and blood.

The next issue was to assess psychopathology in the subjects, which could then be correlated with their report of their family atmosphere and upbringing. This was accomplished in an analogous manner. Following the completion of the interview, Welner dictated a brief summary including a brief diagnostic statement. These paragraphs were placed on file cards and raters asked to Q-sort them on a modified normal distribution of 20 categories, with "1" representing maximal mental health and "20" unqualified schizophrenia. Interrater reliabilities for the three most experienced judges had a median of approximately 0.93. The following are representative examples of differing ranks: 1: an above average mentally healthy person; 5: well within boundaries of normality, slight obsessive and hysterical traits, but on the whole well functioning; 10: neurotic personality with depressive, anxious, and hysterical characteristics; no schizoid or prepsychotic phenomena; 15: very withdrawn, insecure, somewhat suspicious young person, does not present obvious psychotic characteristics; thought structure is pathological to great extent, severely schizoid with impoverished feeling and autistic characteristics; 20: chronic schizophrenia, manifested 20 years.

The next step was to correlate the subjects' reports of their family upbringing with their degree of psychopathology. This was done separately for each of the four groups of subjects. The correlations are shown in Table 1.

TABLE 1. *Correlations between parent-child relationship and adult psychopathology in four selected groups*

Group	N	Correlation	Significance level [a]
Index adoptees	69	0.22	0.05
Nonadoptees	41	0.23	NS
Control adoptees	79	0.34	0.005
Cross-foster subjects	28	0.36	0.05

[a] One-tailed test.

These data are of interest in regard to the question of both rearing factors and development of the schizophrenias and rearing factors and normal child development. If we examine the two groups with a presumptive genetic load for schizophrenia, the index adoptees and the nonadoptees, we find a mean correlation coefficient of 0.23. If we combine the two "nongenetic" groups, we find a mean correlation of approximately 0.36. The difference between these two correlation coefficients approaches but does not reach statistical significance. It is interesting, however, that the difference is in the direction that would be predicted by a genetic hypothesis; namely, that rearing patterns play a greater role in producing normal or psychopathological behavior characteristics in individuals in whom there is no schizophrenic genetic interference with the shaping of behavior by different rearing patterns.

The second point worthy of observation is that in the two groups with no known genetic predisposition to psychopathology, there is a statistically significant relationship between rearing experience and adult psychological adjustment but that the relationship, although statistically significant, does not seem to be causally appreciable. Using a variance model (whose statistical assumptions may have absolutely nothing to do with the real world) we find that in the nongenetically loaded group, familial experience accounts for approximately 13% of the variance in psychopathology. Is the glass half full or half empty? I find the relationship between rearing and adult psychopathology to be surprisingly low and contrary to conventional wisdom. Each reader must decide for him- or herself.

What limitations are there to the study? An important critique is that "true relationships" between family experience and psychopathology may have been spuriously minimized by the research techniques employed. In particular, familial interactions were not directly assessed. What was assessed was the subjects' recollection of the experiences he or she underwent. Furthermore, because of the relative brevity of the interview, the autobiographical material obtained, particularly in regard to description of childhood experiences, was relatively sparse. It is possible that richer material, such as is acquired in the conduct of psychotherapy, might yield different results. Nevertheless, these data are impressive. They strongly suggest that the relationship between child rearing practices and subsequent development of psychopathology may be nowhere near as strong as we have assumed in the past.

SOCIAL CLASS AND PSYCHOPATHOLOGY

The belief that there is a relationship between socioeconomic status (SES) and psychopathology, particularly schizophrenia, is widely held and fairly well documented. A careful review of the data available for schizophrenia led Kohn to conclude that the available data, although supporting this observation, did not support the notion of a simple linear relationship between SES and psychopathology. In medium-sized cities, the relationship between the two variables was accounted for by an increased prevalence of schizophrenia in the very lowest SES, whereas in smaller cities, a relationship between SES and mental disorder is absent.

If a relationship between SES and mental illness does exist, how may it be explained? There are three possible explanations. First, the "sociogenic" hypothesis asserts that there are psychosocial consequences of lower social class membership which foster or at least fail to inhibit the development of psychopathology. These might include grinding economic problems, familial disorganization, inadequate education, maladaptive or inflexible attitudes and values, and the feeling of lack of control over one's life.

A second major explanation is summed up in the phrase "the downward drift hypothesis," wherein mental illness produces social and occupational ineffectiveness, which causes the individual to sink lower in the social hierarchy.

A third explanation is what Rosenthal and I termed the "intergenerational downward drift hypothesis." This hypothesis proposes that there are genetic diatheses to mental illness, and that some mental illnesses affect social competence. As a result of these diatheses operating over time, an evolutionary process occurs with the afflicted subgroups sinking lower in the social hierarchy until their average number reaches a low and stable ecological niche. By way of analogy, if brains and beauty have a genetic component and are considered desirable, if sexual selection occurs, and if the rich are more likely to get what they want, we would anticipate the average upper class individual to be smarter and more physically attractive than the average member of the lower classes.

The adoption studies permit testing of the three hypotheses mentioned above. Such tests have been conducted by Heston and Denney (4) and the NIMH group (18). Both Heston and we examined the sociogenic hypothesis, which proposes that lower social class rearing fosters mental illness. Employing adoptees is advantageous because it eliminates the third hypothesis as a possible explanation; that is, it rules out the possibility that individuals are starting in a lower class because of genetically determined psychological incapacities. These genetic incapacities would be the actual cause of social incompetence, while lower class membership would only be a sign of the genetic diathesis. Both groups obtained the same results. We found that the social class of the adopting parents bore no relationship to the level of psychological health achieved by the adoptee as an adult. An important criticism of the method might be that because of the factors involved in selecting adopting families, the lower class families in these studies were nonrepresentative, having been selected for their potential excellence in child rearing capacities.

The second hypothesis, the downward drift hypothesis, asserts that the putative relationship between lower SES membership and mental illness is the result of the fact that psychiatrically ill individuals sink lower in the social hierarchy. It is not necessary to control for genetic factors to test this hypothesis, although adoption studies still afford an advantage in that in the naturalistic situation, if genetic factors operate, there are more ill members in lower social classes to begin with. If the ill are lower SES, the magnitude of their decline would tend to be less and harder to assess. To test the downward drift hypothesis, Heston examined the relationship between adoptee's own social class and the adults' mental health ratings. A clear-cut positive relationship existed between level of social class and adult mental health: the higher the level of psychological adjustment, the higher the social class. This is a finding in accordance with the narrow downward drift hypothesis, which was examined in the Danish adoption studies in two ways. In the first study, in which all of the adoptees were schizophrenic, the hypothesis was confirmed. In the second, in a population of adoptees whose psychiatric impairment varied from minimal to severe, the hypothesis was not confirmed. The most parsimonious interpretation of the results of these three studies is that downward drift is related to severity of psychopathology and that with mild psychopathology, little or no downward drift occurs.

The third explanation of the social class-psychopathology relationship is the intergenerational downward drift hypothesis. The experimental strategy is to examine the correlation between the adoptee's psychopathology and the SES of their biological parents (which is operationally defined by the occupational and educational level of the biological father). In the Danish studies, no such correlation was obtained, and the hypothesis was not supported. Unfortunately, because of the necessary methodology, the risk of type II error in this study is high. To provide an acid test of the intergenerational downward drift hypothesis, one should randomly select a sample of children at birth (of varying SES) and randomly place them in adoptive homes; such randomization would permit a critical test of the hypothesis. In the Danish study, we obviously did not select our adoptees at random, yanking them from the bosom of their biological families. Rather, we studied individuals whose biological parents had been willing to give them up for adoption. Since it is unusual for upper class parents to place their children for adoption, we strongly suspect that the few upper SES parents who placed their children for adoption represented a deviant sample, possibly skewed toward genetically transmissable psychopathology. Such skewing would mask the presence of intergenerational downward drift. For a further discussion of the sampling biases we could not avoid, and the difficulties so introduced, the original article (18) should be consulted.

SUMMARY

A report of negative results is generally not met with wild interest and excitement. This is particularly so when the obtaining of such results may simply be the result of a type II error, that is, the product of methodology that fails to detect differences that are really present. In the studies of psychiatric illnesses discussed, the methodology employed repeatedly picked up the operation of genetic factors and, because of the logic of the design, should have been as sensitive to familial factors, if present. Hence the risk of the negative results being the result of type II error is small.

Some obvious but occasionally overlooked points should be made. First, the studies reviewed do not document that all instances of the disorders investigated are genetic in origin. Second, the failure to demonstrate that all instances are not genetic does not mean that they are psychosocial in origin. There are a host of environmental biological factors known or suspected to play a role in the genesis of mental illness. These include abnormalities of fetal development, neurological trauma, toxins (such as lead), and possibly other sinister forces (such as slow viral infections). Third, these studies do not rule out the possibility of psychosocially produced phenocopies. Although Schulsinger (13) demonstrated that genetic factors seem to be involved in the etiology of some forms of psychopathy, it may be that Bowlby is right and that one can produce "affectionless psychopaths" by exposing genetically normal children to a suitably impoverished environment. Nonetheless, taken together, these studies support the notion that familial factors do not play an important role in the genesis of some of the better defined and more serious psychiatric disorders.

If these findings are surprising, what may be even more so is that the relationship between family psychopathology in childhood, as perceived by adults, and those adults' own psychopathology, although demonstrable, is not impressive in magnitude. Reservations attributable to design must be taken very seriously here, since it is grossly evident that a tremendous number of cultural attributes are transmitted by the family: language, religion, political stance, philosophy, attitudes, and so forth. Is it possible that a great deal of nonmajor psychopathology is not the product of family experience and family interactions? If the results are to be believed, the answer would be "yes." This should not be entirely unexpected. Correlations between early temperament and later behavior, although statistically significant, are not overwhelmingly high. What is accounting for this lack of a strong relationship remains to be determined. As discussed above, what is not genetic is not necessarily familial, and vice versa. Schools, peer groups, current relationships, and life circumstances may, perhaps, greatly affect current levels of psychopathology. The results, if true, mean we may still have a lot to learn.

In concluding, I hope this review has been useful by increasing the reader's ignorance. I would like to conclude with Mark Twain, that astute observer of human nature, who observed: "It isn't what you don't know that gets you into trouble. It's what you do know that ain't so."

REFERENCES

1. Goodwin, D. W., Schulsinger, F., Knop, J., Mednick, S., and Guze, S. B. (1977): Psychopathology in adopted and nonadopted daughters of alcoholics. *Arch. Gen. Psychiatry,* 34:1005–1009.
2. Goodwin, D. W., Schulsinger, F., Hermansen, L., Guze, S. B., and Winokur, G. (1973): Alcohol problems in adoptees raised apart from alcoholic biological parents. *Arch. Gen. Psychiatry,* 28:238–243.

3. Goodwin, D. W., Schulsinger, F., Hermansen, L., Guze, S. B., and Winokur, G. (1974): Drinking problems in adopted and nonadopted sons of alcoholics. *Arch. Gen. Psychiatry,* 31:164–169.
4. Heston, L. L., and Denney, D. (1968): Interactions between early life experiences and biological factors in schizophrenia. In: *The Transmission of Schizophrenia,* edited by D. Rosenthal and S. S. Kety, pp. 363–376. Pergamon Press, Oxford.
5. Hutchins, B., and Mednick, S. A. (1977): Criminality in adoptees and their adoptive and biological parents: A pilot study. In: *Biosocial Bases of Criminal Behavior,* edited by S. A. Mednick and K. O. Christiansen, pp. 127–141. Gardner Press, New York.
6. Kety, S. S. Rosenthal, D., Wender, P. H., and Schulsinger, F. (1968): The types and prevalence of mental illness in the biological and adoptive families of adopted schizophrenics. In: *The Transmission of Schizophrenia,* edited by D. Rosenthal and S. S. Kety, pp. 413–428. Pergamon Press, Oxford.
7. Kety, S. S., Rosenthal, D., Wender, P. H., Schulsinger, F., and Jacobsen, B. (1976): Mental illness in the biological and adoptive families of adopted individuals who have become schizophrenic: A preliminary report based upon psychiatric interview. In: *Genetics and Psychopathology,* edited by R. Fieve, H. Brill, and D. Rosenthal, pp. 147–166. Johns Hopkins Press, Baltimore.
8. Mendlewicz, J., and Rainer, J. D. (1977): Adoption study supporting a genetic transmission in manic-depressive illness. *Nature,* 268:5618, 327–329.
9. Rosenthal, D., Wender, P. H., Kety, S. S., Schulsinger, F., Welner, J., and Ostergaard, L. (1968): Schizophrenics' offspring reared in adoptive homes. In: *The Transmission of Schizophrenia,* edited by D. Rosenthal and S. S. Kety, pp. 377–392. Pergamon Press, Oxford.
10. Rosenthal, D., Wender, P. H., Kety, S. S., Welner, J., and Schulsinger, F. (1971): The adopted-away offspring of schizophrenics. *Am. J. Psychiatry,* 128:307–310.
11. Rosenthal, D., Wender, P. H., Kety, S. S., Schulsinger, F., Welner, J., and Reider, R. (1975): Parent child relationships and psychopathological disorder in the child. *Arch. Gen. Psychiatry,* 32:466–476.
12. Schuckit, M. A., Goodwin, D. A., and Winokur, G. (1972): A study of alcoholism in half siblings. *Am. J. Psychiatry,* 128:9, 122–126.
13. Schulsinger, F. (1972): Psychopathy: Heredity and environment. *Int. J. Mental Health,* 1:190–206.
14. Wender, P. H. (1972): Adopted children and their families in the evaluations of nature-nurture interactions in the schizophrenic disorders. *Ann. Rev. Med.,* 23:355–372.
15. Wender, P., Rosenthal, D., and Kety, S. S. (1974): Crossfostering: A research strategy for clarifying the role of genetic and experiential factors in the etiology of schizophrenia. *Arch. Gen. Psychiatry,* 30:121–128.
16. Wender, P. H., Rosenthal, D., and Kety, S. S. (1968): Psychiatric assessment of adoptive parents of schizophrenics. In: *The Transmission of Schizophrenia,* edited by D. Rosenthal and S. S. Kety, pp. 235–250. Pergamon Press, Oxford.
17. Wender, P. H., Rosenthal, D., Rainer, J. D., and Greenhill, L. (1977): Schizophrenics' adopting parents. *Arch. Gen. Psychiatry,* 34:7, 777–788.
18. Wender, P. H., Rosenthal, D., Kety, S. S., Schulsinger, F., and Welner, J. (1973): Social class and psychopathology in adoptees: An experimental method for separating the roles of genetic and experiential factors. *Arch. Gen. Psychiatry,* 28:318–325.

Stress and Mental Disorder,
edited by James E. Barrett et al.
Raven Press, New York © 1979.

Psychosocial Modifiers of Response to Stress

C. David Jenkins

Division of Psychiatry, Boston University School of Medicine, Boston, Massachusetts 02118

THE PROBLEM INTRODUCED

A major weakness of most stress research has been its limitation to a two-variable research design: a noxious stimulus is introduced, and a response of discomfort or disease is observed. In the most common study design, participants are defined in terms of the presence of a physical or psychiatric illness, and antecedent stress inputs are then sought through patient's recall of recent life history. Such studies have illuminated the relationship of stressors to physical and mental disorders, but I submit that these simplistic retrospective studies have also generated inconsistencies across different study groups and are unlikely to guide health scientists to more advanced levels of understanding.

We are at the same crossroads neurologists faced when they attempted to apply to the study of central nervous system functioning the simple stimulus-response paradigm which had been so successfully used in the study of reflexes. The two-variable design is inadequate even in the study of nonacute infectious diseases, such as tuberculosis. This classic pulmonary disease does not develop in 98 or 99 of every 100 Caucasian Americans now becoming infected with the tubercle bacillus. The situation is so different for Eskimos and native Americans that one could argue on mathematical grounds that the cultures of these two ethnic groups are a more potent cause of tuberculosis than is the much maligned bacillus.

Similarly, among the so-called stress diseases, why is it that mental disorders develop in so many people with very little prior discernable exposure to stressors? Yet Antonovsky (1) reports from Israel that more than 25% of concentration camp survivors—despite long years of physical suffering, the constant threat of annihilation, and other stressors too rueful to describe—have survived their ordeals without evidence of psychiatric disorder or chronic physical disease.

TOWARD A MORE COMPREHENSIVE RESEARCH MODEL

Selye (10) has described many of the basic principles of stress. In his early work, we note the sharp distinctions he made concerning the natural development of a stress reaction. He noted the marked differences in an organism's reactions to a noxious situation at the stages of alarm, resistance, and exhaustion. These distinctions have often been ignored in studies of stress and mental disorders, despite the fact that psychiatric manifestations are quite different at these three stages.

The stage of alarm is characterized by acute rises in anxiety and fear if the stressor is a threat, or by rises in sorrow and depression if the stressor is a loss. If the stressor is particularly acute and potent, a brief state of shock or feeling stunned or confused may occur. Many of these states are self-correcting if the noxious stimulus is of only brief duration. If it continues, however, the organism will move on to a stage of resistance in which a variety of defenses are called into play. If a persons' perceptual defenses, ego defenses, and problem-solving behaviors are adequate to overcome or escape the noxious situation, no psychiatric symptomatology of a continuing nature will develop. If a person under stress is studied during his or her period of effective defensive reaction, little anxiety, alarm, or mental disorder will be discerned. The primary evidence of the presence of stress may be simply an increased intensity of biological, psychological, and interpersonal defensiveness.

In those circumstances where noxious stimuli are so strong as to overwhelm defenses or are so prolonged as to outlast the energy available for defensive activity, a "pathological end-state" results. I use this term to denote Selye's stage of exhaustion but also to have a broader meaning, which includes any prolonged and relatively irreversible disorder of function which often may result in structural changes. The term as used here does not necessarily imply "adrenal exhaustion" but rather refers generally to a decompensation having poor prognosis, whether this occurs at the biological, psychological, interpersonal, or socio-cultural level.

Pathological end-states are thought to result from the damage caused by stressors against which the organism could not defend. An example of this is the psychotic decompensation seen in war prisoners treated harshly for long periods of time. Alternatively, a pathological end-state may result from a defense that reacts too strongly or continues to react long after the stress has ceased. An example of the latter includes those adult neuroses that take the form of continuing reenactments of childhood traumas. Pathological end-states could also develop from recurrent defensive reactions, which are inappropriate to the nature of the stressful stimulus. Examples of this are found in theories that hold that some cases of peptic ulcer or chronic asthma may represent a physiological response to interpersonal stressors.

At this point we have expanded the two-variable equation—stress–illness—to four variables by taking into account the three stages in the organism's reaction to stress; but there is still something lacking in this theoretical model. The remaining question looks back to a prior point in time: Why is it that among those exposed to a common stress, some defend successfully with minimal effort but others must mount a more heroic defense? The answer must lie in the different capacities of individuals to adapt to specific kinds of challenges or stressors. Again, the field of infectious disease is instructive with its analogous concept of "host resistance." Natural or acquired immunity to an infectious disease enables an organism to withstand an infectious challenge without the discomforts and profound systemic defensive reactions, such as fever, leukocytosis, gamma-globulin production, and reactive hyperglycemia.

Adaptive capacities at the psychological and social level are also important in predetermining whether stressful encounters will precipitate small or large reactions of alarm and defense. The counterparts to host resistance at the psychological level, according to our theory, are ego strength, problem-solving ability, flexibility, and social skills. At the interpersonal level, the adaptive capacity of the individual is raised by positive primary relationships and one's network of social supports. All these levels of adaptive capacity can be thought of as an armamentarium of coping resources. Persons with a strong array of resources are hypothesized to have less likelihood of having a given noxious circumstance override their defenses and lead to pathological end-states of a somatic, psychosomatic, or psychiatric form.

We have thus moved from a two-variable equation involving just stressor and disorder to a more comprehensive paradigm involving five aspects of the interaction of stress with organisms. These five components are reviewed in Table 1.

Thus far, we have given both psychological and biological examples of adaptive capacity, stimulus input, alarm reactions, defenses, and pathological end-states. A comprehensive view of human health and illness requires us to consider the many levels on which human life is lived. Almost all interactions of persons with their environment have interpersonal and sociocultural, as well as biological and psychological, implications. The multidisciplinary schema of Caudill (2) provides a wide-angled lens which enables us to keep in mind the many levels at which experience takes place simultaneously and successively. We include four such levels in this multivariate paradigm: biological, psychological, interpersonal, and sociocultural. These interact in complex ways to determine human health and well-being.

Although the course of human life is by nature holistic, the division of science into separate disciplines has imposed an artificial fractionation on our thinking. Biologists tend to think largely in biological terms. Psychiatrists and psychologists also tend to focus on one level. Family therapists are more likely to include sociocultural than biological factors in their problem-solving. Finally, social scientists are often content to focus on the sociocultural level without reference to the other levels, which provide its foundations.

A multilevel approach is particularly essential in the study of stress and mental disorder. Among many possible examples, consider that (a) stresses on the interpersonal level usually create alarm reactions at the psychological level; and (b) inadequacies of reactive defenses at the sociocultural level can foster development of pathology in biological functioning (6,12). In sum, the typical scenario of the stressful experience involves the participation of several levels of the total human system at each stage of stress input and the organism's reaction thereto. This model is depicted in Table 2.

TABLE 1. *Five aspects of the interaction of stress and the organism*

Class of variable	Example associated with health	Example associated with disease
Adaptive capacity (host resistance)	Problem-solving skills Ego strength	Inexperience Copelessness
Stimulus input ("stressor")	Mild, superficial Brief	Intense, invasive Prolonged
Alarm reaction (immediate distress)	Appropriate to stimulus Used as a cue to action	Inappropriate in amount, kind, or interpretation
Defensive reaction (resistance, adjustment)	Adaptive defense reduces stressor	Maladaptive defense fails to reduce stressor or creates "side effect"
Pathological end-state (disease, decompensation)	Prevented by adaptive capacity or adequate defense	Reduced level of function or structural change

TABLE 2. A model depicting the interaction of stress and the organism

Level	Adaptive capacity	Stressors	Alarm reaction	Defensive reaction	Pathological end-state
Biological	State of physique, nutrition, vigor Natural or acquired immunities	Deprivation of biological needs Excess inputs of physical or biological agents	Arousal—hunger, thirst, pain, fatigue Changes in physiological function	General adaptation syndrome Physiological compensation Shifts in metabolism Changes in pain threshold	Deficiency diseases "Exhaustion" Addictions Chronic dysfunction Structural damage
Psychological	Resourcefulness, problem-solving ability Ego strength Flexibility Social skills	Perceptions and interpretations of danger, threat, loss, disappointment, frustration, or sense of failure or hopelessness Loss of self-acceptance Threat to security	Feelings of deprivation—boredom, grief, sadness Feelings of anxiety, pressure, guilt Fear of danger	Ego defenses—denial, repression, projection Defensive neuroses Perceptual defenses—wishes, fantasies, motives Planning Problem-solving	Despair, apathy Chronic personality pattern disturbances Psychoses Chronic affective disorders Meaninglessness
Interpersonal	Primary relationships including family Network of social supports	Social isolation Lack of acceptance Insults, punishments, rejections Changes in social groups, especially losses	Antagonism, conflict, suspicion Withdrawal Feelings of rejection, punishment	Defensive, rigid social relating Avoidance Assuming sick role Aggressiveness "Acting out" Enlisting social supports	Chronic exploitation Becoming an outcast Imprisonment Permanent disruption of interpersonal ties Chronic failure to fulfill roles
Sociocultural	Values Norms and practices "Therapeutic" social institutions Systems of knowledge and technology	Cultural change Role conflict Status incongruity Value conflicts with important others Forced change in life situation	Communication of concern and alarm Expressive behavior of crowds Mobilization of social structures	Culturally prescribed defenses—scapegoating, prejudice Explanatory ideologies Legal and moral systems Use of curers and institutions	Alienation, anomie Breakdown of social order Disintegration of the cultural systems of values and norms

Needless to say, it would be an overwhelming task for any single research study to provide a comprehensive test of so elaborate a research model. The utility (or nonutility) of this approach can be determined only after a variety of studies have attempted to integrate selected sets of variables representing different cells from the design. A preliminary listing of some of the variables is offered in Table 2.

PRELIMINARY EFFORTS TO TEST THE MODEL

The remainder of this chapter illustrates how a conceptual model, such as the one outlined above, can guide in an analysis of a battery of data speaking to the issue of the relationship between life change events and psychological problems. The data to be presented are drawn from the Air Traffic Controller Health Change Study (ATC-HCS) recently conducted at the Boston University School of Medicine (8). At the time of this writing, only some of the data have received analysis and only in a preliminary way.

The independent or predictor variables considered herein are total life change scores derived by three methods from the 100 possible events included in the Review of Life Experience (ROLE) (5). The ROLE was scored in the standard way for those items that appear on the Holmes and Rahe Schedule of Recent Experience (4). It was also independently scored by the standard system for those items that appeared on the life events questionnaire developed by Paykel et al. (PUP) (7). The third approach to scoring allowed subjects to estimate the amount of stress they experienced as a result of events occurring to them. This rating was made on a continuum of 1 to 99, with the event "child married with parent's approval," "additional person moves into house," and "child died" serving as benchmarks at approximately 10, 50, and 99, respectively, on this scale. Full details of scale development have been presented elsewhere (5).

The outcome variable is derived from the scores on the Psychiatric Status Schedule (PSS) developed by Spitzer et al. (11). This is a structured clinical interview with specified criteria for identifying psychological and behavior problems. It is methodologically superior to both self-report and unstructured clinical judgment. The PSS score distributions have been dichotomized to indicate the presence or absence of a clinically significant disorder (9). Three outcomes will be discussed—elevated scores on subjective distress and on impulse control, and a summary score based on the presence of a significant problem on any one or more of the following five scales: subjective distress, impulse control, alcohol abuse, work role, and mate role. For the most part, we have concentrated on incidence data, that is, the rate of development of clinically significant levels of a psychological problem over a 2- to 2½-year period in men free of that problem at intake into the study and reexamined three times at intervals of about 9 months. Predictive variables were all gathered at intake. This reduces the uncertainty as to which came first, the predictors or the outcome.

The predictor and outcome variables are thus like those in the simple two-variable study design. In the analyses to be presented, however, we have selected variables representative of other parts of the comprehensive 20-cell research model (Table 2) and searched for the ways in which these psychosocial and biological variables modify the relationship between stress and mental disorder.

For each predictor variable discussed, many statistical analyses were run. A good number of these showed no significant trends. Others approached statistical significance but failed to present a definitive picture, often due to small numbers of cases. Finally, an encouraging number of the analyses showed clear relationships, sometimes reflecting the main effects of variables, such as life change or other psychosocial influences, and at other times showing interactions consistent with stress theory and clinical experience.

Alternate approaches to statistical analysis were considered for these data arrayed in three-way contingency tables. The two-way classification of persons, by a life stress variable and a modifying variable, with cases and noncases of a psychiatric problem entering each cell, could be analyzed as two-way analysis of variance performed on rates. This method fails to take adequate account of the sample size in each cell and cannot test for interaction effects since the model assumes the "interaction term" is nonsignificant and utilizes it as the error term by which to test main effects. Use of the minimum modified chi-square was also considered, but the alternative hypothesis which this technique tests (a general interaction term) is not as sensitive as desired to the specific interactions one would hypothesize for combinations of variables under study here.

In this chapter, therefore, for purposes of illustrating the theoretical model (and without claiming a rigorous statistical test of hypotheses), we have proceeded by a simpler statistical procedure. We have calculated a separate chi-square for each level of a modifier variable on the distribution of cases and noncases grouped by ascending amounts of life stress. This procedure addresses the question: "Is amount of life stress associated with probability of new emergences of a psychological problem for this level (high, middle, or low) of the modifier variable?" Modifier variables are selected from the theoretical model to represent adaptive capacity, alarm reactions, or defenses at the various biopsychological and sociocultural levels.

The statistical procedure utilized calls for the calculation of two or three statistical tests in each table, thereby running the risk of generating a greater number of "significant" findings than may actually be present in the data set. We therefore recommend a conservative evaluation of these findings and replication on new study subjects.

RESULTS

A life history characteristic, often hypothesized to affect health, is social mobility. Inasmuch as all participants in the ATC study have the same occupation, measures of social mobility involving occupation were artificially constricted.

There was a wide range of education for both the controllers and their fathers; this provided the opportunity to calculate an index of educational mobility derived by subtracting the ordinal social class rating of the participant's education from the rating of his father's education. Both these ratings were based on the 1 to 7 scale of Hollingshead.

It was hypothesized that educational difference between a man and his father would not only represent a possible disparity in values but also imply an attitude toward that parent. It seems likely that a man who far exceeded his father in education would be more inclined to discount his value system as being "beneath him" or "out-of-date." On the other hand, a man whose father equaled or exceeded him in education might be more likely to place a higher value on him as a role model. The level of a father's education, considered by itself, may also be an index of child-rearing practices. Whatever its process implication, the educational difference between respondent and father would enter the interaction between stress and the organism by increasing or decreasing adaptive capacity. Men the ages of our respondents in general do not live in close proximity to their fathers; thus this variable would operate on the intrapsychic rather than the interpersonal level.

Table 3 shows the relationship between life stress, as measured by the PUP (7) scoring of life events and the incidence of impulse control problems over 2 to 2½ years in men free of such problems at intake. The modifying influence of educational difference on this main effect is also shown.

Table 3 shows that the greater the amount of life change distress, the greater the frequency of new problems in impulse control. Ignoring educational difference, the trend from 10% for those men with 0 to 20 PUP units of life change stress to 23% for those with more than 40 units is significant at $p = 0.02$ by chi-square.

There was also a tendency for ATCs who exceeded their father's level of

TABLE 3. *Relationship of life stress to future impulse control problems as a function of educational differences between subjects and their fathers*[a]

		Life stress past 6 months (%)[c]				
Educational difference[b]	N	Low (N=123)	Middle (N=110)	High (N=101)	Total (%)	P
ATC much higher	51	13[d]	22	24	20	0.69
ATC a little higher	186	15	13	23	16	0.30
Father equal or higher	97	0	11	23	10	0.01
Overall rate		10	14	23	15	0.02

[a] Differences in incidence across educational difference categories ignoring life stress differences are not significant.

[b] Ranked by Hollingshead scale.

[c] Scored by method of Paykel et al., ref. 7.

[d] Percentages indicate the rate of new abnormalities on the PSS of the type indicated per 100 persons in each cell.

education to have higher rates of impulse control problems than those whose fathers went as far or farther in school (right marginal percentages), but these differences were not significant by chi-square. The critical point about Table 3 is that for men who exceeded their fathers in education, level of life stress was not an important correlate of risk for developing an impulse problem. A striking gradient occurs in men not exceeding their father's level of education. For this group, high life stress is associated with a much higher frequency of this type of problem. The significance of the trend in this row of the table is $p = 0.01$. Incidentally, all p values in the last column of these tables refer to the chi-square associated with the difference in percentages across each particular row. They ask the question: "For this level of modifier variable, does amount of life stress associate significantly with incidence of psychiatric problem?"

We next examine a variable at the sociocultural level of the theoretical model. This also antedates the stress-organism interaction and is part of the broad range of adaptive capacities. The variable in question is anomie, the state of normlessness or alienation from society first described by Durkheim in the late 19th century. Our estimate of anomie is based on the scale by Srole, and the research question asked was: "Does the presence of anomie influence whether life stress will precipitate problems in impulse control?" The hypothesis was that anomic persons would have more such problems than persons with greater acceptance of the social ideology. Again, the analysis was confined to incidence data to make it less likely that the recent expression of impulse control problems, and perhaps punishment, might create a temporary reaction of alienation and hostility, thus leading to an artifactual result.

Table 4 shows that persons with low scores on the Srole scale had a 24% rate of impulse control problems over the next three examinations, whereas average and acceptant persons had about half that frequency. These differences do not reach statistical significance for this sample size. For anomic persons, the amount of life stress was not associated with frequency of impulse control problems ($p = 0.50$). Among average and acceptant persons, however, there

TABLE 4. *Relationship of life stress to future impulse control problems as a function of anomie score*[a]

			Life stress past 6 months (%)[b]				
Anomie	Range[c]	N	Low (N=132)	Middle (N=112)	High (N=104)	Total (%)	p
Anomic	5–11	50	27	30	13	24	0.50
Average	12–14	188	7	15	22	14	0.04
"Acceptant"	15–20	110	5	6	26	12	0.01
Overall rate			8	15	22	15	0.02

[a] Differences in incidence across anomie categories, ignoring life stress levels, are not significant.

[b] Scored by method of Paykel et al., ref. 7.

[c] Scores on the 5-item scale: possible range, 5–20.

was a significant association, such that impulse problems emerged among these more conforming men only in the presence of high frequencies of life changes. It therefore appears that anomie is a psychosocial modifier that influences the degree to which life stress eventuates in impulse control problems. The anomic appear to have these problems irrespective of stress, whereas those persons endorsing the social norms tend to maintain adequate impulse control except when stress is high. The overall association between life stress and near-future impulse control problems ($p = 0.02$) comes from the nonalienated portion of the study group.

It should be emphasized that in all tables, the life changes by which men were classified occurred before intake and were inquired about at intake. The development of psychological problems was counted as incidence only in those men who were free of such problems at intake and in whom the problems developed after intake.

The next analysis deals also with a coping resource, but one that operates at the interpersonal level in the theoretical model we have presented. A number of questions were asked of our ATC men regarding whether they sought out social contact at times of stress, whether they felt helped by talking out problems with other people, or, conversely, how much they preferred to work things out all by themselves. Factor analyses of a specially developed item pool led to a scale named "social coping resources." In this next analysis (Table 5), the outcome variable is the occurrence of a clinically notable severity of symptoms on any one of five PSS scales—subjective distress, impulse control, alcohol abuse, work role, and marital role—among men who were free of major problems on all these scales at intake. If one considers the right marginal values in Table 5, one sees that persons in the high, middle, and low thirds on social coping resources had the same incidence of new psychological problems: about 25%. However, the frequencies of such problems for persons in lower, middle, and high ranges of life stress scores show an increasing gradient from 19 to 28 to 32%. This gradient is only marginally significant statistically at $p = 0.10$. Within

TABLE 5. *Relationship of life stress to future psychological problems on the PSS (any of five scales) as a function of level of social coping resources*[a]

| Social coping resources | N | Life stress past 6 months (%)[b] | | | Total % | p for row |
		Low (N = 107)[c]	Middle (N = 76)[c]	High (N = 71)[c]		
Below average	74	15	24	48	26	0.02
Average	95	15	33	23	23	0.23
Above average	80	29	18	28	24	0.55
Overall rate		19	28	32	25	0.10

[a] Differences in incidence across social coping resource categories, ignoring life stress levels, are not significant.

[b] Scored by method of Paykel et al., ref. 7.

[c] Overall sample size is smaller for analyses involving new incidence of any of five psychological problems because more individuals are excluded as cases already prevailing at intake.

the matrix, however, a more interesting and quite logical finding emerges. Although neither life stress nor social coping resources has a significant independent association with psychological problems, a strong association between life stress and psychological problems is visible for those with below average social coping resources. Here the rates of new disorders rise from 15 to 24 to 48%. The significance of this trend is below the 0.02 level. It appears from Table 5 that for this population, life change and life distress correlate with risk of psychiatric pathology primarily in those men whose social coping resources are clearly below average. We have thus identified another potentially important psychosocial modifier in the stress-illness equation.

Although many biological variables are available in the total ATC study, we have selected one hormonal measure for examination here, largely on the basis of its convenience of access in the data sets with which we were working. The secretion of human growth hormone (GH) occurs in brief spiked episodes in response to either stress or specific physiological triggers. The ATC study collected and analyzed serum GHs by procedures described in detail elsewhere (9).

The present data are based on 299 men, each of whom was studied for 2 working days. On each day, 15 blood samples were gathered at 20-min intervals. We were surprised by how infrequently substantial GH responses were observed. Forty-four percent of the men never exceeded the threshold of sensitivity of our laboratory assays, which was 2 ng/ml. At some time during their 30 observations on 2 days, another 30% secreted measurable amounts of GH but in no instance exceeded a reading of 5 ng/ml. Twenty percent had at least one of their readings greater than 5 ng/ml on 1 day only. The remaining 6% (19 people) had at least one reading of 5 ng/ml or greater on each of the 2 days studied. Because of the small number of GH responders and the desire to cross-tabulate them by their life change distress ratings, we have dichotomized the entire sample into those with no measurable response and those with one or more measurable responses greater than 2.0 ng/ml GH.

In Table 6, the impact of life change is indexed by the sum of distress ratings which men applied to the events that happened to them in the prior 6 months.

TABLE 6. *Relationship of life stress to the incidence of impulse control problems as a function of human GH levels[a]*

Human GH (30 readings per man)	N	Life stress past 6 months (%)[b]			Total (%)	p
		Low (N=71)	Middle (N=89)	High (N=69)		
Always ≤ 2.0	105	20	14	22	18	0.65
Ever > 2.0	124	0	13	27	13	0.003
Overall rate		8	13	25	15	0.03

[a] Difference in incidence between human GH Levels, ignoring life stress levels, is not significant.

[b] Scored on basis of self-ratings of distress due to life changes.

This self-rating of distress is the third approach we used to measure life change. In many of the univariate analyses, the self-ratings of distress had stronger predictive value for subsequent illness than did the Paykel and Holmes standardized approaches to indexing total life change. As can be seen from Table 6, there is virtually no association between GH responsivity and future development of impulse control problems when life change distress is ignored (right marginal entries). Separating responders from nonresponders, however, one sees a strong gradient for impulse problems to develop in GH responders who have high stress but for these problems to be a rarity in those who experience only low stress. This trend is significant at the 0.003 level. In contrast, persons with no GH response over these many readings seemed to have a moderate amount of impulse control problems emerging, regardless of their life change experience.

The pituitary system producing GH is rapidly acting. Substantial secretions enter the blood system rather quickly after stress, and our blood studies show the disappearance of the hormone to be rather rapid. GH responsiveness may be a biological expression of the stage of alarm which occurs in immediate response to stress input. It may reflect the rapidity and comprehensiveness with which the body can mobilize itself biologically. It does not seem to be a sustained enough reaction to participate in long-term defenses.

The important suggestion from Table 6 is that features of the endocrine system somehow appear associated, albeit in a selective and interactive way, with the process by which psychosocial inputs (in this case life change distress) may or may not be followed by acting-out behavior of such magnitude as to constitute an impulse control problem, as defined by the PSS.

The final illustration of the model to be presented involved a variable at the sociocultural level. In some circumstances, it could be seen as an expression of adaptive capacity; but in other circumstances, one could consider this variable as part of the broad armamentarium of defenses. Participation in religious activity has been a sociocultural resource which has long been believed by many societies to protect and defend against physical and mental illnesses. Cardiovascular epidemiologists, in both the United States and Israel (3), have reported that the frequency of attendance at religious worship is associated with reduced mortality from coronary heart disease. Guided by this, the ATC-HCS inquired about religious preference and church attendance.

Religious preference had no clear-cut association with the presence or absence of psychological problems. Frequency of attendance at religious services, however, had rather strong associations with various types of psychological problems, as indexed on the PSS. Frequency of church attendance was modestly associated with the subsequent development of impulse control problems, as shown in Table 7. Persons who never attended services had about twice the rate of those who attended monthly or more often. This trend was at the margin of statistical significance ($p = 0.051$).

The question in the present analysis was whether this cultural level of "defense" interacted in some way to modify the relationship between life changes

TABLE 7. *Relationship of life stress to incidence of impulse control problems as a function of frequency of church attendance*[a]

| Attendance | N | Life stress past 6 months (%)[b] | | | | p |
		Low (N = 134)	Middle (N = 115)	High (N = 104)	Total (%)	
Never	57	7	32	20	21	0.18
Once or twice a year	127	12	18	26	18	0.25
Monthly or more often	169	7	6	20	10	0.03
Overall rate		9	15	22	15	0.02

[a] Differences in incidence across church attendance categories, ignoring life stress levels, are marginally significant at $p = 0.051$.
[b] Scored by method of Paykel et al., ref. 7.

and subsequent psychological problems. Table 7 shows that persons with low life change generally had from one-half to two-thirds the incidence of new impulse problems compared to persons with high life change ($p = 0.02$). The increase in these problems with increased life change scores reached significance only for those persons attending services most often. In that category, which contained the largest number of men, those with low and middle amounts of life change seemed singularly protected from future impulse control problems.

SUMMARY

This chapter presents an alternative to the simple two-variable equation which has formed the design for so much past research into the relationship between stress and mental disorder. The theoretical model proposed here does not represent a revolutionary new idea but simply the structuring of what seems to be emerging from clinical experience and stress research. Five of its key points follow: (a) It is essential to distinguish among the stages of the organism's reaction to stress, such as acute discomfort, heightened defensiveness, and chronic residual pathology. (b) The adaptive strengths with which a person enters a stressful situation greatly influence how he or she will react to it. (c) For a person unprepared for a stressful event, the vigor and appropriateness of the defenses may influence whether the person or the stressor emerges as victor. (d) To conduct advanced stress research or to make accurate clinical predictions, one must estimate, at least crudely, the amount of stressful input encountered. (e) As interdisciplinary scientists, we must actively incorporate into our work the reality that the interaction between stress and the organism takes place at many conceptual levels, which can be broadly stated to include (among others) the biological, the psychological, the interpersonal, and the sociocultural.

The theoretical model we have described is admittedly complex. The data analyses presented here demonstrate the feasibility of beginning to test its structure empirically and offer preliminary findings that tend to support its plausibility. The various biological, psychological, and social variables suggested by the components of this model appear to act in powerful ways to modify the relationship between stress inputs and psychiatric outcomes. Although much larger sample sizes are required to generate adequate numbers of illness events so that this complex paradigm can be tested definitively, the preliminary findings presented herein hold promise that this approach can directly advance our understanding of those complex phenomena we call stress, disease, and health.

ACKNOWLEDGMENTS

This research was carried out as part of the Air Traffic Controller Health Change Study, supported by contract #DOT-FA73-WA3211 from the Department of Transportation, Federal Aviation Administration, awarded to Boston University. The views expressed are solely those of the author and do not represent the positions of the Federal Aviation Administration or the Department of Transportation. The author wishes to acknowledge Michael W. Hurst, Ed.D., Robert M. Rose, M.D., and Laurie Anderson, B.A. for their major contributions to the data base used in this report.

REFERENCES

1. Antonovsky, A. (1971): Twenty-five years later: A limited study of the sequlae of the concentration camp experience. *Soc. Psychiatry,* 6:186–193.
2. Caudill, W. (1958): Effects of social and cultural systems in reaction to stress. *Social Science Research Council,* pamphlet no. 14, New York.
3. Comstock, G. W., and Partridge, K. B. (1972): Church attendance and health. *J. Chronic Dis.,* 25:655–672.
4. Holmes, T. H., and Rahe, R. H. (1967): The social readjustment rating scale. *J. Psychosom. Res.,* 11:213–218.
5. Hurst, M. W., Jenkins, C. D., and Rose, R. M. (1978): The assessment of life change stress: A comparative and methodological inquiry. *Psychosom. Med.,* 40:126–141.
6. Jenkins, C. D. (1978): Low education: A risk factor for death. *N. Engl. J. Med.,* 299:95–97.
7. Paykel, E. S., Prusoff, B. A., and Uhlenhuth, E. H. (1971): Scaling of life events. *Arch. Gen. Psychiatry,* 25:340–347.
8. Rose, R. M., Jenkins, C. D., and Hurst, M. W. (1978): Health change in air traffic controllers: A prospective study. I. Background and description. *Psychosom. Med.,* 40:142–165.
9. Rose, R. M., Jenkins, C. D., and Hurst, M. W. (1978): *Air Traffic Controller Health Change Study,* edited by M. A. Levin, Boston University School of Medicine, Boston.
10. Selye, H. (1956): *The Stress of Life.* McGraw Hill, New York.
11. Spitzer, R. L., Endicott, J., Fleiss, J. L., and Cohen, J. (1970): The psychiatric status schedule. A technique for evaluating psychopathology and impairment in role functioning. *Arch. Gen. Psychiatry,* 23:41–55.
12. Weinblatt, E., Ruberman, W., Goldberg, J., Frank, C., Shapiro, S., and Chaudhary, B. (1978): Sudden death after myocardial infarction in relation to education. *N. Engl. J. Med.,* 299:60–65.

Stress and Mental Disorder,
edited by James E. Barrett et al.
Raven Press, New York © 1979.

Discussion, Part IV, and Overview

Joseph Zubin

*University of Pittsburgh and Veterans Administration Medical Center,
Pittsburgh, Pennsylvania 15206*

An analysis of the contents of this volume indicates that the most important concepts discussed in the interface between stress and mental disorder are: life events, vulnerability, crises, and episodes. While life events occupy the center of attention in this volume, it is to be hoped that in the not-too-distant future, a deeper understanding of vulnerability itself will have reached the point where it can serve as the focus of a symposium.

Regarding the chapters in the foregoing section, both Dr. Rose and Dr. Jenkins deal with the stressors provided by the hazardous occupation of air traffic controllers (ATC), an occupation most ingeniously suited to elicit stressful responses in its practitioners since threatening events are continuously in the offing. Dr. Rose deals with the physiological responses, while Dr. Jenkins deals mostly with the psychological and social. Although the data collected on this project are not yet fully analzyed, they already provide opportunities for analyzing the relationship between stressors and psychological dysfunction. These data may cast light on the perennial question of the specific pathway by which a psychologically threatening situation is transduced into a physiological response. It is easy enough to conceive how the injection of a suitable drug will bring about a physiological response, but how does an environmental threat get encoded into a bodily response?

Among the attempts to answer this question are the theoretical frameworks provided first by the James-Lange theory and later by Cannon for fear and anxiety in the "fight or flight" paradigm presumably mediated by the neuroendocrine system. Another attempt is the "conservation and withdrawal" hypothesis of Engle and Schmale (5) for depression mediated by lowered metabolism and increased parasympathetic activity. Selye's hypothesis regarding the sensitivity of adrenocortical hormones to stressors in the environment has not met with universal acceptance (10,11). More recently, however, as Rose points out, other hormones, including growth hormone, prolactin, and testosterone, have been shown to be involved in the responses of the organism to stressors. Whether or not these can serve as general paradigms for the transformation of environmentally originating threats into physiological responses remains to be demonstrated. Perhaps the data on the ATC will provide new leads to solving this problem.

Another type of information which this study is eminently suited to provide is the selection of indicators for the beginnings of crises and their termination. By monitoring the physiological and psychological characteristics of the ATC in situations in which the effects of the stressors become evident, we may be able to discover which of the physiological and psychological changes can serve as markers for the beginnings and ends of crises, miniepisodes, or maxiepisodes.

The partial analysis of the data has thus far proved disappointing to the investigators. To their surprise, they found no relationship between rises in their three physiological indicators (blood pressure, cortisol, and growth hormone) measured during the apparently stressful on-the-job situations and increases in psychological and psychiatric problems. Although in the general literature, and also in this study, increases in the above-mentioned indicators are reported to be predictive of various physical illnesses, they do not seem to be predictive for the psychological area in the ATC. One wonders whether the stresses experienced by the ATC are sufficiently intense to warrant the expectation of a relationship, especially since no actual assessment of the stress has been reported. As Rose points out, the low cortisol levels observed and the absence of growth hormone indicators suggest that most controllers were not under acute stress when tested, at least not as acute as that caused by parachute jumping and upcoming examinations. Why the stress that the ATC undergo is sufficient to trigger physical but not mental distress and/or disorders is a most intriguing question. Is this merely an example of specificity, as Rose argues, or are there any protective mechanisms that operate in the case of mental distress and/or disorders which do not operate in physical disorders? It is to this question that Dr. Jenkins devotes himself; he tries to provide an answer by introducing the concept of moderator variables.

Dr. Jenkins points out that one of the reasons why, in previous investigations, the impact of life event stressors did not invariably lead to reports of discomfort and/or mental disorder was the simplicity of the two-variable design, which is usually employed. He proposes a much broader design along the lines of system-analysis theory and formulates a table in which the various levels of functioning, from the biological through the psychological, the interpersonal and the sociocultural, constitute the ordinate axis and the levels of response suggested by Selye constitute the abcissa axis, giving rise to a 4 × 5 table or 20 rubrics. Unfortunately, Selye's assumptions of the alarm reaction, general adaptation syndrome followed by the "exhaustion" syndrome, have never been generally accepted by biologists (10,11). Whether they will prove suitable for the levels above the biological remains to be seen. However, the test of a model is not whether it is "true" but whether or not it provides hypotheses for testing, which the model does provide. One hypothesis that Dr. Jenkins examines is whether the expected relationship between life event stressors and psychopathology can be modified by moderator variables. Thus he finds that educational mobility, anomie (as measured by the Srole scale), church attendance, and frequency of growth hormone responsiveness modify the expected relationship between life event stressors (as measured by Paykel et al.) and psychopathology, as measured by the Psychiatric Status Schedule (PSS). The educationally less mobile (those who do not excel their fathers) show less psychopathology (impulse dyscontrol) in response to similar life event stressors than do the educationally mobile (those who do excel their fathers). This also holds true of the nonanomic, steady churchgoers, and those who are low in growth hormone responsiveness (those who gave no measurable responses in their serum growth assay).[1]

On the other hand, excelling one's father educationally, scoring high on the anomie scale, irregular or infrequent attendance at church, and high responses in growth hormones tend to make people more vulnerable to life event stressors. Furthermore, the intensity of the stress induced by the life event stressors does not relate to the amount of psychopathology in the vulnerable, whereas those who are not vulnerable to these factors show the expected relationship between intensity of stress and psychopathology. Apparently, the vulnerable are more sensitive and responsive to life event stressors, regardless of the amount of stress involved.

Surprisingly, the degree of utilization of social coping resources (e.g., counseling) does not generally protect against life event stressors. However, the nonutilizers of social coping resources show the expected relationship between degree of life event stressors and psychopathology, while the utilizers do not. Here again the utilizers seem to be more responsive to life event stressors, regardless of the amount of stress induced.

The psychological dysfunction measures used in this study are based on the PSS, which obtains information on the five variables used in this study—sources on subjective stress, impulse control, alcohol abuse, work role, and mate role. Perhaps it would have been more directly informative if data on some of these variables could have been obtained more directly from the work history or daily record of the ATC.

It is interesting that one well-known mediating variable—the type of personality known as Type A (15)—was not considered by the researchers in the ATC studies. It seems a likely candidate for serving as a moderator variable.

If we adopt the vulnerability model for explaining why similar levels of stress do not produce similar dysfunction, we could conclude that mobility in educational level, anomie, and growth hormone responsiveness could be regarded as vulnerability markers for the development of psychological crises in response to life event stressors. Thus those who show upward mobility in education, high level of anomie, poor church attendance, and sensitive growth hormone responsiveness are at greater risk of showing psychopathological behavior, such as impulse control dysfunction, regardless of the level of stress induced by the impinging life event stressors. Whether or not they can also lead to episodes of disorder is not indicated in the reported data.

Dr. Wender's chapter raises several issues that bear directly on the interrela-

---

[1] The life event stress was based on self-ratings of distress due to life change.

tionships between stressors and mental disorder. The question he raises regarding the relative effects of continued stressful niches versus changes in level of stressors on the production of psychopathology has never been adequately answered, but his negative conclusions regarding the role of early rearing practices and socioeconomic status on mental disorders remain debatable. These issues are discussed in the next section.

Interaction Among Life Events, Vulnerability, and Episodes of Illness

The question behind most discussions of life events is: why doesn't the same event produce the same results in everyone? Why do some individuals, when faced with a life trauma, succumb to an episode, while others contain the traumatic effect homeostatically? To analyze the possible answers to this question, we must take a somewhat broader view of the entire problem of the detection and description of psychological dysfunction and mental disorders and their etiology.

Perhaps the most striking progress made in the field of psychopathology has been the emergence of scientifically constructed instruments for the description of psychopathology. Instead of depending on the free-floating interview of the past, we now have, at least for research purposes, systematic structured or semistructured interviews which yield reliable descriptions of a person's psychopathology. We can go even further and provide operational, or at least objective, criteria for selecting the best diagnostic category for a given individual. Once we ask about the validity and significance of the diagnostic category or of the dimensions elicited from the interview, however, we realize that we still lack good answers to these questions. Before we can answer them, we must know the etiology of the disorders. While predictive validity based on outcome, or treatment, can be of help, outcome criteria are so dependent on the ecological niche from which the patient emerges and the one to which he returns that such results are usually not generalizable. Depending for validity on treatment outcome, i.e., whether or not a given treatment produces a specific improvement in a given diagnosis, suffers from the same kinds of problems as outcome in general and is subject to the continual changing armamentarium of treatment methods.

After considering prediction and treatment outcome as validity criteria and realizing that concurrent validity is nothing more than a form of consensual reliability, we have left content and construct validity. We can exclude content validity from further consideration since the currently used interviewing methods do cover the entire waterfront of psychopathology. As for construct validity, we must postulate the constructs involved in the etiology of mental crises and episodes of disorder; this may be the only open road to validity that we now have.

Our ignorance of etiology is truly abysmal. How does one proceed to study etiology under such conditions? The only avenue open is to invent "as if" etiologies in the form of scientific models, develop hypotheses based on these models, and test them for their tenability by direct observations in experimental or naturally occurring situations.

Elsewhere (17) I have proposed six such models ranging from the molecular genetic model to the ecological field model. Each is so wide in scope that only by specifying assumptions and delimiting the scope can psychopathologists make progress.

Such an attempt has been made by providing more specific assumptions for the ecological, developmental, learning, genetic, internal environment, and neurophysiological models (18). However, because each of these models has been standing alone, very rarely interacting with the others, it has become necessary to provide a second order model to integrate them. For this purpose, the vulnerability model has been proposed. According to this model, each of the scientific models of etiology should provide markers in its own domain which differentiate the vulnerable from the rest of the population. Since no one of these models is in itself a sufficient and necessary cause of psychopathology, the vulnerable person is characterized by the interaction among all of these models in the form of the pattern of markers which he possesses across all the models; but this pattern alone is not sufficient to initiate an episode. It must be triggered by some life event stressor, which produces a crisis, which in turn may develop into an episode in the vulnerable (19). What are the implications of this vulnerability model for the future direction of stress research?

The role that stress plays in this vulnerability model is threefold. First, it can serve as a triggering mechanism for eliciting a brief crisis or a longer enduring episode in a vulnerable individual. Second, it can produce an environmentally as opposed to a genetically based vulnerability as a result of an early noxious event often going back as far as the intrauterine existence or childhood, adolescent, or later developmental stress. Third, a persistent continuing stress may also generate a degree of vulnerability sufficient to engender an episode when a triggering event occurs.

Barrett has classified life events according to the first two categories but added an additional category of life events which serves to maintain the disorder once the episode is begun. Here is where behavioral analysis following the learning theory model can be of help, since behavior modification workers establish the contingencies that maintain deviant behavior as the targets for therapeutic intervention.

One of the basic questions implicit in the various discussions and which Barrett raises is whether the triggering events are specific for inducing various types of crises or episodes or whether they are merely happenstances for which no systematic classification or dimensions can be found. He concludes that particular life events and the degree of stress they produce can distinguish between the five subtypes of neurotic disorders he studied.

Thus far we have been content to accept life events at face value without requiring a rigorous definition. But are there any criteria that can be applied to differentiate events that serve as triggers of crises from those that do not?

In searching for criteria to distinguish between life events that serve as triggers and those that do not, the following have been suggested: those that (a) produce losses (exists) or gains (entrances), (b) are undesirable, (c) are novel, (d) are unexpected, (e) are unanticipated, (f) are uncontrollable, and (g) require considerable readjustment of daily routine. Another aspect of the impact of life events, according to Bruce Dohrenwend, is the individual's own subjective rating of the potential stressfulness of an event. While the subjective rating may be a reflection rather than a cause of psychopathology, this rating may indicate the degree to which the individual would find the event subjectively threatening. It would be well to find a common denominator for the criteria by which life events can be defined. Perhaps the impact of the life event on the social network support system which surrounds the individual may serve as the carrier wave on which the criteria listed above can impinge. This may be the common denominator whose constriction or disruption, or even expansion, brings about the crises and/or subsequent episode. One could argue that the other criteria bring about their stressor effect only insofar as they overwhelm the defenses provided by the social network supporting system. This is why, for example, the presence of a confidant protects against depression and why certain losses can be withstood as long as the social network remains intact.

Hammer et al. (8) and Mueller (14) have provided a review of the studies in which the clout of life events can be explained on the basis of their impact on the personal social network. It is interesting to note that of the 43 items in the life event schedule provided by the Social Readjustment Rating Scale of Holmes and Rahe (9), fully 37 (86%) involve reduction in the social interconnectedness of the individual (death of spouse, divorce). Thus the social network serves two functions in our vulnerability model: (a) an etiological function, as one vulnerability marker of the ecotype insofar as a skewed or a constricted social network contributed to by early traumas or by an accumulation of past or present continuing stressful conditions may characterize the individual, and (b) as an agent for absorbing or failing to absorb the impact of immediate life event stressors.

Regarding the question of the valence (either good or bad) attached to the triggering life event, there seems to be a consensus that only the noxious life events have sufficient impact to trigger stress leading to a crisis or episode. Thus the type and quality of the social network which a person develops may serve as a bulwark against the life exigencies which are likely to provoke crises.

It is likely that the social network may serve as a psychosocial index of vulnerability in the same way that consanguinity with a mentally ill person serves as a genetic index of vulnerability. In other words, just as consanguinity with a mental patient identifies the risk of developing an episode on genetic grounds, the social network support in which an individual is imbedded identifies the risk of developing a crisis or episode on nongenetic or environmental grounds.

Dohrenwend (3,4) recently found that self-reporting instruments as screening devices for mental health do not discriminate clinically observed psychopathology from nonclinical cases. It is likely that scores on these techniques measure not psychopathology but demoralization (7) and hence may lead to crises in everyone but to the development of psychopathology only in the vulnerable. If we had measures of vulnerability, we could separate out those for whom the scores on these instruments relate to psychopathology (the vulnerable) from those for whom no relationship to clinically recognizable psychopathology exists (the nonvulnerable).

It is clear in this volume that in addition to the vulnerability to crises and episodes which are based on genetic grounds, there are a considerable number of sources leading to crises, episodes, or deviant behavior in general which are not based on genetics but on life experience. We can classify these experiences as single traumas (such as death of a parent) or as continuing stresses (living in a deprived ecological niche). This nongenetic vulnerability can be related to the various etiological models proposed earlier. In fact, we can postulate etiological bases or etiotypes for each of these models even as we postulate a genotype for the genetic model. Thus we can postulate an ecotype for the ecological model, an auxanotype[2] for the developmental model, a mathetotype[3] for the learning theory model, a chemotype for the nongenetic aspects of the internal environment model, and a neurophysiotype for the neurophysiological model. Certain characteristics, indicators, or markers that indicate vulnerability can be classified under these various etiotypes. It is sometimes difficult to categorize the various markers in accordance with the procrustean schema we have laid down, so that the classification is still highly tentative. Thus for the ecotype we have as examples the following potential markers of vulnerability to psychological disturbance: (a) deviant social networks, (b) anomie, (c) socioeconomic status, (d) overcrowding, and (e) unemployment outside of the home.

One of the most potent arguments for vulnerability markers arising from the ecological model is Brenner's chapter. He claims that the economic cycles are etiological factors in the development of mental disorders (2).

How to integrate the research methodology initiated by Brenner's economic paradigm with the future endeavors in stress research presents a problem. Although the results of Brenner's work are quite impressive, they suffer from the well-known ecological fallacy. Furthermore, the conclusion that rate of unemployment is associated with rate of mental hospitalization is not supported by the data of Kasl. Perhaps the fault lies with the unrepresentativeness of first admission rates, since it has long been recognized that they do not tell the entire story regarding the incidence of mental disorders. On the other hand, Kasl's findings may suffer from the clinical fallacy of basing a generalization on a single case study, reminiscent of the claims that Buergher disease was a Jewish disease, found only in Jews, until the disorder developed in the King of England.

---

[2] Suggested by E. I. Burdock.
[3] Suggested by Kurt Salzinger.

Only by utilizing the broad economic studies as pathfinders for clinical investigations and in turn using clinical results as a basis for verifying the results of economic surveys will we be able to profit from the interaction between these two fields.

For the auxanotype (development) we have as examples the following potential markers: (a) persistent nutritional deprivation in childhood, (b) maternal toxemias during gestation, (c) failure to develop intimacy in friendships during adolescence, (d) lack of confidant in adulthood, (e) loss of mother before age 11 and father before age 17, and (f) parental school truancy or dropout, which Robbins reports as being transmitted to the next generation.

For the learning theory model, the indicators or markers of vulnerability to psychopathology which Jenkins traced out of his data on ATC are: (a) infrequent or no church attendance, and (b) utilization of social coping resources, which are presumably learned behaviors. There is a likelihood that being too realistic about one's social competence may serve as a marker for dysphoria and depression. Mischel (13) reports that the self-ratings of depressives for social competence were more similar to the ratings of observers than was the case with normals and with nondepressed psychiatric patients. This greater similarity persisted even in remission. Thus a certain amount of unrealistic euphoria regarding social competence seems to be necessary for normal adjustment.

For the genetic model itself, the most likely marker is consanguinity with an individual who has had or is now having an episode of mental disorder. The internal environment model provides such markers as monoamine oxidase levels in the blood platelets and growth hormone assays. The neurophysiological model has many potential markers: pupillographic responses, evoked potentials, and reaction time. These and the previously mentioned markers have been discussed elsewhere (20).

The fact that none of these markers is by itself pathognomic of psychopathology necessitates that we consider the patterning of the markers (or their interaction) as the basis for determining vulnerability. As is well known, however, being vulnerable does not necessarily lead to an episode of psychopathology. A triggering life event is needed for eliciting this vulnerability by inducing sufficient stress to produce a crisis. This crisis, which occurs in everyone subjected to stressors, may be contained homeostatically or, if it surpasses the individual's tolerance threshold, develop into an episode. This is where stress and vulnerability meet. The contributions of this volume and their significance for the future inheres in the attempts at classifying and dimensionalizing the life event stressors capable of inducing crises and episodes.

One of the more trenchant contributions in this direction was made in the chapter by Hurst. He examined empirically and to some extent theoretically the content of life event schedules, their scoring, and the clustering of the items of the schedule into sections. After analyzing the present state of the art along these three dimensions, he concludes that it is nearly impossible to develop a universal schedule applicable to all populations and all purposes and that by subdividing the schedule into specific content categories, more focused research becomes possible. His comparison of the different schedules and their scoring with the special schedule developed for the ATC illustrates the importance of content, scoring, and clustering on the outcome of the research.

Dohrenwend (3,4) classifies life events into a triad of pathogenic elements consisting of (a) fateful loss events (bereavement), (b) physical illness and injury, and (c) disruption of social network. He indicates that if these factors overwhelm the internal and external mediating or protective factors, an episode of mental illness will ensue. He raises an interesting problem regarding the effect of extreme traumatic or fateful situations. While most would agree that at least transient psychopathology occurs in everyone under such traumas, opinions differ as to whether severe psychopathology develops in all of those exposed to such traumas. Thus the experience of concentration camp survivors seems to indicate, according to Dohrenwend, that this stress-induced psychopathology persists and even makes them more prone to physical illness and early death. On the other hand, Slater and Slater (16) found that in the survivors of a group of individuals buried by a blockbuster during the London Blitz, although all suffered transient traumas, only those who had a history of previous mental disorder in themselves or their families developed a severe, longer lasting episode.

The findings of Slater and Slater (16) would demand the prior existence of a vulnerability; according to Dohrenwend, no prior vulnerability seems necessary, everyone being at risk of developing a psychopathological episode if the stress is sufficiently severe.

Although Dohrenwend places disruption of social networks on the same level as the other two members of the triad, it could be hypothesized that fateful loss events as well as physical illness and injury bring about their effects at least in part through constriction or alteration of the social network, since bereavement of a loved one certainly is a disruption of the network and physical illness threatens to disrupt or constrain it. This hypothesis can be tested by noting how much of the variance of the stressful life events can be attributed to alteration in the social network.

In addition to the rational logical approaches (one might even call them clinical), there are certain statistical methodological aids that could have been used. First, even the logical categories for clustering life events could be subjected to statistical analysis to determine whether the items in a given cluster are homogeneous and whether any of the items within a given cluster show higher correlations with another cluster. Hurst's objection to the use of covariance between items because they assume or presume a causal connection is somewhat puzzling in this context.

Furthermore, once a set or pattern of items is established by clustering, it might be possible to cluster people according to the established patterns of items. This might produce homogeneous groups of individuals in whom the relationship between life event stress and psychopathology could become clear. Perhaps Lazarsfeld's latent structure analysis or some of the other typological techniques now so popular could be applied to this end (1,6,12). One of the outcomes of such analyses might be an attempt to obtain the factor structure of stress underlying the various dimensions in the clusters of items. This could be based on the actual results of the application of the schedules to a variety of populations as well as on the ratings of experts for the importance or intensity of the items. Perhaps such a factor analysis could answer the question of what the criteria are for designating a given occurrence as a life event. The suggestions listed earlier as criteria for distinguishing an event from a nonevent could be weighed against the factor structure.

An examination of the siblings of the ATC with the same instruments used in the study would cast considerable light on the relationship of vulnerability to the occurrences of life event stressors. Since siblings share not only half their gene pool but a considerable portion of their life experience and ecological influences as well, the role of vulnerability in the life of probands and siblings could be evaluated.

SUMMARY

The role of life event stressors in psychopathology is a relatively new field of investigation. The earlier views tended to regard life event stressors as precipitants of psychopathology; i.e., they tended to precipitate an episode which would have occurred without the life event. Today we tend to classify life event stressors as either triggering events, which initiate an episode in the vulnerable, or as causes in themselves. The primary question facing the investigator is why the same life event stressor leaves some individuals untouched while in others it leads to either a crisis or an episode of mental disorder. This discussion provides a theoretical answer in the form of the vulnerability hypothesis, which assumes that the occurrence of a crisis requires the interaction of a life event stressor and a vulnerable individual, such vulnerability being based on either a hereditary transmitted liability or an environmentally produced or transmitted nonhereditary liability to a crisis, which may develop into an episode in the vulnerable. This vulnerability hypothesis can serve as an integrator for the various types of approaches to the question of the role of stressors in mental disorder, since it encompasses the entire range of liabilities based on ecological, developmental, learning theory, genetic, internal environment, and neurophysiological models of etiology.

To test the tenability of the vulnerability hypothesis, we must discover the markers that differentiate the vulnerable from the nonvulnerable. The work under the various scientific models listed above is providing such markers. Since no single marker is pathognomonic, the search is for patterns of markers that cut across the various models. Thus each of the models and the discipline from which it springs can offer its disciplinary contribution to the interdisciplinary goal of patterns of markers that identify the vulnerable. Once these markers are known, the contingent life event triggers necessary to transform the latent vulnerability into an episode can be determined and therapeutic intervention instituted for preventing either the initial episode or any subsequent episode. After the triggering events are found, families of patients as well as patients themselves can be taught to avoid the occurrence of the noxious events or desensitize the patient to their occurrence if they are inevitable. Advances in mental health are likely to come in the future as in the past not from therapeutic interventions after an episode of psychopathology has occurred but from modification of conditions which lead to psychopathology.

REFERENCES

1. Blashfield, R. K., and Allenderfer, M. S. (1978): The literature on cluster analysis. *Multivariate Behav. Res.,* 13:271–295.
2. Brenner, M. H. (1973): *Mental Illness and the Economy.* Harvard University Press, Cambridge.
3. Dohrenwend, B. P., and de Figueiredo, J. M. (1978): Stressful events of the life course. Paper presented at the Symposium on Aging from Birth to Death. American Association for the Advancement of Science, Washington, D. C.
4. Dohrenwend, B. S., Krasnoff, L., Askenasy, A. R., and Dohrenwend, B. P. (1979): Exemplification of a method for scaling life events: The PERI life events scale. *J. Health Soc. Behav.,* 19:205–229.
5. Engel, G. L., and Schmale, A. H. (1972): Conservation-withdrawal: A primary regulatory process for organismic homeostasis. *Physiology Emotion and Psychosomatic Illness, Ciba Fdn. Symposium 8,* pp. 57–76. Elsevier-Excerpta Medica North Holland, Amsterdam.
6. Fleiss, J. L., and Zubin, J. (1969): On the methods and theory of clustering. *Multivariate Behav. Res.,* 4:235–250.
7. Frank, J. D. (1973): *Persuasion and Healing.* Johns Hopkins University Press, Baltimore.
8. Hammer, M., Makiesky-Barrow, S., and Gutwirth, L. (1978): Social networks and schizophrenia. *Schizophr. Bull.,* 4:522–545.
9. Holmes, T. H., and Rahe, R. H. (1967): The social readjustment rating scale. *J. Psychosom. Res.,* 11:213–218.
10. Mason, J. W. (1975): Psychological stress and endocrine function. *Top. Psychoendocrinol.,* 1–15.
11. Mason, J. W. (1975): A historical view of the stress field. *J. Human Stress,* 1:6–12.
12. Mezzich, J. E. (1978): Evaluating clustering methods for psychiatric diagnosis. *Biol. Psychiatry,* 13:265–281.
13. Mischel, W. (1978): On the interface of cognition and personality. Distinguished Scientist Award Address, American Psychological Association, Toronto.
14. Mueller, D. P. (1979): Social networks *(submitted for publication).*
15. Rosenman, R., Friedman, M., Brand, R., Jenkins, D., Strauss, R., and Wurm, M. (1975): Coronary heart disease in the Western collaborative group study. *JAMA,* 233:872–877.
16. Slater, E., and Slater, P. A. (1944): A heuristic theory of neurosis. *J. Neurol. Neurosurg. Psychiatry,* 7:49–55.
17. Zubin, J. (1972): Scientific models for psychopathology in the '70s. *Sem. Psychiatry,* 4:283–296.
18. Zubin, J. (1978): On breaking the logjam in schizophrenia. Paper presented at the Symposium on Schizophrenia as Psychologists View It Now. American Psychological Association, Toronto.
19. Zubin, J., and Spring, B. (1977): Vulnerability—a new view of schizophrenia. *J. Abnorm. Psychol.,* 86:103–126.
20. Zubin, J. (1979): Chairman's summary Study Group on Markers of Vulnerability to Mental Disorders at Sixteenth Annual Meeting of American College of Neuropsychopharmacology, San Juan, Puerto Rico, Dec. 14–16, 1977. *Psychopharmacol. Bull.,* 15:47–49.

Stress and Mental Disorder,
edited by James E. Barrett et al.
Raven Press, New York © 1979.

General Discussion, Part IV

Dr. Rose: I wish to clarify that we are not saying that with certain combinations of life events along with increased responsivity to work we are bringing about *de novo* impulse disorders. We are saying that, from an operational point of view, we gave these men standardized interviews, and over the course of time certain individuals reported difficulties with the law, had more fights with friends, started using illicit drugs—the items that are specifically listed in the PSS. We observed that during the course of the study, certain men who were previously without symptoms in this area developed or manifested these problems. Obviously, if we went back and obtained more information, we might have found that they had these problems sometime in the past. The model being tested is to ask whether there are ways that individuals may be grouped together in terms of how they respond. Individuals are asymptomatic at one point in time and then later become symptomatic in the sense that they develop troubles behaviorally or interpersonally. We are interested in how individuals may differ in their response to work load or life changes and whether or not one response pattern might be the reappearance of antisocial behavior.

Dr. Elliot Gershon: I'd like to offer some free floating remarks, if I may, to bring in a genetic perspective. The most important thing that we all agree on from studies of the measured effects of illness other than schizophrenia is that they run in families. That means that only part of the population is at risk. The models mentioned in this volume assume that what you have is a factor acting on a population which will randomly strike down persons in the population only in relation to recent life events. That is not the case. I think that it is a mistake to present data on the amount of life events before a depression and not to say whether this is the 15th unipolar episode or the first bipolar episode in the patient's life. The genetic event antecedes all the other events, and care must be taken that we know we are all talking about something that is applicable to everyone or to 1 or 2% of the population.

There is a certain interaction of familial and individual factors worth taking into account. Dr. Winokur mentioned the stormy life of people with certain mood disorders, which may itself engender mood disorders in them or in their relatives. For example, the death of a parent early in life is thought to engender depression. But Dr. Ming Tsuang reports that the death rate of persons who have had depression is quite high in the first decade after discharge from the hospital. If these persons have children, they may transmit to them either a genetic load or the experience of having lost a parent to death. The major cause of death is suicide, but there are also other causes of excess mortality of people with depression. Similarly, you have a familial subculture related to depression, manifested by a number of factors. I think that the life events studies mentioned herein, to the extent that they ignore familial and cultural predictors of vulnerability, and to the extent that they ignore possible biological indicators of vulnerability, with the exception of Dr. Rose's studies, have been unfortunately simplistic in that regard.

Dr. Samuel Guze: I am a firm believer in the importance of repetition, and I therefore want to reiterate something. It has to do with the onset of illness and the strategy of studying stress. There are studies in the literature indicating that psychosocial stressors are important in precipitating clinical manifestations in many disorders; but the significance of these associations is unclear. For example, we know that coronary artery disease begins in the late teens and early 20s. We know this from autopsy studies of young soldiers killed in the Korean and Vietnam wars. Yet if any one of the middle-aged male members of this society were to go out and shovel snow after a snow storm, he would increase his risk of developing a myocardial infarction soon after. The exertion in the cold has little to do with the coronary arteriosclerosis that begins decades earlier, however. The important question is: Why do the changes in the coronaries develop? What makes the heart vulnerable to these processes? We must be sophisticated about similar questions concerning psychiatric conditions. Circumstances that precipitate clinical manifestation may have nothing to do with the cause of the underlying disorder.

Dr. Rose: I think the issue that Dr. Guze is reinforcing is a very valid one. There are several themes or metathemes that have been expressed or argued about in terms of life events or the stress of life. Is it only the big things that count or the small things as well? Is there a continuum? We are asking what the influences are of various kinds of life events, both large and small, on symptomatic behavior which is included under mental disorders.

We studied the air traffic controllers. They were a group of individuals who were functioning on the job, were not hospitalized, and did not have psychotic disorders. No one had a psychotic disorder during the course of the 3 years we were following the men. In addition, these individuals were screened upon entry on the job and their health was reviewed every year by aeromedical examiners.

Our data have potential value and relevance in asking the question whether or not in this group of normal individuals, given a certain range of normality, the paradigm afforded by our study has relevance. We look at what happened to these men in their environment and what happened to them in terms of symptomatic behavior using as reliable a method of assessing symptomatic change as we could. We asked about the relationship between stress events and the development of depressive disorders, for example. I think there is a parallelism between stress and mental illness and stress and mental disorder.

Dr. Bruce Dohrenwend: I am confused about the relevance of the results of the adoption strategies to the inverse relationship between social class and schizophrenia and perhaps some other type of psychopathology. As I understand the adoption strategies, among the things that they cannot be relied upon to clarify is the class relationship. They are most successful in their ability to provide sharp contrast on the genetic side of nature-nurture questions. Their contrast on environmental variables, especially those associated with class, is minimal. The reason is that adoptive families must be stable to qualify for placements; they are rarely among the wealthiest families and probably almost never among the poorest. They represent a very small range of social class positions. Perhaps I might be educated on what I missed in the relevance of the findings from adoption studies to the class relationship.

Dr. Gershon: I cannot defend the adoption studies as being pertinent to social class if all the infants are adopted into one social class and do not have far to move. Although I would think that if the adopting parents are all of one social class and the schizophrenic children are all of a lower social class, it would then indicate that the lower social class of schizophrenia was associated with the disease.

Dr. Bruce Dohrenwend: Dr. Wender was speaking specifically to the stress selection issue of why the disorders are distributed as they are according to social class.

Dr. Gershon: If he finds a downward social mobility associated with the illness, he would then claim the lower social class of schizophrenics might be a consequence of the illness. I don't see where the adoption study is actually necessary to make that point.

Dr. Edward Sachar: If the adoptive families are all of a higher class, and the children who turned out to be schizophrenic all end up in a lower class, it might argue that class was associated with the illness.

Dr. Bruce Dohrenwend: If the person develops the illness, he develops disability and will tend to be selected down or fail to rise up. But demonstrating selection, unless it is a lot stronger than most studies have been able to show, does not rule out an environmental contribution.

Dr. Jonathan Cole: Dr. Wender says there is a correlation between a range of social classes, probably class I to class IV or V. The social class to which you were assigned, that of your adoptive parent, does not influence your future, the extent to which you drop if you become schizophrenic. With lesser degrees of psychopathology, Dr. Wender has observed adopted children and found that those with lesser degrees of psychopathology did not show any drift downward from the social class of the adoptive parents; but it is a correlation relationship and thus not a clean study.

Dr. Rue L. Cromwell: In recent months, I have discussed this point with Seymour Kety. The issue came up at the Second Rochester International Conference on schizophrenia (published in 1978 by Wiley as *The Nature of Schizophrenia*). At that conference, Dr. Michael Goldstein raised the question: "Are not the high risk children of Kety's Copenhagen study given up by biological mothers of lower class origin and adopted by parents of middle class origin?" Kety acknowledged that social class differences may exist between the biological and adoptive parent groups. However, the relevant comparison for genetic inference is between the biological parents of schizophrenic versus control adopted children. In this latter comparison, the socioeconomic differences do not exist. In other words, the genetic inference, comparing index and control parents, is not confounded with the social class differences.

Dr. Eugene I. Burdock: I would like to make a comment related to Dr. Jenkins' presentation of a number of contingency tables, each one analyzed row by row. I think it would be more appropriate to demonstrate a significant overall effect for each table before testing the individual rows in order to minimize the effects of chance.

Dr. Jenkins: We considered several statistical models for analysis of what were actually three-way contingency tables. One could deal with it as a two-way analysis of variance on rates, but then one loses degrees of freedom within cells; this results in an inappropriate analysis for the identification of interaction effects.

Another approach is the minimum modified chi-square approach. We actually ran some of these tables using minimum modified chi-square. This takes a three-way contingency table and then apportions the total chi-square to rows, columns, and interaction. In some of these analyses, we started out with two independently significant main effects and put them into a three-way table. All results were no better than $p = 0.20$ and 0.30. The interpretation of the analysis was that even if one finds a strong effect in some subgroups, if there are other subgroups for which a similar effect does not occur, statistical significance is lost throughout the entire analysis, inasmuch as the main effect model and the interactive model divided the chi-square among them. This obscures the fact that the overall table was most unlikely to reflect a random distribution. We felt that this statistical approach was not sufficiently appropriate inasmuch as we were trying to test specific hypotheses. Such tests could be performed with this row-wise model.

This may in fact be too lenient an approach. The critical issue is to find the correct statistical analysis which answers the specific questions at issue and does not become weakened by a too general test of numerous inappropriate alternative hypotheses.

Dr. James Barrett: In the material that has been presented, I thought a pattern emerged, and I want to draw attention to it. I'm also concerned that some of the remarks have argued for a nonspecificity of stress, that there is little predictability of response to stress except an increased tendency to get ill in some way.

In contrast, the pattern which emerged was that there are certain classes of events that are nonspecific stressors for everyone. These are the events Dr. Bruce Dohrenwend is talking about when he speaks of "the pathogenic triad." They are the events in my data, such as death of a spouse or a child, for which everyone gave a high stress rating if the event was actually experienced. They are the events that received high hypothetical amount of readjustment ratings obtained by Holmes and Rahe. These events are generally significant deaths and major personal illness; they are nonspecific stressors; by that I mean that everyone experiences them as a major assault. I think it is those events that perhaps lead to increased illness of all sorts. In some people they may produce cardiac disease, in others exacerbation of mental disease. Imagine a continuum of events with events of high severity, this severity agreed on by all, at one end. At the other end are events of low or average severity but with a much wider range of perceived stressfulness. The former events do not relate to specific illness but to increased illness of all types. The midrange of events, however (in my data it was the events for which there was high variability about the degree of stress experienced), is where an interaction is taking place, an interaction between these events and something in the individual, a vulnerability, which leads to onset of a specific illness. In other words, here is where specific vulnerability concepts are useful and are going to give the most payoff.

Dr. Barbara Dohrenwend: It seems there are really two kinds of research being done, two kinds of questions being asked about stress and illness, and the fact that these two have been present here has led to a certain amount of confusion and even at times conflict.

Some people are asking: "What are the correlates of illness, and, specifically, is stress a correlate of illness?" For those people the question of how they measure stressors is not critical. What they want is something that will show powerful relationships with illness. They tend to look at measures based on a person's subjective experience of personal events, or on their vulnerability to these events, or on the combination of these, and put these all together.

Others of us, and I must say I identify myself here, are asking a somewhat different question: "What is the impact of the social environment on the individual?" Given this question, we become very concerned with measuring stressors independently of the individual's subjective experience and vulnerability.

I think these two types of research are going along side by side. Maybe if there is another meeting like this in a few years, the two will begin to converge. At this moment, however, I think that they should be recognized as rather separate and different kinds of approaches to the problem of social stress and psychopathology.

Subject Index